eBay
HACKS

Other resources from O'Reilly

Related titles
Google Hacks   Mac OS X Hacks
Amazon Hacks   Windows XP Hacks
TiVo Hacks   Linux Server Hacks
Wireless Hacks

Hacks Series Home   *hacks.oreilly.com* is a community site for developers and power users of all stripes. Readers learn from each other as they share their favorite tips and tools for Mac OS X, Linux, Google, Windows XP, and more.

oreilly.com   *oreilly.com* is more than a complete catalog of O'Reilly books. You'll also find links to news, events, articles, weblogs, sample chapters, and code examples.

oreillynet.com is the essential portal for developers interested in open and emerging technologies, including new platforms, programming languages, and operating systems.

Conferences   O'Reilly & Associates brings diverse innovators together to nurture the ideas that spark revolutionary industries. We specialize in documenting the latest tools and systems, translating the innovator's knowledge into useful skills for those in the trenches. Visit *conferences.oreilly.com* for our upcoming events.

Safari Bookshelf (*safari.oreilly.com*) is the premier online reference library for programmers and IT professionals. Conduct searches across more than 1,000 books. Subscribers can zero in on answers to time-critical questions in a matter of seconds. Read the books on your Bookshelf from cover to cover or simply flip to the page you need. Try it today with a free trial.

eBay
HACKS

David A. Karp

O'REILLY®

Beijing · Cambridge · Farnham · Köln · Paris · Sebastopol · Taipei · Tokyo

eBay Hacks
by David A. Karp

Copyright © 2003 O'Reilly & Associates, Inc. All rights reserved.
Printed in the United States of America.

Published by O'Reilly & Associates, Inc., 1005 Gravenstein Highway North, Sebastopol, CA 95472.

O'Reilly & Associates books may be purchased for educational, business, or sales promotional use. Online editions are also available for most titles (*safari.oreilly.com*). For more information, contact our corporate/institutional sales department: (800) 998-9938 or *corporate@oreilly.com*.

Editor:	Dale Dougherty	**Production Editor:**	Emily Quill
Series Editor:	Rael Dornfest	**Cover Designer:**	Emma Colby
Executive Editor:	Dale Dougherty	**Interior Designer:**	David Futato

Printing History:

August 2003:	First Edition.

Contents

Credits

About the Author

David A. Karp is that dangerous combination of compulsive writer and eBay fanatic.

He discovered eBay in the late 1990s while looking for a deal on an electric cat-litter box. As an avid collector of toys of all kinds, he immediately saw eBay's potential to quench his thirst for second-hand consumer electronics, handmade brass trains, and obscure parts for discontinued products of all kinds. Soon thereafter he began selling on eBay, and now trades religiously, taking breaks occasionally to write books. He still has the litter box.

Educated in Mechanical Engineering at U.C. Berkeley, David consults on Internet technology, user-interface design, and software engineering. Author of six power-user books on Microsoft Windows, including the bestselling Windows Annoyances series, he has also written for a number of magazines, including *Windows Sources Magazine*, *Windows Pro Magazine*, and *New Media Magazine*, and is a contributing editor for *ZTrack Magazine*. Noted recognition includes *PC Computing Magazine*, *Windows Magazine*, the *San Francisco Examiner*, and the *New York Times*.

David spends some of his spare time outside with his camera, but often finds it difficult to tear himself away from a good movie. David likes hiking and skiing, almost as much as he enjoys talking about them. He scored 30.96647% on the Geek Test (*www.innergeek.us/geek.html*), earning a rating of "Total Geek." Animals and children trust him. He can make 15-minute brownies in less than 10 minutes, and never gets tired of the Simpsons.

Contributors

The following people contributed code and inspiration for some of the hacks in this book:

- Todd Larason is a C and Perl programmer currently residing in Portland, OR; he's always interested in new technologies, challenges and obsessions. You can read more about his various obsessions at *www.molehill.org*.

- Samuel L. Clemens (1835–1910) worked as a typesetter between the ages of 11 and 21, during which time he wrote humorous travel letters for regional newspapers. He assumed the pen name Mark Twain (the term used on steamboats as a warning that a river's depth is only two fathoms deep) in 1861 while writing for the Virginia City Territorial Enterprise, and was first made famous in 1864 by the story "The Celebrated Jumping Frog of Calaveras County," which he wrote as a reporter in San Francisco. He is best known for having written *The Innocents Abroad, The Adventures of Tom Sawyer, The Adventures of Huckleberry Finn,* and literally thousands of memorable quotes, several of which adorn the pages of this book. Despite having died 93 years before this book was written, Clemens provided immeasurable inspiration to this, and many other, authors.

Best eBay Pop-Culture References

This is Spinal Tap. The members of the heavy-metal band Spinal Tap (David St. Hubbins, Nigel Tufnel, and Derek Smalls) wax nostalgic on the DVD commentary track of the 1984 Rob Reiner film about the guitars seen in the movie, stating that many of them can now be found on eBay.

The Simpsons (episode BABF22). Homer loses his life savings in the stock market, except for a few remaining dollars he spends on a cowbell. He rings the cowbell gently, only to have it break apart in his hands, and yells "Damn you, eBay!"

Acknowledgments

I'd like to start by thanking Dale Dougherty and Rael Dornfest for coming up with this terrific series of books, and Tim O'Reilly for talking me into writing this particular volume.

Thanks to Dale Dougherty (again) for his guidance and the steadfast idea of exactly what a "hack" should be. Additional thanks to Ruth Kampmann,

Nancy Kotary, and Jim Sumser for their roles in the bizarre series of events that led to the inception of this book.

Thanks to Jeffrey P. McManus and Jeff Huber of eBay for their help with the eBay API, the new "Voyager" search engine, and some other aspects of the marvelous, sometimes mysterious, and always changing computer system behind the curtains at eBay.

I'd also like to thank Todd Larason, who provided code that served as the basis for many of the scripts in Chapter 8.

Thanks to Tim Miller, Katie Woodruff, Michael Eisenberg, Cat Haglund, Dennis Butzlaff, Sara Raymond, and that nice lady who kept bringing us drinks.

Special thanks to Michael Moore, and an extra-special hello to Addie.

Finally, my gratitude and love to Torey Bookstein, whose love and support help warm my soul.

Foreword
This Magic Marketplace

As you will read in this book, eBay is a community, a platform, a social experiment, a successful business, and a microcosm of important Information Age precepts like "network effects," "positive returns to scale," "frictionless economics," even "the changing nature of intellectual property." eBay has a couple of dozen knockout doctoral dissertations lurking in its depths, as well as any number of statutory reforms, sermons, and life-lessons. If you haven't played with eBay yet, you should. If you have played with eBay, this book will enrich your play further.

eBay is becoming the most important way for people to exchange goods. Exchanging goods, exchanging information, and exchanging culture are the three most important activities undertaken by human beings, with the exception of exchanging fluids (without this last exchange, the human race would die off in a generation).

eBay is a uniquely Information Age technology, and as such, it is properly ranked with other technologies that have democratized participation in the fundamental activities of our existence, like the Web itself and Napster.

When the Web was beginning, a lot of Solemn Information Clergy muttered darkly about the inevitable failure of the Internet as a "library" or an "encyclopedia." Libraries are grown-up affairs, filled with serious books written by serious people and carefully cataloged by guardians of human knowledge into hierarchies that express the depth and breadth of all endeavors. The Web has no quality-control mechanism. Any nutbar can pen a few thousand words of lavishly illustrated tinfoil-beanie woo-woo conspiracy theory and post it online, without permission or proofreading. No one seriously attempts to catalog or organize the whole Web into hierarchies anymore—Yahoo! was the last company to make a go at it, and they've quietly deemphasized their effort ever since they realized that keeping pace with the explosive growth of woo-woo tinfoil-beanie conspiracy theories would necessitate hiring every single human being alive and setting them to work cataloging for 14 hours per day.

The best lesson of the Internet is that Napster is better than record labels. Record labels are huge, lumbering, pre–Information Age dinosaurs, thrashing around in the tar as they sink beneath the weight of history while meteors detonate spectacularly overhead. They're incredibly inefficient. They require extraordinary—even unconstitutional!—legal protection to coexist with the Internet. What's more, they've spent a lot of time and money trying to figure out what their customers want from online music distribution, and have utterly missed the fact that hundreds of millions of music-buyers around the world have taken up avid use of file-sharing networks that give them all the music they care to listen to, at a cost that's bundled in with their communications services, day or night, with no "copy-protection" or "rights-management." They've missed the fact that no customer of theirs ever woke up in the morning and said, "Dammit, I wish there was a way I could have less music, and do less with the music I have."

And yet, the Web *is* displacing a lot of the traditional roles played by libraries, despite its typos and madmen. Napster and its progeny *are* becoming the world's preferred means of locating and sharing information, shouting defiance at extraordinarily wicked lawsuits and extraordinarily stupid Acts of Congress. The Priesthood of Information and the Guardians of Music have been displaced by dirty-faced kids whose technology is allowing them to take control of their own information and cultural transactions, and the world is a better place for it.

eBay is a marketplace, and marketplaces are the cradle of civilization. The congress of the market is where all economic theory begins. The Bazaar of the Market is noisome and varied and sticky. Goods sell for one price at one moment, and another price the next. Our modern descendants of the market have had their own priesthoods, like the hyperkinetic hyperacidic floor-traders at the old NYSE who shouted commodities prices out for eight hours a day, running on a lean blend of caffeine and adrenaline.

Buying and selling goods, improving goods, building a business, adding and subtracting value: these entrepreneurial qualities have achieved mythic status in our world. The epitome of these activities is the five-cent lemonade stand: by combining commodity ingredients—sugar, lemon juice, and tap-water—a child can pocket a 400 percent profit on one cent's worth of goods.

Unfortunately, most of us leave the market after our childhoods, revisiting it only long enough to haggle over the price of a car, buy a new house, or throw a yard sale on a summer morning. We forget what it means to be part of that negotiation, that process by which goods and buyers and sellers dance frenziedly about one another, seeking a moment of stability in which a perfect equilateral triangle is formed.

No, most of our transactions are with enterprises like WalMart and Starbucks, slick and faceless entities where haggling is unthinkable, where the passionate intercourse of trade has been neutered, turned into a family-safe, sexless politesse.

eBay makes us all into participants in the market again. It's no coincidence that eBay's first great wave of participation came from the collectibles trade. The collectibles market occurs at the intersection of luck (discovering a piece at a yard sale or thrift shop), knowledge (recognizing its value), market sense (locating a buyer for the goods), and salesmanship (describing the piece's properties attractively). It requires little startup capital and lots of smarts, something that each of us possesses in some measure.

Somewhere, in the world's attics and basements, are all the treasures of history. Someone is using the Canopic jar containing Queen Nefertiti's preserved spleen as an ashtray. Someone is using George Washington's false teeth as a paperweight. Somewhere, a mouse is nibbling at a frayed carton containing the lost gold of El Dorado. A Yahoo! for junk would never break even: you simply couldn't source enough crack junque ninjas to infiltrate and catalog the world's storehouses of *tchotchkes*, white elephants and curios.

And like Napster found the cheapest way to get all the music online, eBay has found the most cost-effective means of cataloging the world's attics and basements. It's attic-Napster, and it has spread the cost and effort around. When you spy a nice casino ashtray on the 25-cent shelf at Thrift Town and snap its pic and put it up on eBay, and when the renowned collector of glass ashtrays, ColBatGuano, bids it up to $400, you have taken part in a market transaction that has simultaneously cataloged a nice bit of bric-a-brac and moved it to a collection where it will be lovingly cared for—and you've left a record of where it is and what it was worth when last we saw it. Buried in eBay's backup tapes is a Blue Book with the last known value of nearly every object we have ever created as a species, from Trinitite (green, faintly radioactive glass fused at the detonation of the first nuclear explosion at Los Alamos, $2.59 a gram at last check) to commodity 40-gigabyte laptop hard-drives ($30 at press-time and falling fast).

Collectors and the junk-pushers who service them have long relied on reputation to manage their relationships. When a picker finds a Hank Williams rookie card at a Volunteer Fire Department Ladies' Auxiliary yard sale at the end of a dusty dirt road and contacts a few customers in Japan, New York, and Frankfurt to arrange for a bidding war and sale, they all need to trust one another. The collectors and the seller need to know that the goods and the cash can be exchanged in confidence before they begin the bidding.

But reputation doesn't scale—that's one of the factors that keeps the laity away from the market's pulpit. No one wants to be the sucker who gives a fellow on the street $500 for a dodgy "diamond bracelet" and ends up with $5 worth of paste-gems. No one wants to get taken by a respondent to a classified car-sale ad who vanishes with your vintage VW Beetle, leaving a rubber check behind.

Geeks have been trying to find a system to allow strangers to trust each other online for decades, and they're still at it. The systems that have emerged are plagued by the need to balance simplicity and accuracy, and being geeks, most engineers have produced reputation systems that require a subtle and rarefied grasp of philosophy and cryptography to get your arms around.

eBay's reputation system is as ingenious as it is simple. It's a streamlined Better Business Bureau, one that's nimble enough to cope with the rapid growth of eBay. And as fascinating as it is when it works, it's even more interesting (and heartbreaking) when it fails, as when a seller with many years' good-standing suddenly lists five $5,000 laptops and disappears with the cash.

The interplay of reputation, buyers, sellers, and goods is what makes auctions so exciting and paradoxical. The more interested bidders there are, the higher the price goes, but high prices attract more sellers, which lowers the closing price of the goods. Add in a few negative feedbacks for some of the bidders and a few more for some of the sellers and you've got an interaction as unpredictable and interesting and mysterious as the weather.

In all this high-minded business about bidding and selling and markets and human striving, it's important not to lose sight of what makes eBay so fiendishly addictive: you can sell anything. You can buy anything. Anything. You can get bargains. You can turn trash into treasure. You can turn your cottage's furnishings into a cottage industry, serving hipster doofuses on the West Coast who've rediscovered seventies kitsch. You can write code that automates this process!

Me, I collect vintage Disney theme park memorabilia. That's my kink. When I started shopping on eBay, this was a manageable habit. I could go through four or five pages of new listings every morning while I listened to the news, and put down a few bids on fright-masks from the Haunted Mansion and cocktail umbrellas from the Tiki Room.

But as eBay grew, the Disney category was overrun with sellers—Disney has made a *lot* of memorabilia over the years—and going through the listings screen by screen became a full-time occupation. So I started to tinker with searches, like this:

```
> disney* -pin
```

That is, "show me all listings containing 'disney' but not 'pin'." Gradually, my search grew, metastasizing into something like this:

```
> disney* -pin -beanie -pinback -classics -baby -wdcc -watch -t-shirt
-tshirt -teeshirt -girl* -CD -DVD -VHS
```

...and so on—it grew to 20 kilobytes, and I'd paste it into my browser every morning and get a shower and dress while eBay's poor servers labored under its demands, spitting out a screen-full of likely items.

But eBay's servers grew more taxed, and my demands grew more taxing. My query started timing out.

And I had to develop a new strategy. I went back through all the items that I found particularly interesting, the things I'd bid on or thought hard about bidding on, and went through their bid histories, noting the names of all the people who'd competed with me for the lots. These people, I reasoned, had good enough taste to bid on the things that I liked, and they apparently have enough spare time to search the listings more thoroughly than I do. Why don't I just take a free ride on their labor?

Which is what I did. I searched eBay for all the auctions that my erstwhile competitors were bidding on and I bookmarked each result. Thereafter, instead of trying to use a series of keywords to locate individual items of interest, I used *people*—people who'd bid against me. By watching what they were bidding on, I was able to discover any number of interesting items up on the block, and whenever I bid in a new auction, I got the added bonus of more names to add to my list of researchers who had the knack for finding the stuff I sought.

This strategy worked altogether too well. Not only did I discover many things I wanted to bid on, I won many of the auctions. Too many. Enough that my once-spacious warehouse loft began to bulge at the seams, and my banker took to phoning me up in the middle of the night to ask me in earnest tones if I'd developed a heroin habit.

If he only knew—I was addicted to something far more fiendish: junque, not junk. I am an unabashed junquie, and eBay is the marketplace of *tchotchkes* where I feed my addiction. I'm happy to welcome you all into the fold. Your habit awaits.

—Cory Doctorow
doctorow@craphound.com

Cory Doctorow is the co-editor of "Boing Boing: A Directory of Wonderful Things" (*boingboing.net*) and is the outreach coordinator for the Electronic Frontier Foundation (*www.eff.org*). Cory is a prolific and award-winning science fiction writer; his first novel, *Down and Out in the Magic Kingdom*, was recently published by Tor books. He is a regular contributor to Wired magazine and a columnist for the O'Reilly Network.

Preface

eBay is more than just a web site. It's a community of millions: people in all parts of the world, all of whom are buying and selling with varying degrees of experience, ingenuity, and, of course, intelligence. eBay refers to the universe it has created as the "eBay Marketplace," which is indeed an apt description.

What makes eBay great is *access*. As a buyer, you have access to things you can't get anywhere else: antique toys, used computer equipment, rare movie posters, handmade clothing, cheap cell-phone accessories, furniture, music, and everything in between. And as a seller, you have access to *buyers* all over the world, willing to shell out money for just about anything you can take a picture of.

eBay has become a vital tool for collectors of all sorts. In my first few weeks of exploring eBay, I found a rare toy train that hasn't been made since I was a kid drooling over pictures in a catalog. In fact, thanks to eBay, I rediscovered a hobby I had loved in my childhood, and met others who have done the same.

Origins

eBay is big. Very big. At any given time, there are over 18 million items for sale, with an average of $680 worth of transactions taking place every *second*. And these numbers will undoubtedly be even higher by the time you get around to reading this.

But like most big things, eBay started out small. As the story goes, eBay was born of a dinner conversation between Pierre Omidyar and his wife, Pam, about PEZ® dispensers. As it turns out, this, like many origin stories, is a myth (this one was cooked up by eBay PR whiz Mary Lou Song); but the fact remains that eBay still has that PEZ-dispenser feel, and that's what keeps customers coming.

What This Book Is...and Isn't

"Hacks" are generally considered to be "quick-and-dirty" solutions to programming problems or interesting techniques for getting a task done. As any experienced eBayer will tell you, there are plenty of tasks involved in buying and selling on eBay, and anything that can be done to make those tasks easier, faster, or more effective will improve your eBay experience significantly.

This book is not a "hand holding" guide. It will not walk you through the process of bidding on your first auction or creating your first auction listing. The fact is that just about anybody can figure those things out for themselves in a few minutes. (If that weren't true, eBay wouldn't have tens of millions of active buyers and sellers.)

But despite the title, this book is also not about "hacking into a system" or anything so nefarious. Quite the contrary: in fact, you'll find in this book a very real emphasis on trading responsibly and ethically, as well as extensive tools and tips for protecting yourself as both a buyer and a seller.

The hacks in this book address the technological and diplomatic challenges faced by all eBay members, written from the perspective of an experienced eBayer who loves challenges as much as solutions.

Essentially, you'll find in this book the tools to help you trade smarter and safer, make more money, and have fun doing it.

Hacking a Dynamic System

"Change is the handmaiden Nature requires to do her miracles with."
– Mark Twain

eBay is constantly evolving and changing to meet the needs of its ever-growing community (as well as its business partners). Every two weeks, in fact, eBay introduces new features and changes to its site. Some changes are subtle, like moving the location of a button or link, or updating an obscure policy. Other changes are much more dramatic.

While this book was being written, for instance, eBay added the Calculated Shipping feature (see "Put a Shipping Cost Calculator in Your Auction" [Hack #45]), substantially changed the licensing and pricing for its Developers Program (see Chapter 8), and introduced an entirely new auction page design. And all of these changes occurred within a period of about 30 days.

There is no such thing as eBay 2.0 or eBay 2.1, a fact that can create quite a challenge for tinkerers. But, by their very nature, hacks are experimental, and not necessarily impervious to breakage or obsolescence. As eBay evolves, some of the hacks in this book may need to be adjusted, fixed, or otherwise massaged to work within the confines of the system. If you encounter a problem, just visit *www.ebayhacks.com* to see if there's a solution (or to suggest one of your own).

Fortunately, whenever eBay closes a door, they try to open a window (or at least a vent), which means that hacking will always be a part of using eBay, and the hacker will always have a home.

Practical Matters

eBay requires only a web browser, an email account, and a sense of adventure. But to use the hacks in this book, you'll want to make sure you have all of the following:

Recent web browser. Your web browser is your portal to the entire eBay universe, so make sure you're not using a browser released before the fall of the Berlin wall. The hacks in this book were designed for and tested on Netscape 7.0 or later, Mozilla 1.4 or later, and Internet Explorer 6.0 or later. These are all free downloads from their respective makers (*netscape.com*, *mozilla.org*, and *microsoft.com*), so no excuses! Earlier web browsers will cause all sorts of problems, such as pages not displaying correctly and forms not working properly. And newer browsers can also prefill forms and remember passwords, which can be very handy on eBay.

Email account. A reliable email account—and an email *address* that is not likely to change in the short term—are vital requirements for using eBay.

Email application. Email is how buyers and sellers communicate with one another, but many eBay members underestimate the need for a reliable program to read and send email. A good email program will do the following:

- Store all sent and received messages *indefinitely*.
- Allow you to search and sort stored messages.
- Include the original message when you send a reply.
- Automatically separate eBay-related email from all other correspondence using filters.

Web-based services such as Hotmail or Yahoo! are not suitable, because they don't store email permanently, and they don't give you sufficient control over spam filters and other features. Instead, try Eudora (*eudora. com*) or Outlook (*microsoft.com*).

Control over your spam filter.   If your ISP filters out your spam, it may be deleting email messages intended for you, such as questions from customers and payment instructions from sellers. See "What to Do When Your Email Doesn't Get Through" [Hack #8] for solutions, including an example of a suitable spam filter.

The ability to tilt your head to the left.   If you are able to correctly interpret smileys ;) and other "emoticons," you can properly discern when someone is kidding. This can mean the difference between being happy with a transaction and filing a dispute with eBay's fraud department.

A digital camera.   If you're going to sell on eBay, you'll need a digital camera, a film camera, a scanner, or some other means of taking photos, as discussed in Chapter 5.

A credit card.   Credit cards are the best means of protection when buying on eBay; see "Send Payment Quickly and Safely" [Hack #29] for details. But even if you don't use it to pay for purchases, a credit card will help you get past some barriers, allowing you sell (see Chapter 4) and have your identity verified (see "Improve Your Trustworthiness Quickly" [Hack #7]).

Fun.   You must have fun on eBay. Otherwise, what's the point?

How This Book Is Organized

This book goes beyond the instruction page to the idea of "hacks"—tips, tricks, and techniques you can use to make your experience with eBay more profitable, more fun, less exasperating, and (if you enjoy such things) more challenging.

On a daily basis, eBay users assume many different roles: consumer, seller, technical support specialist, diplomat, teacher, nuisance, application developer, nuclear safety inspector, web designer, and, of course, hacker. With that in mind, the hacks (and chapters) in this book are divided into four main sections.

Hacks for All

Chapter 1, *Diplomacy and Feedback*
    Feedback in the eBay world is like credit in the real world: you use it to buy and sell things, you build it up over a long time, and you protect it like a first-born child. This chapter introduces eBay's feedback system and describes the many different ways to maintain a good feedback profile and use it to inspire trust in others.

Hacks for Buyers

Chapter 2, *Searching*

The only way to find anything on eBay is by searching, either by typing keywords into search boxes or by browsing through category listings. The hacks in this chapter describe how to find auctions before anyone else does, focus your searches with a variety of tools, and even create an automated search robot.

Chapter 3, *Bidding*

This chapter explains both how bidding is *supposed* to work, and how it *actually* works in the real world. It also discusses how you can use eBay's proxy bidding system to improve your win rate while spending less money.

Hacks for Sellers

Chapter 4, *Selling*

The beauty of eBay is that anything you buy can be sold, sometimes for more than you paid for it. This chapter shows the strategies involved with selling, such as which listing upgrades work best, how to promote your items without spending extra money, how to format your listings with HTML and JavaScript, and how to protect yourself from deadbeat bidders.

Chapter 5, *Working with Photos*

Photos can make or break an auction. This chapter shows you not only how to take good pictures and put them in your auctions, but also includes specific code you can use for cool presentations.

Chapter 6, *Completing Transactions*

The hacks in this chapter will give you the selling tools to help receive payments, ship your packages, and protect yourself while doing it.

Chapter 7, *Running a Business on eBay*

If selling on eBay is your full-time job (or if you just wish it were), the tools in this chapter will help you sell more in less time and with less effort. Streamline listing creation, communications, and checkout, and make more money while you're at it.

Hacks for Developers

Chapter 8, *The eBay API*

To the delight of anyone interested in hacking, eBay's API lets developers write applications to communicate directly with the eBay servers. But it's not just for developers—anyone with a computer or web server and a little time to learn Perl can write (and use) quick-and-dirty scripts to search, retrieve auction information, leave feedback, and much more.

How to Use This Book

You can read this book from cover to cover if you like, but for the most part each hack stands on its own. So feel free to browse, flipping around to whatever sections interest you most.

If you're a Perl "newbie," you might want to try some of the easier hacks (earlier in the book) and then tackle the more extensive ones as you get more confident. If you want more information on Perl, such as the background and documentation not found in this book, see *perl.oreilly.com*. Likewise, go to *scripting.oreilly.com* for more information on JavaScript, and check out *web.oreilly.com* for help with HTML.

Conventions Used in This Book

The following is a list of the typographical conventions used in this book:

Italic

> Used to indicate new terms, URLs, filenames, file extensions, directories, program names, and, of course, for emphasis. For example, a path in the filesystem will appear as */Developer/Applications*.

Constant width

> Used to show code examples, anything that might be typed from the keyboard, the contents of files, and the output from commands.

Constant width italic

> Used in examples and tables to show text that should be replaced with your own user-supplied values.

Color

> The second color is used to indicate a cross-reference within the text, and occasionally to help keep the author awake during late-night writing binges.

You should pay special attention to notes set apart from the text with the following icons:

> This is a tip, suggestion, or general note. It contains useful supplementary information about the topic at hand.

> This is a warning or note of caution. When you see one of these, your safety, privacy, or money might be in jeopardy.

The thermometer icons, found next to each hack, indicate the relative complexity of the hack:

 beginner moderate ![expert thermometer] expert

How to Contact Us

We have tested and verified the information in this book to the best of our ability, but you may find that features have changed (or even that we have made mistakes!). As a reader of this book, you can help us to improve future editions by sending us your feedback. Please let us know about any errors, inaccuracies, bugs, misleading or confusing statements, and typos that you find anywhere in this book.

Please also let us know what we can do to make this book more useful to you. We take your comments seriously and will try to incorporate reasonable suggestions into future editions. You can write to us at:

O'Reilly & Associates, Inc.
1005 Gravenstein Hwy N.
Sebastopol, CA 95472
(800) 998-9938 (in the U.S. or Canada)
(707) 829-0515 (international/local)
(707) 829-0104 (fax)

To ask technical questions or to comment on the book, send email to:

bookquestions@oreilly.com

For more information about this book and others, see the O'Reilly web site:

http://www.oreilly.com

For details about *eBay Hacks*, including examples, errata, reviews, and plans for future editions, go to:

http://www.oreilly.com/catalog/ebayhks/

Code examples, additions and corrections, and other related miscellany can be found at:

http://www.ebayhacks.com/

Got a Hack?

To explore Hacks books online or to contribute a hack for future titles, visit:

http://hacks.oreilly.com

## CHAPTER ONE

Diplomacy and Feedback
Hacks 1–8

eBay is a community of buyers and sellers, not just a mere web site or piece of software. It's a complex social system of which you are an active member. Success on eBay depends not only on your ability to master the technical tasks of bidding and selling, but on your ability to communicate with other eBay members and your willingness to contribute to the community in a positive way.

Feedback is the basis of trust on eBay. Each eBay member has his or her own feedback profile, a public collection of comments left by other eBay members. Each individual feedback comment is tied to a transaction in which the particular member took part. Feedback comments are marked either positive, negative, or neutral, and are added accordingly in the summary that appears at the top of the page.

A member's *feedback rating* is the number representing the sum of all positive comments, minus the sum of all negative comments. (Note, however, that multiple comments left by a single user will never count more than one point.) This number, shown in parentheses after a member's user ID, is a useful tool in determining the trustworthiness and experience level of any given eBay member.

> It's important to note that the feedback rating alone does not give you a sufficient picture of any member's personal history. Before you do business with any other member, make sure to click on the feedback rating to view the member's feedback profile as a whole.

Feedback is taken very seriously on eBay, and with good reason. For example, a seller who deals honestly and fairly with his or her customers will earn lots of positive feedback over the years. Conversely, dishonest or unreliable sellers and deadbeat bidders are likely to earn a higher percentage of negative feedback.

Leaving Feedback

You can leave feedback for another member only if you are both involved in a transaction, namely a completed auction. The actual task of leaving feedback is quite simple; simply go to the completed auction page and click Leave Feedback. Choose a rating (positive, neutral, or negative) and type a "review" in the space provided. You'll then have 80 characters in which to explain what the other eBay member did right (or wrong).

Here are some guidelines for writing appropriate feedback:

Positive. As long as a transaction goes reasonably well, you should always leave positive feedback for the other party.

If you're a bidder, you'll want to reward the seller for shipping quickly, responding to questions promptly, and describing the item accurately; for example:

- "Quick shipping, great deal, overall friendly service. A credit to eBay."
- "Item better than described; trustworthy seller. Highly recommended!"

As a seller, you'll likewise want to leave positive feedback for bidders who pay right away.

- "Lightning-fast payment. Reliable buyer. Thanks for your business!"
- "Quick to pay, friendly emails. This eBayer makes selling a pleasure!"

Negative. Negative feedback is unfortunately overused on eBay, and is, in most cases, unnecessary.

 If at all possible, try to resolve the problem with the other party instead of leaving negative feedback. If you're a buyer, for example, and you're not happy with the transaction, contact the seller to see if he or she will make it right before you give up and post negative feedback. Not only will you avoid possible feedback retaliation, but you might stand to get some money out of it as well.

As a bidder, you should leave negative feedback only if you paid and never received the item, if the seller misrepresented the item and did not offer a refund, or if the seller defrauded you in some way. (Note that unless the seller is also the *manufacturer* of the item, it's not fair to leave negative feedback simply because you don't like the item you purchased. And remember, you can always resell the item if you're not happy.)

- "Seller sent damaged item; completely uncooperative about refund."
- "Warning: seller took money and never shipped. Had to dispute charge."

If you're a seller, you should leave negative feedback only for deadbeat bidders who don't pay. (It's not acceptable to penalize a bidder for returning an item as a result of your mistake.) For example:

- "Bid high and then disappeared! No response to numerous emails."
- "Beware! Bidder paid with a bad check!"

Neutral. While neutral comments don't affect the feedback rating, they carry the stigma of a complaint. For this reason, leave neutral feedback only when you have a legitimate complaint but can't bring yourself to leave negative feedback. For example, neutral feedback might be appropriate for a bidder who repeatedly does not follow payment instructions, or a seller who packs an item so poorly that it arrives damaged. A few examples:

- "Poor packing job, shipping took a long time. Seller slow to respond."
- "Condition wasn't great; seller too busy to care. Not recommended."
- "Bidder took a month to send payment; not responsive to emails."

Overall, remember the purpose of the feedback system when writing feedback for another member. The point of negative and neutral comments is to serve as warnings to other eBay members and to help show a pattern of misconduct. Unless the other person caused you a real problem or cost you money unnecessarily, your feedback comment should be positive and should reward the person for what they did right. Don't use negative or neutral feedback frivolously; for example, don't dock a seller for putting a mailing label on crooked.

Finally, never use feedback as a means of coercion, and don't let other eBay members blackmail you by threatening to leave negative feedback. Any buyer or seller who lets another member get away with murder—simply because they don't want that person to retaliate with negative feedback— does the entire eBay community a disservice.

Deciphering Feedback

As you use eBay, you'll constantly be reviewing other members' feedback profiles, so it's important to interpret the numbers properly. What it usually comes down to is determining a pattern of behavior from the bits and pieces of past transactions.

At the top of a feedback profile page, eBay shows a summary and distribution of past feedback comments, as shown in Figure 1-1.

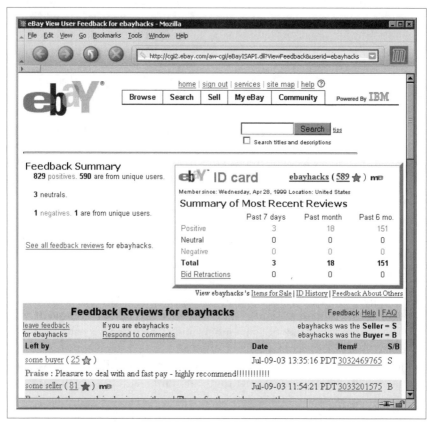

Figure 1-1. The Summary of Most Recent Reviews gives a picture of another member's feedback history

Here you'll see the number of positive, negative, and neutral comments, as well as how many of each were received by the user in the past seven days, the past month, and the past six months. Among other things, this helps add a little perspective to older entries, especially negative ones.

For example, before you bid on any auction, you'll want to check out the seller's feedback. A given seller might have 140 positive comments and 3 negative comments, while another seller might have 612 positive comments and only 2 negative comments. Is the second seller necessarily better than the first? What if both of his negative comments were received in the past week?

On the auction page, a seller's standard feedback rating is supplemented with a "positive feedback" percentage, which is calculated by dividing the number of positive comments by the total number of positive and negative comments. Note that since neutral comments are not part of the equation, a seller with 34 positive comments and 8 neutral comments will have a seemingly perfect positive feedback percentage of 100%. But does this percentage mean this seller is more trustworthy than the aforementioned sellers, with positive feedback percentages of 97.9% and 99.7%, respectively? Of course not.

The point is that numbers alone are not sufficient to gauge the reputation of any single eBay member. Instead, take a moment and investigate. See when the less favorable feedback comments were left and what the posters had to say. For example, the eight neutral comments may have all been left during a week when the seller was in the hospital. By the same token, the three negative feedback comments earned by the first seller may have been left when he was new to eBay and more prone to make mistakes. But if the lion's share of a seller's negative comments were entered within the last week, it might show a pattern of dissatisfaction with an item the user just started selling.

For further information, you can view the auction corresponding to any particular feedback comment by clicking the item number on the right. (Since completed auctions are kept on eBay only for about 90 days, you'll be able to view only the most recent transactions.) Note also that each feedback comment is marked with either S or B, signifying whether the eBay member was the seller or buyer in the specified transaction.

HACK #1 Searching Feedback

Use your browser's Find tool to quickly find complaints or other specific feedback comments in a member's feedback profile.

Feedback is shown in chronological order, with the most recent feedback comments at the top. When scrutinizing a member's feedback profile, it's sometimes helpful to locate specific complaints that other members have left. Unfortunately, feedback profiles can get extremely long, and eBay provides no way of sorting or searching through a member's comments. The simple workaround is to use your browser's built-in search feature.

Start by scrolling down to the bottom of the user's feedback profile page. At the end of the list, you'll see page numbers, allowing you to see older comments. Further down, where it asks "How many feedback comments do you want on each page?" you can specify a larger number, thereby reducing the total number of pages. Choose 200, the maximum, and click View Feedback to show the new, longer page.

Next, press Ctrl-F (or go to Edit → Find in this page) to activate your browser's search tool. To find negative feedback comments, type the word "complaint" in the search field and then click Find.

If the current page has a negative comment, your browser will locate it almost immediately. Click Find repeatedly to cycle through all the negative comments on the page.

> In most browsers, you can leave the Find window open while you flip between pages in the feedback profile. Unfortunately, there's no way to show more than 200 feedback comments on a single page, which would obviously make the search even easier.

You can also search for neutral comments by looking for the word "neutral," and positive comments by looking for the word "praise."

You may also wish to search a person's feedback profile for your own user ID to see if you've left feedback for that person. Likewise, you can use the same technique to search your own feedback profile for another member's user ID to see if that member has left feedback for you.

See Chapter 8 for details on the eBay API, and ways to retrieve and search through feedback with only a few lines of code.

HACK #2   Using Prefabricated Feedback

Save time by storing prewritten feedback for future use.

It won't take you long to get tired of writing feedback comments for the various buyers and sellers with whom you trade. You always end up saying the same thing, so why bother typing it every time?

The solution is simple. Write two generic, all-purpose positive feedback comments, one for buyers and one for sellers, and place them in a plain-text file saved on your hard disk. Remember that each comment can be no longer than 80 characters, including any spaces and punctuation.

Then, when it comes time to leave feedback for someone, open the text file, highlight the appropriate comment, and press Ctrl-C to copy. Then, click the Feedback Review field, and press Ctrl-V to paste.

> Naturally, you can store as many prefabricated feedback comments as you like (variety is the spice of life, after all). Just be careful not to place negative comments too close to positive ones, lest you select the wrong line in haste.

Feedback for Multiple Auctions

Go to My eBay → Feedback → Leave Feedback, and you'll see a list of all closed auctions for which you have not yet left feedback, as shown in Figure 1-2. Simply go down the list, pasting your prefabricated comments for any deserving transactions.

![Feedback Forum screenshot]

Feedback Forum: Rate Your Trading Partners - Mozilla

File Edit View Go Bookmarks Tools Window Help

http://cgi2.ebay.com/aw-cgi/eBayISAPI.dll?GetAndShowTransactions&item=0&nflw=1

Feedback Forum: Rate Your Trading Partners   ⓘ Need Help?

Welcome to the Feedback Forum. Rating other trading partners by leaving feedback is a very important part of trading on eBay.

Please note:
- Once left, you cannot edit or retract feedback.
- Keep your comments factual; avoid personal remarks.
- Be sure to contact your trading partner to resolve disputes before leaving feedback.

You have 23 review(s) to complete.   Find feedback(s) by User ID or item number:

Showing 1 - 23   [   ] Find

Buyer: **some buyer** (77 ★)
Item title: Marklin Z Special Reefer - Olympics / Greece   (3128013703)
End time: Apr-19-03 04:50:34 PDT
Feedback rating: ○ Positive   ○ Neutral   ○ Negative   ◉ I will leave feedback later
Feedback review: [   ] 80 chars max.

Seller: **some seller** (95 ★)
Item title: Little Red Steam Shovel   (3128547694)
End time: Apr-25-03 19:35:14 PDT
Feedback rating: ○ Positive   ○ Neutral   ○ Negative   ◉ I will leave feedback later
Feedback review: [   ] 80 chars max.

Seller: **another seller** (19 ☆)
Item title: Forty Pounds of Pistachios   (3129130544)

Figure 1-2. Leave feedback for dozens of auctions at a time without typing a single word

Make sure to choose the corresponding rating (positive, negative, or neutral) for each transaction, and then click Leave Feedback when you're done.

Right-Click-O-Rama

Users of Windows XP, Me, and 2000 can use their context menus for even quicker access to prefabricated feedback. Start by installing Creative Element Power Tools (*www.creativelement.com/powertools*) and enabling the "Copy file contents to the Clipboard" option.

Next, create at least two plain-text files (one for buyers and one for sellers), each with only a single feedback comment on the first line, and save them to your hard disk. Give each file a name that describes its contents, such as *Standard Seller Feedback.txt* or *Positive Buyer Feedback.txt*.

When you're ready to leave feedback, just right-click one of the files and select Copy File Contents. Then, click the Feedback Review field and press Ctrl-V to paste in the feedback text.

Feedback for International Users

Saving feedback is also handy when you want to have several different prefabricated comments at your fingertips.

For instance, when leaving feedback for an eBay member in another country, you'll probably want to write in the user's native language. And every time you go to the trouble of constructing a comment in a foreign language, you might as well save it for future use. Eventually, you'll have a folder filled with filenames like *Positive feedback for Swedish buyers.txt* or *French feedback comments.txt*.

> If you're not familiar with the member's native language, use a free online translator to help you out, as described in "International Transactions Made Easier" **[Hack #30]**.

See Also

- Some of the auction management tools discussed in Chapter 7 also have features to leave feedback automatically for buyers who have paid.
- See "Leaving Feedback" **[Hack #95]** for details on using the eBay API to leave feedback for other members.

HACK #3 How to Avoid Negative Feedback

Protect your feedback profile—and your reputation—from the proverbial slings and arrows of disgruntled eBayers.

In most cases, negative feedback is unnecessary. And I'm sure that if you just received negative feedback, you'll agree in a heartbeat.

But the reason that negative feedback is unnecessary is that it's usually avoidable. Complaints are usually lodged for one of the following reasons:

A buyer's expectations weren't met. A buyer will leave negative feedback for a seller if the item doesn't arrive quickly, if the item isn't in as good condition as promised, or if the seller isn't responsive to emails.

All of these are avoidable: see "Expectation Management" [Hack #39] and "Damage Control Before and After You Ship" [Hack #70] for tips to effectively prevent customers from being disappointed, both before and after the sale.

But it's important to note that sometimes there's only so much a seller can do to please a customer. For this reason, sellers must also do everything possible to convince their customers—especially inexperienced ones—to communicate any problems or concerns to the seller *before* they go ahead and leave feedback.

If you're the seller, probably the easiest way to do this is to include a note inside all your packages with your email address (and phone number, if applicable) and the assurance that, if the customer has a problem, you'll do everything you can to make the situation right. Sometimes the note alone is enough to make the customer happy.

Deadbeat bidder. A seller will leave negative feedback for a bidder who doesn't pay. If you're a bidder, you can avoid this by quite simply not bidding when you don't intend to follow through and purchase the item. Sellers can usually prevent deadbeat bidders from bidding on their auctions—or rather, prevent bidders from *becoming* deadbeats—by following the tips in "Keeping Out Deadbeat Bidders" [Hack #54].

Communication breakdown. One of the most common causes of failed transactions—and the resulting negative feedback—is one party's inability to email the other. See "What to Do When Your Email Doesn't Get Through" [Hack #8] for a variety of solutions.

Retaliation. A single negative feedback comment will often result in a reciprocal retaliatory feedback. Unfortunately, this is human nature, and there's not much you can do about it. What's worse, though, is that many eBay members don't leave negative feedback where appropriate out of fear of retaliation. See "Withholding Feedback" **[Hack #5]** for an approach that may work in this situation.

Any buyer or seller who lets another member get away with murder, simply for fear of retaliation, does the entire eBay community a disservice. Anyone who tries to blackmail you by threatening to leave negative feedback can be suspended for doing so; see the "SafeHarbor" sidebar for details.

> It might ease your mind to know that in all my years of using eBay, not a single deadbeat bidder who received negative feedback from me has ever retaliated. Not once.

SafeHarbor

SafeHarbor is essentially eBay's policy police. While that sounds like the last thing in the world that would interest a hacker, it's actually quite a valuable tool.

Most of eBay's polices have been put in place to protect buyers and sellers, as well as to maintain the integrity of the marketplace and the level of trust within the community. If you feel that another user is dealing unfairly or abusing the system in some way, you can notify eBay SafeHarbor by going to this address:

http://pages.ebay.com/help/basics/select-RS.html

Some of the situations covered by eBay's policies include:

- Listings for items not in the seller's possession (pre-sale)
- Non-paying bidders and non-shipping sellers
- Fraud, illegal account takeovers, spam
- Feedback extortion

If you'd like eBay to investigate a listing or another member, navigate through the choices on this page, click Continue, and then click Contact Support.

Etiquette and Netiquette

It goes without saying that there are some very simple things you can do on an everyday basis to avoid negative feedback, and most of them involve simple etiquette. For example:

- Be friendly, even if you're not in a friendly mood.
- Write in complete sentences.
- Respond quickly when someone emails you.

- Be patient, and don't panic if you don't get immediate responses to your emails.

- Be forgiving and understanding, especially with new eBay members. Take a little time to educate newbies rather than penalizing them for their inexperience.

- Sellers: treat your customers like gold. Understand that when you have a bidder's money, they can get anxious, suspicious, and downright demanding if you don't reply to their emails quickly.

- Buyers: sellers aren't employed by you, so be nice. Courtesy, gratitude, and patience will go far.

- Be diplomatic, even if it means sometimes swallowing your pride.

See Also

If someone has left negative feedback for you, see "Replies and Followups to Feedback" [Hack #4] for tips to help with damage control, or "Remove Unwanted Feedback" [Hack #6] for a way to have it removed.

HACK #4 Replies and Followups to Feedback
A little damage control will help save a bruised reputation.

The game isn't over when another eBay member leaves feedback for you; you have the opportunity to respond to any feedback comment in your profile. Although this feature is handy for thanking users for leaving you positive feedback, its real value is for damage control when someone leaves neutral or negative feedback for you.

Most people's instinct is to use this tool as a means of retaliation—to "get back" at the other user for leaving a nasty comment. But given the importance of feedback in the eBay community, your main goal should be to use it to lessen the impact of such comments on your own reputation.

For example, consider the following complaint lodged against you, a seller, by an unhappy bidder:

> "Item arrived damaged; very expensive to repair. Lousy seller."

Obviously, this is the wrong response:

> "Stupid buyer! What a jerk for complaining! Now you get nothing."

Think of the message this sends to *other* people, prospective future customers, who might scrutinize your feedback profile. It doesn't address the problem, and since your response shows up only in your *own* feedback profile, it only serves to hurt you. Instead, consider this reply:

> "Please contact me with all problems, and I'll do my best to make it right."

This sends a subtle message to the buyer, should he ever choose to return and view your feedback, but more importantly, it makes it appear to other bidders that *you* are the reasonable one, and this particular customer is nothing more than a crackpot. It also reassures potential customers that you will address problems, and won't just leave your bidders twisting in the wind.

> If you feel the bidder will be understanding and cooperative once you follow up with an email, you may wish to request to have the feedback removed, as described in "Remove Unwanted Feedback" [Hack #6]. Naturally, no bad feedback is the most desirable outcome.

The same approach applies if you're a bidder, and a seller leaves the following feedback for you:

> "Deadbeat! Buyer bid high and never paid. Avoid this guy!"

The common response among inexperienced bidders is often to do nothing, either for fear that something bad will happen to them, or simply because of a lack of familiarity with the system. A response that explains why the aforementioned non-payment might have been reasonable is usually the best choice:

> "Seller never responded to emails, so I gave up and purchased another one."
> "Seller changed the terms of the sale, and I couldn't comply."
> "I was in the hospital getting a finger transplant and couldn't click Pay Now."

But again, when a seller leaves negative feedback for you, the first course of action should be to contact the seller and try to resolve the problem. If everything is worked out, the seller might be willing to cooperate in having the feedback removed. See "Retract Your Bid Without Retracting Your Bid" [Hack #27] for some reasonable approaches a bidder can use to get out of a deal, and usually remain unscathed by negative feedback.

First Reply to Feedback

To reply to feedback left about you, go to My eBay → Feedback → Review and Respond, and a special version of your feedback profile will appear.

Click Respond next to the appropriate comment. (Be careful that you choose the right one, because replies to feedback cannot be retracted.) The Respond To Feedback Left for You page will appear, as shown in Figure 1-3.

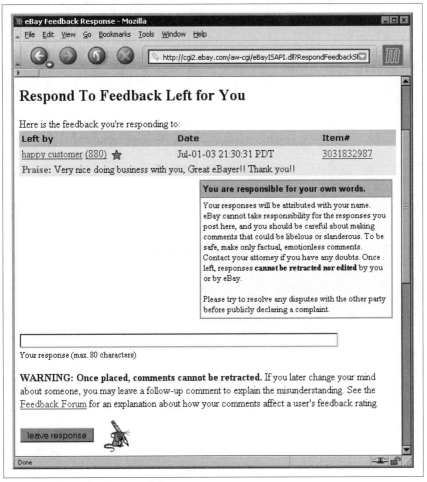

Figure 1-3. Respond to any comments left for you in your feedback profile

Type your reply and click Leave Response when you're done. Note that you can post only one reply to any single feedback comment, so make it count!

Follow Up to Feedback

Once you leave feedback for another eBay user, you can leave a single followup comment that appears beneath your original comment. There are several reasons you might want to do this:

- As a responsible eBay user, you may wish to do damage control on
  another user's feedback profile. For example, if you've left negative feedback for someone and they've since rectified the problem, you can
  return and post a followup, reassuring other people that the issue was
  eventually addressed.

- On the other hand, if you leave a positive comment for someone who
  immediately thereafter causes you trouble (thinking, of course, that it's
  safe to do so), you can amend your comment with a negative followup.

> Although your followup won't have any effect on the user's
> feedback rating, you can precede your followup with the
> word "Complaint:" so that anyone searching for negative
> comments, as described in "Searching Feedback" [Hack #1],
> will see it.

- If you've left feedback for someone, and they've responded to it, as
  described earlier in this hack, you may wish to post a followup
  response. Note that a user doesn't need to have responded to your feedback before you can post a followup comment.

To post a followup comment, go to Site Map → "Review and follow up on
feedback you have left about others" (or go to *http://cgi2.ebay.com/aw-cgi/
eBayISAPI.dll?ReviewFeedbackLeft*).

HACK #5   Withholding Feedback

Know when to hold 'em, and know when to leave 'em.

"The trouble with the global village is all the global village idiots."
– Paul Ginsparg

The biggest flaw (and in some ways, the biggest strength) of eBay's feedback system is the risk of retaliation. You leave negative or neutral feedback
for someone, and they will—without considering the circumstances or
who's at fault—do the same for you. That is the fear, and that is the reason
why many people simply let problems slide.

But the risk of retaliation also reminds people that they are responsible for
their own words; if there were no consequences, people would leave negative
feedback with abandon, and we'd have even more problems on our hands.

I won't deny that the risks sometimes outweigh the gains. Sometimes a bidder has a seemingly legitimate reason for not paying. Perhaps a seller is inexperienced, and while a particular transaction might not have gone very smoothly, it wasn't due to any malice by the seller. Do these people necessarily deserve blemishes on their records? Perhaps not, but they don't necessarily deserve praise, either. In other words, sometimes the best move is no move at all.

Who Goes First

Often the fear of retaliation can work to your advantage. Say you're a seller, and someone has just purchased an item from you. The bidder pays in full, and you go ahead and reward the bidder with positive feedback. But when the bidder receives the item, he's not happy. Since you've already played your hand, the bidder then feels free to file negative feedback, or simply threatens to do so.

On the other hand, if you withhold feedback, the bidder will be much more likely to pursue a diplomatic solution to any problems that come up. Instead of leaving negative feedback, the bidder might politely request a refund, or, better yet, might even go away and not bother you at all.

For this reason, a wise seller will usually wait until the customer has left positive feedback, or at least wait for confirmation that the item has been received and the buyer is happy.

But does the bidder have anything to worry about? If an otherwise happy bidder leaves positive feedback for the seller, isn't there still risk of negative feedback from the seller?

In a word, no. Once a seller has shipped, the seller has everything he or she might've wanted. Unless the bidder does something grievously wrong, the seller has no reason to leave anything but positive feedback.

If There's Doubt

Not everybody retaliates. Some people never even leave feedback, negative or otherwise. If you're worried about retaliation, there's a pretty easy way to predict what any given user will do. Just go to the user's feedback profile page and click Feedback About Others (underneath the summary box) to view all feedback *left* by that user.

Here, you'll be able to easily tell how diligent someone is about leaving feedback, how prone she is to leaving negative feedback, and how likely she is to retaliate if a complaint is lodged against her.

HACK #6 Remove Unwanted Feedback

Use SquareTrade's mediation services to retract feedback.

eBay doesn't kid around when it comes to feedback, and neither do most users. Although eBay is quite clear about stating that every member who leaves feedback is responsible for his or her own words and that, once posted, feedback cannot be retracted, there is indeed a way out.

In fact, there are several circumstances under which a feedback comment can be removed:

- The feedback does not appear to be connected with eBay, the particular member for which it was left, or the particular transaction with which it is associated.

- The feedback contains offensive language, personal identifying information, links to pictures or web sites, or false claims with regard to eBay policies or law-enforcement organizations.

- The feedback was mistakenly left for the wrong user, and the person who left feedback corrects the error and then contacts eBay.

- The feedback was left by someone with false contact information.

- The feedback was used as a means of coercion or blackmail.

- eBay receives a court order finding that the feedback is slanderous, libelous, defamatory, or otherwise illegal, or as a result of a settlement agreement.

- eBay is notified by SquareTrade to remove the feedback, as explained in the next section. If the feedback comment doesn't meet any of the other criteria listed here, then going through SquareTrade is your best choice.

Go to *http://pages.ebay.com/help/policies/feedback-removal.html* for all the legalese associated with eBay's feedback removal policy.

SquareTrade

Any eBay member who wishes to have a feedback comment removed must do so with the cooperation of the person who originally left the feedback.

Here's how it works:

1. The recipient of the unwanted feedback files a case at *www.squaretrade. com* and pays the service fee. There is no time limit.

2. Emails are sent to both parties.

3. Each party independently agrees to have the feedback removed.

4. A mediator at SquareTrade investigates the case.

5. If all conditions are met, SquareTrade sends a removal request to eBay.

The only time things proceed differently is if the other party doesn't respond to any of the SquareTrade emails within 14 days. In this case, a Square-Trade mediator reviews the case, and hopefully dismisses the feedback. The restriction here, however, is that the case must be filed within 90 days of the date of the feedback; this prevents eBay members from attempting to remove old feedback from posters who have long since left eBay and changed email addresses.

What's so terrific about this concept is that it gives buyers and sellers incentive to work things out, even after feedback has been left.

HACK #7 Improve Your Trustworthiness Quickly

Don't let an apparent lack of experience hurt your success on eBay.

"Bad credit? No credit? No problem!"
— Ernie's Used Cars

A low feedback rating can hurt a buyer or seller nearly as much as a feedback profile with an excessive amount of negative comments. Luckily, there are a few things new users can do to gain trust within the eBay community.

Newbie Buyers

Many sellers, primarily those who have had a bad experience with a non-paying bidder, are understandably apprehensive about bidders with low or zero feedback. So, if you see an auction in which the seller has written a warning about such bidders, drop him a quick note by clicking "Ask seller a question," just to let him know you're serious.

If you're a seller, see "Keeping Out Deadbeat Bidders" [Hack #54] for effective ways of dealing with newbie buyers as well as bidders who don't pay.

Newbie Sellers

It's harder to be a new seller on eBay than a new buyer; a seller with low or zero feedback will have a hard time selling anything. Trust, after all, takes on a bigger role when someone else's money is at stake.

The best thing to do (and, coincidentally, the most fun) is to buy a few things before you start selling. Not only is this an easy way to build up feedback, but it will give you some experience in what it's like to be a buyer, which will ultimately make you a better seller.

Note that eBay will also lift some restrictions when you've beefed up your feedback. For instance, once you reach a feedback rating of 10, you'll be able to use the Buy-It-Now feature in your auctions. For those who can't wait, eBay provides the ID Verify service, described in the next section.

When you finally do start selling, make sure to set your payment terms such that your customers will be able to pay safely. If you accept PayPal, as described in "Send Payment Quickly and Safely" [Hack #29] and "Protect Yourself While Accepting Payments" [Hack #67], you'll undoubtedly get more bids from buyers who otherwise wouldn't give you the time of day.

ID Verify

If you're a United States resident and have five dollars burning a hole in your pocket, go to Site Map → ID Verify to begin eBay's ID Verification. The process, which takes only a few minutes, simply involves entering some information that is cross-checked by eBay and VeriSign.

Ultimately, what you get out of it is a little "ID Verify" checkmark icon next to your user ID on eBay. Not everyone will know what it means, but those who click the icon will see the page shown in Figure 1-4.

Trust, as much as any sales pitch, is what will earn bids on your auctions. The ID Verify logo is a bidder's assurance that you are who you say you are. Although it's not a substitute for feedback, the ID Verify icon will help new sellers appear more trustworthy to many bidders.

Negative Feedback

New users are more prone to getting negative feedback, typically as a result of inexperience. If you receive negative feedback, make sure to do a little damage control, as described in "Replies and Followups to Feedback" [Hack #4].

eBay allows you to hide your feedback profile by making it "private," which might appeal to someone who has just received negative feedback. But don't do it; it's a trap! The implication that you have something to hide will be more damaging than any single negative comment.

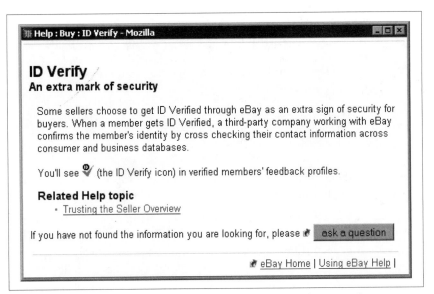

Figure 1-4. This reassuring page is shown to anyone who clicks the ID Verify icon next to your user ID

HACK #8 What to Do When Your Email Doesn't Get Through

Use other means to contact buyers and sellers, and avoid the most common cause of negative feedback.

Email is the life's blood of the eBay community. Sellers use it to send payment instructions to buyers, buyers use it to send questions to sellers, and eBay uses it for just about everything.

Unfortunately, there are times when your email never makes it to the other party, either bouncing back or disappearing into the ether. There are two common reasons why your email may never make it to its intended recipient:

- The other member's registered email address is out of date. In this case, any emails sent to that address should be bounced back to you. (Note that any user can update their registered email address by going to My eBay → Preferences → Change my Email Address.)

- The other member has an overly aggressive spam filter, which might simply delete all email from unknown addresses (including yours). This means you'll never know if your email made it to the recipient.

Any spam filter that deletes email without your approval is ultimately going to lead to a lot of trouble, and possibly some expense and negative feedback. Instead, use a spam filter like SpamPal (*www.spampal.org*) that simply marks suspicious email as spam, so that your email software (discussed in the Preface) can filter it accordingly. Refer to the documentation that comes with your spam filter and email program for details. Also, contact your ISP and make sure they aren't deleting any of your email.

Fortunately, there are a bunch of different tools you can use to send a message to another eBay member, useful for when standard email fails:

Contact an eBay Member form.   Click any eBay member's user ID to send an email via eBay's mail server. This is useful if you suspect that another member's spam filter is deleting your mail, since it's likely to approve all email originating from *eBay.com*. However, since it relies on the member's registered email address, it won't help if that address is wrong.

Use a different ISP.   If you have an email account with another ISP, try sending your email from there. This will also help get around spam filters. If you don't have another account, you can try getting a free backup address at *Yahoo.com* or *Hotmail.com*.

Look in the auction description.   If you're a bidder trying to contact a seller, look in the auction description and payment instructions block to see if the seller has specified an alternate email address. Even if you're not bidding on one of their auctions, the seller may have one or more auctions currently running or recently completed that might contain this information.

About Me.   If the member's user ID is accompanied by a "me" icon, click the icon to view her About Me page, which might also have alternate contact information. See "Make Good Use of the About Me Page" [Hack #48] for details.

Use your photos.   If you're having trouble contacting one of your bidders and you're hosting the auction pictures on your own server, as described in "Host Your Own Photos" [Hack #59], you can use your photos as another means of communication. Simply add large, extremely clear text to one of your photos instructing the bidder to email you immediately. For best results, increase the canvas size and place red text in the whitespace above the image, which will be more obvious than text placed in the photo.

Dynamic text. Also for sellers: see "Dynamic Text in Auction Descriptions" [Hack #51] for ways to put text in your auctions that can be changed at any time, even after the auction ends. This can be very useful in sending messages to bidders who otherwise cannot be contacted via email.

Send a token payment. If the other user has a PayPal account, try sending a token payment of, say, a single penny, and include your message in the Optional Instructions field. Even if the user doesn't receive payment notification email, the payment will appear the next time she logs into PayPal.

Contact Info. Provided that you and the other member are both involved in a transaction, go to Search → Find Members → Contact Info, and enter the member's user ID and item number in the spaces provided. eBay will then email both parties with each other's street address and phone number, which you can use as a last resort.

In nearly all cases, one of these methods will get your message across. Make sure that you inform the other person that you have had trouble sending email, and don't be afraid to request that they take steps to rectify the problem. Strangely enough, people are often indifferent to the situation, but suggesting that yours is probably not the only email that isn't getting through is usually enough to convince the recipient to snap into action.

If you're a seller, and your high bidder isn't replying to your emails, you may have a deadbeat bidder on your hands. See "Keeping Out Deadbeat Bidders" [Hack #54] and "Dealing with Stragglers, Deadbeats, and Returns" [Hack #71] for ways to deal with this problem.

## CHAPTER TWO

Searching

Hacks 9–19

Without the ability to search, eBay would be close to worthless. Think about it: at any given time, there are close to 20 million items for sale on eBay, and that number keeps growing. If you were only able to flip through them like pages in a magazine (a magazine a quarter of a mile thick, mind you), you'd never find anything.

Searching on eBay is an art, often requiring you to think a little creatively. Sometimes you have to get into the minds of other users to predict how they might describe the item you're looking for; other times you just have to be devious.

Now, basic searching on eBay is a piece of cake. Just type a word into eBay's search box and press Enter, or type more than one word to narrow your search. By default, all searches simply cover auction titles, but you can include auction descriptions as well by clicking the "Search titles and descriptions" checkbox.

The hacks in this chapter take it several steps further, covering the advanced search syntax, showing you how to carefully control the scope of your searches, and including several ways to find things that would otherwise elude you. After all, the best deals (and the best finds) are usually the items that most people don't see.

HACK #9 Focus Your Searches with eBay's Advanced Search Syntax

Simplify your searches by making them a little more complicated.

Why should exhaustive searches be so…exhausting? Whether you're performing a quick one-time search or repeating the same search every other day, you can dramatically improve the efficiency of your searches and the relevance of your search results with some simple modifications to your queries.

You could fine-tune your searches by going to Search → Advanced Search, but this can be cumbersome and is mostly unnecessary due to the advanced search syntax.

Excluding Unwanted Results

Simply precede a search term with a minus sign (–) to eliminate any search results containing that term. For example, the query:

```
sunglasses -men's
```

will show all auctions containing "sunglasses" but not "men's", which should, at least in theory, show you a list of women's sunglasses. (Note that there's no space between the minus sign and the term "men's".) This approach is typically more effective than something like "women's sunglasses" because it will also include any auctions for gender-neutral sunglasses.

Naturally, you can exclude multiple terms, like this:

```
sunglasses -men's -children's -ugly
```

The scope of the excluded terms is the same as the scope of the search; that is, if you're searching only titles, the exclusions will apply only to titles. For example, the above example may bring up some auctions with "ugly" in the description, even though it doesn't appear in the title. Only if you're searching both titles and descriptions will eBay look in both places for excluded terms.

> Exclusions open up a little paradox in eBay's search tool. In most cases, expanding a title-only search to include titles and descriptions will increase the number of search results. But when you exclude a word, a title-and-description search may return *fewer* results than the same search performed only on titles. Although this is caused by nothing more than the increased likelihood of finding one of the excluded terms when you search descriptions, I'm still sometimes surprised by it.

Be careful when excluding terms, especially when searching descriptions, because some sellers are sloppy with the words they include in their auctions. For instance, you might type:

```
digital camera -refurbished
```

to eliminate any refurbished (a.k.a. "factory reconditioned" or "factory renewed") cameras from your searches. But any auction that contains the phrase "Brand new; not refurbished" will also be excluded from your search.

Save Time and Typing with Wildcards

Place an asterisk (*) character in or after a search term to match all words that begin with that term. For example, the query:

```
phillips screwdriver*
```

will bring up auctions for "screwdriver" and "screwdrivers". An even better choice is:

```
phil* screwdriver*
```

which will catch the common misspelling "philips" as well.

> As you might expect, if your wildcard searches are too general, you'll get a bunch of irrelevant results. A recent search for "phil* screwdriver*" brought up an auction for a Beatles recording because the auction description mentioned producer Phil Spector and a reference to a joke by John Lennon about a screwdriver.

Since wildcards can also appear in the middle of keywords, you can further focus your search with the following:

```
phil*ips screwdriver*
```

You can also use wildcards with exclusions. For example, if you're looking for women's sunglasses, you might type "sunglasses -men -men's -mens" to exclude results you don't want. But you could also use this much simpler version:

```
sunglasses -men*
```

to exclude all the different variants of auctions for men's sunglasses.

Performing OR Searches

By default, every eBay search is an AND search, meaning that each auction must match each and every search term; the more terms you specify, the narrower your search becomes. But if you're looking for multiple items, or for an item that can be described in several different ways, you can combine your terms into a single OR search.

Terms in an OR search are encased in parentheses and separated with commas. Let's say you're looking for anything by the Beatles or the Bee Gees; you'd type:

```
(beatles,bee-gees,beegees)
```

Note the absence of spaces around the commas and parentheses. You can also combine OR and AND searches; if you're looking for any videos by the Beatles, you might type:

```
beatles (video,videos,dvd,dvds,vhs)
```

Note the inclusion of singular and plural variations of some of the terms, which may or may not be necessary; see "Controlling Fuzzy Searches" [Hack #10] for details.

Looking for Phrases

Enclose phrases in quotation marks, like this:

```
"abbey road"
```

or, to look only for the CD:

```
"abbey road" cd
```

Note that the term "cd" isn't in the quotes, since it could be anywhere in the title or description. Naturally, phrase searches can be combined with exclusions, wildcards, and OR searches. Type:

```
"abbey road" -cd
```

to look for all auctions *except* the CDs. Or, try:

```
("abbey road","white album") -cd
```

to include both these Beatles albums in your searches.

Want to see how valuable the quotation marks are in your searches? Try this search:

```
abbey road -"abbey road"
```

This will show you all auctions with these two words, *except* when they appear together in the phrase "abbey road". When I tried this, the first auction that came up was a signed LP by Barry Manilow. Enough said.

HACK #10 Controlling Fuzzy Searches

Choose when and how plurals and variations of your search terms are used in searches.

For the most part, eBay searches return only listings that match your search terms exactly. That is, if you search for "possum," you won't necessarily retrieve the same results that you would in a search for "opossum."

Historically, to perform a *fuzzy* search, you'd have to include all the variations of a word in the search box manually, like this:

```
(opossum,possum,apossoun)
```

or, to accommodate singular and plural variants, you'd have to type something like this:

```
(antenna,antennas,antennae)
```

The OR search commanded by the use of parentheses, as described in "Focus Your Searches with eBay's Advanced Search Syntax" **[Hack #9]**, takes care of this nicely. But it's not always necessary.

As part of eBay's new search engine (code-named "Voyager" and introduced in 2003), all eBay searches automatically include common plurals and known alternate misspellings of words. For instance, a search for "tire" will also yield results matching "tyre" as well as "tires" and "tyres," rendering the messy OR search unnecessary in this case.

Of course, the inclusion of these variations isn't always desirable. For instance, if you're looking for rooftop antennas for a Pennsylvania Railroad PA-1 locomotive, you wouldn't so much be interested in a book discussing the antennae of Pennsylvania cockroaches. To force eBay to search only for exact matches of words, enclose such terms in quotation marks, like this:

```
pennylvania "antennas"
```

which is practically equivalent to:

```
pennylvania antennas -antennae
```

Whether or not the quotes will be necessary, or whether you'll still need to manually include variations (using parentheses), will depend on the particular search you're trying to perform. eBay's fuzzy searches are based on a hand-selected dictionary of common variations and plurals, meaning that "tire" will match "tyre," but it's unlikely that eBay will go as far as to equate "potato" with "tater."

Punctuation

To simplify searches that would otherwise require very cumbersome search phrases, nearly all forms of punctuation are considered equivalent to spaces in eBay searches. For instance, say you're looking for a 1:43-scale model car; you might expect to have to type the following:

```
car (1/43,1\43,1:43)
```

Instead, all you would need to type is:

```
car 1/43
```

wherein the 1/43 keyword will match "1 43", 1:43, 1;43, 1\43, 1-43, 1.43, 1!43, 1@43, 1#43, 1$43, 1%43, 1^43, 1&43, 1_43, 1=43, 1+43, and 1~43.

Now, say that car is a 1968 Ford GT 40; the appropriate search phrase would then be:

    (gt40,gt-40) 1/43

While gt-40 is equivalent to "gt 40", it won't match gt40 (without any space or punctuation), so the OR search is still needed.

Unfortunately, punctuation doesn't fall under the same rules as variations and plurals, meaning that the quotation marks discussed above won't have any effect on unwanted variations. Furthermore, the equivalence of punctuation also means that the following will not work as expected:

    "gt 40" -gt/40

See "Focus Your Searches with eBay's Advanced Search Syntax" [Hack #9] for more information on search exclusions.

HACK #11 Jumping In and Out of Categories While Searching

Narrow your searches by confining them to certain categories, and filter categories while you browse.

eBay uses an extensive hierarchy of categories to group similar items together. This not only enables sellers to improve the exposure of their auctions, but it helps bidders find what they're looking for and even discover new items.

When you perform a standard search, no thought is given to the categories in which the items are sorted; toaster ovens are listed right alongside antique car parts. By the same token, when you browse a category, you're simply looking at a list of every item placed in that category by sellers, whether it's relevant or not.

Category listings and search results are essentially the same thing: subsets of the massive auction database that is eBay. This means that when you search or when you browse a category, you're really just changing your filtering criteria. Fortunately, you can combine the two quite easily. Think of it as either narrowing a search by confining it to a single category, or filtering a category listing with search terms.

See "Tweaking Search URLs" [Hack #12] for a more in-depth look at categories and how they relate to searches and auctions.

Search Within a Category

Click Browse at the top of any eBay page to view the top-level categories. Choose a category here, and then a subcategory from the assortment displayed on the next page. At three levels deep and beyond you'll see standard category views, including auction listings and a Basic Search field, as shown in Figure 2-1. (Note that you can also jump to a category listing from any auction by clicking the category link at the top of the page.)

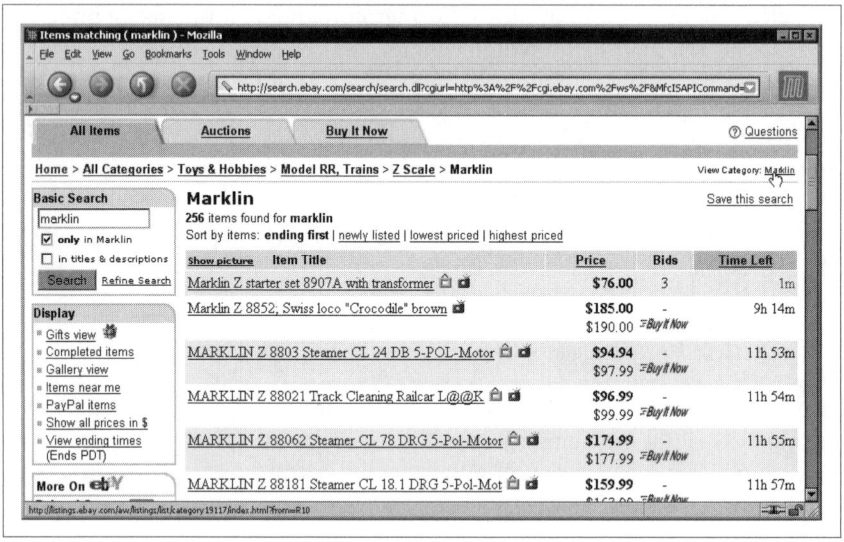

Figure 2-1. Search results and category listings use the same interface, so it's easy to switch between them

Just type your query in the search box, leave the "only in…" option checked, and click Search. Any matching auctions found in the current category (or subcategories, if applicable) will then be shown.

You can jump out of the search and return to the unfiltered category view by clicking the View Category link in the upper right.

Categorize Your Search

Whether you started your search from a category listing or from the search box on another page, a selection of categories with matching auctions will be shown in the Matching Categories box on the left, and the current category (if applicable) will be shown at the top of the page.

You can navigate through the categories without disrupting the search filter. To go up a level, click the higher-level category names at the top of the page.

To drill down to more specific categories and narrow your search, click the desired subcategory in the Matching Categories box.

> The numbers shown in parentheses after the subcategory names represent the number of matching auctions in those categories. However, since different categories are indexed at different times, these numbers may not be entirely accurate. Don't be alarmed if you click "Home Decor (575)" only to find 573 matching auctions inside.

 Tweaking Search URLs

Tap into eBay's massive database right from your own address bar.

eBay is essentially a massive database. Every time you view an auction page, you're just looking at a single database record. Every time you search, you're performing a query. But even if you're not familiar with DB lingo, you can play with eBay's URLs to tweak what you see.

Auction Pages

Many pages on eBay use a standard CGI (Common Gateway Interface) format, which is nothing more than a program name followed by a command and one or more parameters:

```
http://cgi.ebay.com/ws/eBayISAPI.dll?ViewItem&item=3128013703
```

Here, `cgi.ebay.com` is the name of the server, `eBayISAPI.dll` is the filename of the program, `ViewItem` is the command to execute, and `item=3128013703` is a parameter. Any additional parameters are separated by ampersands (&).

In this case, `3128013703` is the auction number. Simply replace this with another valid auction number, press Enter, and you'll see the corresponding auction page. This is typically quicker and more convenient than using the Search page to open an auction by its number.

> Some sellers reference other auctions by simply including the auction number in their descriptions, usually because they don't know how to make links (see "Formatting the Description with HTML" **[Hack #40]**). To view the auction by its number, simply copy and paste the number into the URL, replacing the one that's there.

Search Pages

A typical search page URL looks something like this:

```
http://search.ebay.com/ws/search/SaleSearch?satitle=avocado+green
```

Here, I searched for "avocado green", which you can see in the parameter satitle=avocado+green. Most searches will probably have more parameters, some more self-descriptive than others.

The real value in tweaking the URL is the ability to add or change options otherwise unavailable or inconveniently located in the search interface. One of the most useful of these is the self-evident sorecordsperpage option. Although you can choose this option by going to Search → Advanced Search → Results Per Page, this can be cumbersome, and you can't add it to an existing search you've already built. Instead, simply type the following at the end of an existing search URL:

```
&sorecordsperpage=100
```

Note the required ampersand (&) to separate this parameter from the one that precedes it. (In the old days, you could have up to 200 items on a page, but eBay has since reduced the limit to 100; anything higher will simply be ignored.) Here are some of the other parameters that are worth typing:

Parameter	Description
&sorecordsperpage=*number*	Number of search results to show per page, max=100
&sapricelo=*price*	Show only auctions above or equal to a certain price
&sapricehi=*price*	Show only auctions below or equal to a certain price
&sacategory=*num+num+num*	Restrict results to specified categories; see the next section
&sacategoryex=*num+num+num*	Exclude results from specified categories
&sasaleclass=*class*	Show (1) auctions only or (2) Buy-It-Now listings only
&sapaypal=1	Show only listings that accept PayPal

Searching in Categories

Although there's no way to specify a category directly in the search field, there is a quick way to convert a standard search to a category-specific search without having to drill down through layers of category links. (See "Jumping In and Out of Categories While Searching" [Hack #11] for the long way.)

eBay has thousands of categories (more than 15,000 at the time of this writing), each identified by a unique category number. Although there's no obvious rhyme or reason to the numbering scheme, you may eventually learn the numbers of your favorite categories. The category number is easily found in the URL of the category listing; for example:

```
http://listings.ebay.com/aw/listings/list/category19116/index.html
```

Here, the category number is 19116. (You can also get the number of any category by viewing the complete list at *listings.ebay.com/aw/plistings/list/categories.html*.) To convert a standard search to a category-specific search, simply type the following at the end of the search URL:

```
&sacategory=19116
```

You can specify multiple category numbers by separating them with plus signs, something you can't do by clicking links on search pages.

 Categories are typically restricted to a single nationality. For example, a given category number at ebay.com won't be recognized at ebay.de, even though ebay.de may have an equivalent category that goes by a different number. See "Search Internationally" [Hack #15] for details.

View a Seller's Other Items

If you click "View seller's other items" on any auction page, you'll see a listing of all current auctions by that seller. Although you'll find even fewer options here than on the average search page, there are two important URL options you can tweak.

A seller's auction listing URL looks something like this:

```
http://cgi6.ebay.com/ws/eBayISAPI.dll?ViewSellersOtherItems
                &userid=some_user&since=-1&sort=3&rows=25
```

By default, only current auctions are shown here, but you can change the since parameter from -1 to any number up to 30 to view past auctions up to 30 days old. You can also change the rows parameter to specify how many auctions to show on a page; the maximum is 200.

It shouldn't take long to discover that typing either of these parameters into the URL is far quicker and more convenient than going to Search → By Seller, typing the seller's name, specifying the age and number of auctions to show, and clicking Search. But you probably saw that coming.

See Also

- See "International Transactions Made Easier" [Hack #30] for a way to change the nationality of most eBay pages.
- See "Save Your Searches" [Hack #16] to keep from having to reconstruct the same searches again and again.
- See "Find Similar Items" [Hack #13] for another way to use search URLs.

Find Similar Items

A simple JavaScript tool to quickly list auctions similar to the one you're looking at.

I'm always excited to discover something new while searching on eBay, but I've been around long enough to know that there's virtually no such thing as "one of a kind."

When you've found an item you're interested in, it's often helpful to look for other auctions for similar items, either to compare prices or perhaps to find something better. Typically, this requires opening a search box and typing the name of the item for which to search. Here's a quick hack that will eliminate these steps and list similar items with a single click.

Create a new button on your browser's Links bar (see the "Customizing the Links Bar" sidebar for details) and type the following JavaScript code, all on one line, into the new link:

```
javascript:void(win=window.open(
    'http://search.ebay.com/ws/search/SaleSearch?satitle='+
    document.title.substring(document.title.indexOf(' - ')+3)))
```

Make sure to note the capitalization of the JavaScript code, such as the uppercase "O" in the indexOf keyword. Note also the spaces around the hyphen (' - '). You can name the new link anything you like, such as "Find Similar."

Then, open any auction page and click the new link, as shown in Figure 2-2. (Naturally, the hack won't work on a non-auction page.) A new window will appear with search results matching the title of the auction you were just looking at, which, in theory, should contain at least one auction. At this point, you can modify and repeat the search as needed.

Figure 2-2. View a list of similar auctions by clicking this custom button on your Links bar

Customizing the Links Bar

Modern web browsers such as Netscape, Internet Explorer, and Mozilla all have a customizable toolbar called the Links bar. The Links bar, shown in Figure 2-2, is nothing more than a small collection of easily accessible bookmarks (a.k.a. favorites, shortcuts, links) that you can click to open the corresponding pages.

The easiest way to add a custom button to the Links bar is to simply drag-and-drop the URL shortcut icon (to the immediate left of the URL) onto the bar to add the current page. Or drag any link from any open web page, bookmark, favorite, or Internet shortcut onto the Links bar.

Some of the hacks in this book use JavaScript code embedded in links placed on the Links bar. Although there's no way to create a blank button on the Links bar into which you can type the code, there are other easy ways to create such a link:

- Start by dragging-and-dropping any arbitrary link onto the Links bar. Then, right-click the new link, select Properties, and replace the URL with the appropriate JavaScript code.
- In Windows, right-click on an empty area of your desktop and go to New → Shortcut. Type the JavaScript code into the location field, choose a name, and click Finish when you're done. Then, drag-and-drop the new shortcut onto the Links bar.
- Create a new web page (*.html* file) and place the JavaScript code into an `<a>` hyperlink tag (described in "Formatting the Description with HTML" [Hack #40]). Then, open the page and drag-and-drop the hyperlink onto the Links bar. This is typically more trouble than the other two methods, but it can be an easy way to send the link to others, especially since you can include instructions right on the same page.

How It Works

The first part of the code, `win=window.open`, instructs your browser to open a new window and navigate to the URL that follows. The reason we need Java-Script at all is that part of the URL needs to use information from the auction shown in the current window, something a static link wouldn't be able to do.

Next comes the URL to open. The first part of the URL is taken from a standard eBay search URL, as seen in "Tweaking Search URLs" [Hack #12]:

```
http://search.ebay.com/ws/search/SaleSearch?satitle=
```

The query parameter is then completed by including the title of the currently displayed auction:

```
document.title.substring(document.title.indexOf(' - '),document.title.
length)
```

This last bit of code extracts the auction title from the page title by taking only the text that appears after the hyphen (with spaces on either side) that separates the end date from the auction title.

Hacking the Hack

By default, this hack searches only auction titles. To search both titles and descriptions, add the &sotextsearched=2 parameter to the URL, making sure to place it before the &query parameter, like this:

```
...SaleSearch?sotextsearched=2&satitle=
```

A variation of this hack might be used to search completed auctions instead of current auctions, which may be useful for finding how similar items have previously sold or possibly seeing if the specific item on which you're bidding is being resold. Just change the URL to that of a completed item search, like this:

```
http://search-completed.ebay.com/search/search.dll?GetResult&query=
```

Note that eBay will complain if you try to show complete auctions and search titles and descriptions at the same time, since completed items can be searched only by their titles.

HACK #14 Search by Seller

Easy ways to find items sold by a particular seller.

If for no other reason than to save money on shipping costs, you may find yourself wanting to purchase multiple items from a single seller. Although you can't specify a particular seller when typing into a basic search box, there are three other ways to do it.

View Seller's Other Items

Probably the first thing that occurred to you is to just use the "View seller's other items" link on the auction page. If so, give yourself a gold star. This is typically the easiest way to search by seller because you can see an up-to-date listing of all the seller's current auctions.

Although this is good for perusing, there's no easy way to search here. The only thing you can do is use your browser's "Find on this page" feature

(Ctrl-F), but this isn't exactly a breeze when the seller has over 1,100 open auctions divided into 47 pages of auction listings.

 See "Tweaking Search URLs" [Hack #12] for a way to increase the number of items shown per page, thereby reducing the number of pages.

A Real Search by Seller

The most effective and flexible way to search by seller is to go to Search → By Seller and then use the second, somewhat hidden box at the bottom of the page. If you use the first box at the top of the page, you'll get the same thing as "View seller's other items."

The Multiple Sellers search, shown in Figure 2-3, allows you to do an actual text search on the auctions from one or more specific sellers. Simply type your search in the Search Title box and include the seller's exact user ID in the Multiple Sellers box to conduct your search. You can specify up to 10 sellers by separating their user IDs with commas.

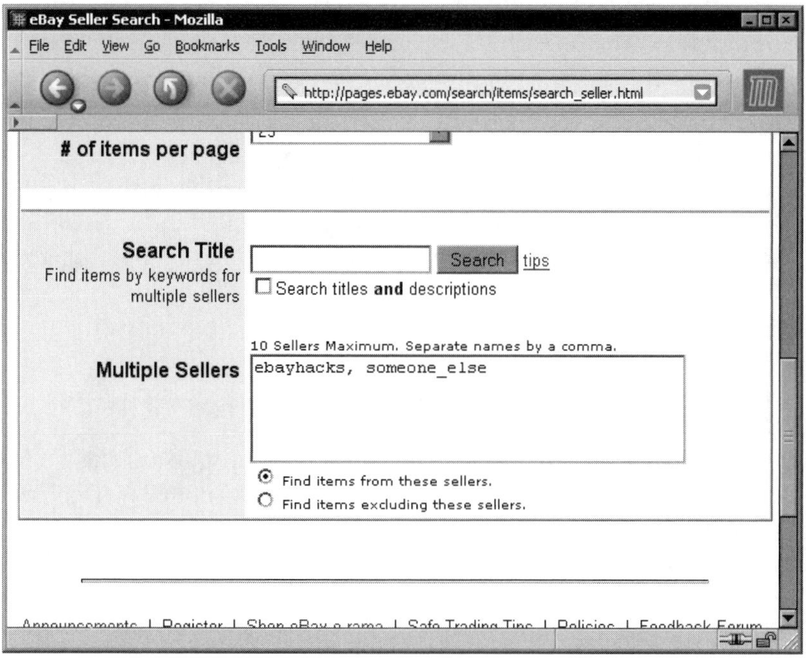

![eBay Seller Search window showing the Multiple Sellers search interface with fields for # of items per page, Search Title, and Multiple Sellers containing "ebayhacks, someone_else", with radio buttons for "Find items from these sellers" and "Find items excluding these sellers"]

Figure 2-3. The Multiple Sellers search, hidden at the bottom of the Search → By Seller page, allows you to specify the seller in a standard keyword search

Click the self-explanatory "Find items excluding these sellers" option if one obnoxious seller appears to be dominating your search results. This is also useful for ruling out sellers with whom you've had previous unpleasant experiences.

eBay Stores

Some sellers have opened *eBay Stores*, an extra-cost option described in "eBay Stores" [Hack #72], in which all of a seller's auctions are shown in a single place. Unlike the "View seller's other items" page, the eBay Stores interface is searchable. Furthermore, sellers can further categorize their auctions and include fixed-price items that don't show up in normal eBay searches.

If a seller has an eBay Store, a little red "Store" icon will appear next to the seller's name on their auctions. Simply click the icon to display the store and search through the seller's items.

The Obvious

Don't forget the most direct approach of all: if you're looking for something, try contacting the seller and asking. More often than not, a seller will have more than what is currently being sold in active auctions on eBay and will be all too happy to sell you something extra.

Case in point: a few years ago, I sold a model locomotive and a few train cars to go with it. The buyer, not yet owning any compatible accessories in the scale, asked me if I had any track to sell. I happily put together an oval of track and included a power pack (transformer), and sold the accessories for a few extra dollars. I sold something I probably wouldn't have bothered to list on eBay, and my customer got a complete train set!

HACK #15   Search Internationally

Use different eBay localizations to look for things outside your home town.

When you search, you're not searching all of eBay; you're searching a subset of auctions made available to your localized version of eBay. Depending on where in the world you live, you may be using any one of the following sites:

Localization	eBay address
Australia	*www.ebay.com.au*
Austria	*www.ebay.at*
Belgium	*pages.ebay.be*

Localization	eBay address
Canada	*www.ca.ebay.com*
France	*www.ebay.fr*
Germany	*www.ebay.de*
Ireland	*www.ebay.com/ie/*
Italy	*www.ebay.it*
Netherlands	*www.ebay.nl*
New Zealand	*www.ebay.com/nz/*
Singapore	*www.ebay.com.sg*
Spain	*www.ebay.com/es/*
Sweden	*www.ebaysweden.com*
Switzerland	*www.ebay.ch*
Taiwan	*www.tw.ebay.com*
United Kingdom	*www.ebay.co.uk*
United States	*www.ebay.com*

Although all these sites share the same global auction database, each one uses the native language and currency of the region it represents. What is dramatically different, however, is the selection of categories, and thus the search indexes.

This means that a search for decorative dog collars at *www.ebay.ch* may yield different results than the same search at *www.ebay.co.uk*.

Expanding Your Search

This limitation on international searches is nothing more than a matter of scope, and the scope can be customized. There are effectively three different levels of scope in eBay searches:

Within your own localization
> The default scope when you search is to look only in the categories that are native to your localization. Some categories are linked to categories on other eBay localized sites, so when searching for dog collars on the U.S. eBay site (*www.ebay.com*), for example, you will most likely see a few auctions priced in euros or Pounds Sterling, as shown in Figure 2-4.

All items available to your country
> Go to Search → Advanced Search, and choose your country from the "Items available to..." listbox. When you search, you'll see more international items, but only those where the seller has intentionally stated that he or she will ship to your country (or, more likely, that the seller will ship "worldwide").

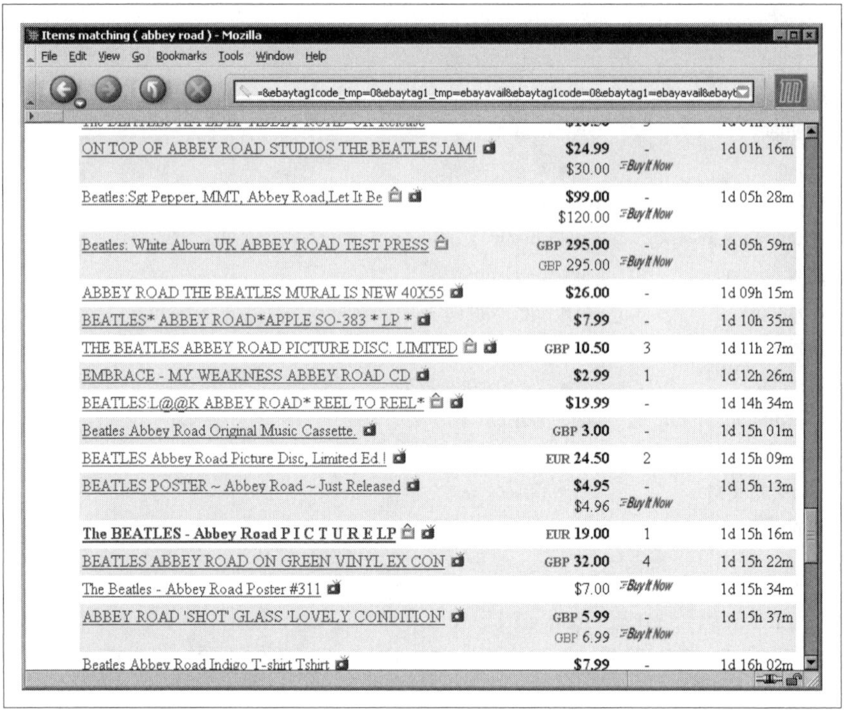

Figure 2-4. International searches show a greater percentage of foreign auctions

All items, everywhere

> Go to Search → Advanced Search, and choose "Any country" from the "Items available to…" listbox. This will show the greatest number of search results, but it's important to realize that your searches may include auctions by sellers who are not willing to ship to your country.

There are several ways to tell if a particular auction is from a different localized eBay than your own, such as the language and currency used throughout the auction page. But there are two auction details to which you should pay particular attention. One is the Shipping section, which lists the parts of the world the seller is willing to ship to (or "worldwide" if the seller has chosen no such restrictions), and the other is the category in which the item has been placed.

Making Sure the Seller Will Ship to You

When performing international searches, you'll inevitably run into sellers who are willing to ship *only* to bidders in their own country or continent. Since international shipping can often be a royal pain in the neck, this is understandable. The problem is that many sellers simply don't bother to change the Shipping option from its default (domestic shipping only) even though they may be happy to ship anywhere.

> Note to sellers: those who are willing to ship to more parts of the world will get more bids. See "Selling and Shipping Internationally" **[Hack #69]** for details.

So the first thing to do is check the description. Sellers who are adamant about not shipping internationally usually say so in big letters, with stern warnings to anyone in another country who dares to bid on their items. But if there's no mention of it, and you really want the item, then all you have to do is ask.

> Since some sellers are intimidated by shipping internationally or may have had bad experiences with bidders from other countries, you should take special care when writing the seller.

Just use the Ask Seller a Question link in the auction page and write something like:

- "Hello! I'm interested in this item; would you be willing to ship to the United States?" Keep it short and sweet, but also make it clear that you're a serious bidder and have every intention of paying quickly.
- "Pourriez-vous possiblement envoyer cet achat chez moi, aux États-Unis? Merci!" If you're writing to a seller who speaks a different language, don't be afraid to write so that they will actually understand you.

With any luck, and assuming you've left plenty of time before the auction closes, the seller should send you a favorable reply. Et voilà!

Viewing Foreign Categories

Each global eBay site has its own selection of categories. Although you can include foreign items in your searches, you can't browse foreign categories from your local eBay site. Naturally, you could switch to any of the foreign sites listed at the beginning of this hack and browse from there, but this can be exceedingly difficult if you don't understand the language.

When viewing any auction native to your local eBay site, you can jump into the auction's category by clicking the category link at the top of the page. But you won't be able to do this for most foreign auctions: the category will still be there, but the link will not. In order to browse a foreign auction's category, you need to view the auction from its native eBay site.

The URL of the auction will look something like this:

```
http://cgi.ebay.com/ws/eBayISAPI.dll?ViewItem&item=3128013702
```

Simply change the domain name to match the native site of the auction. If you're not sure which site to use, simply look at the country specified in the auction details. For instance, to view this from within the French eBay, just change the domain to *ebay.fr*, like this:

```
http://cgi.ebay.fr/ws/eBayISAPI.dll?ViewItem&item=3128013702
```

The currency and language of the site are automatically changed to reflect the localization you choose. More importantly, the category line will become a link, which you can then click to view other items in the same category.

H A C K   Save Your Searches
#16   Different ways to save your complex searches for repeated use.

Ruby's Law states that anything you search for on eBay you will likely search for again. Okay, there is no Ruby, and I just made up the part about the law, but it's still a valid point.

Favorite Searches

The Favorites tab of My eBay is designed to save lists of your favorite searches, favorite categories, and favorite sellers. These lists are on-site and can be accessed even if you're not at home, which can be quite convenient.

To add a new category, click the "Add/change categories" link on the right side of the box. You can save only four individual categories, which can be chosen on the next page. Categories can be removed from the list by marking the corresponding checkboxes and clicking Delete.

The My Favorite Sellers page works similarly to the My Favorite Categories page, except that you type or paste the seller names instead of clicking. Also, there is a delay in adding new sellers to this list; be prepared to wait about a minute before reloading the page to see a newly added seller. You can save up to 30 seller names or eBay Stores (see "eBay Stores" [Hack #72]) on this list.

Probably the most useful of the lists is My Favorite Searches, shown in Figure 2-5, not only because you can save extremely specific and targeted search queries, but because you can save your search directly from the search page. Simply perform a search—any search, including advanced searches or searches on international eBay sites—and click "Add to My Favorite Searches" in the top-right of the search page.

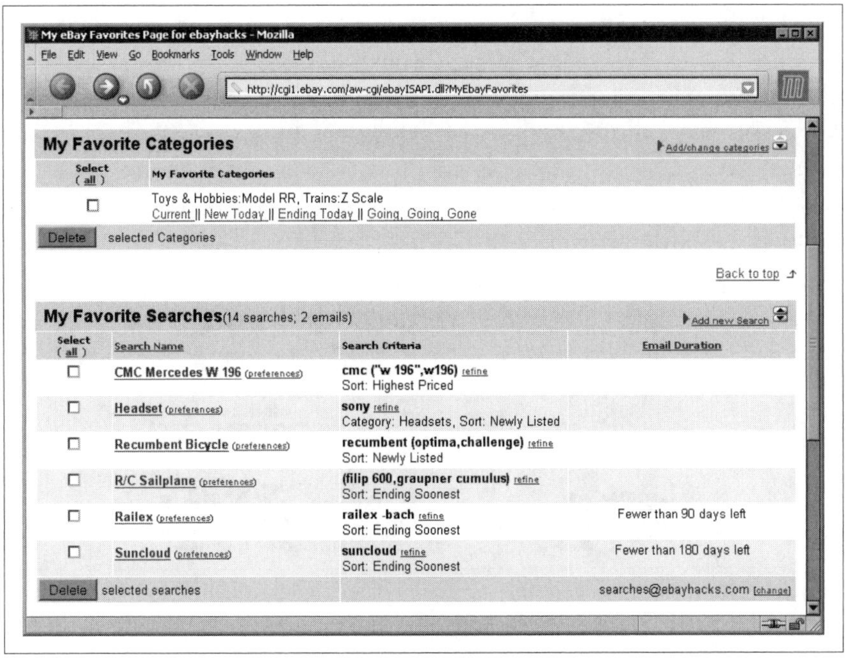

Figure 2-5. The My Favorite Searches list allows you to save up to 15 searches

 Only your search query is saved, not your search results. Each time you click a favorite search, you'll see the most up-to-date search results. To save specific auctions, see "Keep Track of Auctions Outside of eBay" [Hack #24].

Click the search caption to perform the search. Up to 100 different searches can be saved here, 30 of which can be configured to email you daily when new matches are found. Click Preferences to "subscribe" to a daily email notification, as well as rename a search without changing its search criteria. (See "Create a Search Robot" [Hack #17] for a more flexible tool to notify you of new listings.)

Although you can click Refine to change the parameters of an existing favorite search, it's actually easier to simply perform the search normally and make your revisions right on the search page. When you're done, click "Add to My Favorite Searches" again, click "Replace one of these with my new search," and then select the old search caption in the list to replace the old version with the revised search.

Quick and Dirty

Another way to save your searches involves no special features at all. Since all the parameters of a search are stored in the URL (see "Tweaking Search URLs" [Hack #12]), all you need to do is bookmark a search to save it.

Probably the most convenient method is to create shortcuts to your favorite searches by dragging and dropping the Address Bar shortcut icon onto your desktop, as shown in Figure 2-6.

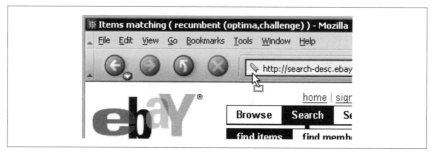

Figure 2-6. Drag the shortcut icon from your browser's Address Bar on your desktop or an open folder to create an Internet Shortcut

Unlike items in the My Favorite Searches list, you can sort your searches alphabetically or by date, or even organize them in multiple folders.

A Little Spit and Polish

Instead of saving your searches as shortcut files, you can just as easily create a custom My Favorite Searches page. Start by opening a blank document in your favorite WYSIWYG web page editor (such as Netscape Composer, which comes free with the Netscape and Mozilla browsers) and placing it side-by-side next to an eBay search window. Then, drag the Address Bar shortcut icon onto your blank web page to create a link to the search; repeat for as many searches as you like.

Your custom search links can then be renamed and organized to your heart's content. When you're done, save the page and then open it in a browser. Or, upload it to a web server so that you (and others) can access it anywhere.

See Also

- "The eBay Toolbar" [Hack #19] allows you to save recent searches right in your browser's toolbar.
- See "Create a Search Robot" [Hack #17] for a way to not only save your search, but to be automatically notified when new matches are found.

Create a Search Robot

#17

Use the WWW::Search::eBay Perl module to perform your searches for you.

A collector in search of a particular item or type of item may repeat the same search, often several times a week. A serious collector, knowing that items sometimes sell within hours of being listed (see "Manipulating Buy-It-Now Auctions" [Hack #26]), may repeat a search several times a *day* for an item. But who has the time?

The Favorites tab of the My eBay page, which allows you to keep track of up to 100 favorite searches (see "Save Your Searches" [Hack #16]), also has a feature to email you when new items matching your search criteria appear on the site. Just check the Preferences link next to the search caption, and then turn on the "Email me daily whenever there are new items" option.

Unfortunately, eBay's new-item notification feature will send you notifications no more than once a day, and in that time, any number of juicy auctions could've started and ended. So I created this hack to do my searches for me, and do them as often as I see fit.

Constructing the Robot

By "scraping" eBay search results with the WWW::Search::eBay Perl module (developed by Martin Thurn), any Perl program can retrieve search results from eBay and manipulate them any way you want. You can download the module for free from *search.cpan.org/perldoc?WWW::Search::eBay* and install it on any computer that has Perl. See the "Installing Perl Modules" sidebar for installation details.

> The WWW::Search::eBay module retrieves search results by parsing eBay's search pages. Since it doesn't use an official programmer's interface (like the eBay API, discussed in Chapter 8), it's vulnerable to even minor changes in eBay's search pages. For this reason, you should routinely check for updated versions of the module, especially if it stops working as expected.

It's easy enough to use the WWW::Search::eBay module to create nothing more than an alternative interface to eBay's own search tool, but the module's real value is how it can be used behind the scenes.

A robot is a program that does automatically what you'd otherwise have to do manually. In this case, we want a robot that automatically performs an eBay search at a regular interval, and then emails us any new listings.

Installing Perl Modules

(*Adapted from* Google Hacks *by Tara Calishain and Rael Dornfest*)

A few hacks in this book make use of add-on Perl modules, useful for turning dozens of lines of messy code into a couple of concise commands. If your Perl script resides on a server maintained by someone else (typically an ISP administrator), you'll have to request that they install the module before you can reference it in your scripts. But if you're the administrator, you'll have to install it yourself.

Installing on Unix and Mac OS X:

Assuming you have the CPAN module, have root access, and are connected to the Internet, installation should be no more complicated than:

```
% su
% perl -MCPAN -e shell
cpan> install WWW::Search::Ebay
```

Note that capitalization counts; copy-and-paste the module name for an exact match. If the install fails, you can try forcing an installation by typing:

```
cpan> force install WWW::Search::Ebay
```

Go grab yourself a cup of coffee, meander the garden, read the paper, and check back once in a while. Your terminal's sure to be riddled with incomprehensible gobbledegook that you can, for the most part, summarily ignore. You may be asked a question or three; in most cases, simply hitting Return to accept the default answer will do the trick.

Windows installation via PPM:

If you're running Perl under Windows, chances are it's ActiveState's ActivePerl (*www.activestate.com/Products/ActivePerl/*). Thankfully, ActivePerl is outfitted with a CPAN-like module installation utility. The Programmer's Package Manager (PPM, *aspn.activestate.com/ASPN/Downloads/ActivePerl/PPM/*) grabs nicely packaged module bundles from the ActiveState archive and drops them into place on your Windows system with little need of help from you. Simply launch PPM from inside a DOS terminal window and tell it to install the module:

```
C:\>ppm
PPM> install WWW-Search-eBay
```

Here's the script that does it all:

```
#!/usr/bin/perl
$searchstring = "railex";
$email = "dave\@ebayhacks.com";
$localfile = "/usr/localweb/ebayhacks/search.txt";
```

```
❷   use WWW::Search;
❸   $searchobject = new WWW::Search('Ebay');
    $query = WWW::Search::escape_query($searchstring);
❹   $searchobject->native_query($query);

    # *** put results into two arrays ***
    $a = 0;
❺   while ($resultobject = $searchobject->next_result()) {
      $a++;
❻     ($itemnumber[$a]) = ($resultobject->url =~ m!item=(\d+)!);
❼     $title[$a] = $resultobject->title;
    }

    # *** eliminate entries already in file ***
    open (INFILE,"$localfile");
      while ( $line = <INFILE> ) {
        for ($b = $a; $b >= 1; $b--) {
❽        if ($line =~ $itemnumber[$b]) {
            splice @itemnumber, $b, 1;
            splice @title, $b, 1;
          }
        }
      }
    close (INFILE);
    $a = @itemnumber - 1;
    if ($a == 0) { exit; }

    # *** save any remaining new entries to file ***
    open (OUTFILE,">>$localfile");
      for ($b = 1; $b <= $a; $b++) {
❾      print OUTFILE "$itemnumber[$b]\n";
      }
    close (OUTFILE);

    # *** send email with new entries found ***
❿   open(MAIL,"|/usr/sbin/sendmail -t");

      print MAIL "To: $email\n";
      print MAIL "From: $email\n";
      print MAIL "Subject: New $searchstring items found\n\n";
      print MAIL "The following new items have been listed on eBay:\n";
      for ($b = 1; $b <= $a; $b++) {
        print MAIL "$title[$b]\n";
        print MAIL "http://cgi.ebay.com/ws/eBayISAPI.
    dll?ViewItem&item=$itemnumber[$b]\n\n";
      }
    close(MAIL);
```

How It Works

The text to search ("railex" in this case) and the email address of the recipient of the notification emails are specified at the beginning of the script ❶. Naturally, you'll want to modify these lines, as well as the $localfile variable, which points to the file in which previous search results are stored.

Next, the WWW::Search::eBay module is referenced ❷ and the search is performed ❹. The $resultobject construct ❺ is then used to enumerate the search results (if any) and retrieve such details as the item number ❻ (taken from the URL) and title ❼ for each auction returned.

All search results are then checked against a list of previous search results ❽, which are stored in a text file ($localfile). Once duplicate auctions have been filtered out, the new auction numbers (if there are any left) are appended to the file ❾.

Finally, a list of new auctions that meet the search criteria is emailed to the email address. You may have to adjust line ❿ to suit your system, either to specify a different location for the *sendmail* executable or to use a different command-line-based email client.

Running the Hack

The search criteria you choose are entirely up to you, but narrow searches make more sense for this hack than broad searches. For instance, my example script targets Railex, a small German manufacturer of handmade brass model trains known for being very difficult to find. At any given time, there may be only a handful of these items for sale on eBay, which means that I may receive a single notification per month, if that. Conversely, a search yielding hundreds of results would quickly fill up your mailbox with dozens of emails with erroneous results. Use some of the other hacks in this chapter to narrow your searches, if necessary.

The best way to run this script is automatically at regular intervals, unless you enjoy waking up at 3 A.M. and typing commands into a terminal. How frequently you run the script is up to you, but it wouldn't make sense to run it more often than you check your email. In most cases, it's sufficient to activate the search robot 3–4 times a day, but given that new auctions can show up on eBay less than a minute after being listed, you can run it once an hour if you like.

Use this script responsibly. If eBay finds that their servers are over-burdened due to abuse by scrapers (which, strictly speaking, violate eBay's terms of service), they might take steps to disable them. See "API Searches" [Hack #83] for a version of this hack that uses the eBay API to perform searches.

If you're using Unix or Mac OS X, type crontab -u *username* -e to set up a *cron* job, where *username* is, not surprisingly, your username. In the editor that appears, add the following four lines:

```
0 0 * * * /home/mydirectory/scripts/search.pl
0 6 * * * /home/mydirectory/scripts/search.pl
0 12 * * * /home/mydirectory/scripts/search.pl
0 18 * * * /home/mydirectory/scripts/search.pl
```

where */home/mydirectory/scripts/search.pl* is the full path and filename of the script. Save the file when you're done. This will instruct the server to run the script every six hours: at midnight, 6:00 A.M., noon, and 6:00 P.M. See *www.superscripts.com/tutorial/crontab.html* for more information on crontab.

If you're using Windows, open the Scheduled Tasks tool, right-click on an empty area of the window, and select New. (This bypasses the cumbersome wizard and goes directly to the so-called "advanced" properties sheet.) Type the full path and filename of the script in the Run field, and then choose the Schedule tab. Turn on the "Show multiple schedules" option, and click New three times. Set up each of the four schedules to run as follows: Daily at 12:00 A.M., Daily at 6:00 A.M., Daily at 12:00 P.M., and Daily at 6:00 P.M. Click OK when you're done.

Assuming all goes well, you should eventually get an email that looks something like this:

```
To: dave@ebayhacks.com
From: dave@ebayhacks.com
Subject: New railex items found

The following new items have been listed on eBay:
Railex Snowplow, RARE
http://cgi.ebay.com/ws/eBayISAPI.dll?ViewItem&item=3128955953

Railex Glaskasten, Green & Black, NEW NR
http://cgi.ebay.com/ws/eBayISAPI.dll?ViewItem&item=3128013702
```

You should continue getting emails as new auctions matching your criteria are listed on eBay; just click the links in the emails to view the auctions.

Hacking the Hack

By default, the `WWW::Search::eBay` module searches only titles. To search descriptions as well, change line ❹ to the following:

```
$searchobject->native_query($query, {srchdesc => 'y'});
```

The search results are sorted by listing date, with newly listed items shown first. You can, of course, sort the results manually, or you can use the `WWW::Search::eBay::ByEndDate` module (part of the `WWW::Search::eBay` distribution) to sort by end date by replacing line ❸ with the following:

```
$searchobject = new WWW::Search('Ebay::ByEndDate');
```

The `WWW::Search::eBay` module is only for searching the U.S. eBay site (*www.ebay.com*). To search non-U.S. eBay sites, use the `WWW::Search::EBayGlobal` or `WWW::Search::EBayGlobal::ByEndDate` modules.

One of the drawbacks to eBay's built-in email notification is that each search generates its own email; have 20 favorite searches, and you'll get up to 20 separate emails every day. In this hack, you can accommodate multiple searches by modifying lines ❶ to ❼ so that the script retrieves a list of individual keywords from a separate file and then compiles a single array from the results of all the searches. That way, you'll only get a single email, regardless of the number of different searches the robot performs.

Once you've been notified of newly listed auctions, you'll most likely want to keep track of their progress, as described in "Keep Track of Auctions Outside of eBay" [Hack #24]. If you want to be a little adventurous, you can modify the search robot script to automatically write new entries to the *track.txt* file used by the *track.pl* script in [Hack #24]. That way, new auctions will automatically show up in your watching list!

H A C K   Find Items by Shadowing
#18
Become an auction stalker and leech off someone else's searching skills.

Often the best deals on eBay are the auctions that most bidders don't find, usually as a result of sellers not knowing what they're selling or not taking the time to promote them properly. The better you become at searching, the more likely you are to find the auctions that are off most bidders' radar. Sometimes, it takes nothing more than dumb luck to stumble upon a great find; occasionally, it helps to rely on other users' dumb luck (and skill) as well.

As much as eBay is a single community of millions of users, it can also sometimes feel like a bunch of micro-communities, each centered around certain genres and auction categories. As you use eBay and become more familiar with the categories in which you're interested, you'll start to recognize individual buyers who, like you, frequently return to eBay in search of more antique pottery, model trains, Ford Model A restoration parts, first-edition Hemingways, or whatever else you might collect.

As soon as someone bids on an item, that bid becomes public record,* even though the bid *amount* is kept private until the auction ends. All you have to do when you see that someone has bid on something in which you're interested is search for other auctions on which he has bid. Not only will you discover auctions for similar items, you'll discover new items that you may not have even known to look for.

To do this, just highlight the bidder's user ID, copy it to the clipboard (Ctrl-C), go to Search → By Bidder, and paste (Ctrl-V) into the Bidder's User ID field. Select No to exclude completed auctions, and click Search. You'll then be shown a list of all public auctions on which that user has bid, whether or not he is the high bidder.

Prevent Bidders from Shadowing You

It's typically in your best interest as a bidder to have as few people as possible see an auction on which you're bidding. Fewer interested bidders means fewer bids, which, in turn, means a lower price and a higher likelihood that you'll win the auction.

Bid shadowing is not common on eBay, but is practiced by some of the more determined users from time to time. The best way to prevent others from shadowing your bids is to bid later in the auction, thereby shrinking the window of time during which other bidders can see where you've bid. See "Snipe It Manually" [Hack #21] for a way to take this to the extreme and effectively eliminate shadowing altogether.

The eBay Toolbar
HACK #19
Expand your browser with eBay's custom toolbar application.

The eBay Toolbar, shown in Figure 2-7, is a free add-on program that provides a handy search box, links to several key eBay pages, and two desktop "alert" features.

Provided you're running a recent version of Windows and using a new version of Internet Explorer or an old version of Netscape Navigator, you can

---

* The exceptions are private auctions and auctions held in localizations with strict privacy laws, such as eBay Germany (*www.ebay.de*).

Figure 2-7. The eBay Toolbar provides several handy tools, primarily useful for bidders, such as two "alert" features not otherwise available to non-toolbar-equipped browsers

download the eBay Toolbar at *pages.ebay.com/ebay_toolbar*. (Users of Mozilla, Netscape 6.x/7.x, Unix, or a Mac of any kind are out of luck.)

In addition to providing handy links to My eBay, the Search pages, the Pay-Pal home page, and other hot spots, the eBay Toolbar also has some features you won't find elsewhere:

- The Search textbox keeps a history of the last few searches you've typed (up to 25), which can be a quick and easy way to save past searches (see "Save Your Searches" [Hack #16]). But you have to use it exclusively, as it doesn't link up with the My Favorite Searches list and it will not save any search typed in the site itself.

- Bid Alerts notify you 10, 15, 30, 60, or 75 minutes before the end of an auction on which you've bid, which is useful if you wish to return to the auction to bid again and ensure a win. Included in the Bid Alerts menu is a handy list of all the open auctions on which you've placed at least one bid; click Refresh Bid List if it appears to be out of date. Click the little arrow next to the eBay logo and click eBay Toolbar Preferences to customize this feature.

- Watch Alerts work just like Bid Alerts, but apply to items in the Items I'm Watching list (see "Keep Track of Auctions Outside of eBay" [Hack #24]), which can be especially useful for sniping (see "Snipe It Manually" [Hack #21]).

- The Bookmarks feature works just like Netscape's Bookmarks button and Internet Explorer's Favorites menu. Probably its greatest strength is that you'll be tempted to fill it with links to eBay-related pages, reducing clutter in your browser's own Bookmarks list.

- Finally, there's a certain cachet to using a customized, feature-rich toolbar right on your browser that simply isn't available anywhere else.

If you're a Windows 95, Mac, or Unix user, or if you use Netscape 6.x/7.x or Mozilla on any platform, there's a very simple alternative to the eBay Toolbar. Both Internet Explorer and Mozilla/Netscape have a fully customizable Links toolbar, which can hold not only links to web pages, but sport neat drop-down menus into which those links can be organized. See "Find Similar Items" [Hack #13] for a snazzy little example.

## CHAPTER THREE

Bidding
Hacks 20–32

The term "auction" evokes a vivid image in most people's minds: a fast-talking auctioneer at a podium, dozens of seated participants, and an assistant parading numbered collectibles across the stage, one by one, as the participants place their bids. The auctioneer quotes an opening price, and participants signal their interest by raising their hands, at which point the bid price is raised by some arbitrary amount. Bidding for each item continues until the current bid price exceeds the amount all but one of the participants is willing to pay.

eBay's bidding system works a little differently. For one, auctions are timed, and close at a predetermined date and time, regardless of the bid price or whether or not everyone has finished bidding.

Secondly, eBay uses something called "Proxy Bidding," a system that somewhat compensates for the fact that the auctions are timed. Instead of placing individual bids on an item, you simply specify a single "maximum bid," and eBay does the rest. Imagine sending someone else to an auction for you, giving them a certain amount of money to bid on a single item. That person, the *proxy*, would place traditional bids until he wins the auction or runs out of money.

Finally, eBay offers "fixed-price" listings, allowing buyers and sellers to skip the bidding process and complete the deal with a single purchase, as though eBay were just another online store. Furthermore, the "Buy-It-Now" feature allows sellers to turn their auctions into a hybrid of sorts, permitting either ordinary bidding or a single purchase. (See "Manipulating Buy-It-Now Auctions" [Hack #26] for more information.) Factoid: About 24% of all listings on eBay end with a Buy-It-Now or fixed-price purchase.

Proxy Bidding

The best way to understand proxy bidding is to see it in action.

A seller starts an auction for an antique pocket watch, and sets an opening bid of $25.00. The duration of the auction is five days; since the auction started at 3:52 P.M. on a Thursday, it is scheduled to end at 3:52 P.M. the following Tuesday. Here's how bidding might proceed:

Time	Bid placed...	Price becomes...	What happened?
Friday 10:00 A.M.	Bidder 1 bids $45	$25.00	First bid; price is set at opening bid price.
Friday 5:30 P.M.	Bidder 2 bids $30	$31.00	Bidder 1's maximum bid is higher than Bidder 2's, so price rises to $1 above Bidder 2's bid.
Sunday 11:15 A.M.	Bidder 3 bids $35	$36.00	Bidder 3 is instantly outbid, just like Bidder 2.
Monday 3:41 A.M.	Bidder 4 bids $60	$46.00	Bidder 1 is finally unseated as the high bidder, and the price is raised to Bidder 1's maximum of $45, plus $1.
Tuesday 1:38 P.M.	Bidder 5 bids $50	$51.00	Another bidder comes along, but her maximum isn't as high as the current high bidder.
Tuesday 3:52 P.M.	Auction ends	$51.00	Bidder 4, who entered the highest maximum bid, wins the auction!

Here, a total of five bidders placed a total of five bids, and the final price ended up at $1.00 more than the second-highest bid. See "Take Advantage of Bid Increments" [Hack #25] for details on the $1.00 increment shown here.

> In any auction with more than one bidder, the final value is always in the neighborhood of what at least two bidders are willing to pay for the item.

The problem with proxy bidding is that bidders are human, and as such, the excitement of winning can cloud their judgment. Furthermore, many bidders still think—and bid—in conventional terms. The next example paints a somewhat more realistic picture of how bidding works, using the same auction as the previous example.

Time	Bid placed...	Price becomes...	What happened?
Friday 10:00 A.M.	Bidder 1 bids $35	$25.00	First bid; price is set at opening bid price.
Friday 5:30 P.M.	Bidder 2 bids $28	$29.00	Bidder 1's maximum bid is higher than Bidder 2's, so price rises to $1 above Bidder 2's bid.
Friday 5:32 P.M.	Bidder 2 bids $32	$33.00	Bidder 2 isn't happy to have been outbid, so he bids again, and is again outbid.
Friday 5:33 P.M.	Bidder 2 bids $38	$36.00	Bidder 2 bids once again, this time finally emerging as the high bidder.
Saturday 1:40 P.M.	Bidder 1 bids $45	$39.00	Bidder 1 returns to auction, discovers that she has been outbid, and raises the stakes.
Monday 9:15 A.M.	Bidder 2 bids $45	$45.00	Bidder 2 is back. Since both bidders have specified the same maximum bid, the earlier bid takes precedence, and the price is set at $45. Bidder 2 gives up.
Tuesday 3:49 P.M.	Bidder 3 bids $50	$46.00	Bidder 3 bids at the last minute and becomes the high bidder.
Tuesday 3:52 P.M.	Auction ends	$46.00	Bidder 3 wins the auction!

Two important things happened in this second example. First, a bidding war took place between Bidder 1 and Bidder 2. Between them, they placed seven bids, but neither won the auction. It would've been much less trouble if each had simply decided how much he or she was willing to spend and then stuck to it.

> The beauty of proxy bidding is that it also accommodates conventional bidding, allowing bidders to enter a single bid or a maximum bid with equal ease. But true proxy bidding is the better choice, because it enforces the concept of picking a maximum and sticking to it.

Second, Bidder 3 saw this war and decided to stay out of it. Instead, she waited until about three minutes before the end of the auction, and then placed her maximum bid. Since there wasn't enough time for Bidder 1 to be notified that she had been outbid, she never bid higher, and ended up losing the auction. Not only did waiting ensure a win for Bidder 3, it avoided further bidding wars, which ultimately resulted in a lower final price. This is called sniping, and is discussed in "Snipe It Manually" [Hack #21].

It's important to point out that sniping doesn't guarantee a win. Quite the contrary, in fact: had either Bidder 1 or Bidder 2 entered a bid higher than $50, either would've won the auction, regardless of Bidder 3's bid. And I'm sure that at least one of the early bidders returned after the auction ended and thought "I would've been willing to pay more than that!"

HACK #20   Sniffing Out Dishonest Sellers
A little research can save you a big headache.

Just because you're paranoid doesn't mean they're not really after you. And just because you take steps to protect yourself doesn't mean that there aren't sellers ready to sell you a lot of hot air. Fortunately, eBay provides a lot of tools to help you discern the good sellers from the bad.

Naturally, feedback (see Chapter 1) should be your first recourse, not only when you suspect a seller of being dishonest, but any time you bid on an item sold by an unknown eBay member. But there are limitations to the feedback system. For one, it relies on the intelligence of past buyers, something you can never count on. It also takes a few weeks for feedback (negative or otherwise) to make its way back to a seller, so a new user—or an old user new to selling—may be able to sell under the guise of a trustworthy seller for up to a month before his reputation catches up to him.

If It Sounds Too Good to Be True…

You've heard it before, and it undoubtedly runs through your head when you're looking at certain auctions: if something sounds too good to be true, it probably is. Now, there are certainly more exceptions to this rule on eBay than at most other places, mostly due to sellers who don't know what they're selling or don't do a good job of constructing the auction. (In fact, I've gotten some great deals—even to the point of effectively getting stuff for free—simply by being more knowledgeable than the seller.) Nonetheless, don't let your desire for a deal cloud your better judgment.

The photo can be a dead giveaway, both to a dishonest seller and to an inexperienced seller who simply doesn't know any better. If the photo appears to be intentionally blurry, doctored, or simply doesn't match the item described in the auction (or other photos of the same item), it should be your first clue that something's fishy. Check out some of the seller's other auctions (both past and present) and look for patterns (or lack thereof); for example, do all the photos have the same background? If they don't, the seller may have snatched them from other auctions or web sites (see "Protect Your Copyright" [Hack #58]). This can either mean that they're selling something they don't have, or merely that they're lazy.

So how do you tell the difference between someone who is trying to rip you off and someone who simply hasn't taken the time to construct a proper auction? Assuming there's still some time left before the auction closes, ask the seller a question. Specific questions, such as those that inquire about an item's dimensions or whether or not it comes with a particular accessory, are good ways to determine whether or not the item described is actually the item you'll receive.

The Shipping-Cost Scam

One of the most common scams is to sell something for pennies, and then make up the difference in grossly inflated shipping fees. Sellers do this for three reasons. First, cheaper items show up higher in search results sorted by price and attract less experienced buyers. Second, eBay's final-value fees are based on the final price only (not including shipping charges), so sellers avoid eBay fees by overcharging for shipping. Third, sellers typically do not refund shipping charges, so if you paid $1.00 for an item and $12.00 to ship it, you'll be unlikely to return it just to get your buck back.

How do you tell whether high shipping charges are legitimate? The giveaway is the "Additional shipping per item" amount, specified in the Payment Details at the bottom of the auction page. If the price seems artificially low with respect to the shipping charges, and it costs nearly as much to ship a second item as the first (e.g., $19.00 for the first item and $17.50 for each additional unit), then you've found a shipping-cost scam.

Naturally, it's up to you to determine if shipping charges are indeed excessive, given your knowledge of the weight and size of the item: $30.00 is a perfectly reasonable shipping charge for a bicycle, but not for a deck of Bicycle playing cards. See "Save Money on Shipping" [Hack #31] for more information.

There's Less Than Meets the Eye

Here's another example of the "if it's too good to be true" scam: someone appears to be selling name-brand consumer electronics for far below their market value, when, in fact, they're selling only *information* on how to acquire the item advertised. If you see a $2,000 camera with a Buy-It-Now price of $8, then it's unlikely you'll be receiving any photographic equipment. Despite the claims made by the seller, all you'll get is an email or CD-ROM with information that is already freely available on the Web. See Chapter 2, especially "Focus Your Searches with eBay's Advanced Search

Syntax" [Hack #9], for ways to eliminate these types of auctions from search results.

> Some sellers start their auctions with a negligibly small opening bid, such as a single cent, merely to encourage healthy bidding (see "What's It Worth?" [Hack #33]). This is not the same as the scam discussed here, and does not necessarily indicate any wrongdoing.

Quick to Unload?

In no time, you'll begin to appreciate the public nature of every eBay member's bidding and selling histories.* For example, you can paste a seller's User ID into the "Search by Bidder" box (see Chapter 2) to see if they're reselling something they've purchased recently on eBay.

Bidder and seller histories can be invaluable, especially if you suspect a seller isn't telling you everything. You may find that the seller indeed bought the item a few weeks ago for only a few dollars, but when reselling, neglected to mention the gaping hole in the side. To find out more, contact the *original* seller to get the whole story. Similarly, if a seller has relisted an item after the original high bidder backed out, try contacting the bidder to see why he or she did not complete the transaction.

Hostile Takeover

eBay's feedback system is useful, but not infallible. Occasionally, an unscrupulous seller will "take over" someone else's account, using that person's good reputation to fool honest bidders. Here's how it works:

1. The seller obtains a list of eBay members' email addresses, typically from a company that sells such lists to spammers (not exactly the pillars of society).

2. The seller sends an email to all the members on the list, carefully designed to look like it came from eBay. See the "Investigating Suspicious Emails" sidebar for ways to determine the validity of any such email you receive.

3. An unwitting recipient clicks a link in the email and is brought to a page that *looks* like an eBay page, into which he types a user ID and password. The server then records the information.

---

* Due to German privacy laws, the bidding and selling histories of eBay members registered in Germany (*www.ebay.de*) are kept confidential.

Investigating Suspicious Emails

eBay never sends emails to their members asking for user IDs or passwords.

You can tell whether a suspicious email actually came from eBay using your email program's View Source feature. Such emails (and corresponding web sites) use JavaScript to spoof the actual URLs of the links. If the URLs in the email or address bar of your browser do not start with something like *pages. ebay.com* or *cgi6.ebay.com* followed by a slash, then you have a fake on your hands. (Beware of sneaky spoofed URLs like *http://pages.ebay.com.fakserver. com* or *ftp://pages.ebay.com@fakserver.com.*)

I've even had an unscrupulous seller go so far as to send an email, under the guise of eBay's SafeHarbor department, informing me of the "legitimacy of his account and transactions." The email went on to say "We advise you to close this specific transaction, the new Western Union and eBay security system allows you to close transactions safely." It would be laughable if it weren't so dangerous.

You can report such emails by going to *pages.ebay.com/help/basics/select-RS. html*, and then selecting Member Problems → Spam → I don't think an email I received is actually from eBay → Continue → Contact Support.

To be on the safe side, never log into eBay using a link in an email; instead, just go to *www.ebay.com* and log in on your own.

4. The crook then uses the user ID and password to log into a valid eBay account. He immediately changes the password and registered email address, and then begins to sell high-priced items under the guise of the unsuspecting user, hoping to use the seller's good reputation to mask his own motivations.

Fortunately, it's usually pretty easy to tell these scams apart from legitimate auctions. First, it's always a deal that seems too good to be true. Second, the seller mysteriously accepts payment only by money order or other postal mail-based payment service with no means of protection (see "Send Payment Quickly and Safely" [Hack #29]). Finally, if you search the seller's past auctions, as described in "Search by Seller" [Hack #14], you'll most likely see a pattern that doesn't match the items currently being sold. For example, if someone who has been selling doll clothes for years is suddenly selling top-of-the-line digital cameras, you've probably found yourself a scam. Report suspicious listings at *pages.ebay.com/help/basics/select-RS.html*.

In short, be a critical thinker, and don't ignore that little voice in your head.

Snipe It Manually

#21   Bid at the last minute to simultaneously ensure that you win the auction and
that you pay the lowest possible amount.

It shouldn't take long to figure out that it's usually better to bid later in the
auction—the later the better. Many eBayers wait until the last few minutes
of the auction to bid, leaving no time for lower bidders to be notified and
respond with higher bids. This is called sniping, and all it takes is a little
nerve and the ability to tell time.

> Sniping leaves no time to read the auction description care-
> fully or to ask the seller any questions you may have. Make
> sure you take care of these things long before the end of the
> auction.

When you've found an auction you want to snipe, the first step is to track
the auction and make note of its closing date and time; see "Keep Track of
Auctions Outside of eBay" [Hack #24] for details. Then, all you need to do is
return to eBay a few minutes before the auction ends and place your bid.

The problem is that many eBay users make a habit of doing this, so you'll
likely have competition. With multiple snipers, the prize often goes to the
bidder who can enter a bid closest to the end of the auction.

With Seconds to Spare...

The most effective snipes occur within 10 seconds of the end of the auction,
leaving no time for other bidders to even see your bid—not to mention outbid you—before it's too late.

Give yourself about two minutes to set up. Start by opening two browser
windows (press Ctrl-N to open a second window), and open the auction
page in both windows. Move and resize the two browser windows so they're
side by side on your screen.

Type your maximum bid in one of the windows and click Place Bid (but do
not confirm your bid on the next page). If necessary, scroll the page so that
the Confirm Bid button is visible and not obscured.

Then, switch to the other window and reload (refresh) the page by pressing
Ctrl-R. Reload it again a few seconds later to see any changes to the current
price and the time left. Repeat this until there's only 10–15 seconds left in
the auction.

If you have a slow connection to the Internet, it will be difficult to reload the page quickly enough to see the status of the auction. Try temporarily turning off images in your browser settings to speed things up. If your connection is exceedingly slow, you'll probably have to increase your sniping margin to 20–30 seconds and hope for the best.

When the time is right, switch back to the other window and press the Confirm Bid button to place your bid. Then, quickly reload the auction page to make sure your bid was accepted. Assuming you entered a sufficiently large bid, you should be the high bidder for the seven seconds that remain. If you cut it close enough, nobody else will even know you've bid until the auction is over.

Ethical Concerns

Some eBay members consider the ethics of sniping to be somewhat dubious in that it may appear unfair to those unfamiliar with the process. This concern is somewhat understandable. It's true that new members will lose auctions to seasoned eBayers at first, either in bidding wars or by sniping, but as they become more experienced, they'll start winning more auctions.

The choice of whether or not to snipe is yours, but in all my years of using eBay, I've never had a single buyer (or seller) contact me and complain about an auction I've sniped. Inexperienced bidders will eventually learn the system and find a method that works for them (sniping or otherwise).

Contingency Plans

Of course, things don't always work out the way we plan. The very nature of sniping leaves little time to correct errors or deal with obstacles, so it's best to prepare for them ahead of time.

For instance, say you want to snipe an item for $25; this bid amount poses no problem two minutes before the end of the option, as the current price is only $17. But if, 20 seconds before the end, the bidding reaches $25, your $25 bid will be refused. Sure, you could anticipate this by bidding $26 instead, but then the same thing could happen. (What really drives me nuts is when I bid $25 and the current price is $24.72; even though my bid is higher, eBay refuses it because it is below the required bid increment. See "Take Advantage of Bid Increments" **[Hack #25]** for further information.)

The best way to combat this—especially if you really want an item—is to open up at least one extra bidding window when sniping. The procedure is the same as ordinary sniping, except on one side you'll have the auction page, and on the other you'll have two (or more) "Confirm your Bid" windows, cascaded so that each is big enough to be functional but small enough that each Confirm Bid button is visible. In the first bidding window, you might type a bid of $25, but have the second window ready to type in a slightly higher bid if necessary.

When it comes down to the wire, you'd click the Confirm Bid on the $25 window as you normally would. If you see the large blue letters confirming that the bid has been accepted, then there's nothing left to do. But if, instead, you see the light-brown letters informing you that your bid is too low or that you've been outbid, you'll be poised and ready to enter a second, slightly higher bid in the extra window.

I know what you're thinking: why not simply enter an inordinately large bid when sniping to completely eliminate the chance of being outbid?

One of the most important but least evident advantages of sniping is that it bypasses the bidding wars that are so common on eBay. Bidding wars typically accomplish nothing more than unnecessarily raising the price of an auction, at which point everyone is bidding more than the item is worth. By bidding at the last minute, you not only eliminate any time for others to outbid you, but you cripple your own ability to bid more than you would normally be willing to pay for the item.

See Also

- See "Keep Track of Auctions Outside of eBay" [Hack #24] for ways to mark auctions for later sniping.
- See "Automatic Sniping" [Hack #22] if you're not going to be around when the auction ends and you don't want to bid early.
- When used in conjunction with "Take Advantage of Bid Increments" [Hack #25], you can cut the price by a few pennies to a few dollars per auction.

HACK #22   Automatic Sniping

Use eSnipe to snipe without actually having to be there when the auction ends.

Sniping is an effective way to increase your odds of winning an auction while simultaneously lowering the final price you pay (see "Snipe It Manually"

[Hack #21]). But there are significant drawbacks to sniping that limit its practical usefulness:

- You have to be in front of your computer, ready to bid, at the exact time the auction ends.

- It's nearly impossible to snipe two or more auctions ending at the same time.

- If your computer crashes or your Internet connection goes down moments before you snipe, you lose.

- You can easily forget to bid, or even become distracted moments before bidding time. (I can't tell you how many times I've been distracted by a doorbell ring or a good song on the radio, only to turn around and find that I've missed my two-minute sniping window.)

The solution, of course, is to simply bid early, and then return to the auction after it's over to find that you've been outbid by 4 cents. Fortunately, there is a better way.

A number of *sniping services* are available that will automatically place a bid for you at a specified time, typically a few minutes or seconds before the end of an auction. Some sniping services are simply standalone programs that run on your computer, but these suffer some of the same limitations as sniping manually—namely, that your home computer be turned on and connected to the Internet at the right time. The better services are web-based, like eBay itself, and operate whether or not your computer is powered up.

> When you use a sniping service, you must share your eBay ID and password so the software can log in and bid for you. While some sniping services are legitimate, there will undoubtedly be some services that use this information unscrupulously. So use caution and do your homework before trusting an unknown service with your eBay login.

The best sniping service available by far is eSnipe (*www.esnipe.com*). It's extremely easy to use, very reliable, and best of all, it works. Just log into eSnipe with your eBay user ID and password, and you're ready to go. To set up a snipe, specify the auction number, the amount to bid, and the buffer time (number of seconds before the end of the auction), as shown in Figure 3-1.

eSnipe will bid for you at the specified time and then send you an email to let you know whether or not the snipe was successful. Naturally, if you were outbid or if your bid wasn't high enough, eSnipe will fail.

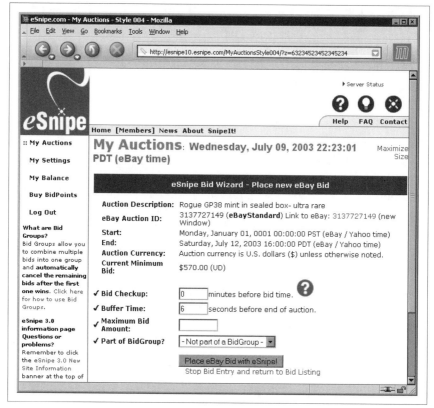

Figure 3-1. Automatic sniping tools like eSnipe bid for you at the last minute

The Catch

There are two drawbacks to using eSnipe. First, it's not free. New users are granted a free trial period, but thereafter eSnipe charges 1% of the final price of the auction, with a minimum fee of 25 cents and a maximum fee of $10.00.* The fees are pretty small, though, and probably pay for themselves with the money saved by sniping. eSnipe fees are paid by purchasing "Bid-Points," which are available at a discount if purchased in bulk.

The second catch is that eSnipe is not smart. It can't read your mind or the minds of the other bidders, nor can it make decisions for you. For instance, if you enter a snipe bid of $54.03 and the price at the time of sniping is $53.99, then eBay will refuse your bid even though it's higher than the highest bid

---

* The fees are per auction; sniping three $2 auctions will cost you 75 cents. The exception is that all foreign auctions have a flat fee of $1 since eSnipe isn't able to do an accurate currency conversion on the fly. Naturally, all quoted prices are subject to change.

(see "Take Advantage of Bid Increments" **[Hack #25]**). If you sniped the auction manually **[Hack #21]**, then you'd be able to make the call on the spot and raise your bid by the required 96 cents. See the sidebar "Where Sniping Can Go Terribly Wrong" for another case.

Where Sniping Can Go Terribly Wrong

Although sniping usually has good results, there are circumstances under which automatic sniping can actually make things worse. Here's a case in point.

I saw a set of Go stones (used in Go, an ancient board game somewhat like chess, but with black and white stones on a 19×19 grid) for auction with an opening bid of $45, so I set up an automated sniping service to bid about $50 for me, seven seconds before the end of the auction. I then promptly forgot about it; that is, until I received an email from the service shortly after the end of the auction.

It appeared that the seller had extended the auction another three days and lowered the price to $40. This happened sometime after I placed my snipe bid, so I was none the wiser until it was too late. Not wanting a bid retraction to show up in my feedback profile, I let the bid stand. And since the price had been lowered and I was the only bidder, I felt like I was in a good position.

Then, another bidder came along and bid repeatedly until my $50 bid had been trounced, something that wouldn't have happened if my bid had not yet been placed (or if I had retracted the errant snipe). Since my bid was placed early, the other bidder felt compelled to outbid me, thus raising the price of the set over what I was willing to pay.

I ended up losing the auction, and the other bidder ended up paying too much, all because of what can go wrong with sniping. Had I sniped manually, I would've known to postpone my bid. Or, had I simply bid at the time I entered my snipe bid, the seller wouldn't have been able to extend the auction in the first place.

eSnipe offers a Bid Checkup feature, an automated email sent at a specified time before the end of the auction to notify you of any potential problems with your pending snipe, but the real-world usefulness of the feature is limited, since you probably won't be around when it arrives. Personally, I've found the Bid Checkup email to be somewhat of a nuisance, as it only means I get two email messages notifying me of a failed snipe instead of just one. Fortunately, you can specify 0 (zero) in the Bid Checkup field to disable the feature.

Put eSnipe on Your Toolbar

If you find yourself using eSnipe more frequently, you may want to streamline the bid entry process. Instead of opening up eSnipe, logging in, and then typing or pasting the auction number into the form, you can use eSnipe's SnipeIt feature.

Start by clicking SnipeIt! on eSnipe's toolbar and following the prompts on screen. Eventually, you'll be given a link that you can drag onto your browser's Links toolbar. (The link is the same for all supported platforms and browsers, but the screenshots in the instructions are different.)

To snipe an auction, navigate to the auction page on eBay and click the SnipeIt link on your Links toolbar. A small window will appear with all information filled in for you; just specify a bid amount and press "Place eBay Bid with eSnipe."

See Also

- See "Snipe It Manually" [Hack #21] for the old-school approach to sniping.
- See "Conditional Sniping with Bid Groups" [Hack #23] if you want to bid on several auctions but win only one.

Conditional Sniping with Bid Groups

#23   Automatically discard future snipes once you win an auction.

One of the best features of eSnipe is its ability to cancel one or more future snipes once you win an auction (see "Automatic Sniping" [Hack #22] for more information on eSnipe).

Say you want to buy a PDA. Since PDAs are a common commodity on eBay, you'd likely be happy winning any one of a dozen different auctions for the same model. But if you were to snipe them all with eSnipe, you run the risk of winning more than one auction. The solution is to use eSnipe's Bid Group feature.

Start by clicking the Bid Groups tab on the eSnipe site, and then clicking Create New Bid Group, as shown in Figure 3-2. Type a name for the new group under Brief Name and click Create New Folder (the Long Name and Description fields are optional).

Next, pick one of the auctions on which you want to bid and begin placing an eSnipe bid as you normally would. The only difference is that you must

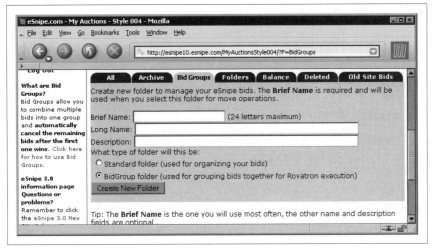

Figure 3-2. eSnipe's Bid Groups feature allows you to snipe multiple auctions until you win one

choose the name of the Bid Group you just created from the "Part of Bid Group?" field. Repeat the process for the other auctions in the group.

eSnipe will bid on each of the auctions in the Bid Group, one after another, until it wins one. As soon as an auction has been won, the pending bids from all remaining auctions will be canceled.

Keep Track of Auctions Outside of eBay

HACK #24

Use eBay's auction-tracking tools, or create a flexible auction-watching tool better than anything eBay has to offer.

If I bought everything on eBay I wanted, I would've gone broke long ago. But I'm also a collector, and as such, I routinely track many auctions in my various fields of interest, whether or not I actually intend to bid on them.

I would argue that keeping track of auctions is among your most important tasks as a bidder—especially for items you've won—if for no other reason than to ensure that you eventually receive everything you've paid for. Tracking auctions is also an essential part of sniping (see "Snipe It Manually" [Hack #21]) as well as selling (see "What's It Worth?" [Hack #33]). If you're really after something specific, you may want to track completed auctions that didn't sell so you can find them easily when they're relisted. And sometimes you may want to keep track of an auction's progress purely for the sake of curiosity.

Using eBay's Tracking Tools

The Bidding/Watching tab of My eBay is where most people turn to track their auctions. The Items I'm Bidding On list and the Items I've Won and Items I Didn't Win lists are all updated automatically whenever you place a bid or an auction on which you've bid closes, respectively. These lists include all the vitals, such as the auction titles, amounts of your bids, end dates, and closing prices.

By default, the Items I've Won and Items I Didn't Win lists show only auctions that have ended in the past few days, but you can increase their range to up to 30 days by typing the desired number of days in the box at the top of each list. And like search results, all the lists on this page can be sorted by clicking the hyperlinked column headers.

> You can clean out these lists by ticking the checkboxes next to one or more auction titles and clicking Delete. However, when you delete an auction, its entry disappears into the ether with no means of retrieval; instead, you'll have to search by bidder for your own auctions (see Chapter 2) to get a complete listing of your bids. A better way to shorten these lists is to simply decrease the number of days back they go.

The Items I'm Watching list, also on the Bidding/Watching page, is a very handy tool, but it works somewhat differently from the others. It will remain empty until you choose to "watch" an auction: simply go to any auction (or fixed-price listing) page and click "Watch this item." A message then appears confirming that item is now being tracked in My eBay; click the link to view the updated list. The Watching list is easy to use and adequate if you never track more than a few items at a time.

> The eBay toolbar **[Hack #19]** sports a few additional features that work in conjunction with the Items I'm Watching list, such as watch alerts and bid alerts that remind you when auctions you're watching or have bid on are about to end.

If You Want It Done Right…

As useful as eBay's tools are, I've found that none of them completely meets my needs. For example:

- You can watch a maximum of 30 auctions at a time. When you reach the limit, you have to manually delete watched items before you can add more.

- Auctions appear in the lists for no longer than 30 days, even though they remain in the eBay system for about 3 months.

- You can't add completed auctions to your Watching list (although closed auctions do remain in your Watching list for 30 days).

- There's no way to prioritize items in your Watching list, which would be useful for differentiating items on which you're planning to bid and those about which you're simply curious.

- There's no way to add auctions to the Items I've Won list, which would be useful if you've decided to complete a transaction outside of eBay.

- The Bidding/Watching page can be cumbersome to use. For example, the way entries are divided into auctions won, auctions lost, etc., has a certain logic to it, but doesn't necessarily end up being as convenient as a single, unified list of auctions would be.

These limitations have prompted me to come up with something better: a fully customizable, web-based, off-site list of auctions with none of the limitations of eBay's tools. The following is based on a tool I created for my own use and have used every day since.

There are two parts to this hack: a Perl script, used to store and display your personal list of auctions, and the link, used to activate the script and add the auction at which you're currently looking.

The Link

The first task is to create an easy way to add any given auction to your custom list, an alternative to the Watch This Item link on auction pages. This is accomplished by placing the following snippet of JavaScript in a button on your browser's Links bar (make sure the text appears all on one line):

```
javascript:void(win=window.open('http://www.ebayhacks.com/exec/track.pl?
    do=add&auction='+location.href+'&title='+document.title,'Hack'))
```

You can name the new link anything you like, such as "Watch Auction" or simply "Track." (See "Find Similar Items" [Hack #13] for more information on the Links bar.)

The first few bits of the code are used to instruct your browser to open a new browser window and execute the code inside the parentheses, but it's the stuff that follows that concerns us. First comes the URL of your tracking tool, so you'll need to change www.ebayhacks.com to the name of your own server, /exec to the name of your executable folder (often /cgi-bin), and track.pl to the filename of your script (discussed in the following section).

The second half of the URL, after the question mark (?), is composed of three arguments that are passed to your script, separated by ampersands (&):

```
do=add&auction='+location.href+'&title='+document.title
```

JavaScript automatically inserts the auction URL (location.href) and page title (document.title) as arguments to pass to the script. One of the neat little tricks of this code is how it works with eBay's auction URL, which also includes arguments separated by ampersands:

```
http://cgi.ebay.com/ws/eBayISAPI.dll?ViewItem&item=3125058177
```

When this URL is passed to your script with the other arguments, it is automatically split into these two arguments:

```
auction=http://cgi.ebay.com/ws/eBayISAPI.dll?ViewItem
item=3125058177
```

and thus the auction number is conveniently separated for us!

The Script

The second half of this hack is a script written in Perl, which interprets the information it receives from the JavaScript link (see the previous section), stores all your auctions in a file, and then displays a properly sorted list.

> This script requires the Time::ParseDate Perl module, part of David Muir Sharnoff's *Time-modules-2003.0211* distribution (*search.cpan.org/perldoc?Time::ParseDate*), which is necessary to convert eBay's date notation into something Perl can understand. (See "Create a Search Robot" **[Hack #17]** for installation instructions.) Also required is Steven E. Brenner's *cgi-lib.pl* Perl library (*cgi-lib.berkeley.edu*), used to parse the arguments passed from the JavaScript link.

```perl
#!/usr/bin/perl

# *** includes ***
use Time::ParseDate;
use POSIX qw(strftime);
require("cgi-lib.pl");
&ReadParse;

# *** variables ***
$selfurl = "http://www.ebayhacks.com/exec/track.pl";
$localfile = "/usr/local/home/ebaylist.txt";
$timeoffset = 0;
$url = "http://cgi.ebay.com/ws/eBayISAPI.dll?ViewItem&item=";
@formatting=("color=#EE0000 STYLE=font-weight:bold",
             "color=#000000 STYLE=font-weight:bold", "color=#000000");
```

```
    $i = 0;
    $exists = 0;
❸   $numlevels = 2;

    # *** read stored list ***
    open (INFILE,"$localfile");
      while ( $line = <INFILE> ) {
        $line =~ s/\s+$//;
        $i++;
        ($enddate[$i],$priority[$i],$item[$i],$title[$i]) =
                                             split(",", $line, 4);

        # *** see if passed auction number is in list already ***
        if (($item[$i] ne "") && ($item[$i] eq $in{'item'})) { $exists = $i; }
      }
    close (INFILE);

    # *** add latest auction to list, if valid ***
    if (($in{'auction'} =~ "ebay.com") && ($in{'item'} != "") && ($exists==0)) {
      $x = index($in{'title'}, "(");
      $y = index($in{'title'}, ")", $x);
      $z = index($in{'title'}, "-", $y);

❹     $title = substr($in{'title'}, $z + 2);
      $enddate = parsedate(substr($in{'title'}, $x + 6, $y - $x - 7));

      $i++;
      ($enddate[$i], $priority[$i], $item[$i], $title[$i]) =
                                     ($enddate, 2, $in{'item'}, $title);
    }
    elsif (($in{'do'} eq "promote")) {
      $priority[$exists]--;
      if ($priority[$exists] < 0) { $priority[$exists] = 0; }
    }
    elsif (($in{'do'} eq "demote")) {
      $priority[$exists]++;
      if ($priority[$exists] > 2) { $priority[$exists] = 2; }
    }
    elsif (($in{'do'} eq "delete")) {
      splice @enddate, $exists, 1;
      splice @priority, $exists, 1;
      splice @item, $exists, 1;
      splice @title, $exists, 1;
      $i--;
    }

    # *** update list ***
    if (($in{'do'} ne "")) {
      open (OUTFILE,">$localfile");
        for ($j = 1; $j <= $i; $j++) {
          print OUTFILE "$enddate[$j],$priority[$j],$item[$j],$title[$j]\n";
        }
```

```
    close (OUTFILE);

    print "Location: $selfurl\n\n";
    exit( 0);
}

# *** sort list ***
@idx = sort criteria 0 .. $i;

# *** display list ***
print "Content-type: text/html\n\n";
print "<table border cellspacing=0 cellpadding=6>\n";

for ($j = 1; $j <= $i; $j++) {
  $formatteddate =
        strftime("%a, %b %d - %l:%M:%S %p", localtime($enddate[$idx[$j]]));
```
⑤
```
  $formattedtitle = "<a href=\"$url$item[$idx[$j]]\" target=\"_blank\"><font
            $formatting[$priority[$idx[$j]]]>$title[$idx[$j]]</font></a>";

  if (strftime("%v", localtime($enddate[$idx[$j]])) eq
                                        strftime("%v", localtime(time))) {
```
⑥
```
    $formattedtitle = "<li>" . $formattedtitle;
  }
  if ($enddate[$idx[$j]] < time) {
```
⑦
```
    $formattedtitle = "<strike>" . $formattedtitle . "</strike>";
  }
  else {
    $timeleft = ($enddate[$idx[$j]] - time) / 60 + ($timeoffset * 60);
    if ($timeleft < 24 * 60) {
      $hoursleft = int($timeleft / 60);
      $minleft = int($timeleft - ($hoursleft * 60));
      if ($minleft < 10) { $minleft = "0" . $minleft; }
```
⑧
```
        $formattedtitle = $formattedtitle .
                    " <font size=-1>($hoursleft:$minleft left)</font>";
    }
  }

  print "<tr><td>$formattedtitle</td>";
  print "<td><font size=-1>$formatteddate</font></td>";
```
⑨
```
  print "<td><a href=\"$selfurl?item=$item[$idx[$j]]&do=promote\">+</a>";
  print " | <a href=\"$selfurl?item=$item[$idx[$j]]&do=demote\">-</a>";
  print " | <a href=\"$selfurl?item=$item[$idx[$j]]&do=delete\">x</a></td>";
  print "</tr>\n";
}

print "</table>\n";

sub criteria {
  # *** sorting criteria subroutine ***
  return ($priority[$a] <=> $priority[$b] or $enddate[$a] <=> $enddate[$b])
}
```

Save this script as *track.pl* and place it in your web server's *cgi-bin* directory, as described in "Generate a Custom Gallery" [Hack #94]. Note that the $selfurl and $localfile variables ❶ must be modified to match the URL of your script and the location of the local file in which the auction titles are to be stored, respectively. Also, you may need to adjust the $timeoffset variable to compensate for the time zone difference between eBay time (Pacific time) and your computer's clock; e.g., enter 3 if you're in Eastern time (GMT − 5:00).

Running the Hack

With the script in place and the JavaScript link at the ready on your browser toolbar, all that's left is to try it out. Open any auction page on eBay and click the "Track" link on your Links bar. A new window will open, and the auction you were just looking at will appear at the top of the list, as shown in Figure 3-3. Repeat this for as many auctions as you like; there's virtually no limit. You can even track completed auctions and auctions that you haven't won.

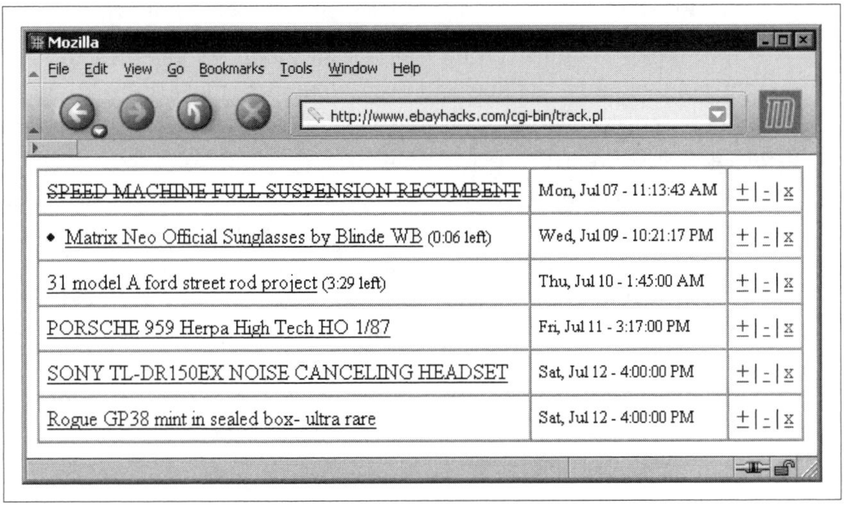

Figure 3-3. Track and prioritize auctions with this flexible web-based tool

Click the title of any auction to open the eBay auction page in a new window. Click the [x] link to delete the entry.

Auctions can be prioritized; all new entries start out at the lowest priority and are shown in normal font. Click the [+] link to promote an auction and make its title bold. Click [+] again to promote the auction to the highest level and make its title red and bold. Likewise, click [-] to demote any entry. Higher-priority items appear higher in the list, and all auctions within a certain priority level are sorted by their closing date. I use the lowest priority for auctions on which I don't intend to bid, the medium priority for items I want, and the highest priority for items I've already bid on and won.

> Sellers often lower the Buy-It-Now prices of running auctions that haven't received bids, sometimes repeatedly. If you really want an item, it's a good idea to check back a few times before the end of the auction to see if you can snag it before someone else does. (See "Manipulating Buy-It-Now Auctions" [Hack #26] and "Make Changes to Running Auctions" [Hack #50] for more information.)

You can see this hack in action at *www.ebayhacks.com*.

Hacking the Hack

Naturally, you'll want to customize this hack to suit your needs, which is really this tool's greatest advantage over eBay's Bidding/Watching page. Among the more interesting ways to hack this script are the following:

- If you're familiar with HTML, you can add pictures and text to your heart's content. Add shading and even column headers (for sorting) to the table. Replace the [+], [-], and [x] links ❾ with more interesting icons, and add a splash of color to the page.

- You can have as many different levels of prioritization as you like. Three levels suit my needs just fine, but you can add more by increasing the $numlevels variable ❸. (Keep in mind that lower numbers mean a higher priority.) The only other thing you'll need to maintain is the @formatting array ❷, which contains snippets of HTML code (one for each priority level) that visually differentiate one priority level from another. For details, look up the <font> structure in any HTML documentation (or see "Formatting the Description with HTML" [Hack #40]).

- Using the $item[$idx[$j]] variable ❹, you can also add links to bid, leave feedback, and view the bid history.

- To support multiple users, include another argument in the JavaScript link (Part 1), such as &user=cletus. Then, simply append the username to the filename to create a different auction list file ❶ for each user, like this:

```
$localfile = "/usr/local/home/ebaylist_\L$in{'user'}.txt";
```

- For simplicity, the script retrieves the auction title ❹ by parsing the arguments passed to it from the JavaScript link. The main caveat is that if the title contains an ampersand (&) or pound sign (#), the title will be broken apart, and all you'll get is the first portion. Also, the script determines the closing time and date by further parsing the title, and may not work with titles from non-U.S. sites that use a different date notation.

  A more bulletproof (and only slightly more complex) solution to both of these problems would be to use the eBay API to retrieve the auction title and end date, as described in "Track Items in Your Watching List" [Hack #86]. This would also enable you to reliably read the seller's name, the current price, and other auction details, all without having to resort to parsing.

- The script also contains code to add a little "richness" to the tool. For example, completed auctions have crossed-out titles ❼, auctions ending today are marked with round bullets ❻, and any auction ending within 24 hours shows the time left to bid ❽. I've found these additions to be quite helpful for my purposes, but you may have different needs. For example, if you're in front of the computer only during the day, you can configure the script to highlight auctions ending after 5:00 P.M. so you know you'll have to bid early or set up an automatic snipe (see "Automatic Sniping" [Hack #22]).

- The pop-up window can be customized by modifying the JavaScript code. For example, add the following to the JavaScript line:

  ```
  ,'width=400,height=300,menubar=no,status=no,resizable=yes,scrollbars=yes'
  ```

  Place the code after 'Hack' but before the two closing parentheses. Make sure to include the comma and enclose the parameters as a whole in single quotes as shown. More information on these parameters can be found in any JavaScript documentation, under the window.open statement.

HACK #25 Take Advantage of Bid Increments

A slight adjustment to your bidding strategy will help you save money and win more auctions.

Every auction has a minimum bid, a dollar amount shown just above the Place Bid button on the auction page, as shown in Figure 3-4. If the auction hasn't received any bids, the minimum bid is the same as the starting bid. Otherwise, the minimum bid is equal to the current price plus a bid increment.

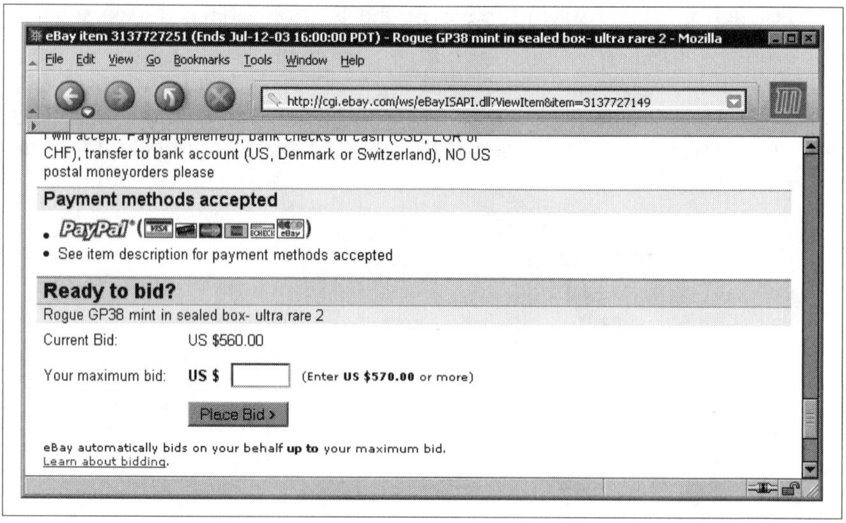

Figure 3-4. The Bidding Section shows the current bid increment and minimum bid

Bid increments, at least in theory, prevent bidders from outbidding one another by a single cent, and are calculated as follows:

Current price	Bid increment
$0.01 – $0.99	$0.05
$1.00 – $4.99	$0.25
$5.00 – $24.99	$0.50
$25.00 – $99.99	$1.00
$100.00 – $249.99	$2.50
$250.00 – $499.99	$5.00
$500.00 – $999.99	$10.00
$1000.00 – $2499.99	$25.00
$2500.00 – $4999.99	$50.00
$5000.00 and up	$100.00

For example, an auction currently at $68.45 will have a minimum bid of $69.45 ($1.00 more), so you wouldn't be able to bid $69.00 even though it's higher than the current price.

Bid increments also come into play when calculating the current price. If there's more than one bidder, the current price is equal to the second-highest bidder's bid plus the bid increment. So if someone bids $114 and someone else bids $157, the current price will be $116.50 ($114 + $2.50), and the minimum bid for future bidders will be $119 ($116.50 + $2.50).

As more bids are placed, the current price continues to rise, always equal to the second-highest bid plus the bid increment. But it gets more interesting when someone places a bid very close to the high bidder's maximum bid. The bid increment rule is compromised by another rule: eBay will never raise the current price above the highest bidder's maximum bid. Here's how this works:

- If someone bids $156.80 on this auction, it will raise the current bid to $157, even though it's only 20 cents above the second-highest bidder's maximum.

- If a subsequent bidder enters a bid of $157, the current price will be exactly $157. The original bidder will still be the high bidder, because earlier bids take precedence over later bids of the same amount.

- If the later bidder bids $157.01, the current price will be raised to $157.01 (one cent above the previous high bid), and the newcomer will become the high bidder.

This loophole effectively allows you to outbid another bidder by as little as a single cent. But why is this important, and how is this useful?

Outbidding the High Bidder

Bid amounts are always kept hidden until an auction closes. As described above, however, you can easily determine the second-highest bidder's maximum bid by subtracting the bid increment from the current price. Only the high bidder's maximum remains elusive.

Most bidders type whole, round numbers when bidding, primarily out of habit and sometimes out of laziness. You can take advantage of this by guessing a high bidder's maximum and adding a penny.

For example, if an auction with a starting bid of $7.99 has only one bidder, the current price is $7.99. If that bidder is relatively new to eBay (having a feedback rating of, say, less than 30), that bidder most likely typed either $8 or $10 as a maximum bid. Although you couldn't bid $8.01, as the minimum bid would be $8.49, you could bid $10.01 and have a pretty good chance of outbidding the other bidder by a single cent. Contrast this to a bid of $15.00, which would result in a final price of $10.50 ($10 plus the 50-cent increment). You've just saved 49 cents.

More experienced bidders won't type whole numbers, but they will likely be just as predictable. If you want to outbid someone by a single cent, try searching for past auctions they've bid on (see Chapter 2); look at the bidding history of *closed* auctions they *didn't* win, and you'll see their exact bids. Look at two or three old auctions, and you'll likely find a pattern.

Understanding bid increments is also extremely useful if you bid and don't end up as the high bidder. If, after you bid, the current price ends up *lower* than your bid plus the bid increment (you bid $40 and the price rises to $40.17), then the high bidder's maximum bid is equal to the current price (in this case, $40.17). This means that all you need to do is place one more bid of at least $41.17 to put yourself in the lead. Combine this with sniping [Hack #22], and you've won the auction!

Take It One Step Further

You can take steps to prevent other bidders from outbidding you by one cent (and they will) while allowing you to more readily outbid others. Instead of bidding whole, round numbers, make a habit of bidding odd numbers, such as $10.07 or $11.39. That way, if someone bids $10.01 or $11.01, respectively, you'll still be the high bidder. Likewise, you'll also be more likely to outbid others who type bid amounts like $10.01.

HACK #26 Manipulating Buy-It-Now Auctions
Save money with the loopholes of the Buy-It-Now feature.

The Buy-It-Now feature that appears in some auctions allows a bidder to bypass the bidding process and end an auction early at some predetermined price. Whether or not this is a good deal for the buyer, however, depends on the Buy-It-Now price the seller has chosen.

The Buy-It-Now option remains visible on the auction page until the first bid is placed, after which it disappears. (The exception is reserve-price auctions, where the Buy-It-Now will be available as long as the reserve hasn't been met, regardless of the number of bids.) There are several ways to use this to your advantage.

Start with the Obvious

Some of the best deals I've gotten on eBay have been Buy-It-Now items, where the seller specified too low a Buy-It-Now price, and I snatched it before anyone else got a chance. If you see a good price, why wait? Just click Buy-It-Now and end the auction without bidding.

> There may be a reason that an auction has a low Buy-It-Now price; make sure you read the auction description carefully before you commit. Buyers have the same obligation to complete Buy-It-Now transactions as those that end normally.

Sort your search results by Newly Listed, and the newest Buy-It-Now auctions will appear first. This gives you a good chance to catch early deals, as they're unlikely to last more than a few hours.

Undercut the Buy-It-Now Feature

Auctions with too high a Buy-It-Now price are just as common as those with a low Buy-It-Now price. But there will always be some yahoo who doesn't know any better, and will come along and buy these items anyway. If, however, you place a bid right away—say, the minimum amount—the Buy-It-Now option will disappear, and bidding will proceed normally. This will not only give you a chance to win the item for less than the Buy-It-Now amount, but will also give you more time to decide whether you really want the item. (This is an example of when it pays to bid early, a strategy contrary to that of "Snipe It Manually" [Hack #21].)

This works best on auctions with artificially low starting bids, because bidding is likely to exceed your first bid and you'll be under no obligation to buy. For example, a few weeks ago, I undercut an auction with a Buy-It-Now of $12 by bidding the minimum of $1. The item ended up selling for less than $5, but it could easily have sold for $12 if someone who really wanted it got there before I did.

> Let this be a lesson to sellers to choose their starting bids and Buy-It-Now prices carefully. Had the seller in this example set the starting bid at $6 and the Buy-It-Now at $9, I would've likely bought it at $9. I would've been happy to get a deal, and the seller would've gotten twice as much for the item. See "What's It Worth?" [Hack #33] for similar strategies.

Naturally, you're running the risk of the bidding exceeding the original Buy-It-Now price. But if the Buy-It-Now price were more than you were willing to pay, you would've lost the auction either way.

There's also a chance that the auction won't get any other bids, and you'll end up winning the item with your starting bid. Assuming the bid was low enough, you should be happy to get a good deal. However, if you suspect that you may be stuck with something you don't want, you should probably retract your bid (see "Retract Your Bid Without Retracting Your Bid" [Hack #27]).

Let's Make a Deal

Buy-It-Now is an optional feature, chosen by sellers on a per-auction basis. A seller may not wish to include a Buy-It-Now price if she is unsure of the value of the item, or if she doesn't want to scare away bidders with too high a price. The Buy-It-Now option is also available only to sellers with a feedback rating of 10 or higher, so sellers new to eBay won't be able to include it even if they want it. And as stated at the beginning of this hack, the Buy-It-Now feature disappears once bids have been placed on the auction.

For whatever reason, there will be auctions without a Buy-It-Now price, but that doesn't mean you can't "buy it now." Simply contact the seller and make an offer in exchange for ending the auction early.

Beware: there are good and bad ways to broach the subject. As in many aspects of using eBay, diplomacy is very important here. The idea is to get what you want, but also to make it worth the seller's while.

Here are some *good* ways to request a Buy-It-Now:

- "Do you have a Buy-It-Now price for this item?" This is polite and non-confrontational, and the seller will typically respond with a price or ask you what you'd be willing to pay.

- "Would you consider adding a Buy-It-Now price to this auction?" This is similar to the previous example, except that it doesn't send the message to the seller that you're trying to circumvent eBay's rules. Use this only if the auction hasn't yet received any bids. (See "Make Changes to Running Auctions" [Hack #50] for details on how sellers can do this. Remember, sellers with a feedback rating of less than 10 will not have this option.)

- "Would you be willing to end the auction early for $250?" Pique the seller's interest by including a specific offer in your first email. Even if it's too low, you can always raise it later.

About half the sellers I've contacted with offers like these end up agreeing, and the other half have preferred to wait. In nearly all cases where a seller has declined to sell early to me, though, I ended up buying the item for less than my original offer. Let this be a lesson to both buyers and sellers!

Here are some examples of what *not* to do:

- "Would you sell me the item for the current bid price?" Why would any seller sell at the current price when they can wait and most likely get more money? Remember, make it worth the seller's while, or they won't give you the time of day.

- "I'll give you 50 bucks for it." The tone here is condescending and aggressive, and most sellers will respond poorly to it (if at all). Furthermore, if the bidding has been healthy and your offer is not much higher than the current price, the seller will probably take it as an insult that you'd expect them to sell so cheaply. You're asking the seller a favor, so be nice!

- "What would it take to end the auction early?" Again, the tone is too aggressive, and the message offers the seller nothing for her trouble. Furthermore, it pressures the seller to quote a price right away, which is never good. Sellers put in this position will quote you a higher price for fear of quoting too low. It's much harder to haggle a seller down than to increase a low opening offer.

If a seller seems disagreeable to the whole idea, you're unlikely to convince them otherwise (unless you offer so much money that it's no longer worth *your* while).

 You can often determine a seller's disposition before you write by simply reading the auction description. If the seller's tone is relaxed and positive, then she'll be more likely to make a deal. If the prose is stiff and curt, the seller will likely want to proceed "by the book" and let the auction play out.

Assuming the seller agrees, you'll have three choices. One, you can wait for the seller to add a Buy-It-Now price to the auction, and then purchase the item normally. Just make sure to check the auction page frequently and purchase it as soon as the option becomes available, lest someone beat you to it.

If the seller can't use Buy-It-Now for whatever reason, you can always bid and become the high bidder, with the understanding that the seller will then end the auction early and sell to you at the agreed price (regardless of the closing price of the auction). This allows both you and the seller to leave feedback for one another and use eBay's other services.

The other option is for the seller to cancel all bids, end the auction early, and then sell to you outside of eBay. The seller may prefer this, as it will save the eBay fees* normally charged to successfully completed auctions, but there will be little advantage for the buyer. Any transactions not completed through eBay aren't eligible for feedback, fraud protection, or any other services.

 ## Retract Your Bid Without Retracting Your Bid
#27 Back out of an auction before it's too late.

There are a lot of reasons why you might want to back out of an auction after bidding. Obviously, if you make a mistake and bid the wrong amount or bid on the wrong auction, you'll want to retract that bid before the auction ends and you're obligated to pay.

But there are other reasonable circumstances under which you may change your mind about an auction. Sellers can make changes to the description or photos, even after the item has received bids (see "Make Changes to Running Auctions" [Hack #50]), and such changes may affect your desire for an item or your ability to pay for it. Or, if you lose your job and find your daughter needs braces, your desperate need for that 42" plasma TV may become slightly less desperate.

eBay takes bidding very seriously, to the point of imposing restrictions as to when and under what circumstances you can retract a bid. This is understandable, considering the scams a small minority of eBay users have propagated; look up "buying offenses" in eBay's Help for an exhaustive list (and lots of ideas, too).

By the Book

The easiest way to retract a bid is to use the "Retract my bid" form. Simply enter the auction number, choose one of the prewritten excuses from the list, and click Retract Bid. (It doesn't really matter which reason you choose; the end result will be the same.) All your bids on the auction will be canceled, and the auction's current price will be adjusted accordingly.

 Not surprisingly, you can't retract a bid *after* an auction ends under any circumstances. Keep this in mind any time you bid, and especially when you snipe (see "Snipe It Manually" [Hack #21]).

---

* Strictly speaking, it's against eBay policy for any users to intentionally circumvent the fee system. But eBay also can't prevent members from completing transactions any way they choose, even if the end result is a coincidental lowering of the fees eBay ultimately receives.

The problem is that any bid retractions will be shown on your feedback page for six months, and while it doesn't actually affect your feedback rating, excessive bid retractions may make you appear less trustworthy and certainly less serious. Furthermore, a pattern of bid retractions may arouse the suspicions of eBay's investigations department; at the extreme, your account may be suspended if eBay suspects abuse of their system.

This is also where eBay's restrictions come into play: during the last 12 hours of an auction, you are not allowed to retract any bid placed *before* the final 12 hours.* Furthermore, if you bid in those last 12 hours, you can only retract your bid within one hour of placing it. Note that because of this restriction, sellers are not allowed to make certain changes to their auction within the last 12 hours.

Getting Help from the Seller

If you find that you need to retract a bid but either don't want to or, due to eBay's restrictions, are unable to, you can still contact the seller and ask to have your bid canceled. A seller can cancel any bid on his or her auction at any time, and for any reason.

Keep in mind that you're asking a favor of the seller by requesting to have your bid canceled, so be especially polite and apologetic. Here are a few examples of good excuses:

- "Would you mind canceling my bid? I just read your auction more carefully and discovered that I'll be unable to pay. I'm sorry for the inconvenience." The last thing the seller wants is a deadbeat bidder, so make him feel it's in his best interest to cancel your bid. But try not to give the impression that you simply didn't read the description before you bid.

- "Could you possibly cancel my bid on auction #3125058177? I made a mistake in my bid, but since there are fewer than 12 hours left in the auction, eBay won't let me retract." eBay's bid retraction rules can be a little confusing, so don't be afraid to educate the seller on eBay policies.

The decision of whether to grant your request is completely up to the seller, and there are valid reasons why he may not agree. For example, if there's more than one bidder, canceling your bid may lower the current price. Or the seller may be desperate to unload the item, and if you're the only bidder, you're his ticket to freedom.

---

* The idea is to curb two different kinds of bidding abuse: shill bidding (where a friend of the seller bids to raise the price) and bid shielding (where a friend of the high bidder bids high and then retracts so the auction ends with an artificially low price).

If you're not the high bidder or if the reserve hasn't been met, then you're under no obligation to buy anyway. The seller knows this and probably won't cancel your bid in this case, especially if the current price of the auction will be affected.

The following excuses will probably just anger the seller, and should be avoided:

- "I just bought another one of these from another seller on eBay, and I no longer need yours." You should never bid on multiple auctions when you only intend to pay for one, and sellers know this. If you're currently the high bidder, the seller may let your bid stand just to teach you a lesson. (See "Conditional Sniping with Bid Groups" [Hack #23] for a safe way to bid on multiple auctions.)

- "I noticed another auction with a lower price, so I'd rather bid on that one." This is a slap in the face, and a clear indication to the seller that you're wasting his time. Again, he may leave your bid intact out of spite alone.

Like much of using eBay, getting out of sticky situations requires diplomacy, careful wording, and an understanding that you won't always get your way.

Getting Out of Your Obligation

eBay is a community built on trust, as well as an understanding by buyers and sellers that successfully completed auctions are legally binding contracts. But it's also naïve to expect that all sellers are trustworthy and all transactions can go smoothly. Sometimes, you need to back out.

The easiest—and worst—way to back out of an auction is to simply not pay. Ignore all a seller's emails and the eventual payment reminders and warnings from eBay. Do this once, and you'll get a nasty, negative feedback comment from the seller. Do this three times, and you'll be suspended from eBay indefinitely.

Only the seller can release you of your obligation to pay for an auction you've won, so it's typically a matter of delicate diplomacy to try to convince a seller to consider the auction void and not retaliate with negative feedback or non-paying bidder filings.* See the previous section for some examples of approaches that work and some that don't.

---

* See "Dealing with Stragglers, Deadbeats, and Returns" **[Hack #71]** for tools available to sellers for dealing with deadbeat bidders.

If you decide not to complete a transaction because you suspect fraud of some sort (see "Tools for Dealing with Fraud" [Hack #28]), the first thing you should do is contact the seller and express your concerns. For fear of eBay cracking down and possible legal consequences, the seller will probably just let it drop and not retaliate with negative feedback. At this point, you can proceed to contact eBay and ask them to investigate the seller. If the seller is suspended or the auction voided, the obligation will disappear, as will the seller's ability to leave feedback for you.

If, on the other hand, there is really nothing wrong with the seller or the auction, you should do everything you can to complete the transaction. If it turns out that you simply no longer need or want the item, you can always resell it on eBay, possibly for more than you paid!

HACK #28 Tools for Dealing with Fraud
Your last resort to get your money back.

eBay provides two tools to help buyers deal with suspected fraud by sellers, mostly to the end of retrieving any money sent. These should be used only as a last resort, if diplomatic efforts fail and if the buyer didn't use a payment method with built-in protection (see "Send Payment Quickly and Safely" [Hack #29]). These tools can also be used by sellers who suspect fraud by buyers.

The first tool is the Fraud Alert form (*crs.ebay.com/aw-cgi/ebayisapi. dll?crsstartpage*), which is little more than a moderated discussion between buyer and seller. The two parties air their complaints in a private forum on eBay's site and, in some cases, resolve the dispute themselves; the prying eyes of the typically silent eBay moderator act as a stern parent separating two kids in the back seat.

If you wish to pursue a fraud investigation, you can also file a report with SquareTrade (*www.squaretrade.com*). SquareTrade is a separate company, but has a partnership with eBay and offers dispute resolution services at no charge. (See "Remove Unwanted Feedback" [Hack #6] for another service provided by SquareTrade.)

Note that eBay's buyer and seller protection services are available only to participants in officially completed auctions. This means that if you weren't the high bidder in an auction or if the reserve wasn't met, you won't have access to these services.

Sleuthing Tools at Your Disposal

An eBay user who knowingly commits fraud will undoubtedly take steps to hide his or her true identity, but there are a few things you can do to learn more about who you're dealing with:

- Start with the obvious: check the user's feedback profile and look for a possible pattern of behavior. Next, contact any other buyers and sellers with whom the user has completed a transaction. Use the buyer search and seller search to find relevant auctions for the last 30 days, or use the auction numbers in the user's feedback page to view auctions up to 3 months old.

- Use the Find Contact Info form (Search → Find Members → Contact Info) and enter the user's ID and the auction number, and eBay will email you the phone number and mailing address on file for that user. The user will also receive a notice that you've requested the information. But don't be surprised if Mr. John Doe lives at 123 Fake St. in Springfield.

- If the user has an unusual domain name (as opposed to something common like *aol.com* or *hotmail.com*), the domain itself may provide more insight. Use a Whois tool, such as the one at *www.netsol.com/cgi-bin/whois/whois*, and find out who owns the domain behind the user's email address.

- If you've received any email from the user, look for any IP addresses in the email headers. For example, you might see something like this:

  ```
  Received: from mx22.sjc.ebay.com (mxpool11.ebay.com [66.135.197.17])
  ```

  where 66.135.197.17 is the IP address of one of the computers responsible for routing the email to you. In this case, the IP address is a machine at eBay, but if the user emailed you directly, his IP address will show up somewhere in the headers. If the machine name (here, mxpool11.ebay.com) doesn't appear next to the IP address, use the NSLookup tool to resolve the address.

> NSLookup is a program included on most modern computers, such as those running Windows XP/2000, Unix, or Mac OS X. Just go to Start → Run, type nslookup 66.135.197.17, and click OK. If you don't have NSLookup on your system, you can use an online NSLookup gateway (try *www.his.com/cgi-bin/nslookup* or *www.webreference.com/cgi-bin/nslookup.cgi*).

The computer name is often useful in determining the user's own domain, or at least his ISP (such as *aol.com* or *notmyrealdomain.com*). Use the Whois tool to find out more about the domain in the machine name.

- Try searching Google for the user's name, email address, postal address, phone number, zip code, or anything else you know.

- Use eBay's forums to reach out to other eBay users for help. You may even find someone else who has had dealings (negative or otherwise) with the user in question. See "Keep Tabs on the eBay Community" [Hack #81] for more information.

HACK #29 Send Payment Quickly and Safely
The best—and worst—ways to pay for an auction.

It's your money, and you can do anything you want with it. That said, I don't want to see any of you stuffing dollar coins up your nose or sending cash through postal mail.

Electronic payments have become the most popular method of paying for auctions on eBay, and for good reason—sending money online is by far the safest, quickest, and cheapest way to pay, for both buyers and sellers.

When choosing an auction to bid on or when deciding how to pay for an auction you've won, look for any payment method that can be funded by a credit card. Although some people are downright terrified of transmitting credit card numbers over the Internet, credit cards are undoubtedly the safest way to pay online. You can dispute any unauthorized charges with your credit card company with a simple phone call, which is much easier than trying to find out what happened to a check you mailed six weeks ago. Some cards even offer extended buyer-protection services such as replacement insurance.

Sellers choose which payment methods to accept, so make sure you can abide by the payment terms specified in an auction before you bid. If there is more than one of a particular item you want on eBay, look for the seller who accepts the type of payment you want to use.

Avoid auctions by sellers with overly restrictive payment terms. A seller who accepts only cash and money orders, for example, may have something to hide, or at least will be more of a hassle to deal with than a seller who accepts online payments. (Let this be a lesson to sellers, too: if you want more bids, give your customers more ways to pay.)

PayPal: The eBay Way

PayPal allows you to send a payment to almost anyone with an email address, regardless of whether or not the payment is for an eBay auction. Just go to *www.paypal.com*, log in, click Send Money, and type the amount to send and the email address of the recipient. See the "Signing Up with Pay-Pal" sidebar if you don't yet have a PayPal account.

Signing Up with PayPal

To get a free PayPal account, just go to *www.paypal.com*, click Sign Up, and follow the instructions. They'll ask for the usual information, such as your name, address, email, and a username and password. What may not be clear, however, is that the amount of additional information you provide drastically affects your standing on PayPal, and thus your ability to send and receive auction payments.

First, there are three different types of accounts: Personal, Premier, and Business. A Personal account, the default, allows you to send and receive money at no charge, but comes with severe restrictions on the amount of money you can send and the types of payment you can receive. If you're serious about eBay, you'll need to upgrade to a Business or Premier account. Although the "upgrade" paradoxically means that PayPal will begin charging a percentage of all payments you receive, the restrictions will be lifted, and you'll be able to do things like accept credit card payments. And sending money will continue to be completely free, regardless of the type of account you have. (Note that Business and Premier accounts are essentially the same thing—the only real difference is the name seen by buyers and sellers with whom you conduct transactions.)

If at all possible, you'll want to link a credit card to your PayPal account. Not only will this allow you to pay for auctions with your credit card, but you'll be able to "confirm your address," a step required by many sellers (see "Protect Yourself While Accepting Payments" **[Hack #67]** for an explanation). Also, you'll want to link a checking account into which you can transfer money you've received from auction payments.

Once a serious competitor to eBay's now-defunct BillPoint system, PayPal is now owned by eBay, and their services are tightly integrated into eBay's checkout system. If a seller accepts PayPal payments, a PayPal logo will usually appear in the Payment section of the auction details or underneath the auction description. If you're the high bidder, simply click the PayPal logo or the Pay Now button at the top of the auction page to go to the PayPal site (*www.paypal.com*) and complete the transaction. Note that if there's no Pay-Pal logo, it doesn't necessarily mean the seller doesn't accept it, only that he perhaps didn't take the time to choose the correct options when constructing his auction. Look in the description itself or in the Payment Instructions box for clues; if in doubt, simply ask.

Your PayPal account has its own balance, like an ordinary bank account. Any payments you receive are added to your PayPal balance, which can then be transferred to a bank account or used to fund other auction payments.

You can fund your payment with a credit card, electronic bank account transfer, PayPal balance, or eCheck.* You can even fund payments with airline frequent-flyer miles or other "partner" awards; see *anythingpoints.ebay.com* for details. Although the default funding method is electronic bank transfer (if available), you can choose to use a credit card on a per-payment basis, as shown in Figure 3-5.

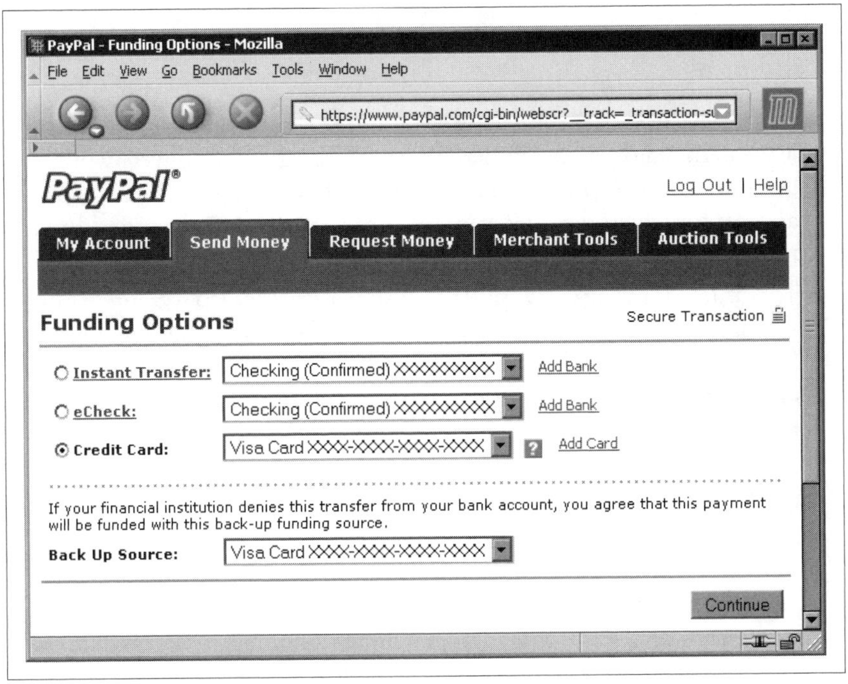

Figure 3-5. Click the More Funding Options link to fund your PayPal payment with a credit card

---

* An eCheck is just like a bank account transfer except that it takes about a week for the funds to clear. If you have the option to do a real transfer, there's no reason to ever send an eCheck.

Because PayPal has different types of accounts, a seller may have a restriction on how you fund your PayPal payment. New PayPal users with "Personal" accounts can receive all payments funded by a bank transfer for free (up to a limit), but will not be able to receive large payments or any payments funded by a credit card. More serious sellers upgrade to a "Premier" or "Business" account so they can receive all types of payments, but pay a small percentage (about 3%) on all payments they receive.

> PayPal automatically notifies sellers when they receive payments, but these emails can sometimes be delayed or even lost. Make sure to contact your sellers directly to be certain they're aware of your payment.

Alternative Online Payments

There are plenty of other ways to pay for an auction, useful if the seller doesn't (or can't) accept PayPal payments. Each has its own advantages and disadvantages:

BidPay

BidPay (*www.bidpay.com*) allows you to use your credit card to purchase a Western Union money order online. This is great for buyers who want the protection offered by their credit card company, but have won an auction for which the only way to pay is to send a money order through postal mail. This is often the best choice for international payments.

There are drawbacks to BidPay, however. Sending payments through postal mail can delay shipment by several days. And the buyer pays all fees (BidPay costs sellers nothing). BidPay can be used only to pay for eBay auctions, and is notorious for canceling payments without explanation.

C2IT

C2IT allows you to send electronic bank transfers from your checking account to the checking account of any other user for a flat fee. This is especially useful for sending payments to eBay members in Germany and other European countries, where many sellers accept only electronic bank transfers for auction payments. Although it's a Citibank service, you don't need a preexisting Citibank account to send or receive C2IT payments.

Although it's much safer than sending cash, money orders, or checks through postal mail, C2IT doesn't offer the kind of buyer protection that a credit card–funded payment service offers. And while the $10 fee is a tiny fraction of what most U.S. banks charge, it's rather pricey for small payments.

Credit Cards

Sellers who are also credit card merchants will be able to accept your credit card directly, without the use of an online payment system like PayPal. While paying directly has little advantage for buyers, it may be the best choice if the seller doesn't accept PayPal.

> If you frequently use your credit card online, you may wish to get a separate credit card only for online purchases. That way, if your credit card number is ever stolen, you'll still be able to buy groceries at the Piggly-Wiggly down the street.

The main hurdle to paying directly with your credit card is finding a safe and convenient way to transmit your credit card number and expiration date to the seller. The seller may provide a web site address, but make sure the little yellow padlock on your browser's status bar is glowing and in the "locked" position (see Figure 3-6); this is your browser's way of telling you that your connection to the server is secure and appropriate for transmitting sensitive information like credit card numbers. Also, look at the address of the page, and make sure you know where your information is going. While some sellers have their own secure web sites, others use third-party checkout services like AuctionWatch (*www. vendio.com*) and Ándale (*www.andale.com*). If you're not familiar with the company, look at their home page to learn more before you send them any sensitive information.

![Screenshot showing two browser window sections with "an eBay company" text, "999-2003 PayPal. All rights reserved." and a yellow padlock icon in the status bar]

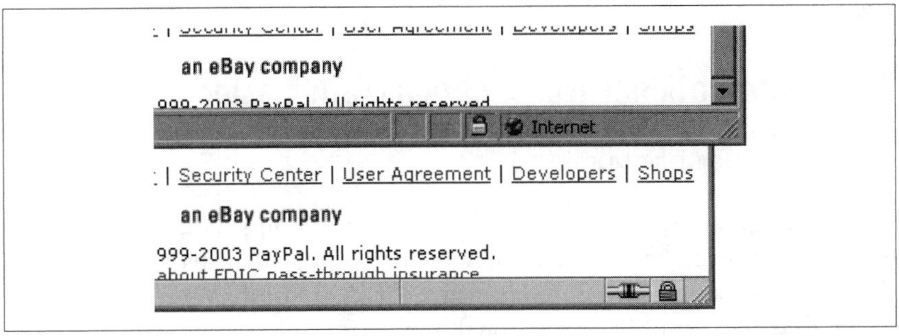

Figure 3-6. The little yellow padlock tells you that you are using a secure connection

You can also phone or fax your order, if you still remember how to use such devices. The last resort is to email your payment information, but given that email is insecure, unreliable, and not even a little private, it's a poor choice. If you must use email, try breaking your number into multiple emails: send the first eight digits and expiration date in one message, then send the second eight digits in another message an hour later.

Convince a Seller to Play by Your Rules

Nearly all sellers who refuse online payments like PayPal do so for one of three reasons. First, inexperienced sellers may simply not know how to accept such payments; in this case, you can politely offer to walk them through it. Second, a previous bad experience may have turned a seller against online payment services, and it's unlikely that a single anxious buyer will change his mind. Finally, the seller may simply not want to pay the associated fees—this is where you have the most latitude.

Nothing speaks to people like money. PayPal takes about 3% of any payment a seller receives. Some sellers refuse PayPal payments merely to avoid paying the fees, despite the fact that the PayPal logo on their auctions will almost certainly get them more bids. If this is the case, the seller may happily accept your payment if you offer to pay the fees yourself.

Not wanting to waste money, you'll want to calculate the amount to send so that the seller receives exactly the requested amount. Assuming PayPal takes 2.9% plus 30 cents for each transaction,* the total amount to pay is calculated as follows:

$$total = \frac{(subtotal + 0.30)}{1 - 0.029}$$

So, if you need a seller to ultimately receive $53.25 (the *subtotal*), you'd send a *total* of $55.15, or an additional $1.90. The seller is happy, and you get the additional security and convenience of paying online for less than two bucks.

International Transactions Made Easier

#30   Tools to help overcome the hurdles and gotchas associated with trading with members in other countries.

Everything gets a little more complicated when trading across international borders. Language barriers, currency confusion, payment hassles, and high shipping costs are all common problems. Here are some of the tools at your disposal to help simplify international transactions.

---

* This is the standard rate charged to PayPal users with Business and Premier accounts. As always, your seller's mileage may vary.

View Auctions on Your Native eBay

Although eBay has several international sites, all auctions are contained in the same global database. For example, if you're looking at an auction on the German eBay, like this one:

```
http://cgi.ebay.de/ws/eBayISAPI.dll?ViewItem&item=3128013702
```

You can simply change the domain from *ebay.de* to *ebay.com*, for example, and you'll see the auction details in more familiar terms:

```
http://cgi.ebay.com/ws/eBayISAPI.dll?ViewItem&item=3128013702
```

The currency used for the starting bid, current price, and minimum bid will all be automatically converted to your native currency. Additionally, the end time will be changed to your country's local time, and the payment and shipping terms will be translated into your native language. Almost every part of the auction page is changed—except for the auction description.

Enter the Babel Fish

If the auction description is not in your native language, you'll have to translate it manually. The easiest way is to copy and paste the description (or auction URL) into an online translator, such as the following sites (all free):

- AltaVista Babel Fish (*babelfish.altavista.com*)
- FreeTranslation (*www.freetranslation.com*)
- Dictionary.com Translator (*dictionary.reference.com/translate*)

The languages supported by these tools, collectively, include Chinese (Simplified and Traditional), Dutch, English, French, German, Greek, Italian, Japanese, Korean, Norwegian, Portuguese, Russian, and Spanish.

Keep in mind that these automated translations are performed on the fly and are based primarily on strict definition conversions, and are therefore far from perfect. Still, they will help you get the gist of the description, and even translate your email messages to sellers (and buyers).

> When emailing other eBay members in a language you don't speak fluently, be sure to include both your assisted translation and the original text in your native language. That way, the likelihood that your recipient will receive something like "bite the wax tadpole" will be somewhat more remote.

Paying and Shipping Over Great Distances

Sellers in other countries are typically less likely to accept the payment methods used in your own country. For example, fewer sellers outside of North

America are able to accept PayPal or credit cards, and virtually nobody outside Europe uses electronic bank account transfers. With fewer choices, buyers often resort to less secure payment methods.

Compound the less secure shipping with the other risks inherent in sending money to other countries—such as the fact that the language barrier and great distance makes it more difficult to get your money back if the seller doesn't ship—and buying internationally becomes downright dangerous.

If the seller doesn't accept online payments or credit cards, your choices are pretty much restricted to the following:

International Postal Money Order
> If you need to send a check or money order, probably the best choice is an international postal money order, as the recipient will be able to cash it without any additional fees (which you'd have to pay). Although there's no practical way to retrieve your money once the check is cashed, you can at least get your money back if the money order is lost in the mail.

Electronic Bank Account Transfer
> When buying from Germany and some other European countries, a bank account transfer is the fastest way to pay. Although it's secure in terms of the money safely reaching the recipient, buyers have virtually no protection if the seller doesn't ship. If you must use an electronic transfer, the best choice is C2IT (*www.c2it.com*); see "Send Payment Quickly and Safely" [Hack #29].

Cash
> A fool and his money are soon parted, a process that is significantly accelerated if you send cash through the mail. That said, I have been forced to pay with cash a few times (never large amounts), and I've only been burned once; someone stole the money and the recipient received an empty envelope. If you must pay with cash, use an ordinary envelope —not a package—so that your payment will most likely not be opened by customs.

Finally, give some thought to the shipping options (if any) offered by the seller; don't just choose the cheapest one. For example, I purchased a $300 item from a seller in Japan, for which I paid with an international postal money order. The seller had good feedback, but I didn't want to take any chances. My shipping choices included surface shipping for about $50 and EMS (Express Mail) for $80, but rather than go for the cheaper method and risk the package arriving after I could leave feedback for the seller, I decided it was worth the extra $30 for the security of getting the package within a week.

Save Money on Shipping

Save the seller time, get your item sooner, and cough up less money for shipping.

I hate being ripped off, and one of the most common rip-offs on eBay is inflated shipping charges. The problem is that most sellers who overcharge for shipping don't even know they're doing it.

Sellers want to cover all their costs, so it's the buyer who ends up footing the bill for packing materials, shipping charges, insurance, and the bagel the seller ate while waiting in line at the post office. But even those who charge only for shipping charges may still be charging their buyers too much, simply because they don't know a cheaper or more efficient shipping method.

The problem is that most sellers don't care how much they spend on shipping because, in theory anyway, the buyer is the one paying for it.

 If you don't know what method of shipping a seller is using, just ask. You have a right to know what you're paying for, and many sellers will be willing to use a cheaper (or faster) shipping option if you request it.

A Little Knowledge Can Be Dangerous

Fortunately, every buyer has access to the same tools sellers use to estimate shipping costs. The first thing to do when quoted a shipping charge that seems a tad high is to look it up for yourself.

The three largest couriers in the U.S. are FedEx (*www.fedex.com*), UPS (*www.ups.com*), and the United States Postal Service (*www.usps.com*), and all three have online shipping-cost calculators. (Most couriers in other countries have similar services; see "International Transactions Made Easier" [Hack #30].)

Typically, all you need for a shipping-cost quote are the origin and destination zip codes and the weight of the package.* The origin zip code can be found in the seller's address, usually included with any payment instructions; if not, just ask. The destination zip code is simply your zip code, which you already know (hopefully). If you don't know the weight of the item, just take a guess. Make sure to include extras like insurance and residential delivery surcharges when choosing your shipping options.

---

* Some shippers ask for the package dimensions, but these rarely affect the price quoted. If in doubt, just make an educated guess.

Armed with the actual cost to ship your item, possibly from several different couriers, you now have two options (assuming your quote is better than the seller's). Either you can contact the seller and request a different shipping method, or better yet, you can offer to take care of shipping yourself.

Excuse Me While I Take Over

People are creatures of habit, and as such require a bit of careful persuasion before they'll change their routine. This is especially true of sellers, who won't want to spend any extra money or time on you or your package. If you want to save money to ship your package, you have to make it worth the seller's while to play by your rules.

As described in "Cheap, Fast Shipping Without Waiting in Line" **[Hack #68]**, the fastest and cheapest way to ship a package is almost always to use a pre-paid shipping label. Using the same technique, you can create a shipping label addressed to yourself, and then email the label to the seller.

> Before asking the seller to ship with your prepaid label, make sure there's a drop-off location nearby. Type the seller's zip code into your courier's online location finder to find the closest drop-off box or counter. Most often, there will be one within a mile or two; if not, you may have to scrap your plan. Note that you can often schedule a pickup if there's no drop-off location close to the seller, but this often comes at substantial extra cost.

Before you snap into action, ask the seller if she would be willing to ship your way. Here are a couple of examples of such a request:

- "Would you be willing to use a prepaid shipping label I send you? All you'd have to do is affix the label to the package and drop it off. I'd save money, and you wouldn't have to wait in line at the post office. If this sounds OK, just email me the weight and dimensions of the package."

- "I have a shipping alternative that should save you time and save me money. All I need from you are the weight and dimensions of the package, and I'll do the rest. Simply affix the prepaid label I send you, and drop off the package at a local courier counter. Let me know if that's all right with you, and I'll get started."

> Diplomacy tip: don't make demands. You're asking the seller a favor, so be polite and encouraging, and make sure to let her know that she can refuse without any ill will. If the seller feels she has a choice in the matter, she'll be more likely to agree.

More often than not, the seller will agree, happy to save time by not having to put together a label and stand in line at the courier counter. (For sellers who refuse, you may still be able to give them your courier account number, or at least request a cheaper shipping method.)

The next step is to prepare the label, a simple procedure outlined in "Cheap, Fast Shipping Without Waiting in Line" [Hack #68]. But instead of printing the label on your own printer, you'll need to create a file that can be emailed to the seller. PDF files are perfect for this; see the sidebar "Turn Shipping Labels into PDF Files" for details.

Once you've created the PDF file with your shipping label, simply email it as an attachment to the seller. Include instructions in your email for obtaining the latest version of the Adobe Acrobat Reader from *www.adobe.com* if they don't have it already. Make sure to specify one or two nearby drop-off locations, obtained from your courier's online location finder, as described earlier in this hack. Better yet, send a link to the courier's web site so the seller can see the map and any nearby alternatives.

If all goes well, the seller will print out the label, tape it to the package, and drop off the package as instructed. You'll be able to track the package from the courier's web site, and the seller will be out of the loop.

H A C K   #32   Dealing with Disappointment: Getting Refunds

How to get your money back when an item isn't all it was made out to be.

In some ways, eBay is no different from any other store. Whether it's a brick-and-mortar shop down the street or an online superstore across the country, sometimes you don't get what you were expecting and you want your money back.

Getting your money back requires three things: knowing what your rights are, understanding what policies and requests are considered "reasonable," and most of all, knowing what tools you have at your disposal if the seller is less than cooperative.

Sellers: see "Expectation Management" [Hack #39] for easy ways to reduce the likelihood of returns, and "Dealing with Stragglers, Deadbeats, and Returns" [Hack #71] for tips on getting your money back.

Turn Shipping Labels into PDF Files

The Portable Document Format (PDF), created by Adobe Systems, allows for the exchange of documents without losing formatting, and is ideal for creating shipping labels that can be emailed. Anyone can view a PDF file with the free Adobe Acrobat Reader software, available at *www.adobe.com*; odds are you already have it installed on your system.

A PDF file can be created from any application, including your web browser (where you'll likely create your labels). Simply print as you normally would (File → Print...), but instead of printing to your printer, print to a PDF printer driver.

On any modern Mac, you can create a PDF file from your browser's Print dialog. But on any other platform, you'll need a PDF printer driver such as the full version of Adobe Acrobat (not the reader), a commercial product available at *www.adobe.com*.

Windows users can also create PDF files using the free Ghostscript software:

1. Start by installing Ghostscript (*www.cs.wisc.edu/~ghost/*) and GSview (*www.cs.wisc.edu/~ghost/gsview/*).

2. Install a free PostScript printer driver (*www.adobe.com/products/printerdrivers*) and make sure it's set to "print to file." Go to Control Panel → Printers → right-click the Postscript driver → Properties → Ports → click FILE:, and click OK.

3. Create your label (see "Cheap, Fast Shipping Without Waiting in Line" [Hack #68]), and print it to your PostScript printer driver. Choose a filename (such as *label.prn*) when prompted.

4. Start GSView and open the *.prn* file you just created. Go to File → Convert, select the *pdfwrite* device, choose a resolution of 600, and click OK. Choose a filename (such as *label.pdf*) when prompted.

Alternatives to Acrobat and Ghostscript include Create Adobe PDF Online (*cpdf.adobe.com*), a subscription-based service; JawsPDF (*www.jawspdf.com*); and PDFMail (*www.pdfmail.com*). All of these have free trials.

Diplomacy Tactics

It's the seller who sets the return policy for any given auction, so before you write the seller and complain, you'll need to check the auction description and the seller's About Me page (if applicable) to see if the seller has outlined a policy on returns. For instance, the seller might accept returns only under certain circumstances, or might not accept returns at all. Other sellers will be more understanding, accepting returns within three days of receipt, or offering refunds on everything except shipping.

Next, see if the problem (your reason for wanting a refund) is stated in the auction. For example, if the seller wrote that the item is missing a wheel in the description, then said missing wheel is not a valid reason for return. Sellers should not be held responsible because a bidder didn't read the auction description.

Finally, contact the seller and let him know that you're not happy with the item you received. Your first email will set the tone for the entire conversation, so try to avoid sounding angry or unreasonable. Instead, be calm, understanding, and thoughtful. For example:

- "I received the item yesterday; thanks for the quick shipping. Unfortunately, its condition was somewhat worse than described in your auction. Would you be willing to accept a return?" This is friendly, even to the point of thanking the seller for something he did right. It also cuts to the chase and specifically outlines a valid reason for return. Also, it makes no demands, which will make the seller much more receptive to your request.

 Including photos of the problem (including any damage or excessive wear) will help your case significantly. See Chapter 5 for information on taking good photos of items.

- "I've been examining the item you sent, and it appears to be a different model than the one you advertised in your auction description. I'm afraid I'm going to have to return it." This is a little more direct than the first example, but still contains an acceptable amount of level-headed diplomacy. It also leaves no room for interpretation; you're clear in what you want, and you're only awaiting return instructions. Naturally, this assumes that the seller's return policy allows returns in this case.

- "The item I received is missing a few accessories, a fact that wasn't stated in the auction description. Would you be willing to accept a return, or at least offer a partial refund?" This approach is extremely valuable, as it makes the seller feel empowered by giving him a choice. It also provides a solution (the partial refund) that both parties may prefer: the seller doesn't have to give you all your money back, and you don't have to hunt for another item.

Most sellers will be understanding and cooperative, especially if you were smart and bought only from those with good feedback profiles. But less scrupulous sellers will try any number of excuses to avoid having to give you some or all of your money back. For instance:

- "I've sold plenty of these, and nobody else complained." This response is common, but is easily defeated by responding with "If you've had no trouble selling these items in the past, it should be equally easy to resell this one after I've returned it."

- "I'm sorry, this is an 'as is' item, meaning no returns." Although this is perfectly valid, it doesn't necessarily relieve the seller of all obligations. For instance, if the item was misrepresented in the auction or damaged in shipping, you are entitled to a refund even for an "as is" auction.

- "Although the item isn't exactly what you expected, it should be every bit as good and work equally well." Don't let a seller pull a bait-and-switch on you. You have every right to get what you paid for and to insist on a refund if you don't.

- "I can give you a full refund, minus all shipping charges and eBay fees." Most sellers understandably don't refund shipping charges, but you shouldn't have to pay to ship an item both ways if you're returning it due to the seller's mistake. Also, sellers can get refunds from eBay for final-value fees if the item is returned, so they should never charge you for them.

Sending Things Back

Assuming you can come to an agreement with the seller about the terms of your return and subsequent refund, the next step is to return the item to the seller. Here are a few tips:

- Confirm the return address with the seller before you send it back. Don't use the return address on the package or the seller's payment address without first double-checking with the seller.

- Never send a package without a tracking number; see "Cheap, Fast Shipping Without Waiting in Line" [Hack #68] for details.

- Don't sit on the package; get it out within 48 hours of contacting the seller.

- Tell the seller when you're sending the package back so that he knows to expect it. Make sure he understands that you expect a refund as soon as he receives the returned package. And if you use a tracking number, there will be no "misunderstandings."

If all goes well, you should have your money back shortly. See the next section if it doesn't go as planned.

When the transaction is complete, think twice about the feedback you leave for the seller. If the return was handled gracefully, reward the seller with positive feedback. Use neutral feedback only if the return was a hassle, and negative feedback only if you got no refund at all. This is important, because as a member of the eBay community, you want to reinforce—with all sellers —that accepting returns is in their best interest. If there's a stigma equating returns with negative feedback, then no seller will ever accept a refund. See "Withholding Feedback" [Hack #5] for further information.

> If you've paid via PayPal, don't let the seller send your refund like a normal payment—otherwise, you and the seller will both have to pay the ~3% PayPal fees. Instead, make sure the seller knows to use PayPal's Refund feature.

If All Else Fails...

This is the part of the hack where I say, "You paid for this item with a credit card or PayPal, right?" And you say, "Yes, of course I did!"

When you use a credit card or PayPal, you can, as a last resort, dispute a charge under the following circumstances:

- The item you received was not as the seller had described it in the auction, and the seller is uncooperative in accepting a return.
- You returned the item, you have proof the seller received it, but you have not yet received your money back.
- The item never arrived, and the seller is uncooperative.
- You suspect fraud or intentional misrepresentation (see also "Tools for Dealing with Fraud" [Hack #28]).

If you paid for the item with PayPal, you can use PayPal's Buyer Complaint Form; just log in to PayPal, go to Help → Contact Us → Contact Customer Service, and then choose Protections/Privacy/Security → Buyer Complaint Process. Unfortunately, PayPal's Buyer Protection Policy only covers purchases you never received. Despite the presence of the "Item Not as Described" option, don't use it: it's a trap! If you select "Item Not as Described" during the process, PayPal will close the case and you won't be given a second chance.

If you paid for the item with a credit card (including via PayPal), simply contact your credit card company and dispute the charge. You'll have to carefully explain the situation (include relevant emails and all tracking numbers), but in most cases you should get a full refund whether the seller is cooperative or not. No other payment method offers this level of protection.

Don't dawdle when it comes to filing charge disputes, but don't file them frivolously, either. Although you'll typically have only 30–60 days in which to file a dispute, it's always better to handle it directly with the seller, so try to be patient. Sometimes filing a dispute is enough to convince a seller to cooperate, at which point the dispute can be simply canceled.

But the real beauty of eBay is that, no matter what the circumstance, you can turn around and sell just about anything. And if you do it right, you'll probably get more than you originally paid!

## CHAPTER FOUR

Selling
Hacks 33–54

People will buy *anything*. The old adage "one person's trash is another's treasure" has never been more true than on eBay. And for this reason, you'll find that people will *sell* just about anything. From antique pottery to broken pieces of the Berlin Wall, from computers to cell phone batteries, from collectible dolls to human organs, you'll find a rich assortment of junk and jewels at the world's largest flea market.

Selling on eBay is a piece of cake. Just click the Sell button at the top of any eBay page and follow the prompts. When you're done, your auction will start, and other eBay users can bid on it.

The hard part, however, is the stuff eBay *doesn't* tell you, such as how to get more bids and more money for your items, how to get the most bang for your buck when using the extra-cost listing upgrades, how to hide search keywords in your auctions, how to make deals with bidders, and how to customize your auction descriptions with JavaScript, HTML, forms, and other goodies. The hacks in this chapter are designed to help you get more money for your items, communicate more effectively with your customers, and have more fun while you're at it.

See Chapter 5 for photo-related hacks, Chapter 6 for completing the transaction, and Chapter 7 for streamlining hacks to help you run a business on eBay.

HACK #33 What's It Worth?

Determine an item's current market value using eBay's Completed Items search and set your price accordingly.

On eBay, research is money. A seller who knows how much an item is worth will be able to choose the selling options more appropriately, and as a result, get more money for it. And a buyer who knows the worth of an item will more readily recognize a good deal, and as a result, spend less money. Fortunately, there are tools at your disposal to help determine an item's worth in about 20 seconds.

Investigate the Market

Any item on eBay is worth only what someone is willing to pay for it. Fortunately, for almost every item sold on eBay, an identical or similar item will have been sold within the last month or two. And given the public nature of eBay's past auctions, it's easy to find out the health of the current market for your item before you list it.

Start with a standard search (see Chapter 2), and locate any auctions for items similar to the one you're selling. Click "Completed items" in the Display box as shown in Figure 4-1, and then click "highest priced" to sort the listing by final price in descending order. Note that eBay's Completed Items search is a title-only search (descriptions of closed auctions aren't indexed), so you'll typically want to use simpler (broader) search queries than you'd use for active items.

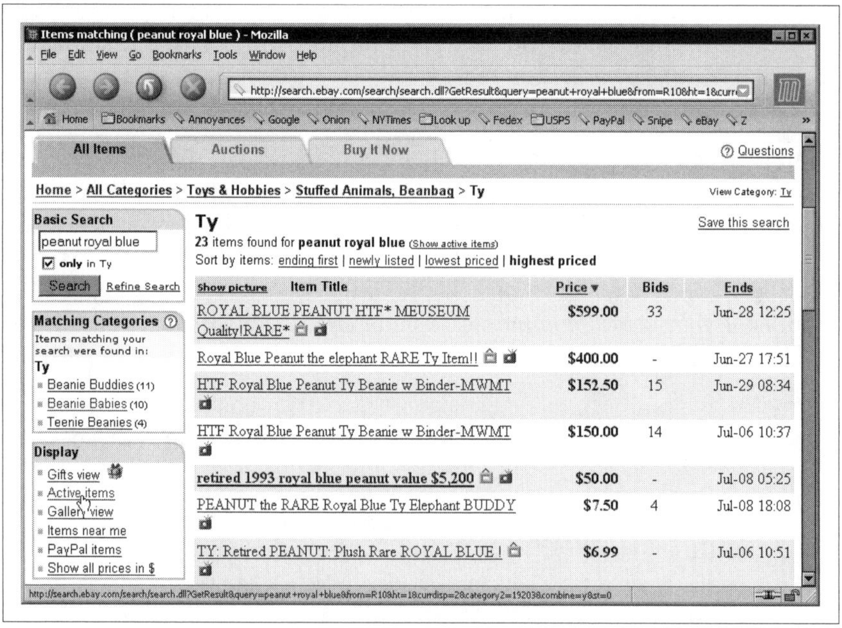

Figure 4-1. A quick search through recently completed auctions, sorted by price, will give you a good idea of what your item is worth

Only the closing price of a successfully completed auction matters, so pay attention only to auctions that have received at least one bid. Even if the seller had a reserve that wasn't met (see "Reserve Judgment" [Hack #35]), the closing price will give you a picture of what buyers might be willing to bid for your item.

> Completed auction listings are goldmines of information, and not just for finding closing prices. For example, you can find out how the top-selling completed auctions have been categorized and titled, and build off past sellers' experiences. And if you're really determined, you can even track running auctions for items similar to those you're selling, so you can see first-hand when the market is good and when it's not. See "Keep Track of Auctions Outside of eBay" [Hack #24] for details.

It's important to realize that some markets will be more stable than others. For example, there's always an extremely healthy interest in laptops, PDAs, digital cameras, and other popular consumer electronics, especially since there are retail stores to help set prices. But markets for collectibles are typically more volatile, since the value of a given item is influenced more by its rarity and the people who happen to be visiting eBay that week than the item's original price or its quoted value in some collector's handbook.

An item's *perceived value* is the most important factor of its market value. If you're selling a rare antique toy, and yours is the only one like it on eBay, then it will likely fetch a fortune. But during a week in which several examples of a supposedly rare item are being sold, its perceived value will be lower. If your research shows that the market for your item appears to have bottomed out, it usually pays to wait two or three weeks until those items currently on eBay have been sold off, and a new batch of hungry buyers makes their way to the auction block.

> When you see a rare item getting a lot of bids on eBay and you have one just like it to sell, it's best to wait until the other auction ends before listing yours. Otherwise, you'll undermine the perceived value of your item by flooding the market, and you'll end up splitting bids with the other seller. Plus, if you time it so that your item appears in search results within a few hours of the close of the other auction, you'll be the happy recipient of bids from all the hungry eBayers disappointed at losing the other seller's auction.

The Empty Restaurant

Inexperienced sellers often make the mistake of setting the starting bid of an auction equal to the amount they expect—or hope—to get for their item. Other sellers forgo research and set the starting bid at a single dollar, relying on the market to set the price. Of the two, the second approach is the better choice for the lazy seller, because you're virtually guaranteed to sell your item.

The key is to remember the empty-restaurant syndrome. When strolling down the street looking for a good restaurant, are you more likely to enter an empty restaurant or a crowded one? If you're like most people, you'll go for the crowded restaurant, even if there's a wait.

Bidders on eBay think the same way. Consider two auctions for the same item, one starting at $20 and other starting at $300. Assuming the market value of the item is at least $300, the first auction may receive 20 bids and close at $330 while the second may get only two bids and close at a measly $305. Why? Not only will the lower-priced auction attract more bidders early on and appear higher in search results sorted by price, its perceived popularity will buoy its perceived value toward the end of the auction.

So, by that logic, should you start all your auctions at a single penny? Of course not. Instead, you'll want to temper this approach with the following concepts:

- When selling an item of limited appeal—when you might expect only one or two bidders to be interested—you'll want to set your opening bid much higher. Remember, if your starting bid is $5 and you get only a single bidder, the closing price will be $5, even if the buyer entered a maximum bid of $150.

- If you don't know how much your item will sell for, but you don't want it to sell for too little, you can use a reserve price auction. See "Reserve Judgment" [Hack #35] for details.

- Use the Buy-It-Now option to set two prices for your auction: the artificially low starting bid price, and the full amount you'd like to get for your item. Hint: an especially eager bidder might be willing to pay a few extra dollars to get the item sooner. See "The Strategy of Listing Upgrades" [Hack #36] for more information on the Buy-It-Now option.

- The Buy-It-Now price disappears once the first bid is placed, but there are ways to get around this. The most common method is to use a reserve price, which will keep the Buy-It-Now price visible until the reserve has been met. The problem with this is that your bidders may mistake the Buy-It-Now price for your reserve price, and as a result may simply be scared off.

Another workaround—which is *not* recommended—is to simply state your Buy-It-Now price in the auction description, instructing bidders to contact you directly if they're interested. Not only does this violate eBay policy, but it may also appear to bidders as though you're trying to scam them (see "Sniffing Out Dishonest Sellers" [Hack #20]).

> Generally speaking, it's OK for a bidder to make a direct offer to a seller (see "Manipulating Buy-It-Now Auctions" [Hack #26]), but it's not acceptable for a seller to use eBay's resources to solicit an off-eBay transaction. See also "Let's Make a Deal" [Hack #52].

Of course, if you choose your Buy-It-Now price wisely, keeping it around longer won't be much of an issue.

- eBay's listing fees are based on the starting bid you choose: the lower the starting bid, the lower the cost to list. Fees are not calculated proportionally, however, but rather according to a tiered pricing structure. For example, a fixed fee of 30 cents is charged for all auctions under $10, which is why you see so many auctions starting at $9.99. The next cut-off is at $25, so $24.99 is also a common starting price. Note that it rarely pays to use a lower starting bid just to save a few cents on eBay fees, however. Go to *pages.ebay.com/help/sell/fees.html* for descriptions of all current fees.

- Setting a starting bid of $1.00 or even $0.01 is a clear sign to the more experienced bidders that you expect heavy bidding for your item, and some bidders might pass it up as a result. Instead, a slightly higher, arbitrary starting bid like $20 might be a better choice. This is low enough to encourage healthy bidding, but *looks like* a starting bid entered by someone who doesn't know what they're selling. Auctions like these tend to especially catch the attention of advanced eBay members who will wait until the end of the auction to bid (see "Snipe It Manually" [Hack #21]).

If nothing else, these examples should illustrate why it's so important to know the market value of your item before you sell.

To Bundle or Not to Bundle

#34   A simple approach to choosing how and when to bundle your items for sale.

One of the most common mistakes sellers make on eBay is selling too many things together as a "lot." Sure, it's easier to list fewer auctions, but bundles are usually worth much less than the same items sold separately, and may even be less likely to sell.

One of my favorite eBay anecdotes involves a single auction for a large lot of model trains, for which I paid approximately $800. I then turned around and sold about *half* the collection, all told, for about $800. I estimated the value of the remaining items to be about $1000, all of which I effectively got for free. (This is similar, in concept, to arbitrage, but relies more on skill than on simply taking advantage of inefficiencies in the marketplace.)

Obviously, the original seller of the collection would've earned quite a bit more money had he listed each item separately. But how could he have known?

The most direct approach is to compare the expected value of a collection with the total expected values of the separate items, as described in "What's It Worth?" [Hack #33]. But this can take a lot of time, and you'll be hard-pressed to find another auction with exactly the same items.

So instead, just ask yourself this question: *How likely is it that any single bidder will want all of the items I'm selling?*

Bidders who buy large collections or lots typically do so with the intention of reselling some or all of the items. Since they'd only do this if there were profit in it, it's unlikely that anyone would pay the full value of such a collection. However, if there's a good chance that a single person will want to keep all of the items you're selling, then you very well may get what they're worth.

> Never bundle unrelated or incompatible items. For instance, say you'd like to sell two camera lenses, each for a different brand of camera. It should be obvious that they should be sold separately, but even experienced sellers sometimes try to sell odd things like these together. In this case, anyone who bids will likely be interested in only one of the lenses, and as a result won't bid higher than that single lens is worth.

Accessories can go either way. Sometimes, adding $50 worth of accessories to an item will increase the desirability of the item by at least that much, if not more. Other times, it won't make a lick of difference.

Take, for example, a $300 handheld computer, sold along with a $40 memory card, $25 leather case, $10 screen protector, and $150 worth of software. Here, knowledge of the market will save you time researching the value of each item. Accessories like used leather cases (at least the cheaper ones), used screen protectors, and especially the software are all pretty much worthless when sold separately, but will probably raise the value of the handheld. Why? Because it is likely that any single bidder will actually want all of those things, and will pay more to avoid having to buy them separately. You might fetch a few more dollars for the memory card if it's sold separately, but it might also raise the value of the handheld by $25–$30. If you have several memory cards, include one with the handheld, and sell the rest separately.

Naturally, the market for your particular item will be different, but this should give you an idea of the methodology used to determine the practicality of bundling related items.

Leveraging Dutch Auctions

If you have a large quantity of an inexpensive item, you may be inclined to sell the entire lot in a single auction. But who is going to want 4,000 pairs of shoelaces, even if you do offer them all at the low, low price of only $200? Naturally, it also doesn't make sense to list them separately at 5 cents apiece, but there are other options.

Probably the best choice is a Dutch auction, but not necessarily the kind you might expect. The nature of a Dutch auction suggests that if you have 4,000 items, you enter a quantity of 4,000, wherein a single bid buys a single item. But then you'd be back where you started—handling up to 4,000 different customers at a nickel a piece.

Instead, try selling 400 bundles of 10 for $4.00 each. So a single bidder would be able to buy 10 pairs of shoelaces for $4.00, 20 pairs for $8.00, and so on. You'll have to build only one auction, you'll get eight times as much money per shoelace, and you'll be much more likely to get any money at all for your bizarre collection.

HACK #35 Reserve Judgment

Use a reserve-price auction for items with unknown value or limited appeal.

One of eBay's greatest strengths is the lengths to which its policies go to protect its millions of users, both buyers and sellers. One of the best known of these policies is the reserve price, which subsequently gets overused.

A reserve price is a dollar amount the seller specifies, below which he or she is under no obligation to sell. For example, you might want to sell a car for at least $15,000. But if you set the starting price at $15,000, you might not get as many bids as with a starting price of $100 (see "What's It Worth?" [Hack #33]). A reserve effectively allows you to start the bidding at $100 while protecting yourself from the auction closing with too low of a bid. If a reserve is set at $15,000, and no bids exceeding that amount have been placed by the end of the auction, then neither the seller nor the high bidder is under any obligation to complete the transaction.

Bidding on a reserve-price auction proceeds just like a normal auction, with two exceptions. First, a notice stating whether or not the reserve price has been met is shown next to the current price at the top of the auction page. Second, if the reserve has not been met and a bidder enters a bid that exceeds the reserve, the current price is automatically raised to the reserve price.

The reserve is never made public, which is essential for it to work as intended. Keeping the reserve price secret allows the seller to decide whether to sell the item at the end of the auction at whatever price bidders have set.

The problem with a reserve price is that it can scare away bidders who feel that they have no chance of winning the auction, and as a result the final price will often be lower than if there were no reserve at all. For this reason, you should use a reserve price only under these circumstances:

- If you don't know the value of the item, a reserve still allows healthy bidding with minimal risk to the seller. However, in most cases you can determine the realistic market value of your item by using eBay's Completed Items search, as described in "What's It Worth?" [Hack #33].

- For items of limited appeal for which you expect only one or two bidders, a reserve might help you get more money. For instance, consider an auction with a $1 starting bid and a $20 reserve, on which a single bidder enters a $25 proxy bid. Since eBay raises the current price to the reserve price when the reserve has been met or exceeded, the price will rise to $20. Without the reserve, the closing price would otherwise stay at $1. This approach might be useful if you're relisting an item that previously didn't sell with a high starting bid.

But that's about it. Sellers often use reserves for other reasons, most of which don't turn out to be terribly good ones. For example:

- If there's a lot of competition, a seller might use a reserve to permit an arbitrarily low starting price, which would rank the auction more favorably in search results sorted by price. Unfortunately, any gains in visibility will likely be negated by the lower overall appeal of reserve-price auctions.

- On non-reserve auctions, the Buy-It-Now price disappears once the first bid has been placed; on reserve-price options, it remains visible until the reserve is met. Some sellers add a reserve price simply to keep the Buy-It-Now option available longer. The problem with this approach is that the Buy-It-Now price looks to bidders like the reserve price (even if it's not), which may scare them away. If you want to set your reserve equal to your Buy-It-Now price, it's best to use a fixed-price listing instead.

If you do end up using a reserve price in your auctions, you may want to explain a few things to your bidders. First, many less experienced bidders don't really understand how reserve-price auctions work, so you might want to include something like this in your auction description:

> "Attention bidders: don't let the reserve scare you. If you're interested in this item, just go ahead and bid as though there were no reserve. If your maximum bid is not over the reserve, you'll know right away, and you won't be under any obligation to buy. If your bid exceeds the reserve, the current price is automatically raised to the reserve price, and you'll have a shot at winning the auction!"

You might also want to reassure your bidders that you're a serious seller by explaining that you might be willing to sell to the high bidder even if the reserve isn't met. In fact, for vehicles in eBay Motors, sellers can use the "Second Chance Offer" to do just that.

The Strategy of Listing Upgrades

#36 Perform a simple cost/benefit analysis to determine which listing options to use.

An extra-cost listing upgrade pays for itself if it increases the auction's closing price by at least the cost of the upgrade. But no upgrade is a guarantee, and it can be difficult to predict which ones will be effective without first doing a little research.

For example, the Gallery option, which includes a tiny photo of your item in search results (shown in Figure 4-2), costs 25 cents. Presumably, a Gallery photo increases traffic to an auction, which can lead to more bids and a higher closing price. But it also takes time to prepare a proper Gallery image (see "Create a Good Gallery Photo" [Hack #64]), and while 25 cents doesn't sound like much, listing fees can add up fast. So, you may want to be selective with the Gallery and other listing upgrades you use.

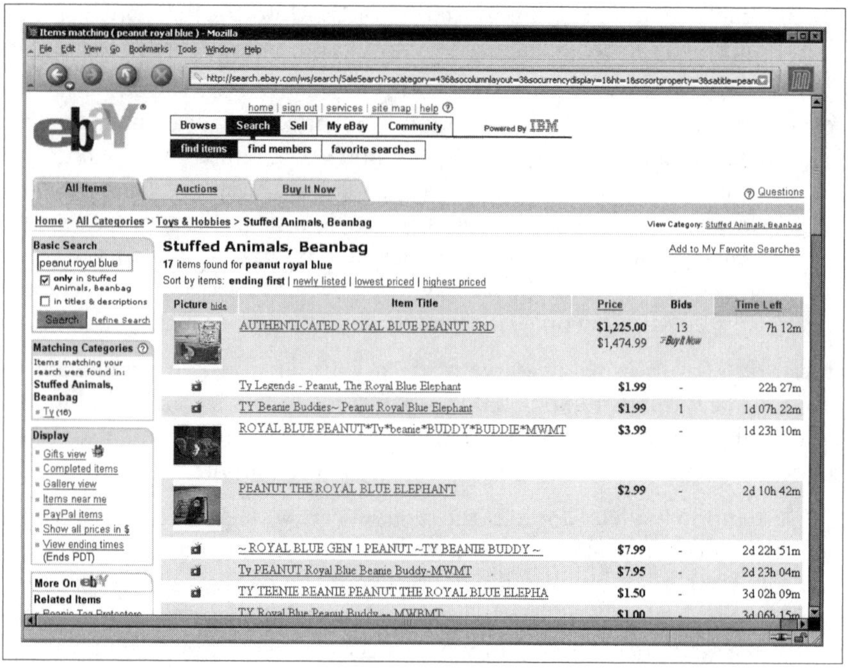

Figure 4-2. The Gallery option is sometimes worth the cost and trouble if it ultimately raises the closing price

Table 4-1 lists the available listing upgrades, their costs, and recommended minimum prices for which they should be used. (Note that some of the fees are different for specialty items, such as autos and real estate.)

Table 4-1. Available extra-cost listing upgrades

Listing Upgrade	Cost	Minimum price (recommended)	Affects search results	Affects listing page
Buy-It-Now	$0.05	$0.00	✓	✓
10-Day Listings	$0.10	$10.00	✓	✓
Gallery	$0.25	$25.00	✓	
List in Two Categories	2 × listing fee	$35.00	✓a	
Bold	$1.00	$50.00	✓	
Scheduled Listings	$0.10	$50.00	✓	✓
Extra Photo Fee	$0.15	$50.00		✓
Gift Services	$0.25	$50.00	✓	✓
Reserve Price	$2.00	$100.00		✓
Listing Designer	$0.10	$100.00		✓
Highlight	$5.00	$500.00	✓	

Table 4-1. Available extra-cost listing upgrades (continued)

Listing Upgrade	Cost	Minimum price (recommended)	Affects search results	Affects listing page
Featured in Category	$14.95	$500.00	✓	
Featured Plus	$19.95	$500.00	✓	
Featured in Search (Stores)	$19.95	$1,000.00	✓	
Featured in Gallery	$19.95	$5,000.00	✓	
Featured on Home Page	$99.95	$100,000.00		

ª Listing in two categories affects only category listings, not search results.

Whether or not any particular upgrade is appropriate for your item depends on several factors, as well as a certain degree of luck. With a little research (see the next section), you'll be able to make more informed decisions that will have greater impact on the success of your auction. But if you don't want to take the time, you can use the "Minimum price" column in Table 4-1 as a quick-and-dirty guideline. For instance, if you expect your item to sell for about $40, there's little point in paying $20 to have it Featured. By the same token, if you're selling a $1500 item, then that extra $20 doesn't sound like so much, as it might end up getting you an extra $100 for your item.

> From time to time, eBay offers specials on listing upgrades, such as "Free Bold Day" or "Gallery for a Penny." Such deals are typically advertised in search results listings and on the Announcements board, so keep your eyes open.

Statistics and Research

From time to time, eBay publishes statistics regarding the effectiveness of the more popular listing upgrades. For example, in February 2003, eBay estimated that the Gallery option, on average, increased bids by 13% and the final price by 11%. Likewise, the Bold option reportedly increased both the number of bids and the final price by 39%.

What these statistics *don't* say is that there were likely other factors that helped increase the closing prices of these auctions. For example, sellers who took the time to add the Bold or Gallery options to their auctions were probably also diligent enough to write proper titles and descriptions and take good photos. This doesn't necessarily mean that listing upgrades won't help you get more money for your items, but merely that any claims that a listing upgrade will increase the price of your auction should be taken with a grain of salt.

Since your item will likely be competing for bidders with other auctions, the upgrades you choose should depend largely on those used—and not used—by your competition. Start by performing a quick search for your item, as well as browsing the category in which your item will be placed, and see what other sellers are doing to promote their items (see Figure 4-3).

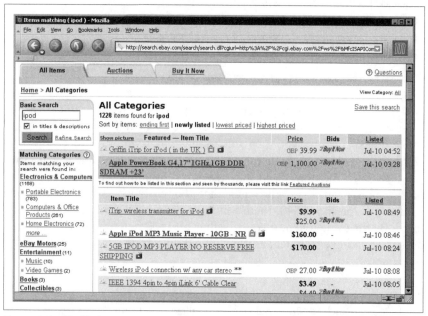

Figure 4-3. *If half of your competition has paid extra to be Featured in search results, your item may be buried if you don't, and as a result, your auction will receive fewer bids*

If you're selling a rare collectible or a one-of-a-kind item, you might find few sellers in your category using the Bold or Gallery upgrades. But for more common items, such as computers, just about every auction title will be Bold, and about a third will be Featured in Search or Featured in Category.

> Also helpful is the Completed Items search, described in "What's It Worth?" [Hack #33], to see which upgrades were used in the most successful completed auctions.

But that's all the help eBay will give you. If you want a little more analysis and summary, try the Andale Research tool (*www.andale.com*), shown in Figure 4-4; it's a pay service via a monthly fee, but you can get a handful of trial uses for free.

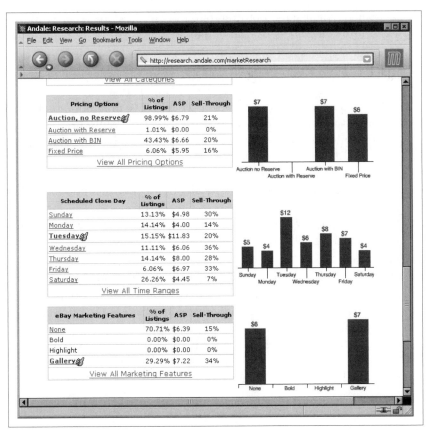

Figure 4-4. The Andale Research tool provides a targeted summary of the success rate of completed items matching your search query

Instead of basing its statistics on averages across all of eBay, the Andale Research tool gathers up-to-date results matching your specific search query using eBay's Completed Items search. It's nothing earth-shattering, but statistics such as the Success Rate by eBay Feature—the percentage of successful sales by listing upgrade—can be somewhat enlightening.

However, the most reliable research you can do is on your own auctions. See "Track Your Exposure" **[Hack #38]** for details.

Upgrade Analysis

Some listing upgrades are more effective than others, but the most expensive options don't always provide the biggest gains. As a rule, the most effective listing upgrades are those that affect your auction's visibility in search results, making them stand out from the rest. Here's a brief analysis of the extra-cost listing upgrades eBay has to offer:

Buy-It-Now

The Buy-It-Now feature allows you and a bidder to complete the transaction early at a price you set (see "Manipulating Buy-It-Now Auctions" [Hack #26]). But it can also be a very effective promotion tool, with the Buy-It-Now icon and price appearing in search results just below the opening price. Set the Buy-It-Now a little *under* the item's market value, and you'll likely make a sale to a shrewd buyer within a few hours of listing. Or set the Buy-It-Now a little *over* the item's market value, and you might get a bite from a hungry bidder in a hurry. If nothing else, a carefully chosen Buy-It-Now price might subconsciously suggest a price to early visitors, even if they don't end up using it. At only 5 cents, it's not much of a gamble.

10-Day Listings

eBay charges the same listing fee for 3-day, 5-day, and 7-day auctions, but a 10-day listing will cost you an extra dime. The theory is that the longer the auction is active, the more bidders will see it, and the more bids you'll get. In most cases, the extra exposure is easily worth the extra 10 cents. But its effectiveness is somewhat offset by the implied "urgency" of a short 3- or 5-day auction, which might encourage bidders to bid earlier—and higher.

Gallery

See "Create a Good Gallery Photo" [Hack #64].

List in Two Categories

It costs twice the normal listing price to include your item in two categories, so the risk increases with the starting bid. Since it has no effect on search results, this upgrade won't necessarily double your exposure as eBay claims, but it will usually help. Use this upgrade only if there are two equally appropriate categories for your item; otherwise, it's typically unnecessary.

Bold

The Bold option simply displays your auction title in a bold font in search results and category listings. To see how effective this upgrade is, try any search on eBay and see how the bolded auctions stand out. Bold makes auctions harder to miss when there's a lot of competition. However, if most of your competition is already using Bold, you might need something more aggressive, such as Featured Plus.

Scheduled Listings

The start time is an important factor in the amount of exposure your auction gets, since it affects when it shows up in Newly Listed and Ending First search results. By default, a listing starts as soon as you complete the Sell Your Item form, but if you're up writing auction descriptions at 3:00 A.M., you may wish to pay an extra 10 cents to schedule your auctions to start at a more reasonable time. But you can save your dime by using a listing tool to prepare your auctions ahead of time; see "Streamlining Listings" [Hack #73].

Extra Photo Fee

If eBay is hosting your photos, the first photo is free; any additional photos cost 15 cents apiece. But you can include as many photos as you like at no cost if you host them yourself; see "Host Your Own Photos" [Hack #59] for details.

Gift Services

If you're willing to gift-wrap your item, include a gift card, use express shipping, or ship to a recipient other than the buyer, you can pay an extra 25 cents to advertise these services. Don't expect the little gift icon to get you any extra bids, though, except perhaps during the holidays. If you want to save money, you can simply say you'll gift-wrap your item in the auction description.

Reserve Price

See "Reserve Judgment" [Hack #35].

Listing Designer

For an extra 10 cents, you can use one of eBay's predesigned templates for your auction. But with a little knowledge of HTML and some imagination, you can create a unique look for your auctions without paying any extra fees, as described in "Framing Your Auctions" [Hack #42].

Highlight

The Highlight feature changes the background color behind your auction title in search results and category listings. In most cases, though, it's barely noticeable, and hardly worth the $5 fee. But if most of your competition is already using the Bold and Featured upgrades, then Highlight might give you enough of an edge to pay for itself.

Featured

"Featured" is the only upgrade that actually affects your *ranking* in search results (see Figure 4-3). If your item normally appears on a given page in search results or a category listing, then it will also appear in the l section at the top of the page. There are five types of Featured s:

l in Category

cts category listings only. At only $5 more, Featured Plus (next) is a much better choice.

Featured Plus

Affects search results and category listings; probably the best choice for most sellers.

Featured in Search

Affects searches in eBay Stores only (see "eBay Stores" [Hack #72]); despite the name, this upgrade has no effect on standard searches.

Featured in Gallery

Affects the General Gallery only (go to Site Map → Gallery), and then only periodically. Use this only if you're desperate.

Featured on Home Page

For about $100, your auction *might* appear in the small Featured Items box on the eBay home page (*www.ebay.com*). But there is no guarantee that your item will ever actually appear in this list; and even if it does appear, the odds that the person who sees it will actually be interested enough in your item to bid is so astronomical that this option is a gamble at best. It might be worth the cost if you're selling real estate or promoting a pyramid scheme; otherwise, it's a complete and utter waste of money.

HACK #37 Putting Keywords in Your Auction

Hide keywords in your title and description to increase your exposure without violating eBay's keyword spamming rules.

The title is the single most important part of your auction, as it is the only basis for standard searches on eBay. You have 80 characters with which to simultaneously describe your item and include as many search keywords as possible, so don't waste them.

Say you're selling a camera, and you want to attract as many bidders as possible to your auction. The following approach should help you construct the best possible title.

Start by including the full manufacturer name, product name, and model number, like this:

```
Nikon F100
```

If you were to put only "Nikon" in the title, any searches for the model name ("F100" in this case) wouldn't bring up your item. Next, make sure to state what the item actually is:

```
Nikon F100 35mm Camera
```

One of the more common mistakes sellers make is not actually stating what the item *is* in the title or even the description. Think about it: without the word "camera" in the title, searches for "nikon camera" wouldn't bring up your item.

 eBay goes to great lengths to help sellers describe their auctions. If you're not familiar with a certain category, check out eBay's seller's guide for the section. For instance, eBay's Art Seller's Guide (*pages.ebay.com/artsellersguide*) suggests that the word *art* is consistently one of the top five search terms.

Next, you'll want to compensate for common variations by including them right in the title:

```
Nikon F100 F-100 35mm Camera 35 mm
```

Note that I expanded out the model number to cover both "F100" and "F-100", as well as "35mm" and "35 mm" (with the space), all of which are different in eBay searches. Note, however, that I placed "35 mm" (with the space) after "camera", because I wanted to maintain the order of the words "35mm Camera" to accommodate phrase searches in quotes (see "Focus Your Searches with eBay's Advanced Search Syntax" [Hack #9]). For the same reason, you wouldn't want to type something like "F100 Nikon".

Next, if the manufacturer is known by other names (or other spellings), include them as well:

```
Nikon F100 F-100 35mm Camera 35 mm Nikkor
```

Finally, if there's room, think about other things your bidders might be looking for. Remember, the title not only seeds search results; it must also compel bidders to view your item when it's shown in search results and category listings. For instance, if it comes with extras or is brand new, say so:

```
Nikon F100 F-100 35mm Camera 35 mm TWO Nikkor Lenses Lens BRAND NEW
```

As before, I included variants of important words. I used "Lenses" to make it clear that multiple lenses were included, and "Lens" to catch any searches for "Nikon Lens" or "Nikkor Lens". (Note that including plurals of your search terms may or may not be necessary, depending on the particular terms you're using; see "Controlling Fuzzy Searches" [Hack #10] for details.)

> Be judicious with your use of capital letters. In most cases,
> putting the entire title in ALL CAPS is unnecessary, and will
> just seem obnoxious to your bidders. But a few choice words
> in all capitals will not only emphasize those words, but will
> help separate them from other words in the description with-
> out having to resort to unnecessary punctuation and preposi-
> tions like "with." A good mix of upper- and lowercase will
> stand out better than an otherwise homogeneous title.

In this last example I used the word "TWO", although I could've instead
used the number 2 and had two more characters for other keywords. I did it
because I had the space to spare and I wanted to emphasize that I'm including multiple accessories. But, depending on your needs, you might make a
different decision.

Naturally, your ability to squeeze more words into the title will vary with the
item being sold and which words you think people are likely to use in
searches. If you run out of room, you'll have to start prioritizing. Remove
the less common words, phrases, and monikers and embed them in the
description, discussed later in this hack.

Title Don'ts

eBay's support for "fuzzy" searches is very limited, so in most cases, only
exact matches will bring up your auction in search results. For this reason,
never abbreviate:

    Nikon F100 Cam. with two lenses, and other xtras

For the same reason, be careful not to misspell the name of your item, or
nobody will find it. This, of course, doesn't include *intentional* misspellings
you might include to accommodate your spelling-challenged bidders.

Next, avoid wasting space with prepositions ("with"), conjunctions ("and"),
and punctuation (commas, periods, semicolons, and quotes). In most cases,
nothing more than a single space is needed to separate words in your titles.
But don't take it too far; a lot of sellers make the mistake of squishing all
their words together, like this:

    NikonF100 withtwolenses extrabatteries,freeshipping brandnew

This auction won't show up in any searches, ever, and is so difficult to read
that few people will bother opening it in category listings. Do this only if you
want to completely hide your auction from bidders.

Don't abuse keywords by using them to spam search results. A common practice is to include the word "not" followed by other manufacturer names, like this:

```
Nikon F100 Camera not Canon Olympus Minolta
```

The idea is to increase the item's visibility by having it show up in a wider variety of searches, a plan that usually backfires for several reasons. First, anyone searching for a different manufacturer is very unlikely to be interested in your item. Second, this is in violation of eBay's keyword-spamming rules, and is grounds to have your item removed. Third, this practice will probably end up annoying the very customers you're trying to attract. Finally, these superfluous keywords are a total waste of space that could otherwise be used to include relevant keywords that will attract bidders who might actually bid on your item.

Here's an especially bad title:

```
\/\/\/\/\ Nikon F100 35mm Camera ***** @ LOOK @ ***** \/\/\/\/\
```

Obviously, this is a total waste of space. Lots of fluff is consuming space that could be used to include more keywords. And when was the last time you searched for the word "LOOK" anyway? But a lot of sellers do this; a recent title-only search on eBay for the word "LOOK" actually generated 65,480 results.

In most cases, the asterisks and other symbols are also wasteful, but if you have the space to spare (which is rare if you do it right), a little decoration may actually help your item's visibility in category listings, much like extra-cost listing upgrades such as Bold and Highlight (see "The Strategy of Listing Upgrades" [Hack #36]).

The Description

The description is used (obviously) to describe your item. But it's also the only other part of your auction that is indexed by eBay's search, so you'll want to make sure to insert any relevant search terms that you weren't able to fit in the title.

Since there's no size limit for the description, you can use as much space as you like with keywords, variations, alternate spellings, and anything else you can think of. The catch, of course, is that description text comes into play only in "title and description" searches.

The only big "don't" when it comes to auction descriptions is keyword spamming, which essentially involves listing a bunch of search keywords unrelated to the actual item being sold. As in the title, keyword spamming is grounds for removal of your listing.

As a seller, you have something at stake when other sellers flood category listings and search results with irrelevant auctions. Not only does this annoy bidders, but it forces them to include exclusions in their search queries (see "Focus Your Searches with eBay's Advanced Search Syntax" [Hack #9]) that might inadvertently exclude your listing as well. If you suspect that a seller is keyword spamming, you have every right to report the listing by going to *pages.ebay.com/help/basics/ select-RS.html.*

To avoid *looking* like a keyword spammer (even when you're not), you'll want to embed your keywords in your descriptions rather than blatantly listing them at the end. This is a much better way to "hide" keywords than, say, making them invisible with white text, as described in "Formatting the Description with HTML" [Hack #40].

For instance, consider an auction for a used camera. Here's a paragraph that surreptitiously hides intentional misspellings, variations, specific phrases, and other keywords, all of which have been set apart in a different color:

"You are bidding on a like-new Nikon F3 35mm camera, complete with all the original paperwork, three Nikkor lenses (a 28-80 mm zoom lens, a 55mm macro lens, and a 105mm Nikon lens), and the original Nikkon warranty card. I've had the F-3 for only a few months, during which time I've only used FujiChrome 35-mm film with it. I've decided to go digital. Being a photo nut, I also have some other photographic equipment for sale this week, such as a used Canon, and some other cameras as well, so check out my other listings.

Note that since description searches also include titles, you don't have to duplicate keywords in your description that already appear in your title.

Track Your Exposure
#38   Make sure your listing is findable before it's too late.

You have at your disposal all the tools available to your bidders, which means that you should be able to locate your auctions in only a few seconds. If you can't, neither can they.

Furthermore, listing upgrades like Bold, Highlight, and Featured Plus (see "The Strategy of Listing Upgrades" [Hack #36]) can double or triple the cost of listing an auction on eBay, but until you can see the effect, it's hard to determine if your money has been well spent.

Start by doing a quick search, not only for the specific keywords in your title but for anything that your customers might type to find items like yours. If your item doesn't appear when it should, take a moment to add any necessary keywords (see "Putting Keywords in Your Auction" [Hack #37]).

Where Is an Item?

eBay provides another handy tool, specifically used to locate a single item in eBay's various category listings. Go to Site Map → Where Is an Item, and enter the item number of the auction you wish to track.

Figure 4-5 shows the results, which list the category and the page number on which the item currently appears, as well as the results for the Ending Today, New Today, and Going, Going, Gone listings, if applicable.

Figure 4-5. Use the "Where is an item" tool to see where your item is listed

The category links shown on the "Where is an item" page will take you right to your item in the listings, automatically scroll down the page as necessary, and highlight your listing in yellow. This is done with a special URL, like this one:

```
http://listings.ebay.com/pool2/plistings/list/all/category7276/page2.
html?finditem=3135119134&from=RO#findit
```

To display the listing as it would normally appear, just remove the finditem=3135119134 and from=R0 parameters, as well as the #findit anchor reference, like this:

```
http://listings.ebay.com/pool2/plistings/list/all/category7276/page2.html
```

This will show you how your item truly looks to bidders, including the Highlight upgrade you might've spent money on.

Counters

If you want to see the number of people who have viewed a single item, you can add a counter to your page. A counter is simply a dynamically generated image residing on a server that keeps track of the number of times the image is requested. You can show the counter right on the page, or you can select the "Hidden" counter so that only you can view the statistics. You can view all your counter totals, choose a different visual style, and even reset your counters by going to *www.andale.com*.

> Counters are free, but you probably won't want to use them unless you really need them, as they can sometimes slow the loading of your page (especially for bidders using slow connections).

On its own, a counter isn't much more than a curiosity, but when used on different auctions with different listing upgrades, you can get a terrific idea of how well your extra-cost upgrades are working.

For instance, you can list three auctions, all identical except for the installed listing upgrades. Buy a Bold upgrade for one, add a Gallery photo to another, and use no special upgrades on the third. Assuming all three auctions start and end at the same time, the counters on each auction will accurately reflect the differences in each item's visibility, and the eventual closing prices will show you the bottom line.

HACK #39 Expectation Management

A few carefully chosen words in your auction descriptions will help avoid unhappy buyers, returns, and negative feedback.

"If you lend someone $20 and never see that person again, it was probably worth it."

Most sellers would agree that an eBay transaction can be considered successful if the bidder pays promptly, leaves positive feedback, and then disappears. Naturally, this happens when the bidder is happy. Unhappy bidders, on the other hand, have complaints, want refunds, leave nasty feedback, and, all told, make themselves a general pain in the neck.

When a bidder is displeased, it's usually because of a failure by the seller long before the customer even places a bid on the item. It's the seller's job to describe the item so that the eventual buyer will be pleased with it, even if it means pointing out its flaws.

Think about it: every time you're happy or unhappy with a transaction, it's because the experience either met or failed to meet your expectations. The higher the expectations, the harder it is to meet them. The key is to strike a balance between making your product look good and setting reasonable expectations.

Consider the following when writing your auction description:

- If you would like to categorize an item as "like new," say it's in "mint condition" instead. The phrase "like new" means "indistinguishable from brand new." No matter how good it looks to you, the person who's just laid down $1,500 of their hard-earned money will expect more than you'll probably be able to deliver.

- If the item has been used, say so; don't expect your bidders to realize this simply by scrutinizing your blurry photos or noticing that you set a low starting bid.

- Mention all flaws, regardless of how insignificant. Whether or not the flaws are important is beside the point. Rather, it's the blunt honesty that will win the trust of your bidders, and ultimately get you more money for your items (and happier bidders to boot).

- If you're selling something belonging to someone else, say so. Otherwise, your bidders will expect *you* to have full knowledge of its history and will hold you accountable for any flaws you don't specifically mention up front. Anything you know about the item's history (such as previous owners, repairs, or accidents) should be mentioned in the description, along with the current condition of the item. Or, if the item has had a relatively cushy life—surviving no accidents and requiring no repairs—then say so.

- If it's dirty, clean it. If you don't want to take the time to clean it, say that it's dirty in the description. Or, better yet, say something like "With a good cleaning, this item will be as good as new!"

- If you're selling clothing, stuffed animals, dolls, camping gear, or anything else that can trap odors, be sure to mention whether the items were kept in a smoke-free environment. Your non-smoking customers will thank you either way.

- Measuring tapes are cheap and plentiful. Be sure to include the dimensions of your item, especially if you're not that familiar with it. This is not so much for the bidder's convenience, but rather to help ease (or confirm) your bidders' fears that you might've miscategorized your item. For instance, if you're selling your grandfather's model trains and you're not sure of the scale (HO, N, Z, etc.), then you run a pretty good chance of getting it wrong. If you include the dimensions, your bidders can be sure of what they're buying, long before they receive it and have to send it back.

- Don't forget to mention the inclusion (or exclusion) of the original box, manuals, accessories, warranty card, paperwork, price tags, or anything else your bidders might expect to get with your item.

- See "How to Keep Your Item from Looking Pathetic" [Hack #55] for tips on taking good photos that will simultaneously sell your item and inspire trust in those who would pay for it.

- Don't say "the photo says it all." The photo *never* says it all.

- Finally, your tone sets an expectation with your bidders as to what you'll be like to deal with. Be inviting and friendly, and invite inquiries from interested bidders. Write in complete sentences. See "Keeping Out Deadbeat Bidders" [Hack #54] for ways to protect your interests in the auction description, and "Diplomacy 101: Answering Dumb Questions" [Hack #53] for everything else.

Although it may sound trite, honesty is indeed the best policy. By selling on eBay, you are joining a community. By dealing fairly and honestly, you will build a good reputation, attract more bidders, and contribute positively to that community. This will, in turn, improve your reputation and attract more bidders. Plus, you'll make lots of cash.

H A C K   Formatting the Description with HTML

#40   Use HTML tags to turn a drab block of text into an interesting, attractive, and effective sales tool.

As a seller on eBay, you're expected to wear a lot of hats: diplomat, market researcher, salesperson, and yes, even web designer. Since eBay auctions are web pages, your description area can be decorated with the same fonts, colors, images, links, and tables found on any other web site.

> If you're already familiar with HTML, you'll probably want to skip this primer and just use it as a quick-reference. The rest of the hacks in this chapter contain more meaty HTML code.

Rapid HTML Primer

For many sellers, the introduction to HTML comes in the disappointment of seeing a carefully formatted description seemingly mutilated by eBay. For example, this text:

```
Antique steam shovel toy:
    real working treads
    working shovel, turn crank to raise
    glossy red lacquer
in immaculate condition!
```

will look like this when viewed on an eBay auction page:

Antique steam shovel toy: real working treads working shovel, turn crank to raise glossy red lacquer in immaculate condition!

The fault lies not with eBay, but with the way web browsers interpret plain text. All spacing, alignment, and line breaks are effectively ignored in favor of the HTML code that is the basis of formatting in all web pages.

HyperText Markup Language (HTML) consists of plain text interspersed with markup tags. A *tag* is a special formatting keyword enclosed in pointy brackets (also known as carets and greater-than and less-than symbols). For instance, simply place the <br> tag in your text to insert a line break, or <p> to insert a paragraph break. For example:

```
real working treads<br>working shovel, turn crank to raise<br>glossy red
lacquer
```

Tags that modify text actually require two parts: a tag to turn the formatting on and another to turn it off. For example, the <center> tag, used to center-justify text and images, requires a corresponding </center> tag later on to restore the default left justification. Other tags that work like this include bold, <i>italics</i>, and the <table></table> structure, all described in the next sections.

HTML Quick Reference

Table 4-2 shows some of the more tags* you'll use in your auction descriptions, and how they'll appear on the auction page.

---

* For a complete listing of all HTML tags, consult an HTML reference such as *www.w3.org* or *HTML & XHTML: The Definitive Guide* (O'Reilly).

Table 4-2. *HTML tags that affect spacing and alignment*

Goal	HTML Code	Preview
Line break	`First line Second Line`	**First Line** **Second Line**
Paragraph break	`First line<p>Second Line`	**First Line** **Second Line**
No break	`My <nobr>red steam shovel</nobr>`	**My** **red steam shovel**
Horizontal line, centered	`First section<hr>Second section`	**First section** ———— **Second section**
Center-justify	`<center>In the middle</center>`	**In the middle**
Right-justify	`<p align=right>way over</p>`	**way over**
Indent	`<blockquote></blockquote>`	*See the next table*
Start a bulleted list (unordered list)	`<ul><li>item A<li>item B</ul>`	• **item A** • **item B**
Start a numbered list (ordered list)	`<ol><li>item A<li>item B</ol>`	1. **item A** 2. **item B**

Display preformatted text with all line breaks and spacing	`<pre>Color: Red`
	`Size: Small`
	`Age: Really old</pre>`
		`Color: Red`
		`Size: Small`
		`Age: Really old`

Display text in a scrolling marquee	`<marquee>Bid Now!</marquee>`	**w! Bid No**

So using some of these tags, we can fully reproduce the steam shovel description as intended:

HTML Code	Preview
Antique steam shovel toy: `<blockquote>real working treads work-` `ing shovel, turn crank to raise glossy red` `lacquer</blockquote>` in immaculate condition!	Antique steam shovel toy: real working treads working shovel, turn crank to raise glossy red lacquer in immaculate condition!

Better yet, let's use bullets:

HTML Code	Preview

Antique steam shovel toy:
`<ul><li>real working treads<li>working`
`shovel, turn crank to raise<li>glossy red`
`lacquer</ul>`
in immaculate condition!
	Antique steam shovel toy:
	• real working treads
	• working shovel, turn crank to raise
	• glossy red lacquer
	in immaculate condition!

Note that the individual tags don't have to be on separate lines, but it would sure make the code easier to read. Table 4-3 shows the commonly used HTML tags that affect the appearance of text.

Table 4-3. HTML tags that affect fonts and appearance

Goal	HTML Code	Preview
Bold	Shipping is \Free\	Shipping is **Free**
Italics	it's \<i>really\</i> important	it's *really* important
Subscript	Drink H_{2\}O	Drink H_2O
Superscript	Turn 180\^{o\}	Turn 180°
Set the font	\<font style="font-family: courier">Mono-spaced\</font>	Mono-spaced
Set the font size	\<font style="font-size:120%"> Big\</font> or \<font style="font-size: 80%">small\</font>	**Big** or small
Set the font color	It's \<font style="color:white"> invisible\</font>!	It's !

Tags can be combined to achieve just about any effect. Take care when nesting HTML tags, however, so that structures do not improperly overlap. For example, this is wrong:

```
The <i>coldest <b>winter</i></b> I ever spent
```

But this is correct:

```
was <i>a summer in <b>San Francisco</b></i>
```

Essentially, tags that are opened *first* should be closed *last*.

> If you want to test your HTML code before placing it into your auction, simply type it into a plain text editor. Save the file with the *.html* filename extension and open it in your favorite web browser. Reload/refresh to see changes as they're made.

Images and Links

An image of any size, from a tiny icon to a full-size photo of what you're selling, can be inserted anywhere in your text using the \<img> tag, like this:

```
<img src="http://pics.ebay.com/aw/pics/navbar/ebay_logo_home.gif">
```

In this case, the image URL points to a GIF file on eBay's *pics.ebay.com* server that happens to be the eBay logo itself. See "Host Your Own Photos" [Hack #59] for information on placing your photos on the Web and referencing them from your auctions.

By default, the image will appear inline with the text, which typically doesn't look very professional. Instead, you can left-justify or right-justify the image and the text will wrap around it:

```
<img src="http://pics.ebay.com/aw/pics/navbar/ebay_logo_home.gif"
align=right hspace=4 vpsace=7 border=1>
```

Also shown in this example are the hspace and vspace parameters, which specify invisible horizontal and vertical margins in pixels, and the border parameter, which places a black line around the image with the thickness also specified in pixels.

Hyperlinks are created by placing the <a> (anchor) structure around ordinary text, like this:

```
<a href="http://www.ebayhacks.com/">click here</a>
```

Here, the text "click here" will automatically appear blue and underlined in your auction, and when clicked will navigate to the URL *http://www. ebayhacks.com/*. Make sure to include the closing </a> tag to end the hyperlink.

> Always test each and every one of your links before placing them into your auction descriptions. The last thing you want is 20 confused bidders emailing you because you mistyped a URL in one of your links.

Of course, you don't want your bidders to click a link and leave your auction, never to return. To have the link open in a new window, leaving your auction description window intact, include the target="_blank" parameter:

```
<a href="http://www.ebayhacks.com/" target="_blank">click here</a>
```

Note that the <img> and <a> tags can be combined to make clickable images; see "Make Clickable Thumbnails" **[Hack #60]** for details.

Tables

Tables are easy to create and are a great way to organize information in your auction descriptions. A table is defined with a single <table></table> structure with one or more <tr></tr> and <td></td> structures contained therein. For instance, this code defines a simple table with two rows and two columns:

```
<table width=90% border=1>
  <tr>
    <td>Color:</td>
    <td>red lacquer with chrome trim</td>
  </tr>
```

```
    <tr>
      <td>Dimensions:</td>
      <td>3 inches high, 4 inches long</td>
    </tr>
  </table>
```

Each `<tr></tr>` structure defines a row in the table, and each `<td></td>` structure defines a single table cell inside that row. Once a row is complete, another row begins. The resulting table looks like this:

Color:	red lacquer with chrome trim
Dimensions:	3 inches high, 4 inches long

Note that text and images should never be placed outside the `<td>` tags. Use indents, like in the example above, to make the code more readable and to help you keep track of your rows and columns.

Using nested tables, you can create a nice-looking box to highlight important information:

```
<table border=0 cellspacing=0 cellpadding=0 width=40% bgcolor=#000000>
  <tr><td>
    <table width=100% border=0 cellspacing=1 cellpadding=3>
      <tr><td bgcolor=#CCCCCC align=center>
        <b>Condition of this item</b>
      </td></tr>
      <tr><td bgcolor=#FFFFFF>
        Brand new in the original box with all original paperwork.
        <br>Batteries are not included.
      </td></tr>
    </table>
  </td></tr>
</table>
```

which should look something like this:

Condition of this item
Brand new in the original box, with all original paperwork.
Batteries are not included.

The bgcolor parameter in the `<td>` tag sets the background color; the six-digit code is explained in "Customize Auction Page Backgrounds" [Hack #41].

Tables are also often used to make simple bars and stripes. For example, to include section headers that match those on eBay auction pages, use this code:

```
<table width="100%" border="0" cellpadding="0" cellspacing="0">
<tr><td bgcolor="#9999CC">
```

```
    <img src="http://pics.ebay.com/aw/pics/x.gif" width=1 height=1>
  </td></tr>
  <tr><td bgcolor="#EEEEF8" nowrap>
    <img src="http://pics.ebay.com/aw/pics/x.gif" width=6 height=1>
    <font face="Arial" size="3"><b>
      Your Title Goes Here...
    </b></font>
  </td></tr>
  </table>
```

Table cells with background colors set with the aforementioned bgcolor parameter can be fine-tuned with transparent, single-pixel images (like *x.gif* here) used as spacers.

Using a WYSIWYG Editor

For more complicated page layouts, you may wish to use a graphical web page editor such as Netscape/Mozilla Composer (free from *www.netscape. com* or *www.mozilla.org*), HTML-Kit (free from *www.chami.com/html-kit*), or any word processor (Wordperfect, Word, etc.).

The problem is that web page editors are all designed to generate complete HTML pages, not snippets to be inserted into other pages, which means that the generated HTML code must be modified before it's inserted into your auction description. Otherwise, your page may not display correctly and may even interfere with people's ability to bid on your item.

 If you've generated a page with a Microsoft Office application such as Word, Excel, or Powerpoint, the resulting HTML will be clogged with extraneous codes that should be removed. The easiest way to do this is to use the Microsoft Office HTML Filter, available for free at *www.microsoft.com/ downloads*.

First, open the generated HTML file in a plain text editor (e.g., Notepad on Windows) so you can see the HTML tags. The actual body of the page will be contained within a <body></body> structure, so all you need to do is delete everything before the opening <body> tag and the closing </body> tag, as well as the tags themselves. Then, select everything that's left (Ctrl-A), copy it to the clipboard (Ctrl-C), and paste it into the description field of the Sell Your Item form at eBay (Ctrl-V).

eBay also provides a WYSIWYG auction description editor as part of the Turbo Lister auction listing tool; see "Streamlining Listings" **[Hack #73]**. But if you want to use the same design for all your auctions, you'll still need to be somewhat familiar with HTML, so you can create clean code that can be used again and again.

Customize Auction Page Backgrounds

#41 Make your item stand out with a little personalization of the auction page using JavaScript.

Although the description area occupies only a portion of the auction page, it's possible to include code with the ability to reach out and affect the entire page.

Why would you want to do this? Well, as the theory goes, a more distinct auction will get more attention from bidders. However, anyone who looks at your auction has already given you their attention, so the effect will not be earth-shattering. Still, a little tweaking may make your auction look nicer, or at least let you express your own personal style and have a little fun with your auctions.

 Never build an auction such that it will be rendered inoperable if a bidder has disabled JavaScript support in his or her browser. For instance, if you place white text on a dark background but the background remains white due to the JavaScript code not working, then all you'll have is white text on a white background and a very frustrated bidder.

This code, when placed anywhere in your auction description, will change your auction's background color:

```
<script language=javascript><!--
document.bgColor='blue';
--></script>
```

Valid colors include aqua, black, blue, fuchsia, green, gray, lime, maroon, navy, olive, purple, red, silver, teal, white, and yellow. For more control, you may wish to use RGB (red-green-blue) color coding instead, like this:

```
document.bgColor='#C5D0EE';
```

The six-digit color code (here, C5D0EE) is comprised of three pairs of hexadecimal numbers, ranging from 00 (zero, no color) to FF (256, full color). Each pair represents the amounts of red, green, and blue to be used, respectively. For instance, #FF0000 is solid red (no green or blue components), and #FF00FF is purple (red and blue, but no green). Likewise, #000000 represents solid black and #FFFFFF represents solid white.

Convenient color tables can be found at *www.utexas.edu/learn/html/colors.html*. If you have Adobe Photoshop, you can mix colors in the Photoshop color picker, and the corresponding hex code will appear right next to the red, green, and blue values.

Unfortunately, the eBay logo and menu bar that appear at the top of auction pages aren't intended to be used with colored backgrounds and will have an unsightly white matte instead of the ideal transparent background.

To change your auction's background wallpaper image, insert this code into your auction description:

```
<script language=javascript><!--
document.body.background='http://www.ebayhacks.com/pictures/stone.gif';
--></script>
```

Simply replace http://www.ebayhacks.com/pictures/stone.gif with the full URL of the background image you wish to use. See "Host Your Own Photos" [Hack #59] for details on making your photos available to use as wallpaper.

 ## Framing Your Auctions
HACK #42
Use tables and carefully aligned images to place decorative frames around your auction descriptions.

A little extra decoration will give your customers that warm, fuzzy feeling they need to open their wallets and bid a little higher, or so the theory goes. At the very least, frames may help your auctions look a little more polished and inviting.

For a fee, eBay's Listing Designer will do this for you. But unless you want to look like a mindless automaton by using someone else's predesigned templates right out of the box, you'll want to take a few minutes to design your own.

The Table

It all starts with a single table, which positions the frame across the top, bottom, and sides, holding your content snugly inside. While you're designing the table, turn on the border so you can see more clearly what's going on.

```
<table style="width:100%" cellpadding=0 cellspacing=0 border=1>
<tr>
  <td width=25>top-left</td>
  <td>top-middle</td>
  <td width=25>top-right</td>
</tr>
<tr>
  <td width=25>left side</td>
  <td>

Your content goes here...
```

```
<br><br><br><br><br><br><br><br><br>

    </td>
    <td width=25>right side</td>
</tr>
<tr>
    <td width=25>bottom-left</td>
    <td width=25>bottom-middle</td>
    <td width=25>bottom-right</td>
</tr>
</table>
```

The resulting table shown in Figure 4-6 is our placeholder for the eventual design. Note the `width=25` parameters in the left-hand and right-hand columns, which can be changed to accommodate whatever images are eventually placed inside.

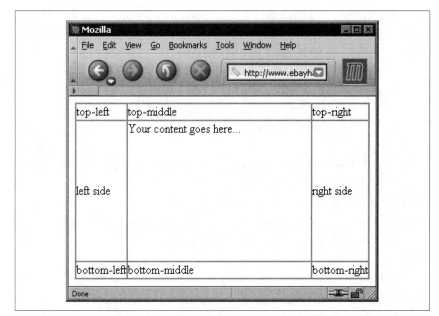

Figure 4-6. This simple table provides the structure for a decorative frame around an auction description

> Early versions of Internet Explorer and Netscape are notorious for improperly resizing table cells and trying to automatically adjust the cell widths based solely on content. If your table doesn't appear to be responding to the `width=25` parameters as it should, try filling the center cell with lots of text, which should give it the "bulge" it needs to squeeze the sides into position.

The Images

In most cases, you'll need eight images—one for each corner, and one for each side—all hosted on an off-site server. See "Host Your Own Photos" [Hack #59] for details.

The corner images stay put, but since the width of the browser window and the height of your content cannot be taken for granted, our side images (top, bottom, left, and right) should be designed so that they are either stretchable or repeatable.

To make an image stretch to fill its container (in this case, a table cell), specify 100% for the width if it's a top or bottom piece, or for the height if it's a left- or right-hand piece. For example, place this in the top-middle cell:

```
<img src="http://www.my.server/my_top_image.jpg" width=100% height=25>
```

Since the image will be stretched, you'll want to do this only with images comprised of solid colors, and nothing that will look bad if distorted in one direction.

> Make sure not to leave any spaces between the opening `<td>` tag and the `<img>` tag and between the `<img>` tag and the closing `</td>` tag; otherwise, those spaces will appear as gaps between the pictures.

On the other hand, you may want to have a single image repeat like wallpaper, which is accomplished by modifying the `<td>` tag, like this:

```
<td background="http://www.my.server/my_top_image.jpg">
```

Naturally, repeating images should be designed as such, with an edge that provides a smooth transition to the adjacent image.

Putting It Together

For the full effect, the theme of your decorative border should relate to the item being sold. When selling photographic equipment, for instance, a film-based theme, like the example that follows, would be appropriate.

Uncut film makes an excellent border because it's comprised entirely of a very simple, repeating pattern. So the image need only contain a single frame, and the browser will do the rest. Figure 4-7 shows a completed border with four film canister images and film extending down the sides of the auction, accommodating long and short descriptions with ease.

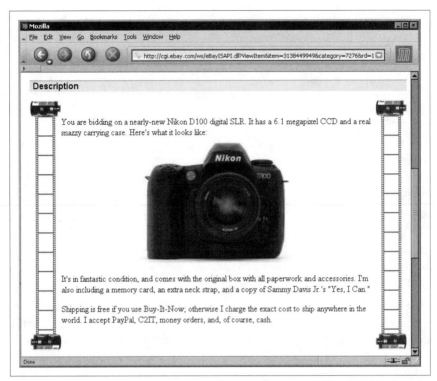

Figure 4-7. The completed frame with four film canister images and a single film frame image repeated down both sides

Here's the code for this frame:

```
<table style="width:100%" cellpadding=0 cellspacing=0 border=0>
<tr>
  <td width=60><img
    src="http://www.ebayhacks.com/pictures/film_canister_top.jpg"></td>
  <td></td>
  <td width=60><img
    src="http://www.ebayhacks.com/pictures/film_canister_top.jpg"></td>
</tr>
<tr>
  <td width=60 background="http://www.ebayhacks.com/pictures/film.gif"
              width=60> </td>
  <td>

Your content goes here...

<br><br><br><br><br><br><br><br><br>

  </td>
  <td width=60 background="http://www.ebayhacks.com/pictures/film.gif"
              width=60> </td>
```

```
    </tr>
    <tr>
      <td width=60><img
        src="http://www.ebayhacks.com/pictures/film_canister_bottom.jpg"></td>
      <td></td>
      <td width=60><img
        src="http://www.ebayhacks.com/pictures/film_canister_bottom.jpg"></td>
    </tr>
    </table>
```

The canister images, `film_canister_top.jpg` and `film_canister_bottom.jpg`, are referenced by the `<img>` tags in the corner cells, providing a weird "scroll" effect. You could even replace two of the canisters with jagged film edges for more realism, if that's what you're after.

The film strip, `film.gif`, appears as the background of the two side cells. Note the use of the   code (non-breaking space) in the side cells to convince browsers that there's content to display; otherwise, the cells (and their backgrounds) might not show up at all.

The widths of the left and right columns are set at 60 pixels to match the width of the film canister images. To get the 38-pixel-wide film to line up, 11 pixels of whitespace was added to each side. Make sure to get all the dimensions right, or unsightly gaps or misalignments could ruin the effect.

Overriding eBay's Fonts and Styles

#43 Use Cascading Style Sheets to change the look of more than just the description.

The `<font>` tag, introduced in "Formatting the Description with HTML" [Hack #40], allows you to set the font for any block of text. But it won't have any effect on text outside the `<font></font>` structure, which means you can never control the appearance of any text outside the description area (e.g., the rest of the auction page). Instead, you'll have to use Cascading Style Sheets (CSS) if you want to apply your styles to the entire page.

The following code, for instance, will turn all text on the page green:

```
❶  <style>
❷  BODY,FONT,TD,A {
       font-size: 10pt !important;
       font-family: Verdana,Arial,Helvetica !important;
❸     color: green !important;
    }
    </style>
```

Here's how it works. First, the `<style></style>` structure ❶ sets apart our CSS definitions, which will take effect regardless of where the code is placed on the page. Next, a single CSS definition ❷ lists the HTML tags to modify with our new styles. In this case, we are applying our styles to all <body> text, as well as to any text inside <font></font> tags, <td></td> tags (used for tables), and <a></a> tags (used for links). If you don't want to modify link colors, for instance, just remove ,A from line ❷.

The actual styles applied are listed between the curly braces { }, separated one per line for clarity. This includes the font size, the typeface, and, of course, our glorious green color ❸. The !important keywords ensure that our styles override any other styles defined elsewhere in the page, which is why even the section headers and the light gray text in the "Time left" section are overpowered by our choice.

If you feel that making all text the same color is a little drastic, you can customize it further:

```
<style>
BODY,FONT,TD {
    font-family: Verdana,Arial,Helvetica !important;
    color: blue !important;
}
A {
    font-family: Verdana,Arial,Helvetica !important;
    color: orange !important;
}
</style>
```

This sets all ordinary text blue, except for links, which will appear orange (this will look pretty awful, by the way). Note the absence of font-size style, which will ensure that the original size of all text is preserved.

> For a complete list of all the CSS styles you can use, you'll need dedicated CSS documentation such as *Cascading Style Sheets: The Definitive Guide* (O'Reilly), or the official W3C CSS specification (*www.w3.org/Style/CSS/*).

You can also use this technique to alter other aspects of the page. Don't like the blue shading section headers? Well, you can do something like this:

```
<style>
TD { background-color: white !important; }
</style>
```

You may find this particular solution somewhat extreme, since it removes the shading used in every table on the page. But it will give you a taste of the power of CSS.

See "Customize Auction Page Backgrounds" [Hack #41] for further auction-page hacking.

Override Other Sellers' Hacks

You'll eventually encounter an auction that has been hacked up pretty well, possibly by a seller with even worse taste than you. Fortunately, you may still have some control over the pages you view with your own browser.

Have you ever opened a page with a text/background combination that rendered the page nearly impossible to read? Here's a quick fix: just press Ctrl-A to highlight all text on the page. This will make all text appear white on a dark blue background, which will likely be a significant improvement.

You can set your browser preferences to favor your own color choices over those made by web site designers, but this can be a pain to turn on and off as needed. Instead, you may wish to set up a user stylesheet, a set of carefully constructed preferences and rules that will trump any crazy code like the stuff at the beginning of this hack. User stylesheets are supported by Netscape 6.x/Mozilla 1.x and later, and Internet Explorer 5.x and later.

See Also

Probably the best source for information about user stylesheets is Eric Meyer's "CSS Anarchist's Cookbook" at *www.oreillynet.com/pub/a/network/2000/07/21/magazine/css_anarchist.html*. There, you'll find ways to "wreck" tables, disable banner ads, and render font coding pretty much useless, all worthwhile pursuits for the anarchist in each of us.

  ## Annoy Them with Sound

#44   Drive away your bidders by putting background music and sound effects in your auctions.

Although I despise sound in web pages, I feel compelled to show you how to do it properly so you don't pick up any bad habits on the street.

The number-one rule to remember when including sound or music in web pages is to provide a means of turning it off. Otherwise, your bidders will eventually discover the workaround by themselves…and they probably won't come back.

Some Call It Elevator Music

You can insert background music (in either *.wav* or *.midi* format) into your auction with this line of code:

```
<bgsound src="http://www.ebayhacks.com/files/aah.wav" loop=1>
```

where the `loop` parameter specifies the number of times to play the sound. The problem is that the `<bgsound>` element has no controls: no way for your customers to turn off the sound or adjust the volume. In other words, a poor choice.

The more general-purpose `<embed>` tag can do everything `<bgsound>` does, but it also includes a controller box:

```
<embed src="http://www.ebayhacks.com/files/aah.wav" hidden=false
autostart=true loop=true></embed>
```

The `loop=true` parameter can be replaced with `playcount=3` to play the sound a specified number of times and then stop. Go to *www. htmlcodetutorial.com* for further documentation on embedded objects.

When to Use Sound

Sound can be useful when text and photos just won't do. For example, if you're selling a music box, you may want to include a clip of the music it plays, especially if you don't know the name of the song. Or, if you're selling a product that modifies sound (such as a car exhaust silencer), your customers will appreciate being able to hear, first-hand, what it sounds like with—and without—your product. And obviously, if you're selling music on CD, tape, record, or DVD, you may want to include a short clip to entice your bidders.

Even given these perfectly legitimate uses for sound in your auctions, it still makes sense to give your bidders control over the sound, rather than simply having it play automatically in the background.

Hacking the Controller

The actual audio controller that appears on the page depends entirely on the browser plug-in currently configured to handle sound objects. (Note that users without an appropriate plug-in installed will just see an empty box and won't hear any sounds at all.) Instead of using the default controller, which is usually large and rather clumsy, you can integrate the controls into your auction description quite nicely.

Making Sound Files

Any modern computer can record sound; all you need is a microphone to record ambient sounds, or the proper cables to connect to a stereo and record audio from a tape, record, or DVD. Just use your computer's sound recorder application, record a few seconds of audio, and save it into a *.wav* file.

The exception is audio CDs, which can simply be inserted into your computer's CD drive; as long as you have the proper software, any audio track can then be "ripped" to create a *.wav* file. Nearly all CD recorder software supports this, as do advanced sound applications such as Sound Forge (available at *www.sonicfoundry.com*). Or, if you simply want to use canned sound effects, go to *www.freeaudioclips.com*.

Either way, you'll need to ultimately host your *.wav* file on a web server, as described in "Host Your Own Photos" [Hack #59], before you can reference it with the code in this hack.

First, we need to modify the <embed> tag to hide the default controller, turn off the autostart feature, and give it a name, mySound, that we can reference with JavaScript:

```
<embed src="http://www.ebayhacks.com/files/aah.wav" hidden=true
autostart=false loop=false name="mySound" mastersound></embed>
```

Since it's now hidden, it doesn't strictly matter where you put the <embed> tag. In most cases, it's probably best to place it at the end of the auction description so browsers will load the rest of your auction before the sound file. Next, include these links in your text to control the audio:

```
<a href="javascript:document.mySound.play();">Listen</a>
to the music made by this music box. When you're done, you can
<a href="javascript:document.mySound.pause();">Pause</a> or
<a href="javascript:document.mySound.stop();">Stop</a> the music.

( Volume: <a href="javascript:document.mySound.setVolume(33);">Soft</a> |
<a href="javascript:document.mySound.setVolume(66);">Medium</a> |
<a href="javascript:document.mySound.setVolume(100);">Loud</a> )
```

The "controller," in this case, will simply appear as ordinary text links in your auction description. The text links can also be replaced with images to make a fancier controller.

Quick-and-Dirty Links

If you find that a controller in your description is overkill, you can simply link to your audio files directly, like this:

```
<a href="http://www.ebayhacks.com/files/aah.wav">Listen</a> to the music
made by this music box.
```

The problem is that about a third of your bidders will get a download prompt and nothing else, and will probably not know where to go from there. If you choose this solution, you'll want to include a bit of instruction, telling them to save the files on their desktops and then double-click the icons that appear.

Put a Shipping Cost Calculator in Your Auction

#45 Use an HTML form and a little JavaScript to provide accurate shipping costs to your customers on the fly.

One of the advantages of understanding HTML is the ability to add functionality to your auction descriptions without having to rely on extra-cost services or—gasp—the intelligence of your bidders.

A shipping cost calculator, placed right in your auction description, will allow you to avoid setting a single, fixed shipping cost (which can scare away frugal bidders), and still avoid the burden of having to quote shipping costs to everyone who asks.

Probably the easiest way to provide self-service shipping cost information is to include your zip code and the weight of your item right in your auction description. Your bidders can then punch that information and their own zip code into a courier web site, such as *ups.com* or *fedex.com*, and get an accurate cost to ship, as well as any available shipping options (insurance, overnight, etc.). The problem is that it's easy for the bidder to make a mistake or choose the wrong shipping options, which can cause all sorts of problems.

Fortunately, there are many more streamlined solutions, ranging from services provided by eBay to custom HTML-based calculators.

eBay's Calculated Shipping

eBay offers sellers its own shipping calculator, a feature introduced in the middle of 2003. When listing your item, just choose the "calculated shipping" option. Specify your zip code, the weight and dimensions of your item, and a single shipping method, and eBay will allow your bidders to determine shipping costs on their own.

The calculated shipping feature, however, is rather limited. First, it uses software provided by Connect Ship, a UPS company, so only UPS and U.S. Postal Service rates are supported. Second, it works only for buyers and sellers in the continental United States. Finally, sellers can choose only a single shipping method when listing the item, so bidders will have no choice when using the tool (which can be good or bad, depending on your perspective).

> The biggest advantage to Calculated Shipping is probably also its biggest drawback. For the bidder's and seller's convenience, the calculated shipping cost is automatically inserted into the bidder's invoice, which means that it will be used when the bidder completes the Checkout procedure. This means that the bidder can send payment without any post-auction input from the seller, even if the shipping quote is incorrect. See "Opting Out of Checkout" **[Hack #49]** for more information.

Calculated Shipping can also combine shipping costs for multiple auctions won by the same bidder, although the accuracy of the calculation should never be taken for granted. As the seller, you'll want to have an active role in helping your bidders complete transactions by sending accurate totals and payment instructions promptly. Otherwise, you'll be deluged with complaints from impatient bidders who have sent incorrect payments and who blame you for their mistakes.

Whether eBay's Calculated Shipping option is sufficient or not is entirely up to you. But anyone outside the continental United States, anyone shipping internationally, or anyone wishing to ship with another courier may want to pursue a different solution.

A Custom Front-end

Regardless of where you live, where you ship, or what courier you use, you can provide a simplified front-end (interface) to your courier's web site and significantly reduce the possibility of errors.

Start by opening the web site of your courier's shipping cost calculator. For example, go to *wwwapps.ups.com/cost* if you're shipping with UPS (though this procedure should work with most couriers' web sites). Then, calculate the cost to ship a 5-pound package from San Francisco, California (zip 94102) to Honolulu, Hawaii (zip 96801). When you're done, you'll end up with a page showing the total cost to ship using each of the available services (UPS Next Day Air, 2nd Day Air, etc.). The rather long URL of the page should look something like this:

```
http://wwwapps.ups.com/QCCWebApp/controller?origcountry=US
   &origcity=&origpostal=94102&destcountry=US&destpostal=96801&destcity=
   &destResidential=NO&packages=1&iso_language=en&iso_country=US
   &dropOffChoice=DO&billToUPS=no&container=02&length1=12&width1=12
   &height1=12&length_std1=IN&weight1=5&weight_std1=LBS&value1=100
   &ratesummarypackages.x=18&ratesummarypackages.y=6
```

As described in "Tweaking Search URLs" [Hack #12], everything after the question mark (?) is simply a collection of parameters, each separated by an ampersand (&). For example, the parameter destpostal=96801 specifies the destination zip code.

The next step is to translate this URL into an HTML form:

```
❶ <form method=get target=_blank
                 action=http://wwwapps.ups.com/QCCWebApp/controller>
   <input type=hidden name=origcountry value=US>
   <input type=hidden name=origcity value=>
❷ <input type=hidden name=origpostal value=94102>
   <input type=hidden name=destcountry value=US>
❸ <input type=textbox name=destpostal value="">
   <input type=hidden name=destcity value=>
   <input type=hidden name=destResidential value=NO>
   <input type=hidden name=packages value=1>
   <input type=hidden name=iso_language value=en>
   <input type=hidden name=iso_country value=US>
   <input type=hidden name=dropOffChoice value=DO>
   <input type=hidden name=billToUPS value=no>
   <input type=hidden name=container value=02>
   <input type=hidden name=length1 value=12>
   <input type=hidden name=width1 value=12>
   <input type=hidden name=height1 value=12>
   <input type=hidden name=length_std1 value=IN>
❹ <input type=hidden name=weight1 value=5>
   <input type=hidden name=weight_std1 value=LBS>
   <input type=hidden name=value1 value=100>
   <input type=hidden name=ratesummarypackages.x value=18>
   <input type=hidden name=ratesummarypackages.y value=6>
❺ </form>
```

Each parameter in the URL receives its own <input> tag as shown. For a shortcut, use your text editor's search-and-replace function to do the work for you. First, replace all occurrences of "=" with " value=" (including the preceding space), and then replace all occurrences of "&" with "><input type=hidden name=" (not including any of the quotation marks).

All of the fields here are hidden (with the exception of destpostal); this means that you can customize them by hacking into the code, but your bidders won't see anything. For instance, change the value for origpostal ❸ to your own zip code, and the value for weight1 ❹ to the weight of the item currently for sale. The one visible field (with the type option set to textbox) is destpostal ❷, into which your bidders will type their own zip codes to get a shipping cost quote. Note that our test zip code, 96801, should be removed so that the bidder sees only an empty zip code field.

> Note that all of these parameter names may be entirely differ-
> ent for the particular URL you dissect. If you're uncertain
> about a particular ambiguously named parameter, just look
> at its value for clues.

Finally, the site address and executable name are placed inside the <form> tag ❶, and the corresponding </form> tag is placed at the end ❺.

When you're done, simply place the code right into your auction description along with a sentence of instruction, such as "Type your zip code here and press Enter for your shipping cost," immediately above it. You may also want to set apart this code by placing it in its own HTML table, like the one in Figure 4-8; see "Formatting the Description with HTML" [Hack #40].

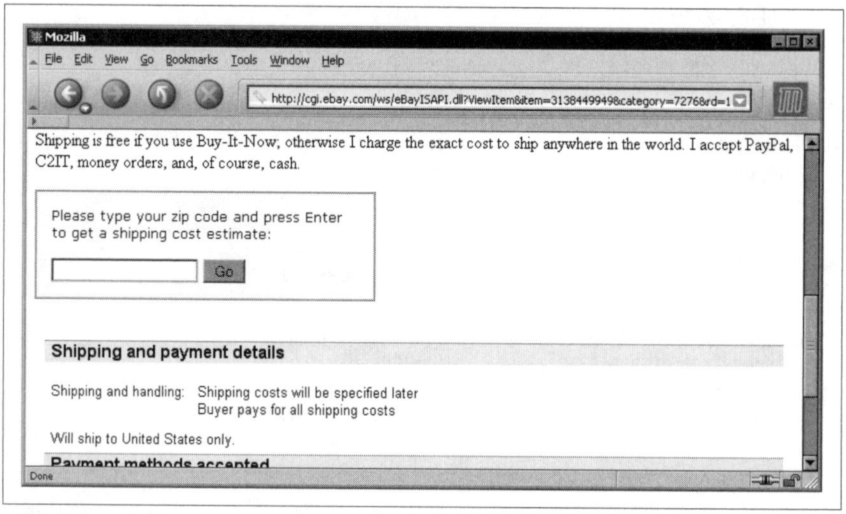

Figure 4-8. A simple shipping cost calculator allows your bidders to get a shipping quote without asking you

Naturally, this code can be reused and placed in all your auctions; just change the weight on line ❹ for the specific item being sold. Make sure to test it from time to time, however, since the courier may change their web site at any time, and probably without personally notifying you first.

The Zonalyzer Calculator

The Zonalyzer calculator doesn't utilize any external web sites, but rather encapsulates all of the rate tables and functionality right in the code. Of course, since including rate tables for all locations would make the script needlessly complicated, only the rate tables that apply to your location are included. This means that the code must be generated for each person who uses it.

To generate a free shipping cost calculator, go to *www.zonalyzer.com* (Figure 4-9) and follow the prompts. When you're done, just copy and paste the code into your auction description. Or, to test the code, paste it into a text editor, save it as an HTML file, and open the file in your web browser.

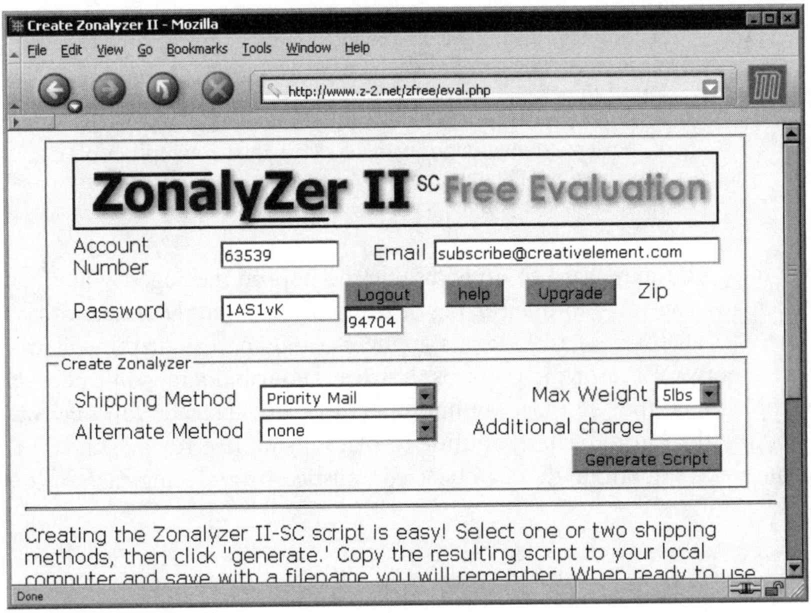

Figure 4-9. Use Zonalyzer to generate a personalized shipping cost calculator for your auctions

One of the nice features of the Zonalyzer calculator is that it lets you add a "handling" fee, a fixed dollar amount that is automatically added to every shipping cost quote. It also lets you restrict the shipping options to one or two different types, so your bidders won't expect something you can't deliver. Finally, since it doesn't rely on an external site, it won't go down without notice.

On the down side, Zonalyzer supports only a small handful of couriers and shipping types, and then only for shipments originating from the U.S. It also relies entirely on JavaScript, and won't appear at all if your bidder has disabled JavaScript support. Finally, courier rate tables do change, so you may have to regenerate your calculator code from time to time.

Hacking Zonalyzer

The Zonalyzer code is automatically generated from the information you provide in the Zonalyzer wizard, but the customization doesn't have to end there. Once you have the code, you'll have free reign to modify, simplify, or expand the tool to your heart's content.

> Because the code is as compact as possible, it may be missing some of the line breaks and indentation normally used to make such code more readable. As a result, you may need to spread things out before you begin hacking, a task most easily accomplished by simply inserting a line break after most of the semicolons found in the code (with the exception of those used in if statements). Make sure to create a backup of the code before you mess with it.

One thing you may want to do is disable the pop-up messages, which your bidders (or you) may find annoying or troublesome. Simply delete (or comment out) all three of the alert statements, and the calculator will work more silently. Without the pop-ups, however, your bidders won't necessarily know when they've typed an improper zip code. Instead, you may want to modify the error-checking routine to place a simple error message in the output field, something that can be accomplished by replacing each of these lines:

```
alert("Please enter a valid Zip Code!");
alert(t+" is not a valid Zip Code!");
```

with the following:

```
return "bad zip";
```

Being a minimalist, I typically prefer simple black-and-white boxes to the more colorful schemes provided by the Zonalyzer wizard. Fortunately, the appearance of the box is determined by a lone HTML tag that looks something like this:

```
<table style="color:black; width:255; background-color:yellow; font-size:12;
border:thin solid indigo; font-family:arial; cursor:hand">
```

The parameters in the `<table>` tag, separated by semicolons, follow CSS (Cascading Style Sheets) rules and are therefore fairly self-evident and easy to change. For instance, to have a basic black-and-white table using the default font of the page, change the line to the following simplified version:

```
<table style="width:255; border:thin solid black;">
```

Finally, you may wish to add additional restraints to the calculations, such as a minimum charge, maximum charge, or a surcharge to certain locations. This can be done in the loadZoneFinder( ) function; this is responsible for calculating the toTSH[i] variable, which ultimately is the shipping cost shown to the bidder. For example, to impose a minimum charge of $5.00, change this line:

```
toTSH[i]=fmtCUR(Number(shC[i])+addAMT);
```

to the following:

```
var minimum=5;
toTSH[i] = fmtCUR(Number(shC[i]) + addAMT)
if(toTSH[i] < minimum) { toTSH[i] = minimum; }
toTSH[i] = fmtCUR(toTSH[i]);
```

If you're using Zonalyzer II or one of the other more advanced calculators, the function name and code specifics may be different, but the methodology is the same.

FreightQuote

For shipping heavier items, such as furniture and appliances, you can use FreightQuote, a free shipping cost calculator available at *www.freightquote. com*. Although it isn't self-contained, it's still fairly compact and rather professional-looking. Just make sure you're able to ship with one of their affiliated shippers before you insert their calculator in your auctions.

Allow Visitors to Search Through Your Auctions
HACK #46

Put an HTML search form in your auction description to make it easier for your customers to find other items you're selling.

The "View seller's other items" link on auction pages leaves a lot to be desired. Lacking the flexibility of standard search results or category listings, it simply lists your other running auctions with no convenient way for bidders to search through the titles, and no way at all for bidders to search your descriptions.[*] Since you'll get more money for items that are easier to find, a seller search box right in your description will help advertise your

---

[*] See "Tweaking Search URLs" [Hack #12] for a few tricks for bidders using this page. Sellers can also open an eBay Store [Hack #72] to add some functionality to their lists of running auctions at an added cost.

other auctions. Figure 4-10 shows a custom search-by-seller box preconfigured to show only your auctions.

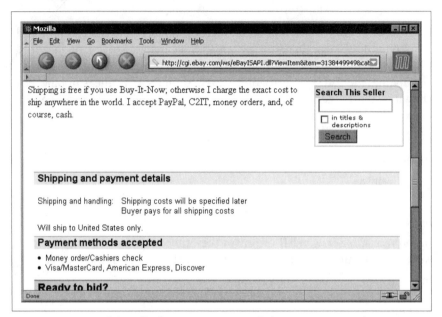

Figure 4-10. A search-by-seller box in your auctions helps promote your other items

To put this box in your auction, simply place the following code somewhere in your auction description:

```
<table cellpadding=0 cellspacing=0 border=0 width=150><tr>
  <td bgcolor="#ffcc00" rowspan=2 width=1%>
  <img src="http://pics.ebay.com/aw/pics/s.gif" width=2></td>
  <td height=2 bgcolor="#ffcc00" valign=top width=98%>
  <img src="http://pics.ebay.com/aw/pics/s.gif"></td>
  <td background="http://pics.ebay.com/aw/pics/listings/sliver_1x22.gif"
      rowspan=2 valign=top align=right width=1%>
  <img src="http://pics.ebay.com/aw/pics/listings/yellcurve_22x20.gif"
      width=22 height=21 align=top></td></tr>
  <tr><td colspan=3 bgcolor="#ffe680">
  <font size=2 face="arial, helvetica, sans-serif">
  <b>Search This Seller</b></font></td></tr>
</table>

<table cellpadding=0 cellspacing=0 border=0 width=150>
  <tr><td bgcolor="#ffcc00" width=1%>
  <img src="http://pics.ebay.com/aw/pics/s.gif" width=2></td>
  <td width=2> </td><td width=98%>
```

❶ ```
    <form action="http://cgi6.ebay.com/aw-cgi/ebayisapi.dll" method=post>
    <input type=hidden name="MfcISAPICommand" value="SearchBySellerReDirect">
    ```
    ```

```
  <input type=hidden name="include" value="1">
❷ <input type=hidden name="sellerList" value="my_user_id">

  <table cellpadding=1 cellspacing=0 border=0 width=100%>
    <tr><td colspan=2>
❸     <input maxlength=300 name="searchTitle" size=17 value="">
      </td></tr><tr><td valign=top>
❹     <input type=checkbox name="descriptionSearch">
      </td><td><font size=1 face="Verdana, Arial, Helvetica, sans-serif">
      in titles & descriptions</font>
      </td></tr>
    <tr><td colspan=2>
      <input type=submit value="Search">
      </td></tr><tr><td colspan=2 height=3>
      <img src="http://pics.ebay.com/aw/pics/s.gif"></td></tr>
  </table>
❺ </form>

  </td><td bgcolor="#ffcc00" width=1%>
  <img src="http://pics.ebay.com/aw/pics/s.gif" width=2></td>
  </tr><tr><td bgcolor="#ffcc00" colspan=4 height=2 width=1%>
  <img src="http://pics.ebay.com/aw/pics/s.gif" width=2>
  </td></tr></table>
```

Simply replace my_user_id on line ❷ with your own user ID to confine the search results to your own running auctions. The code can otherwise be used exactly as is.

Since this box has a genuine eBay look, complete with the yellow lines and even the "in titles & descriptions" checkbox, it's somewhat more complicated than it needs to be. In fact, the actual search form is comprised only of the code between lines ❶ and ❺. But the official eBay appearance will make your bidders more comfortable using it, and will make your auction look more professional.

Hacking the Hack

Naturally, you can customize your search box to suit the style of your auctions by replacing all the code above line ❶ and below line ❺ with a custom table, such as the one described in "Formatting the Description with HTML" [Hack #40]. Just be careful about the code in the <form></form> structure.

As it is, the box will appear left-justified in your auction description. To center it, simply place a <center> tag at the beginning and a </center> tag at the end. Although you can similarly right-justify the box by placing the code between <p align=right> and </p> tags, it's better to place it all inside a *floating table* instead so that the rest of your text wraps around it. Just place the following code at the beginning:

```
<table cellpadding=0 cellspacing=0 border=0 align=right hspace=4>
<tr><td>
```

and then close this table with the following code at the end:

```
</td></tr></table>
```

Don't let your bidders forget where they came from. Instead of the search results appearing in the same window, you can have the search open a new window simply by adding the target=_blank parameter to the <form> tag on line ❶, like this:

```
<form action="http://cgi6.ebay.com/aw-cgi/ebayisapi.dll" method=post
target=_blank>
```

To turn on the "in titles & descriptions" checkbox by default, which will most likely increase the number of search results your bidders see (and improve the exposure of the corresponding auctions), just add the checked parameter to the <input> tag on line ❹, like this:

```
<input type=checkbox name="descriptionSearch" checked>
```

Finally, if you have a lot of different auctions open concurrently, you may want to help your bidders out by suggesting a search query. For instance, if you're selling a wireless phone product, you may want to pre-enter the search word "wireless" in the search field (line ❸):

```
<input maxlength=300 name="searchTitle" size=17 value="wireless">
```

Although this will likely reduce the number of search results your bidders see, it will show them more targeted, relevant auctions that are more likely to interest them. In this way, you'll have a chance to sell multiple items to a buyer who otherwise would've purchased only a single item from you.

HACK #47 List Your Other Auctions in the Description

Capitalize on a single auction's popularity by using it to promote your other items.

As suggested in "Allow Visitors to Search Through Your Auctions" [Hack #46], it's beneficial to make your other running auctions as accessible as possible so that your bidders will be more inclined to purchase multiple items from you.

The first thing you'll want to do is tell your customers that they can save money (in the form of shipping expenses) by purchasing multiple items from you at the same time. Probably the simplest and most effective way to do this is to place the following HTML code in your auction descriptions:

```
<a href="http://cgi6.ebay.com/ws/eBayISAPI.
dll?ViewSellersOtherItems&userid=my_user_id">Check out my other auctions</a>
- bid on multiple items and save on shipping!
```

This link is effectively no different from the "View seller's other items" link that eBay provides, except that your message suggests to customers that they have something to gain by clicking through. And since you customize the link, you also have the advantage of being able to pre-sort the listing and even show more auctions on a single page; see "Tweaking Search URLs" [Hack #12] for details.

Specific Product Links

The next step up is to actually link to specific auctions in your description. This is most useful if you're selling an item and a bunch of related accessories separately. For example, an auction for a PDA might contain this HTML code:

```
Note that I'm also selling a genuine leather case for this PDA <a
href="http://cgi.ebay.com/ws/eBayISAPI.dll?ViewItem&item=3116521524">here</
a> and a travel charger <a href="http://cgi.ebay.com/ws/eBayISAPI.
dll?ViewItem&item=3116521523">here</a>. Bid on multiple items and save on
shipping!
```

Then, in the auction description for the aforementioned travel charger, you might include something like this:

```
Note that I'm also selling the PDA that uses this charger <a href="http://
cgi.ebay.com/ws/eBayISAPI.dll?ViewItem&item=3113167823">here</a>. Bid on
multiple items and save on shipping!
```

The resulting links, shown in Figure 4-11, are much more convenient and conspicuous than the simple list of auctions hidden behind the "View seller's other items" link. Your bidders will be able to quickly flip between your related auctions, and you'll probably get more bids as a result.

There is one catch, however. The item numbers in the links are assigned when the auctions begin, so you can't include complete links to auctions that haven't started yet. Instead, just type your links without the auction numbers, like this:

```
<a href="http://cgi.ebay.com/ws/eBayISAPI.dll?ViewItem&item=">here</a>
```

Then, once the auctions have started, go back and revise the descriptions, inserting the corresponding auction numbers as needed. See "Make Changes to Running Auctions" [Hack #50] for details.

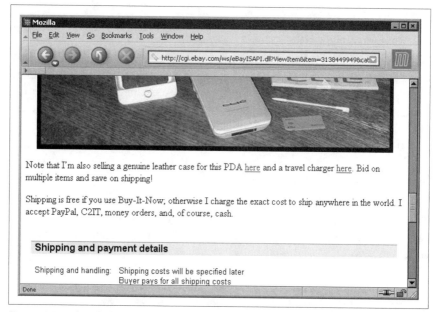

Figure 4-11. Place links to related auctions right in your auction descriptions to increase the likelihood that buyers will purchase multiple items from you

Java-Based Galleries

Although the targeted links in the previous section are often the most effective method for linking to your other auctions, they do require a good amount of extra time and attention for each auction in which they're used. Busy sellers who don't want to invest the extra work may instead prefer to place automated galleries in their auction descriptions.

For a monthly fee you can use the Andale Gallery (shown in Figure 4-12), an interactive, Java-based browser that allows your customers to browse through your other items without even leaving your auction page. It's automatically updated with your current auctions, so very little customization is required.

A free trial of the Andale Gallery is available at *www.andale.com*. A similar tool, AuctionLynxx, is available at *www.auctionhelper.com*. Although these add-ons are overkill for small sellers, those running a business on eBay will probably appreciate the slick, store-like feeling they afford.

Create a Custom "Gallery"

The Andale Gallery is essentially a scrolling viewport with dynamic (changing) content. Using iframes, discussed in "Dynamic Text in Auction

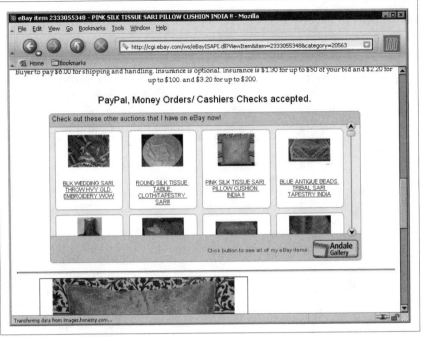

Figure 4-12. Include the Andale Gallery in your auction descriptions

Descriptions" [Hack #51], you can create your own custom gallery. All you need to do is reference a page with a list of your auctions, optionally with Gallery photos.

Of course, you could place your "View seller's other items" page inside the iframe, but your bidders would only see the huge eBay logo and menu bar; they'd have to scroll down for the actual list. Instead, you'll want a more abbreviated list, like the one described in "Generate a Custom Gallery" [Hack #94]. Or, check out "Make Money by Linking to eBay" [Hack #77] and "List Your Auctions on Another Site" [Hack #78] for a way to have eBay pay you for linking to your own auctions.

HACK #48 Make Good Use of the About Me Page

Set up a static page on eBay for all the stuff that would otherwise clutter up your auction pages.

Many sellers make the mistake of including pages and pages of payment and shipping terms, only to supplement it with a single sentence about the item itself. No wonder bidders never read descriptions!

I hate clutter, whether it's on one of my own auctions or someone else's. I like to reserve the space in my auction descriptions for information about the item being sold, mostly because bidders have a limited attention span, and I, as a seller, have a limited amount of time to prepare my auctions.

eBay allows any user to build a static page right on the eBay web site—separate from their auctions—with whatever content he or she wants to make public. Although anyone can put together an About Me page by going to Site Map → About Me, it's sellers who will benefit most from this feature.

> Since the About Me page is separate from auctions, its content can be modified at any time, even after your auctions have received bids. See "Make Changes to Running Auctions" **[Hack #50]** and "Dynamic Text in Auction Descriptions" **[Hack #51]** for more information.

Although you can maintain your own web page on any off-eBay site, there are significant advantages to using the About Me feature. For one, the information on the page will appear more trustworthy to your bidders because it looks like part of the eBay site, complete with the eBay logo and menu bar. Second, a link to your About Me page will appear next to your user ID whenever your ID appears on eBay. And finally, you'll be able to insert dynamic, eBay-specific content in your page, as follows.

Just Say No to Templates

When you use the About Me feature for the first time, eBay presents a selection of different templates that you can choose from to frame your page. The next step involves filling in about a dozen fields with your personalized information (see Figure 4-13), such as a title, welcome message, something called "another paragraph," and some of your favorite links. You can also choose to display recent feedback and a list of your items for sale, right on the page.

If you want to have full control over the look of your page, you can skip the setup page by clicking Preview at the bottom of the page. Then, on the next page, click "Edit using HTML." You'll then be shown a single edit box, pre-filled with the HTML code from your current About Me page. You can proceed to modify or replace this code as you see fit. See "Formatting the Description with HTML" **[Hack #40]** for assistance in this area, as well as information on using a WYSIWYG web page editor to create pages like this.

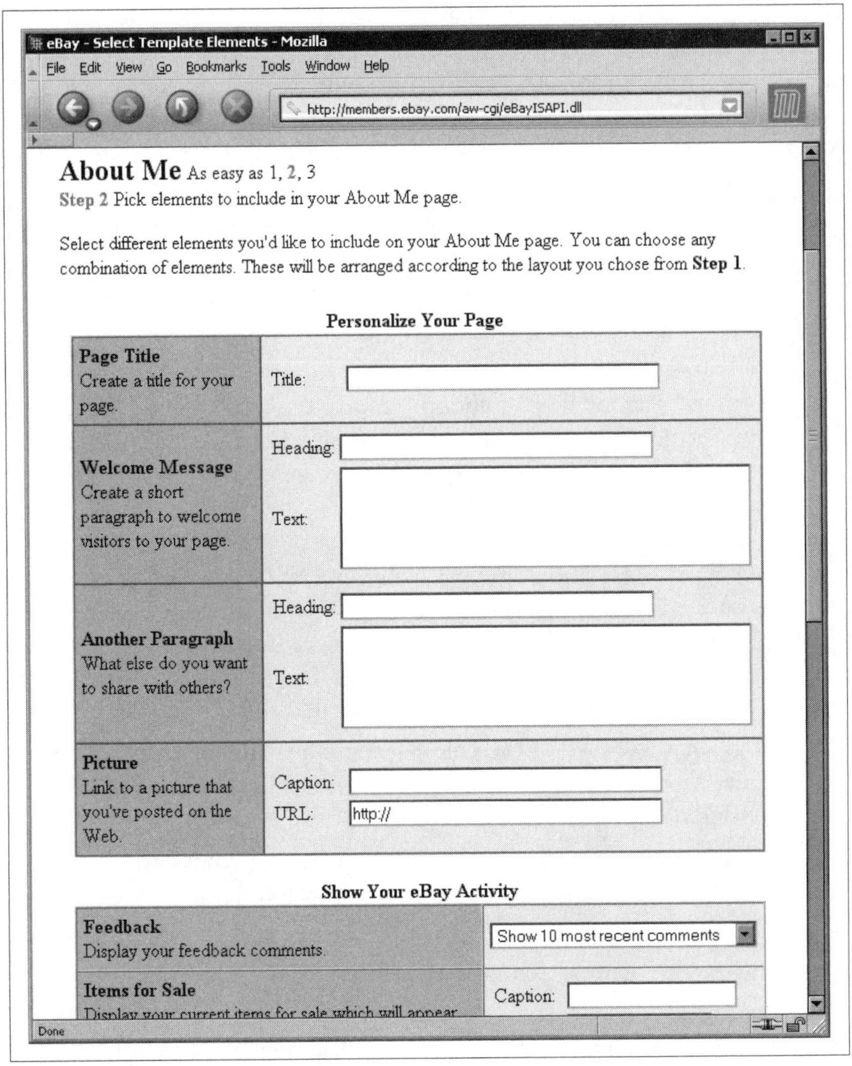

eBay - Select Template Elements - Mozilla

File   Edit   View   Go   Bookmarks   Tools   Window   Help

http://members.ebay.com/aw-cgi/eBayISAPI.dll

About Me As easy as 1, 2, 3

Step 2 Pick elements to include in your About Me page.

Select different elements you'd like to include on your About Me page. You can choose any
combination of elements. These will be arranged according to the layout you chose from **Step 1**.

Personalize Your Page

Page Title Create a title for your page.	Title:
Welcome Message Create a short paragraph to welcome visitors to your page.	Heading: Text:
Another Paragraph What else do you want to share with others?	Heading: Text:
Picture Link to a picture that you've posted on the Web.	Caption: URL: http://

Show Your eBay Activity

| **Feedback** Display your feedback comments. | Show 10 most recent comments |
| **Items for Sale** Display your current items for sale which will appear | Caption: |

Done

*Figure 4-13. The About Me setup page is the first thing you see when you build an About
Me page, but it doesn't afford the flexibility of the optional HTML editor interface*

Once you leave the template interface, you won't be able to
go back without "starting over," which effectively deletes
your page and returns you to the blank slate provided when
you first started. For this reason, you should always keep a
copy of your custom About Me page in a text file on your
computer. Just highlight all the text in the edit box (Ctrl-A),
copy to the clipboard (Ctrl-C), and paste into your favorite
text editor (Ctrl-V). Do this every time you modify your page.

Since the page is hosted on the eBay site, you'll have access to features not otherwise available if you were to host the page yourself. Using specialized HTML tags, you can insert eBay-specific content, such as recent feedback and a list of your running auctions. In all, five tags are available, each with a selection of options to further customize your page.

<eBayUserID>

> Instead of putting your email address in your About Me page, you can take advantage of eBay's privacy features. Having your bidders contact you through the Contact an eBay Member form will reduce the spam and other nuisance emails you might otherwise get. For example:
>
> > <ebayuserid nofeedback nomask>
>
> The nofeedback and nomask options remove the feedback in parentheses and the icons that would normally appear after your user ID. If you want more flexibility, you can include a hard-coded link to the same page, like this:
>
> > <a href="http://cgi3.ebay.com/aw-cgi/eBayISAPI.
> > dll?ReturnUserEmail&requested=*user_ID*">contact me</a>

<eBayFeedback size=n>

> Use this tag to include a table with some recent feedback you've received; specify size=15 to show the last 15 comments. You can further customize the table with the following additional options:
>
> - alternatecolor=red (the color of the *upper* line of each comment; see "Customize Auction Page Backgrounds" [Hack #41] for a list of supported colors)
> - color=white (the color of the *lower* line of each comment)
> - border=1 (the width, in pixels, of the table border)
> - tablewidth=100% (the width of the table, as a percentage of the width of the browser window)

<eBayItemList>

> This tag places a table with a list of your running auctions right in your text, similar to the "View seller's other items" page. You can customize the table with these options:
>
> - sort=n (where *n* can be 8 to show newly listed auctions first, 2 to show the oldest auctions first, 3 to show the auctions ending first, or 4 to show the lowest-price items first)
> - since=n (include a positive number for *n* to show completed items, up to 30 days old)

- category=*n* (restrict the listing to items in a single category; see "Tweaking Search URLs" [Hack #12] for more information on the category number to include here)

- border, tablewidth, and cellpadding (see <eBayFeedback>, above)

<eBayMemberSince>
<eBayTime>

These two tags display the date you first registered and the current date in eBay time, respectively.

You might use <eBayMemberSince> like this:

```
eBay member since <ebaymembersince format="%B %d, %Y">
```

and you'd see something like "eBay member since May 31st, 2003" in your About Me page. The idea is to imply a certain level of trustworthiness, corresponding to the length of time you've been buying and selling on eBay. But since this date never changes, there's no reason you can't simply type it directly onto your page.

Since <eBayTime> doesn't necessarily show either the seller's local time or the bidder's local time, but rather only the current time in eBay's time zone (Pacific time, GMT-8:00), its usefulness on this page is limited.

The codes used in the format string are as follows. To format the date, include %A for the day of the week (%a to abbreviate), %m for the month number, %B for the month name (%b to abbreviate), %d for the day of the month, and %Y for the year (%y for only two digits). Likewise, to format the time, type %I for the hour (%H for 24-hour clock), %M for the minute, %S for the second, and %p for the appropriate "AM" or "PM" text. (Note that the codes are case-sensitive; %Y is different from %y.)

Referencing the About Me Page

Once you've built an About Me page, a little "me" icon will appear next to your user ID (right after the feedback rating) wherever your ID appears on the eBay site. Another user can simply click the icon to view your About Me page. But you can also link directly to your About Me page in your auctions using this simple URL:

```
http://members.ebay.com/aboutme/user_ID/
```

If you want eBay's little "me" icon to appear in your link, use this code:

```
See <a href="http://members.ebay.com/aboutme/user_ID/" target=_blank><img
src="http://pics.ebay.com/aw/pics/aboutme-small.gif" border=0></a> for
payment and shipping terms.
```

If your About Me page is complicated or lengthy, you may want to divide it up with named anchors. For instance:

```
<a name="shipping"></a>
My Shipping Terms...
<p>
<a name="payment"></a>
My Payment Terms...
```

You can then jump to any anchor on the page by placing a # sign at the end of the URL, followed by the anchor name. For example, you may want to place this code in your auction description:

```
Please read my <a href="http://members.ebay.com/aboutme/user_ID/#shipping">
shipping terms</a> and my <a href="http://members.ebay.com/aboutme/user_ID/
#payment">payment terms</a> before you bid.
```

This would create two links, each to a different part of your About Me page.

Opting Out of Checkout

#49   Keep the personal touch in your transactions by disabling eBay's controversial Checkout feature.

The direct communication between buyers and sellers is one of the main reasons that eBay works as well as it does, and one of the things that makes eBay fun. In 2001, eBay took an unfortunate step toward circumventing that communication by introducing the Checkout feature, which angered and alienated (at least temporarily) many of its most loyal users.

But the biggest problem with Checkout is that it allows the winning bidder to complete the transaction without having to wait for the seller to send payment instructions. For example, a bidder in another country can pay for an auction for which the seller has specified a fixed shipping charge intended only for domestic shipments. The result is a frustrated seller and a confused bidder, not to mention a transaction that has to be redone.

> Sellers should think twice before including their postal address in their auctions. In addition to privacy concerns, this would allow buyers to mail their payments without any input from sellers. This is especially troublesome because a payment sent via postal mail is much more difficult to rescind than an electronic payment like PayPal. And bidders who have to resend payments typically blame sellers for the hassle.

Initially, the Checkout feature was designed to funnel more users into eBay now-defunct BillPoint auction payment system (and away from its rival, Pay Pal), as it allowed bidders to choose BillPoint as a payment option whether or not the seller was willing to accept BillPoint payments. Almost overnight, eBay had thousands of angry sellers threatening to leave eBay.

Well, it seems that fate is not without a sense of irony. Within six months, BillPoint was history, and eBay had acquired PayPal. But the Checkout problem remains, now simply funnelling bidders into PayPal instead (albeit only if the seller has chosen to accept PayPal).

Figure 4-14 shows what your customers see at the top of completed item pages when the Checkout feature is in full force.

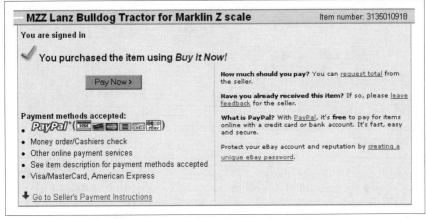

Figure 4-14. What your customers see when you use eBay's Checkout feature

Since eBay doesn't let you prioritize your payment methods or link to off-site Checkout services (introduced later in this hack), PayPal will always be shown more prominently than any other payment method.

Disabling Checkout

Although it isn't obvious by any stretch of the imagination, Checkout is indeed optional for sellers. Whether or not you decide to use it will depend on your needs and how the Checkout system fits with the way you like to do business.

To formally disable the Checkout feature, go to My eBay → Preferences → Update Checkout Preferences, and choose the "No, do not display eBay's Checkout button" option. Any changes to your Checkout preferences affect

ted thereafter, which means that there's no way to disable
out for current or recently completed listings.

ually a two-tiered system, and the Checkout Preferences
half the battle. If you've specified PayPal as one of your
forms of payment when listing your item, your customers will still
see the Pay Now button shown in Figure 4-15.

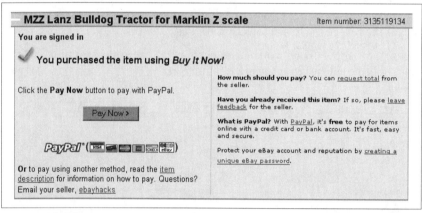

Figure 4-15. *What your customers see when you've disabled Checkout but left PayPal* *active*

All that's actually changed is that bidders can now "check out" only if they're paying via PayPal; no other payment options will be displayed. This is useful for sellers who wish to accept only PayPal payments.

Disabling PayPal

The Pay Now button will be visible on all completed auctions for which Pay-Pal is an accepted payment method, even if Checkout is disabled.

Although PayPal can be very convenient for both buyers and sellers, there are situations where it can't (or shouldn't) be used, at least not until the bidder and seller have worked out the details of the transaction.

> Since PayPal protects only sellers who accept payments from buyers with "confirmed addresses," sellers may wish to restrict PayPal sales to customers in the United States (see "Protect Yourself While Accepting Payments" [Hack #67]). Unfortunately, the Pay Now button gives all winning bidders the impression that they can pay with PayPal, regardless of their location or ability to complete the transaction.

At this point, the only way to get rid of the Pay Now button—and put all payment methods on equal footing—is to remove the PayPal option from your listings. You can do this in the Sell Your Item form as well as the Revise Your Item form (explained in "Make Changes to Running Auctions" [Hack #50]).

Turning off the PayPal option doesn't mean that you can't accept PayPal payments; it simply disables the link between PayPal and eBay. One unfortunate consequence of this, however, is that your auctions won't be included in searches for PayPal-only items. To help compensate for this, you may wish to place a PayPal logo prominently in your auction description.

When both the Checkout and PayPal options have been disabled, your completed auctions will look like the one in Figure 4-16.

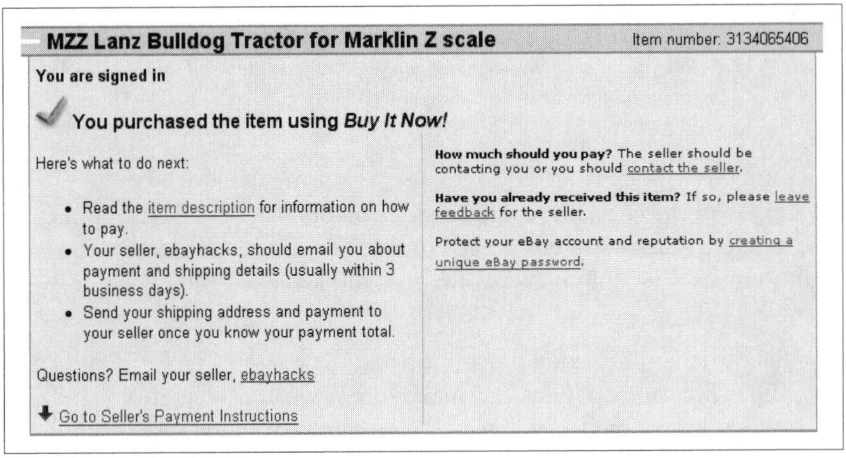

Figure 4-16. *What your customers see when you've both disabled Checkout and removed PayPal as an official payment option*

This third option—with neither Checkout nor PayPal in effect—is probably the most convenient for sellers who wish to use off-eBay checkout services (described later in this hack). But with no automated way for a bidder to send his or her mailing address, this is the least convenient setup for bidders.

The fourth scenario involves reenabling Checkout, but leaving the PayPal option inactive. As shown in Figure 4-17, the resulting page now looks as it did before, complete with the Pay Now button. But any customer who uses Pay Now will be able to send nothing more than their mailing address and intended method of payment to the seller. This is effectively the best choice for sellers who don't want to receive payments until they've sent their bidders payment instructions, but who also want to take advantage of eBay's automated Checkout system.

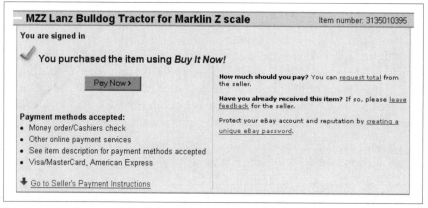

Figure 4-17. *What your customers see when you've enabled Checkout, but disabled PayPal as a payment option*

Payment Instructions

Regardless of the checkout configuration you choose, you should explain to your bidders exactly what they need to do to complete the transaction, both in the auction description and in the special Payment Instructions box. For example:

> "Please read the auction description and the payment terms in my About Me page carefully, and make sure you can pay before you bid. – – – Winning bidders will receive payment instructions via email. If you're the high bidder and you don't receive an email from me within 24 hours after the close of the auction, you may have an overly aggressive spam filter. Adjust your email account settings and then contact me for instructions. – – – Thanks for bidding!"

Since you're limited to 500 characters in the Payment Instructions box and you're not permitted to use HTML, you'll need to be concise and a little creative to communicate the most important information to your winning bidders. For instance, notice the repeating dashes to help separate paragraphs.

See Also

- Sending Payment Instructions [Hack #66]
- What to Do When Your Email Doesn't Get Through [Hack #8]
- Streamlining Checkout and Payment [Hack #75]

HACK #50 Make Changes to Running Auctions

Keep your auctions looking and performing their best with post-listing revisions.

We all misspell words from time to time, but where auction titles and descriptions are concerned, innocent typos can adversely affect sales. eBay allows you to modify your auctions once they've been started, but certain revisions may not be allowed, depending on when you submit them and whether the item has received any bids.

For example, eBay understandably doesn't let you change the description once someone has bid on your auction,* but you can *add* to the description. Any supplemental text and photos are placed at the end of the description, accompanied by a date and timestamp, making it clear to your bidders exactly what you added and when. Additionally, since eBay doesn't allow bidders to retract their bids within the last 12 hours of an auction (see "Retract Your Bid Without Retracting Your Bid" [Hack #27]), further revisions normally available to sellers are prohibited during that time. Table 4-4 shows possible revisions to a running auction; a checkmark indicates when each revision is allowed.

Table 4-4. When aspects of an auction can be changed

Revision	Before 1st bid	After 1st bid	Last 12 Hours	Completed Items
Bold	✓	✓ (nonrefundable if removed)	✓ (nonrefundable if removed)	
Buy-It-Now	✓	vehicles with a reserve price only		only using second-chance offer
Calculated shipping	✓			change in invoice only
Cancel bids		✓	✓	
Categories	✓	✓		
Counter	✓	✓	✓	
Description	✓	add to only	add to only, unless it has also received a bid	
Duration	✓	only by ending early	only by ending early	

* Note that canceling bids, as described in "Keeping Out Deadbeat Bidders" [Hack #54], will not restore your ability to make changes to the auction description.

Table 4-4. *When aspects of an auction can be changed (continued)*

Revision	Before 1st bid	After 1st bid	Last 12 Hours	Completed Items
End listing	✓	✓	✓	
Featured	✓	✓ (nonrefund-able if removed)	✓ (nonrefund-able if removed)	
Gallery	✓	✓ (nonrefund-able if removed)	✓ (nonrefund-able if removed)	
Gallery photo	✓	✓	✓	
Gift services	✓	✓ (nonrefund-able if removed)	✓ (nonrefund-able if removed)	
Highlight	✓	✓ (nonrefund-able if removed)	✓ (nonrefund-able if removed)	
Item location	✓			
Listing format (auction vs. fixed-price)	auctions only, using Buy-It-Now			
Payment details	✓	add to only		change in invoice only
Payment instructions	✓			change in invoice only
Pictures (if hosting on eBay)	✓	add to description only		
Pictures (if hosting yourself)	✓	✓	✓	✓
Private auction	✓			
Quantity	✓			
Reserve price	✓	vehicles only, can be removed or lowered once		vehicles only, use second-chance offer
Shipping details	✓	add to shipping destinations only		change in invoice only
Starting price	✓			
Title	✓			

Most revisions can be made by clicking the "Revise your item" link at the top of the auction page, or by going to Site Map → Revise my item and entering the auction number. There are a few exceptions, such as "Fix my gallery image," all of which appear in the "Manage My Items for Sale" section of the eBay site map.

If you find that a revision you need to make is prohibited by eBay policy, your final resort is to go to Site Map → End My Listing, cancel all bids, end the auction early, and then relist the item. eBay will refund your listing fees (minus any listing upgrade fees) from the first auction if the relisted auction sells, so it should ultimately cost you nothing but time.

There are ways to sneak around eBay's auction revision policies, of course, as long as you don't do anything egregious like changing what the auction is for after the high bidder has bid.

- If you host your own photos, you can change them at any time, even after the auction has ended. All you need to do is make sure you don't change the photo filenames. See "Host Your Own Photos" [Hack #59] for more information.

- See "Dynamic Text in Auction Descriptions" [Hack #51] for ways to change your auction description when eBay won't otherwise allow you to do so.

- Your About Me page is separate from your auctions and can be modified at any time, regardless of the status of your auctions. This makes it ideal for your payment and shipping terms, contact information, and details about your business; see "Make Good Use of the About Me Page" [Hack #48] for more information.

Dynamic Text in Auction Descriptions

#51
Use inline frames to change the text in your auction descriptions, even after bids have been placed.

Once bids have been placed on an auction, eBay severely restricts the changes that the seller is allowed to make (see "Make Changes to Running Auctions" [Hack #50] for details). Probably the most prevelant restriction is the auction description itself, which can only be added to once the auction has received its first bid. Fortunately, you can use iframes (inline frames) to work around this.

> Any text not hardcoded into your auction description will not be indexed by eBay Search, so you'll want to restrict dynamic text to material not specific to the item being sold (such as payment terms or information about your company).

An inline frame is like a web page within a web page. To try it, place the following code right in your auction description:

```
<iframe src="http://www.ebayhacks.com/myiframe.html"
        style="width:350;height:200;" align=left>
```

```
<a href="http://www.ebayhacks.com/myiframe.html" target=_blank>Click
here</a> to view additional information about this auction.
</iframe>
```

The web page designated by the src parameter in the <iframe> tag will load in a window 350 pixels wide and 200 pixels high, as shown in Figure 4-18.

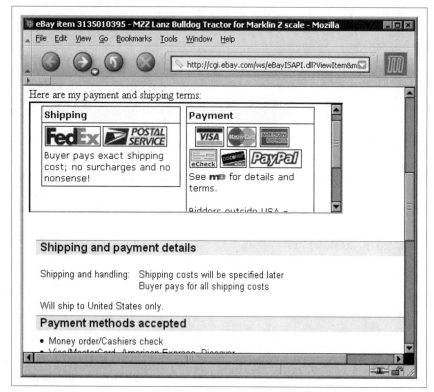

Figure 4-18. Use an inline frame to place an external web page in your auction description that can be changed, even after the auction receives bids

The page you reference can be any page on any web site, but you'll most likely want to place one of your own pages in the iframe. See "Host Your Own Photos" [Hack #59] for more information on hosting your own web pages (HTML files). In this example, the page is named *myiframe.html* and is located on *www.ebayhacks.com*.

Unfortunately, support for iframes among the browsers currently in use is a little sketchy, especially in older versions. You can accommodate users viewing your auction with iframes-challenged browsers by including alternate text between the <iframe> and </iframe> tags, like the link to the page in the example above.

You can fine-tune the appearance of your `<iframe>` with the following styles and parameters (others exist, but these are the only ones that can be counted on):

Parameter	Description
`style="width:n; height:n;"`	Specify the width and height of the box, in pixels or percentages
`style="margin:n;"`	Specify the horizontal and vertical distance between the iframe content and its border
`style="border:n;"`	Specify the border width; use 0 to turn it off completely
`scrolling=no`	Turn off the scrollbars; note that the viewport can still be scrolled by clicking and dragging to select text inside
`align=left | right | top | middle | bottom`	When you align the iframe to the `left` or `right`, the exterior text wraps around the box; otherwise the box is placed in-line with the text, and the `align` parameter only affects whether surrounding text is aligned to the `top`, `middle`, or `bottom` of the box

Now, you can set apart the iframe with a thick border or added whitespace by simply enclosing it in a table, but in your auctions you probably want it to blend in as much as possible with the surrounding text. In that case, try this:

```
<p>
<iframe src="http://www.ebayhacks.com/myiframe.html" scrolling=no
        style="width:100%;height=200;margin:0;border:0;">
<a href="http://www.ebayhacks.com/myiframe.html" target=_blank>Click here</
a> to view additional information about this auction.
</iframe>
<p>
```

First we have a paragraph break `<p>` tag before and after the iframe. Next, we have no `align` parameter, and a width set to 100% (equal to the width of the page). Next, the scrollbars are turned off for obvious reasons, and the margins and border are both set to zero so that the text in the iframe lines up with the rest of the auction description.

The only guesswork is in the `height` parameter, which unfortunately must be set to a static value. You'll see the problem when you resize the browser window: if the page is too wide, you'll be stuck with extra space at the bottom; if the page is too narrow, the height won't be sufficient to hold all the text. Ideally, the height of the box should automatically adjust to the size of the contents of the iframe—which, not surprisingly, is something we can accomplish with a little added JavaScript.

Start by simplifying the `<iframe>` tag by removing the height style:

```
<iframe src="http://www.ebayhacks.com/myiframe.html" scrolling=no
     style="width:100%;margin:0;border:0;" id="myIframe">
```

Also new is the `id="myIframe"` parameter, which assigns a name (`myIframe`) to the iframe that we'll use later. Next, the JavaScript code that does the resizing is actually placed in the referenced HTML file:

```
     <html>
     <head>
     <script type="text/javascript">
     function resizeIframe() {
❶       parent.document.getElementById('myIframe').height =
                 document.getElementById('myContent').scrollHeight;
     }
     </script>
     </head>
❷     <body style="margin:0;border:0"
                 onload="resizeIframe()" onResize="resizeIframe()">
❸     <div id="myContent">

     Your content goes here...

❹     </div>
     </body>
     </html>
```

Here's how it works. The visible content of the page—all of it—is placed inside the `<div></div>` structure, ❸ to ❹, which defines a layer named myContent. (The layer acts like a taut rubber band, stretching to the edges of its contents and allowing us to calculate the overall height of the text.)

The single line of JavaScript code ❶ sets the height of `myIframe` object on the *parent* page (the auction, in this case) to be equal to the height of the myContent layer.

Finally, the `<body>` tag ❷ executes the JavaScript code by running the resizeIframe function when the page is first loaded and also whenever the page is resized. The `style` parameter in the `<body>` tag helps reinforce the marginless, borderless appearance, as illustrated in Figure 4-19.

If all goes well, the iframe will automatically resize to fit its contents and will look just like another paragraph in your auction description. But since its contents are stored in an off-site file, the paragraph can be modified at any time, including after the auction has received bids, and even after it has ended!

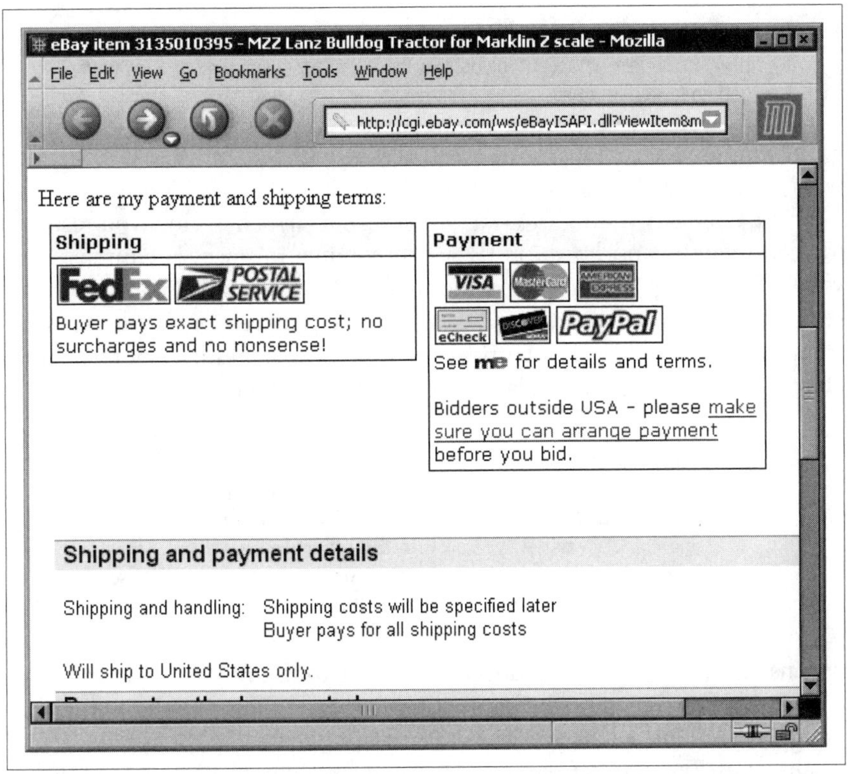

Figure 4-19. A dynamically resizing, borderless iframe placed in your auction description will blend in with the rest of the text

How to Tell Dynamic from Static Text

So, if you're a bidder, how can you tell that you're looking at a page with dynamic text in an iframe? Just press Ctrl-A to select all the hardcoded text in the auction, and any blocks of dynamic text will stand out like a sore thumb.

If you're concerned that a seller has included dynamic text describing something important, simply highlight the text with the mouse, copy it to the clipboard (Ctrl-C), and paste it into a text editor (Ctrl-V) for safe storage.

If you suspect that a seller is using dynamic text for deceptive reasons (e.g., to defraud bidders), report the auction to eBay by going to *pages.ebay.com/help/basics/select-RS.html*.

Let's Make a Deal

#52   How to handle impatient bidders without losing customers and without getting kicked off eBay.

From time to time, bidders will contact you with special requests, such as those suggested in "Manipulating Buy-It-Now Auctions" [Hack #26] and "Retract Your Bid Without Retracting Your Bid" [Hack #27]. How you respond to such requests and how you decide to conduct business is entirely up to you, but you'll want to be careful about some of the steps you take. As a seller on eBay, you'll have to walk a fine line between protecting yourself from dishonest bidders, not upsetting your honest bidders, not violating eBay policy, and not wasting large amounts of your time.

> See who you're dealing with by taking a moment to look at their feedback and investigate their history, a process explained in "Diplomacy 101: Answering Dumb Questions" [Hack #53]. That way, you'll know whether you should trust the bidder or add the bidder to your Blocked Bidder list (see "Keeping Out Deadbeat Bidders" [Hack #54]).

For instance, an impatient bidder might want to use Buy-It-Now on one of your auctions, even though the item has received bids and the option has disappeared from the page. The following are a few different approaches to dealing with this type of request, each with its own advantages and disadvantages:

- Assuming you know the value of your item (see "What's It Worth?" [Hack #33]), you should be able to look at the current bids—as well as the relative success of your competition—and predict how much you're ultimately going to get for your item. Your auction may indeed be on track to fetch a higher amount than your original Buy-It-Now price, in which case you'll want to politely tell the bidder that you prefer to let the auction run its course. Naturally, you'll run the risk of not getting as much as the bidder is offering, or, at the very least, driving the bidder away by making him wait.

- If you cancel all bids on an auction, the Buy-It-Now price will reappear, and the bidder in question can buy the item. Unfortunately, this approach is not without risks. First, you'll need to get the timing right; if the bidder isn't quick enough, someone else may place a bid and the Buy-It-Now price will once again disappear. But what's worse is the possible flight risk; if the bidder doesn't end up using Buy-It-Now, you've essentially canceled a bunch of honest bids on your item for no reason.

- You can also make an under-the-table deal with the bidder, agreeing to end the auction early for a certain dollar amount. But this, too, is fraught with peril. First, eBay may consider this to be a violation of their "fee avoidance" policy, and as a result may suspend your account. Second, since it is an off-eBay transaction, it won't be covered by eBay's fraud protection policies, and neither you nor the bidder will be able to leave feedback.

 As a seller, you should never solicit an off-eBay transaction from your bidders, either in your auction descriptions or in any eBay-related emails. There are several reasons for this, not least of which is that it's a common practice by scammers and spammers (see "Sniffing Out Dishonest Sellers" [Hack #20]) and may unsettle otherwise interested customers. It would also violate several eBay policies put in place to protect bidders. This doesn't mean that you can't agree to such requests from bidders, only that you should be careful about how you proceed.

- Probably the safest approach is to create a second listing, identical to the first. When it's ready, send the URL to the bidder and instruct him or her to use the Buy-It-Now option promptly (before anyone else bids). Only when that auction has closed successfully should you cancel bids on the original auction and end it early. This way, you and the bidder can complete the transaction officially and enjoy the protection of eBay's buying and selling policies. And if the bidder backs out, you can simply end the superfluous listing or modify it to accommodate a different item.

Although the preceding example is the most common request of this sort, it's not the only one you'll receive. Bidders often contact sellers to ask for alternative colors, versions, etc., as well as related items and accessories, and a cooperative seller can stand to make quite a bit of extra money. Just be careful about how much you reach out to bidders.

If you're selling shoes, for example, it's generally acceptable to mention that you have other sizes and colors, either in other auctions (see "List Your Other Auctions in the Description" [Hack #47]) or for sale in your online store. But this is different from posting a "dummy" auction whose purpose is to simply direct customers to your off-eBay store. Bidders won't buy it, and eBay won't tolerate it.

Diplomacy 101: Answering Dumb Questions

Good and bad ways to handle communications with seemingly lazy or dim-witted bidders.

No matter what you do, you'll never get all your bidders to read your auction descriptions, shipping terms, or payment instructions as carefully as you'd like them to, if at all. As a result, you'll occasionally get a bidder who looks at an auction entitled "Antique Royal-Blue Vase," sees the large photo of a royal-blue vase, and then writes you to ask what color the vase is.

OK, it's not usually that bad, but sometimes it seems like it is. The first thing to remember is how easy it is to miss even the most obvious piece of information. Instead of antagonizing your bidder with the all-too-familiar, "It's blue, like it says in the description," try one of the following:

- "The vase is a deep royal blue that almost looks purple in low light. The glaze seems a little darker at the bottom." Not only does this answer the bidder's question respectfully, it presumes that the bidder was looking for more information than simply, "it's blue."

- "The vase is royal blue. The photo in the auction actually has a pretty good reproduction of the color, so please let me know if it doesn't come through." This not only (kindly) reminds the bidder that there is a photo, but it helps inspire trust that the photo is accurate, a fact the bidder may not have wanted to take for granted. It also suggests a legitimate reason for the bidder asking the question in the first place; namely, that the photo might not have loaded properly on the bidder's computer.

Instead of driving your bidders away, you'll be sending them the message, so to speak, that a transaction with you will be a pleasant one, that you're trustworthy, and that your item is as you've described it. See "Sniffing Out Dishonest Sellers" [Hack #20] for some of the tactics that your bidders might be using.

>
> It may seem like a no-brainer, but when replying to a bidder's question it's important to use your email program's Reply feature so that the original message appears at the bottom of your response. This way, the bidder doesn't receive an email that simply says "Yes," with no further clue as to what question you're answering. Strangely, this simple bit of "netiquette" is basically ignored by even the most experienced sellers—don't be one of them.

Next, remember that for every bidder who writes you with a question, there will be 10 potential bidders who don't bother. Either they bid without asking, only to be disappointed later, or they move on and bid on someone else's auction instead. For this reason, it's best to be a little proactive. If a bidder asks a question that isn't answered in your auction description, go ahead and revise the auction to include the extra information, as described in "Make Changes to Running Auctions" [Hack #50]. And if you find that several bidders are asking a question that you feel is already addressed, there must be something unclear about it. There's certainly no harm in going back to the auction and trying to clarify.

Finally, as a seller on eBay, it's often your job to act as a teacher, instructing your bidders on basic bidding concepts, your payment terms, and some of the more confusing eBay policies. After all, a bidder's first dumb question is not likely the the last.

Check Out Your Bidders

When an unfamiliar eBay user makes contact, you may want to take a moment to figure out who he or she is before you reply. For example, if your auction states that you won't ship internationally, and someone from Iceland* is inquiring about your item, you'll want to let him know that you can't ship to him. But how do you know where these bidders are located? Well, you'll have a pretty good clue if someone asks, "How much to ship to Iceland?" but otherwise you'll have to do a little investigating.

Start by going to Search → Find Members, type the bidder's user ID into the Feedback Profile box, and click Submit. (For a shortcut, just open any member's feedback page and replace the user ID in the URL with that of the member you're investigating. See Chapter 1 for more information on feedback.) The country where the member is registered is shown right in the summary box at the top of the page.

> While you're at it, take a look at the member's feedback rating. If the member has an excessive amount of negative comments, now may be an excellent time to make sure that bidder can't bid on your auctions. See "Keeping Out Deadbeat Bidders" [Hack #54] for details.

The country specified on the Feedback page is not foolproof, however. If you're suspicious, just look at the bidder's email address, which will appear

---

* For my beloved readers in Iceland, please substitute *Greenland* here.

at the top of the email they've sent you. Unless the bidder's domain is *.com*, *.net*, *.org*, or *.edu*, the TLD (top-level domain) will contain a country code (such as *.uk* for the United Kingdom, *.de* for Germany, or *.ca* for Canada).

Finally, if you want to be as thorough as possible, go to Search → Find Members and look at the User ID History box. If the bidder has ever changed his or her user ID, the change will show up here. If nothing else, one of the past user IDs may be another email address, which could provide another clue as to the bidder's country of origin.

HACK #54 Keeping Out Deadbeat Bidders
A little diplomacy will help keep out deadbeats and still allow healthy bidding on your auction.

"Good judgment comes from bad experience, and a lot of that comes from bad judgment."

One of the most frustrating aspects of selling on eBay is dealing with winning bidders who don't pay. Not only are non-paying bidders a waste of the seller's time and money, they end up ruining honest bidders' chances of winning the auction.

You can always tell a seller has been recently burned by a deadbeat from the harsh warnings in their auction descriptions:

- "Don't bid if you don't intend to pay!"
- "Serious bidders only."
- "If you have zero feedback, email before bidding or your bid will be canceled!"
- "A non-paying bidder will receive negative feedback, lots of threatening email, and a note to your mother."

The problem with all of these is that they typically do more harm than good. For example, you should *never* tell visitors not to bid on your item, regardless of your intentions. The tone is angry and threatening, and sends a message (even to honest bidders) that dealing with you will likely be a less than pleasant experience. Besides, your average deadbeat bidder probably won't read your description anyway.

Instead, start by thinking about why someone may not pay after winning an auction, and then find a diplomatic way to weed out such bidders.

In most cases, it will be new eBay users—with a feedback rating of less than 10 or so—who end up bidding and not paying, a fact due largely to their inexperience rather than any kind of malice. For instance, new bidders will often wait until after they've bid to read the auction description and payment terms (if they read them at all). Or, a bidder might bid and later discover that he or she no longer needs or wants your item. And since inexperienced eBay users typically don't know how to retract bids or communicate with sellers, nor do they understand that they can simply resell something they don't want, they simply disappear, hoping that the problem will go away if they ignore a seller's emails.

Naturally, there are also those clowns who bid with no intention of paying. This is actually quite uncommon, and such abusers of the system don't last long on eBay. If you suspect that someone with a vendetta against you might bid on one of your auctions just to leave feedback, you may want to update your Blocked Bidder List (described later in this hack).

So how do you tell the difference between honest bidders and dishonest deadbeats? Go to Search → By Bidder, enter the bidder's user ID, and click Yes to include completed items. If the user's bidding history seems reasonable (a few bids, all along the same lines), then he is probably a legitimate bidder. However, if the user is bidding as though it were going out of style, trying to buy up as many high-priced items as possible, then you've likely found yourself a deadbeat.

An Ounce of Prevention…

Since the problem of deadbeat bidding is most often caused by a lack of experience, any notes of warning in your auction description should instead be welcoming and instructional. Think of it as educating your bidders on eBay basics:

- "Attention new bidders: please read the auction description carefully and make sure it's what you want before you bid."

- "Please read my payment and shipping terms to be sure you can complete the transaction before you place your first bid."

- "If you have any questions about this auction, please contact me before you bid."

Not only do these examples encourage bidders to bid on your auctions, they enforce the practices that will help ensure that they're happy once they've paid and have received their items, which will reduce the likelihood of negative feedback and having to deal with returns. See "Expectation Management" [Hack #39]] for more ideas.

Finally, to avoid misunderstandings that can lead to non-paying bidders, take steps to make sure your payment and shipping terms are as clear as humanly possible. See "Make Good Use of the About Me Page" [Hack #48] and "Formatting the Description with HTML" [Hack #40] for ways to remove clutter and set apart important policies in your auction descriptions, respectively.

Being Proactive Behind the Scenes

Probably the best approach to preventing deadbeats is to be a little sneaky about it. Instead of relying on bidders to effectively censor themselves (which they won't), simply let them bid freely. After all, only the intentions of the *high bidder* count; all lower bids—even those placed by deadbeats in the making—only serve to raise the final auction price.

Check back and review the status of your running auctions every few days. If you see any eBay users with zero feedback or the little "new user" icon next to their user IDs, just send them a quick note to verify that they're serious. If you don't get a reply in a day or two, cancel their bids and let them know why.

Now, if any of your auctions has a high bidder with a *negative* feedback rating (less than zero) or a feedback profile with excessive negative comments, don't feel bad about canceling their bids and blocking them from bidding on any of your auctions.

Canceling Bids and Blocking Bidders

Canceling bids is easy...and fun! With the ability to cancel a bid at any time and for any reason, a seller yields tremendous power (over his or her own running auctions, anyway).

To cancel a bid, go to Site Map → Cancel Bids on My Item, and follow the prompts. All bids placed by the specified bidder will be canceled, and the auction price will be adjusted accordingly. (You can also cancel all bids on an auction in one step by going to Site Map → End my listing.)

Once a user's bids have been canceled, you'll have the opportunity to add that user's ID to your Blocked Bidder List, available at Site Map → Blocked Bidder/Buyer List. The list is simply a textbox with the user IDs of all the bidders you don't want bidding on your auctions, separated by commas. Note that although blocking a user prevents the user from placing any future bids on your auctions, it has no effect on any open bids placed by that user on any running auctions, so you may want to check your running auctions when you're done for any remaining bids that need to be canceled.

eBay doesn't allow you to automatically block bidders based solely on their feedback rating, which is a good thing. After all, every eBay user has to start somewhere. Don't assume every new user is going to be a deadbeat, but don't expect new users to understand all the ramifications of bidding, either. If you get stuck with a deadbeat bidder, they'll usually shape up with a little diplomacy and motivation; see "Dealing with Stragglers, Deadbeats, and Returns" [Hack #71] for more information.

Timing is important when canceling bids. Canceling a bid too early is usually pointless, since the user is likely to be outbid by someone else, and the cancellation would just lower the final price needlessly. Canceling too late is also not a good idea, since it would keep the final price artificially high close to the end of the auction, which might scare off bidders planning to snipe. A good window in which to cancel bids is typically about 20–30 hours before the end.

Regardless of the timing, there's usually no benefit to canceling bids by a user who isn't currently the high bidder, with two small exceptions. First, unless you block a bidder, he can bid again and become the high bidder. Second, if the high bidders retract their bids, then a once-trailing bidder can take the lead. Of course, bidders cannot retract their bids in the last 12 hours of an auction, so that particular threat is minimal.

Working with Photos
Hacks 55–64

There are no two ways about it: a photo can make or break an auction.

Attractive, clear, well-composed photos will excite your customers and get you more money for your items. Poor photos, however, will make your item —and therefore your auction—less desirable. And having no photo is tantamount to auction suicide. None of this should surprise you. But there's a lot to think about when it comes to taking photos, transferring them to your computer, preparing the files, and putting them in your auctions.

See "How to Keep Your Item from Looking Pathetic" [Hack #55] and "Mastering Close-Up Photography" [Hack #56] for tips on taking good auction photos.

Getting Photos into Your Computer

Probably the biggest hurdle that most sellers face is getting photos into their computers. In most cases, this involves an investment, not only of money for equipment, but of time taking photos and preparing them properly. If you do it right, though, the investment will more than pay for itself in a very short time.

The first step involves taking the photos, as explained in "How to Keep Your Item from Looking Pathetic" [Hack #55]. Naturally, this requires a camera, and in this department you have several options:

Digital camera

Easily the best choice for taking auction photos, a digital camera allows you to see your results immediately and get your photos online quickly.

Better digital cameras have better optics and take higher-resolution photos (more megapixels); the one you choose depends on your budget and your needs. But since the largest auction photos are typically no bigger than 800×600, which translates to only about 0.5 megapixels, the camera's resolution will not be that important. If you're shopping for a camera specifically for shooting auction photos, look for one with a good macro (close-up) lens.

 All digital cameras come with cables for transferring images to your computer. Often, however, a digital film reader will be quicker and more convenient. Look for a USB-based memory card reader that accepts all major memory card formats, including CompactFlash, SecureDigital, Memory Stick, Memory Stick Pro, SmartMedia, and xD Picture cards.

If a digital camera seems expensive, consider that the extra money you'll get for your items by having good photos will more than pay for a digital camera (which you can buy used on eBay!).

Video-conferencing camera

An alternative is to buy a video-conferencing camera—the kind that sits on top of your monitor and connects directly to your USB port. Since they have no internal memory, no LCD screens, and no optics to speak of, these cameras are remarkably cheap (with prices starting at under $10), and most support taking snapshots of at least 640×480. Make no mistake, however—the quality is pretty lousy, so it should be used only if you have no other choice at the moment.

Film camera

Never fear—film purists among us will not be left out in the cold. Flatbed scanners are cheap and relatively easy to use, and allow you to transform any print into an image file in about a minute.

Furthermore, many film developers include CDs (or floppies) with film processing, sometimes at no additional cost. The quality is nothing to write home about, but it's convenient nonetheless. You can also send your undeveloped film to an online photo service, such as Kodak's Ofoto (*www.ofoto.com*) or Shutterfly (*www.shutterfly.com*). In a few days, you'll be able to download high-quality scans from their web site.

Any way you do it, however, you'll be subject to the limitations of film photography, namely the film and developing costs, and, of course, the wait. With digital, you know right away if the picture came out, which can be especially hard to predict when taking close-up auction photos.

Image Editors

Regardless of how you take your photos and get them into your computer, you'll eventually end up with one or more image files. But before you send them to eBay or upload them to your web server (as described in "Host Your Own Photos" [Hack #59]), you'll need to prepare your images, and for that, you'll need an image editor.

A good image editor will be able to do the following:

- Read, write, and convert all popular image file formats (see the next section)
- Basic image manipulation, such as crop, resize, and rotate
- Basic touch-up, including clone, line, and text tools
- Basic color adjustments, such as contrast, brightness, and color balance
- Batch processing (converting or modifying a group of files in one step)

Here are some of the image editors currently available, including both free and commercial applications:

Adobe Photoshop (www.adobe.com)
Easily the best photo editor available, Photoshop will do just about anything you'll ever need when it comes to processing auction photos. The Windows and Macintosh versions are practically identical, meaning that the Photoshop-specific instruction in this book (which covers Version 7) should be easy to follow. The down side is that Photoshop is rather expensive, and is probably overkill for most eBay sellers.

Adobe Photoshop Elements (www.adobe.com)
Essentially a scaled-down version of Adobe Photoshop, Photoshop Elements offers many of the basic functions—without the sophistication or the steep learning curve—of its older cousin at a fraction of the price.

Jasc Paint Shop Pro (www.jasc.com)
Although not nearly as capable as Photoshop, Paint Shop Pro's strengths lie in its support for every conceivable image format and its ability to easily and quickly convert between them. Supports Windows only.

VicMan's Photo Editor (vicman.net/vcwphoto)
A free image editor for Windows with a good assortment of tools.

IrfanView (www.irfanview.com)
Also free, IrfanView is a basic image viewer with some image manipulation tools.

The Gimp (mmmaybe.gimp.org)
A free image editor for Unix, Windows, Macintosh, and even OS/2!

iPhoto and MS Paint
iPhoto and MS Paint are free image editors that come with Mac OS X and Windows, respectively. Although they support only rudimentary functionality, these programs have the significant advantages of being free and already installed on your computer.

Most of the specific instruction in this chapter covers Photoshop and, where applicable, Paint Shop Pro. Although most image editors work similarly to these programs, the usage and location of the various features will likely be a little different. Refer to the documentation included with your favorite image editor for details on its tools and capabilities.

Image Formats

Of all the different image file formats, the only one you should ever use for your photos is the JPG (pronounced "jay-peg") format. JPG files support 24-bit color, which is sufficient to reproduce all the hues you'll ever need for auction photos. JPG files also support compression (discussed in the next section), which means that they will be smaller and will load more quickly than the same images stored in most other formats.

Other image file formats you might encounter include:

GIF

GIF files support only 8-bit color (256 shades with an adaptive palette), which makes for pretty lousy photos. But GIF also has "lossless" compression (as opposed to the lossy compression used by JPG), which means that it's a better choice for logos, drawings, and text. GIF images are supported by all web browsers.

BMP

The Windows Bitmap format is the default format used by MS Paint, the rudimentary image editor included with Microsoft Windows. Not all web browsers support BMP files, and with good reason—the BMP format doesn't support compression, so even the smallest photos consume huge amounts of data. Never put BMP images in web pages.

TIF (or TIFF)

TIFF is the default file format for many flatbed scanners. If your scanner supports JPG but your JPG scans look bad, it's because your scanner software doesn't allow you to adjust the JPG compression, explained in the next section. In this case, your best bet is to save your scans as TIFF files and convert them with a suitable image editor (covered in the previous section).

PNG

The PNG format has all the advantages of JPG with some of the added features of GIF (such as animation). Unfortunately, the format was established years after the web browser, so many older browsers don't support it. In a few years, when the older browsers have mostly disappeared, PNG files will be a better choice.

Any decent image editor should be able to convert files between any of these image file formats.

Preparing Images for eBay

Before you put a photo in your auction, you'll want to take the following steps:

1. Crop the image to remove anything that isn't for sale.

2. Resize the image. If you're using eBay's Picture Services to host your photo, the image doesn't need to be any larger than 400×300 (or 800×600 if you're using the "supersize" option). Although eBay will shrink your photo down for you, it will turn out better if you do it yourself. Plus, you'll have less data to send when it's time to start the auction.

   If you have access to a web server and can host your own photos [Hack #59], you have more freedom as to the size of your photos. But it's still a good idea to keep your images no larger than 800×600; otherwise, your bidders may be annoyed by photos that take too long to load and run off the sides of their screens.

3. If necessary, touch up the photo using any of the techniques outlined in "Doctoring Photos" [Hack #57].

4. Save your photo as a JPG file. See the sidebar "Dialing in the JPG Compression" for more information.

When your photos are ready to go, the last step is to put them on the Web so they will appear in auction photos. The easiest way to do this is to use eBay's Picture Services, which allows you to upload the files to eBay as part of the Sell Your Item form. If you want more control, however, you may want to host your own photos [Hack #59].

HACK
#55   **How to Keep Your Item from Looking Pathetic**
A simple approach to taking great photos of your items.

Simply put, good photos will get you more bids and more money. An attractive, clear, well-composed photo will excite customers and inspire trust in your bidders that you're selling what you say you're selling.

On the other hand, if your photos are blurry, poorly lit, too small, or too cluttered with junk, your bidders will not be nearly as impressed. Not surprisingly, bad photos will make your item look pathetic, and as a result your auction will get fewer bids and less money (if it sells at all).

Composition

Start with a neutral background, like an empty table or section of the floor. A little texture (like wood or fabric) can be nice, but don't overdo it. Avoid

Dialing in the JPG Compression

The JPG file format supports adjustable "lossy" compression, which means that some information is lost when the image is compressed. The higher the level of compression, the more data is thrown away, and the worse the resulting photo will look. Conversely, a lower compression level will provide crisper photos, but at a cost: the resulting files are larger and take longer to load.

A good compromise is somewhere in the middle, with a slight bias toward better quality. The confusing part is that different programs represent compression levels differently. For example, the "quality" setting in Adobe Photoshop ranges from 0 to 12, with 7 typically being a reasonable compromise. In Paint Shop Pro, the "compression factor" ranges from 1 to 99, with 15 being a good compromise. And digital cameras typically have three settings: Fine, Normal, and Basic, with Normal often being the best compromise.

You may wish to perform a few experiments before settling on a single compression level. For instance, one of the example 300×225 photos in this chapter saved with the lowest quality setting (representing the highest level of compression) produced a 17 KB file and a miserable-looking image. Conversely, the same image saved at the highest quality setting (and least compression) produced a 50 KB file. While the high-quality image looked excellent, it was virtually indistinguishable from the same image saved with a medium-quality setting of 7, which topped out at only 27 KB (roughly half the size).

Naturally, your mileage will vary with the photos you take and the software you use. Note that eBay's Picture Services, explained in "Host Your Own Photos" [Hack #59], tends to over-compress photos, which may be reason enough to host them yourself.

carpet, which can make your item look dirty and shabby. And nobody is going to want something that is seen sitting in the dirt.

A shiny, reflective base, like a mirror or the top of a silver file cabinet, will make smaller items look like they're in a professional showroom. A close-up shot with only a little depth of field, as explained in "Mastering Close-Up Photography" [Hack #56], will throw any unwanted background reflections out of focus.

Your item will be lost in the photo if it's in front of a busy pattern or other high-contrast background. Remove all unnecessary clutter from the photo; it should be crystal-clear to your customers exactly what they're bidding on.

Shoot from an angle to illustrate that you're selling a three-dimensional object. An object photographed slightly askew will look much better than if it's perfectly centered and aligned with the edges of the photo. Figure 5-1 shows the same object shot at two different angles, one of which looks much better than the other.

Figure 5-1. Photograph your items from an angle to make them look more attractive

Make sure the photo is in focus. Most digital cameras let you zoom in to inspect the detail of your shots using the built-in LCD screen. If you're shooting with film, you'll want to take a few insurance shots to ensure at least one good one. (Instant feedback is one of the best reasons to shoot digital.)

Show the entire item—fully assembled—in at least one photo, preferably the first. Don't take it apart unless you feel it's important to show an internal feature or to illustrate the way the item goes together.

Case in point: Not too long ago, I purchased a toy car on eBay from a seller who included only a single, rather small photo of the item. To illustrate that one of the wheel bolts was missing, the seller physically removed one of the wheels and placed it underneath the vehicle to prop it up. The photo made it look more like a pile of junk than a car, and as a result, I got it for less than half the price the model typically fetched. When the car arrived, I simply attached the wheels and reveled at the great deal I had gotten. Although the seller was probably just trying to set a reasonable expectation, as detailed in "Expectation Management" [Hack #39], he went too far, and his car looked simply pathetic.

Photographing Collections

If you're selling a collection of items, or if there are included accessories, include at least one photo showing the entire collection together. Figure 5-2 shows a handheld computer (PDA), together with a bunch of included accessories. The group shot makes your bidders feel like they're getting a lot for their money, and it clearly illustrates exactly what is included with the auction.

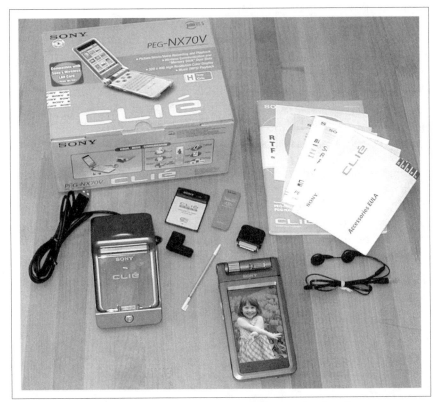

Figure 5-2. A carefully aligned group shot shows bidders exactly what they're getting

Lighting

Don't rely entirely on your camera's flash to sufficiently illuminate your object, or half your item will appear in shadow. You don't need professional-quality studio lighting, only a desk lamp or overhead light to serve as a second light source. But if there's too much light, any detail in the item might get washed out. Figure 5-3 shows the same item photographed with different amounts of light.

Figure 5-3. You can see the most detail if the object is lit from at least two sources

Finally, if you're taking multiple photos, shoot each one as if it will be the only thing your bidders see. Given how unreliable Internet connections can be, any single photo might indeed be the only thing a bidder sees!

HACK #56 Mastering Close-Up Photography

Control the depth of field to get a perfect close-up every time.

Nothing helps more than close-up photos to compensate for the fact that bidders can't see your item in person. A good close-up photo will show detail (a really good close-up will show the texture of the paint), and will also allow you to adequately explain any flaws or damage. Different ways of shooting close-up photos will yield different results.

Understanding depth of field is the key to shooting good close-ups. Depth of field is the distance between the closest object in focus and the furthest object in focus, as illustrated in Figure 5-4.

Several things affect the depth of field:

Distance from the object

The further the distance between the camera and the object, the closer your lens will be focused to infinity, and the wider the depth of field will

Figure 5-4. Depth of field is the width of the plane in which your subject will be in focus

become. Bring the camera closer to the object to narrow the depth of field.

Focal length
   A wide-angle lens will increase the depth of field, and a telephoto lens will decrease it. This means that if your camera has an optical zoom lens (not a digital zoom), you can zoom *out* to put more of your object in focus, or zoom *in* to throw more of your object out of focus.

> As you zoom out, hoping to increase the depth of field, you might be inclined to walk toward your object to keep the frame full. Unfortunately, these two actions work against one another. Instead, let the object get smaller in the frame and simply crop the photo later.

Aperture

If you're using an SLR (digital or film), you'll likely have control over the f-stop. A smaller aperture (larger f-stop) will increase the depth of field, and a wider aperture (smaller f-stop) will decrease the depth of field. This allows you to adjust what's in focus without zooming or moving the camera.

Extension tube

Although it's almost certainly overkill for auction photos, an extension tube inserted between an SLR camera and the lens will increase the macro (close-up) capability of your lens and reduce the depth of field to almost zero. The wider the angle of the lens, the closer you'll be able to focus. For example, with a 55mm extension tube and a 40mm lens, I'm able to focus on the dust on the lens glass!

So how does depth of field come into play when taking close-up photos? First, when shooting an ordinary close-up, the depth of field will likely be too small, and it will seem nearly impossible to get your item in focus. So, for example, you can try moving away from the object to bring more of it into focus, as described above. Figures 5-4 and 5-5 show the same object with a narrow and a wide depth of field.

If you're shooting a shiny or reflective item, or shooting with a reflective backdrop (see "How to Keep Your Item from Looking Pathetic" [Hack #55]), you'll want to reduce the depth of field. That way, any objects reflected in your item will be thrown out of focus, and your bidders will be able to see the subject itself more clearly.

Finally, if you're shooting a sculpture or other large object with a complex shape, you might have a hard time getting everything in focus without bringing in too much of the background. In this case, you'll want to fine-tune the depth of field so that the entire subject is in focus, but nothing else.

Figure 5-5. Increase the depth of field to bring more of an item into focus

Doctoring Photos

HACK #57

Techniques and tools for fixing up your photos after they've been taken.

There's more to image preparation than simple crops and rotations. When presentation really matters, you may want to take a few extra minutes to make your auction photos look perfect.

> Be careful not to doctor the photo so much that it misrepre-
> sents the item being sold. Try to strike a balance between
> making your photos look professional and setting a reason-
> able expectation with your bidders; see "Expectation Man-
> agement" [Hack #39] for details.

The following tools are available in most of the more capable image editors,
but their names and usage may vary slightly:

Clone Tool

Use the clone tool to copy one part of an image to another part, useful
for removing dust and unwanted reflections.

Start by choosing an area to clone. In Photoshop, click while holding the
Alt key. In Paint Shop Pro, click while holding Shift. Then, start draw-
ing on a different part of the image. The horizontal and vertical distance
will be held constant, so if you move a half-inch to the left, you'll be
cloning the area a half-inch to the left of the spot you originally selected.
Figure 5-6 shows an image doctored with the clone tool.

*Figure 5-6. Use the clone tool to touch up small areas of your images; here, the table edge
and a few scratches were removed with cloning*

Skew, Distort, and Perspective Tools

Photoshop supports a variety of linear distortion tools, useful for fine-
tuning the perspective of your item. Start by selecting a portion of your
image (or the entire image), and then go to Edit → Transform → Perspective. Drag any of the eight handles with your mouse to distort the selection, and click any tool in the toolbox to commit (or reject) the change.
The Skew and Distort tools work the same way, but the distortions they
permit vary slightly.

Drop Shadows

Although somewhat old-school, drop shadows are handy for making small photos stand out, especially thumbnails (see "Make Clickable Thumbnails" [Hack #60]). Although Photoshop has a feature to automatically add a drop shadow to any layer, here is a more general procedure that will work in any image editor:

a. Start by floating the layer containing your image. Press Ctrl-A to select all, Ctrl-X to cut, and Ctrl-V to paste the image into a new layer.

b. Enlarge the canvas of your image slightly, enough to accommodate the shadow; say, 20 pixels on the right side and bottom.

c. Duplicate the layer by going to Layer → Duplicate Layer, and then move the lower layer down and to the right slightly.

d. Go to Image → Adjustments → Brightness/Contrast, and turn both the brightness and contrast all the way down. The lower layer will turn completely black.

e. Finally, perform a Gaussian blur (Filter → Blur → Gaussian Blur) on the lower layer; adjust the radius to achieve the desired effect.

Auto Levels

Most image editors allow you to adjust the individual levels of red, green, and blue, as well as the brightness and contrast of an image. If all you want to do is make the image look more balanced, you can let your image editor do all the work by using the Auto Levels tool (in Photoshop, go to Image → Adjustments → Auto Levels or press Shift-Ctrl-L). It's nothing more than a mathematical operation so it's not always perfect, but most of the time it does a pretty good job.

HACK #58 Protect Your Copyright
Prevent other sellers from stealing your photos.

Taking a good-quality photo of each and every item being sold can be extraordinarily time consuming, not to mention practically impossible for items still in their boxes or not in the seller's immediate possession. As a result, many sellers resort to hijacking other sellers' photos for use in their own auctions.

The problem is that photo theft can be extremely damaging, and not so much because of mere copyright law (although it does apply).

A big part of any auction's desirability is its uniqueness. The more uncommon an item appears to bidders, the more valuable it becomes. When bidders see the same exact photo in two different auctions, not only are the implied scarcity and value of the item severely weakened, but the integrity of both sellers becomes suspect. And unless it's painfully obvious, most bidders won't distinguish between the thief and the seller whose photos were pilfered; a single theft of an image will hurt both sellers.

Protecting Your Image

My inspiration for this solution was a hot-dog vendor in my college town. On a shelf next to the broiler sat an old black-and-white television set, with the words "Stolen from Top Dog" written in permanent marker on its side.

The idea is to mark your photos so that they're unusable by other sellers, but in a way that doesn't adversely affect your own auctions. This is accomplished quite simply with a bit of text superimposed right on your photos.

The text should be carefully placed so that it doesn't obscure the subject but also can't be easily removed by the thief (such as with the clone tool in "Doctoring Photos" [Hack #57]). Often the easiest way to do this is with large, translucent text right over the center of the image, as in Figure 5-7.

Figure 5-7. Tagging your photos with your eBay user ID is an effective deterrent against image theft

The specific text you use is up to you, but it should include a copyright sym-
bol (©) and your eBay user ID. The user ID is important, as it indicates that
the photo belongs in your auction and no one else's.

Disable Right-Click

The right mouse button is what most people use if they want to save an
image on a web page. If you want to take an aggressive stance on image
theft, you can disable your customers' right mouse buttons for your auction
photos. Just include this code somewhere in your auction description:*

```
<script language="JavaScript1.1"><!--

function lockout() {
    for (var i=0; i < document.images.length; i++) {
①      document.images[i].onmousedown = norightclick;
②      document.images[i].oncontextmenu = nocontextmenu;

    }
}

function norightclick(mousebutton) {
    if (navigator.appName == 'Netscape' &&
                   (mousebutton.which == 3 || mousebutton.which == 2)) {
③      alert("Please don't steal my pix.");
        return false;
    }
}

function nocontextmenu() {
④  event.cancelBubble = true;
    event.returnValue = false;
    return false;
}

⑤ if (document.layers) {
    window.captureevents(event.mousedown);
    window.onmousedown=norightclick;
}

// --></script>
⑥ <body onLoad="lockout();">
```

Here's how it works. The lockout function sets two rules for the page: any
time a user clicks an image on the page, the norightclick function is run ①,

---

* Based on code snippets by Martin Webb (*irt.org*).

and any time a user opens a context menu on an image, the noncontextmenu function is run ❷. Later on, the <body> tag ❻ calls the lockout function only when the page has completely loaded, otherwise, the for loop would miss any images that haven't yet finished loading.

The norightclick function then blocks the right click with a warning message ❸, but only for Netscape and Mozilla browsers. The nocontextmenu function disables the context menu with no warning ❹, but only for Internet Explorer. The two browsers are handled differently because only Internet Explorer supports the oncontextmenu event. (And, to cover all our bases, there's a bit of code to handle older versions of Netscape ❺.)

This code is by no means foolproof. Any knowledgeable or determined user can disable JavaScript, or view the page source, or perform a screen capture, or simply drag-and-drop images off the page (for browsers that support it). But most users who steal images do so because they don't know any better, and this script gets the point across.

Other Ways to Protect Your Copyright

Here are a few other ways to protect your images from being stolen:

- If you're hosting your own photos, take them down right after your auctions close to reduce the window during which other sellers might find and steal your images. But this could arouse the suspicions of your winning bidder, and would weaken the marketing power of any photos in your completed auctions that might otherwise help drive bidders to your current items.

- If you're really concerned about image copyright, you can use CopySafe Pro (available at *artistscope.com*), a Java-enabled image viewer. It may be overkill for simple auction photos and it's not foolproof, but it may be the additional security you're looking for.

- Some image editors, like Photoshop, support invisible watermarking, a method by which images can be marked and later identified for copyright infringement. Image thieves won't ever know it's there, but it can be useful for proving that theft has taken place.

Reporting Image Thieves

The most effective means of protecting your images is to simply report any auctions in which another seller has used one of your images without permission.

You can try contacting the offending sellers directly, but you may not get that far. A few sellers have gotten downright hostile after I asked them to remove photos they've stolen from me. Plus, if their auctions have received bids, they may not be able to change the photos (or may simply not know how).

To report an auction, go to *pages.ebay.com/help/basics/select-RS.html*. On the Rules & Safety Support page, select Questionable Content on eBay → Potentially Infringing Issues → Use of Images, Text or Links without Proper Permission. Click Continue and then click Contact Support on the next page. Finally, specify the offending item number(s) in the first box and explain the offense in the second box. Be sure to include the item number of your original auction in the second box to show that it was you who posted the image first.

eBay typically takes 2–3 days to investigate and respond to claims. In the case of content theft, eBay will simply remove the offending auction and explain the situation to the seller (assuming you've sufficiently proven your case).

Host Your Own Photos

HACK #59

Bypass eBay's photo restrictions by hosting auction photos on your own server.

Any photos that appear in your auctions must be stored on a web server somewhere; which one you use is up to you. When you use eBay's Picture Services, you're instructing eBay to store your photos on their own dedicated picture server and link them to your auction automatically. While this is the easiest and most convenient way to host photos, it's also fraught with limitations.

Hosting photos off-eBay has tons of advantages over using eBay's Picture Services (ePS). For instance, you can:

- Include as many photos as you like in any auction at no additional charge.
- Include photos of any size with no "supersize" fees. With ePS, photos are limited to 400×300, or, for an additional fee, 800×600 (supersize).

Large photos are more striking and show much more detail than small ones, and will end up getting you more bids. The problem with eBay's supersize photos is that they appear only when bidders click the Supersize Picture links beneath the thumbnails. If you host your own photos, you can put the large versions right in the auction (as many as you like), so your bidders don't have to click to see them. This is especially helpful if you choose to create a photo collage [Hack #63].

- Control the quality (compression) settings of your JPG photos. ePS has a tendency to over-compress photos, which reduces detail and increases fuzziness.

- Use very long or very wide images that don't conform to the standard 4:3 aspect ratio. These would otherwise be shrunk beyond recognition to conform to eBay's 400×300 size limit.

- Make changes to photos while an auction is running, even after it has received bids. You'll also have control over how long the images remain in your auctions after they've closed.

- Place your photos directly in the text of your auction descriptions or use a more creative photo presentation, such as "Make Clickable Thumbnails" [Hack #60], "Construct an Interactive Photo Album" [Hack #61], or "Show a 360-Degree View of Your Item" [Hack #62].

- Reuse the same photos for multiple auctions without having to upload them repeatedly.

- Include logos and section headers right in your text.

All that's required to host your own auction photos is access to a web server on which you have an account. If you don't have access to your own server, see the sidebar "Looking for a Good Home."

Sending Photos to the Server

In most cases, an FTP program is required to transfer your images from your computer to your web server. (The exception is when you're using a dedicated picture hosting service that requires you to upload photos through a web page.)

Although nearly every modern computer comes with a command-line FTP client, you'll probably want something a little friendlier and more streamlined. Popular FTP programs include Fetch for the Mac (*fetchsoftworks.com*) and WS_FTP for Windows (*ipswitch.com*). All you'll need is the hostname (the name or address of the server), and your username and password.

Looking for a Good Home

If you want to host your auction photos outside of eBay but you don't have access to a web server, never fear—there is always help for those who need it.

Start with your ISP. Most Internet providers offer free web space to their customers, so you might have 20 MB or so of space with your name on it (literally). However, some ISPs specifically lock out image hosting, so if your photos don't load in your auctions, that's probably why.

If your ISP turns you away, you have other options. There are a number of companies that offer space (for a fee) specifically for hosting auction photos, such as *ipix.com*, *pongo.com*, *pixhost.com*, *inkfrog.com*, *eaph.com*, and *andale.com*. But since one of the goals of this hack is to save money by hosting the photos yourself, you may want to look elsewhere.

Some of the sites that offer free auction picture hosting include *freepicturehosting.com*, *easypichost.com*, *boomspeed.com*, and *villagephotos.com*. Each site works a little differently, so make sure to read the fine print.

When selecting a site to host your images, there are a few things to look for. First, make sure the images can be placed in your auctions; you don't want your customers to have to click a link to see your photos (because they won't). Second, since most free sites are advertising-supported, you'll want to make sure the ads don't interfere with your auction (and never pay for image hosting with ads). Finally, the site you choose shouldn't impose the same (or worse) restrictions on your photos that eBay does (see the beginning of this hack).

If you're resigned to paying for image hosting, consider paying for *web* hosting instead. Simple, no-frills web space is often the best choice, whether you pay for it or get it free with your Internet connection. You'll not only be able to insert photos into your auctions with none of the nonsense that accompanies most image hosting services (ads, logos, restrictions), but you'll also be able to use this space to host an entire web site, including the CGI programs detailed in other hacks in this book.

Users of most modern versions of Windows (Me, 2000, and XP) can also access FTP servers right from Explorer by typing this URL into Explorer's address bar:

```
ftp://my_server.com
```

where *my_server.com* is the hostname or IP address of your FTP server. If you want Explorer to log you in automatically, include your username and password in the URL, like this:

```
ftp://username:password@my_server.com
```

The FTP server then acts like any ordinary folder, where files can be drag-dropped, deleted, renamed, or moved into subfolders.

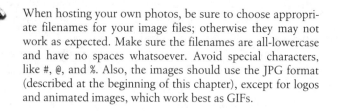

> When hosting your own photos, be sure to choose appropriate filenames for your image files; otherwise they may not work as expected. Make sure the filenames are all-lowercase and have no spaces whatsoever. Avoid special characters, like #, @, and %. Also, the images should use the JPG format (described at the beginning of this chapter), except for logos and animated images, which work best as GIFs.

Placing Photos in Your Auctions

The most direct way to include a photo in one of your auctions is eBay's Sell Your Item form. On the Pictures & Details page, choose "Your own Web hosting" and then specify the full URL of your photo:

```
http://my_server.com/my_folder/image.jpg
```

where *image.jpg* is the filename of the photo, *my_folder* is the name of the folder in which the image file is stored, and *my_server.com* is the hostname. No HTML is required to specify your photos this way, which makes it especially convenient; your images will simply appear beneath your auction description.

If you have more than one photo or if you prefer to place your photos directly in your auction text, use the <img> HTML tag to reference them, like this:

```
<img src="http://my_server.com/my_folder/image.jpg">
```

You can include as many pictures as you like, but it's up to you to present them in an attractive and efficient manner. Figure 5-8 shows some photos placed right in the text; see "Formatting the Description with HTML" [Hack #40] for more information on the <img> tag, including parameters to control alignment and text wrapping.

> If you want to place your photos directly in your auction text (using some of the other hacks in this chapter), check the box that says, "The description already contains a picture URL for my item." Otherwise, the little green "picture" icon won't appear next to your item in search results and category listings, and bidders may·pass you by.

Other means of image presentation include "Make Clickable Thumbnails" [Hack #60], "Construct an Interactive Photo Album" [Hack #61], and "Show a 360-Degree View of Your Item" [Hack #62].

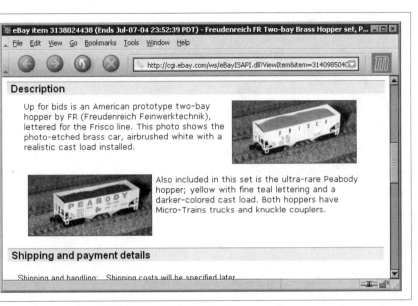

Figure 5-8. A self-hosted photo appears beneath the auction description unless you insert it into the text with HTML

HACK #60 Make Clickable Thumbnails

Use thumbnails for more professional-looking auction photos that load more quickly.

If you're hosting your auction photos [Hack #59], you have the freedom to include as many images as you like at no additional charge. But you're also responsible for inserting those photos into your auctions and presenting them in a way that is efficient and appropriate.

An average eBay auction page is about 40 kilobytes in size, not including any photos you might include. (There's also about 50 KB of JavaScript code and 15 KB of eBay images, but these will be quickly cached and ultimately loaded only once.) The size of an average, medium-sized JPG file is about 50–60 KB, which more than doubles the amount of data your bidders will have to load to view your auction.

Thumbnail photos are much smaller than their full-size equivalents, both in physical dimensions and in the amount of data that must be transferred. This means that by replacing several full-size photos with thumbnails, your auction will not only appear tidier but will load faster as well.

Preparing the Images

Thumbnails are nothing more than smaller versions of full-size images, so you'll need to make two versions of each photo.

> Don't even think about using the width and height parameters of the `<img>` tag to "shrink" down large photos. Not only will your images look awful, but they'll load much more slowly than true thumbnails.

Start by duplicating each of your image files. In Windows, for example, highlight all the images you wish to duplicate, drag them with the right mouse button to another part of the same folder window, and select Copy Here.

Next, rename your thumbnails appropriately. For example, if one of your images is named *front.jpg*, name the thumbnail image something like *front. small.jpg* or *front_thumb.jpg*. Remember to follow the naming conventions outlined in "Host Your Own Photos" **[Hack #59]**.

> An easy way to rename large groups of files quickly is to use Power Rename, a component of Creative Element Power Tools, available at *www.creativelement.com/powertools* (Windows XP, 2000, and Me only at this time). Among other things, Power Rename allows you to do search-and-replace operations on groups of filenames, even creating duplicates in the process.

Finally, open the newly created duplicates in your favorite image editor and shrink them down. A good size for thumbnails is 100 pixels in the larger dimension, but you can certainly make them smaller or larger as you see fit. Anything smaller than 50 or 60 pixels, however, will probably be too small, and anything larger than 200 will probably be unnecessarily large.

In most cases, your thumbnails will look best if they're all the same size. If you're placing them side by side, you might want them to be all the same height; if you're stacking them, you might want to make them all the same width. But probably the most effective approach is to pick a size to use for each photo's larger dimension.

> If you're using Windows XP, you can use Microsoft's Image Resizer utility, freely available at *www.microsoft.com/ windowsxp/pro/downloads/powertoys.asp*, to resize a bunch of photos in a single step.

When your images and corresponding thumbnails have been prepared, upload them to your server (see "Host Your Own Photos" [Hack #59]).

Putting Thumbnails in your Auctions

To put a single thumbnail image in your auction description, use the following bit of HTML:

```
<a href="http://www.ebayhacks.com/pictures/view1.jpg"><img
    src="http://www.ebayhacks.com/pictures/view1_small.jpg"></a>
```

Simply replace http://www.ebayhacks.com/pictures/view1_small.jpg with the complete URL of the thumbnail image, and replace http://www. ebayhacks.com/pictures/view1.jpg with the URL of the full-size image. (See "Formatting the Description with HTML" [Hack #40] for more information on the <img> and <a> tags.)

To right-align or left-align your thumbnail in the description, simply include the align=right or align=left parameters, respectively, in the <img> tag, like this:

```
<img src="http://www.ebayhacks.com/pictures/view1_small.jpg" align=right>
```

You can use tables to group a bunch of thumbnails together. Not only does this impose some structure on your images, but it permits captions, which require the alignment only tables can afford. For instance, the following code shows four thumbnails—with captions—aligned in a simple 2×2 table:

```
<table cellpadding=10 cellspacing=0 border=0>
<tr><td align=center>
  <a href="front.jpg" target=_blank><img src="front_small.jpg"></a>
  <br>The front of the car
</td><td align=center>
  <a href="glovebox.jpg" target=_blank><img src="glovebox_small.jpg"></a>
  <br>The spacious glove compartment
</td></tr>
<tr><td align=center>
  <a href="fender.jpg" target=_blank><img src="fender_small.jpg"></a>
  <br>The dent in the fender
</td><td align=center>
  <a href="dog.jpg" target=_blank><img src="dog_small.jpg"></a>
  <br>The dog I found in the back seat
</td></tr>
</table>
```

(Note that the URLs have been removed from this example for clarity, but they're needed nonetheless.) The resulting table is shown in Figure 5-9.

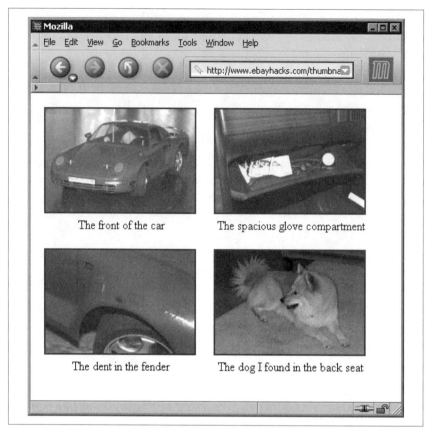

Figure 5-9. A simple table helps you align thumbnail images and their captions

The target=_blank parameters in the <a> tags in the preceding example force the full-size images to open in new windows, thus leaving the original auction page intact. Another way to do this is via JavaScript:

```
<script language="JavaScript">
  function newWindow(url,width,height) {
    flags = "width=" + width + ",height=" + height +
        ",resizable=no,scrollbars=no,menubar=no,toolbar=no,
        status=no,location=no,alwaysraised=yes";
    window.open(url, "mywindow", flags);
  }
// --></script>

<a href="http://www.ebayhacks.com/pictures/front.jpg"
    onClick="newWindow('http://www.ebayhacks.com/pictures/view1.jpg',
    300,225);return false;"><img
    src="http://www.ebayhacks.com/pictures/front_small.jpg"></a>
```

Instead of simply opening an ordinary browser window, this JavaScript code will display the image in a smaller, tidier window, sized to fit the image, and will reuse the window for each successive image that is viewed. Note that there's still an <a> tag, allowing the code to work even if JavaScript is disabled; the return false; statement is used later on to deactivate the link when JavaScript is active.

There are plenty of other ways you can customize your thumbnails. For instance:

- Change the border width of the thumbnails by placing the border=n parameter in each <img> tag, where n is the number of pixels (2 is the default).
- Add whitespace around your thumbnails by using the hspace and vspace parameters, introduced in "Formatting the Description with HTML" [Hack #40].
- Further decorate the table containing your thumbnails; see "Framing Your Auctions" [Hack #42] for details.
- See "Construct an Interactive Photo Album" [Hack #61] for another way to put thumbnails in your auction.

HACK #61 Construct an Interactive Photo Album

Use JavaScript to save money and get a better photo album to boot.

eBay provides a "photo album" feature, which allows your bidders to view multiple photos right in the auction by clicking thumbnails. However, this feature is available only if you're using eBay's Picture Services to host your photos, which means you're paying extra for rather limited photos.

If you're hosting your auction photos, as described in "Host Your Own Photos" [Hack #59], all you need is a little JavaScript to accomplish the same thing. See "Make Clickable Thumbnails" [Hack #60] for another approach, as well as some background information on preparing the thumbnail images used in this hack.

The Hack

Simply place this code in your auction description:

```
<table cellpadding=10 cellspacing=0 border=1>
<tr><td>
    <img src="view1.jpg" border=0 name="view">
</td></tr>
<tr><td align=center>
```

❷   ```
     <img src="view1s.jpg" border=1
             onClick="document.images['view'].src='view1.jpg';">
     ```
❸    ```
     <img src="view2s.jpg" border=1
             onClick="document.images['view'].src='view2.jpg';">
     </td></tr>
     </table>
     ```

This creates a simple, two-cell table, shown in Figure 5-10. The upper cell contains the first of several images, and the lower cell contains the thumbnails for all images.

Figure 5-10. This simple photo album gives photos hosted off eBay a classy presentation

Lines ❷ and ❸ specify the two thumbnails, but they're not linked to their larger counterparts with <a> tags as in "Make Clickable Thumbnails" [Hack #60]. Instead, the following JavaScript code—activated by the onClick event —changes the image ❶ in the upper cell:

```
document.images['view'].src = 'view2.jpg';
```

The code is simple enough, but its greatest strength is its flexibility.

Hacking the Hack

The first thing to do is put your own images in the photo album. Start by replacing *view1.jpg* on line ❶ with the full URL of the first image you wish to appear in the album. Then do the same for each of the thumbnails, *view1s.jpg* and *view2s.jpg* on lines ❷ and ❸. Finally, specify the full URLs for the corresponding full-size images, replacing *view1.jpg* and *view2.jpg*.

> In theory, your full-size images can all be different sizes, but in practice this can cause problems on some browsers. To allow your bidders to view all the images properly, make sure all your JPGs have the same pixel dimensions.

You can have as many thumbnails as you'd like—simply duplicate line ❷ or ❸ for each additional image. The table is designed to accommodate a virtually unlimited number of thumbnails without modification; for instance, if there are more thumbnails than will fit on a line, they will simply wrap to the next line. If needed, use the <br> tag to insert line breaks between groups of thumbnails.

As it is, this photo album will not function if support for JavaScript is disabled in a bidder's browser. To make the hack work even if JavaScript is disabled, change your thumbnail code (lines ❷ and ❸) to the following:

```
<a href="view1.jpg"><img src="view1s.jpg" width=60 height=45 border=1
onClick="document.images['view'].src='view1.jpg';return false;"></a>
```

This works because of the added <a> tag that links the thumbnail image to the full-size image, as described in "Make Clickable Thumbnails" [Hack #60]. Next, the return false; statement is placed at the end of the onClick event, which disables the link if JavaScript is active. This has the added benefit of showing bidders the little "hand" cursor, so they know the thumbnails can be clicked.

For an extra fee, eBay will give you a "slide show" of your images, which is nothing more than a photo album on a timer. See "Show a 360-Degree View of Your Item" [Hack #62] for a way to make your own timed slide show.

Show a 360-Degree View of Your Item

HACK #62

With a few photos of your item and a little JavaScript code, you can wow your customers with that showroom feel.

One of JavaScript's greatest strengths is its ability to manipulate images on a web page, allowing you to turn an otherwise static auction page into an interactive selling tool. In addition to being much cooler than eBay's built-in slide show feature, it's completely free and limited only by the amount of time you want to spend preparing your images.

Taking the Photos

The most challenging part of creating an interactive 360-degree view of your item is taking the photos, which really isn't all that difficult. The goal is to take photos of all sides of an item so that when they're viewed consecutively, like frames in a movie, it looks like the object is spinning. In most cases, you won't need more than four or five images. Having more frames will produce a smoother effect, but will take longer to load.

There are two basic approaches to taking the photos:

Stationary camera
> To produce a "spinning" effect, simply mount your camera on a tripod and point it at your item. Take a photo, rotate the item 90 degrees, take another photo, rotate it again, and so on. For a smoother effect, place your item on a turntable or lazy susan, commonly available at hardware and houseware stores.

Stationary object
> If you're photographing a large item, like a car or piece of furniture, or if you simply want that "walkaround" effect, then you can literally walk around your item and photograph it from each angle. For the best effect, use a tripod to keep the height and angle consistent, and use a ruler or measuring tape to maintain a consistent distance from the object.

Either way you do it, you'll want your photos to be as evenly spaced as possible. If you're taking only four frames, each photo should be 90 degrees apart (72 degrees for five frames, 60 degrees for six frames, 45 degrees for eight frames, and so on). Figure 5-11 shows four sides of an object photographed with a stationary camera.

If you don't have a tripod, do your best to keep the angle, height, and distance from the object as consistent as possible—otherwise, your object will jump and the rotation will look sloppy. Also, don't mix portrait and landscape shots.

Preparing the Images

The more consistent your images are, the better the animation will look. For instance, the object you're photographing must appear to be the same size in each photo. If you used a tripod to take the photos, this will be a snap; otherwise, you may have to crop the photos to make them all proportional. The lighting should also be consistent; you can correct slight aberrations in expo-

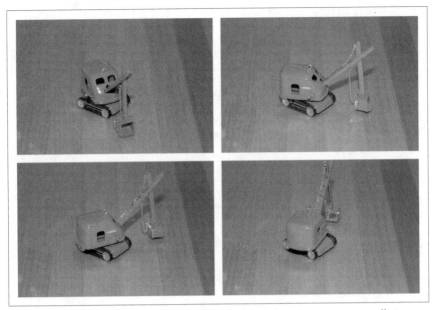

Figure 5-11. Four sides of the object photographed with a stationary camera will give you a "spinning" effect

sure by using your image editor's Auto Levels tool (in Photoshop, go to Image → Adjustments → Auto Levels).

All your images must have the same pixel dimensions. To allow the animation to run smoothly, your images should be small so that they load quickly. Don't bother making them bigger than 400 pixels wide (for the larger dimension); 300 pixels is even better. See "Make Clickable Thumbnails" [Hack #60] for an easy way to resize a bunch of pictures.

When you're done, upload all the photos to your web server, as described in "Host Your Own Photos" [Hack #59].

The Hack

Simply place this code in your auction description to include an interactive 360-degree view of your object:

```
<script language="JavaScript"><!--
var lastimg = "1";

view1 = new Image(300,225);
view2 = new Image(300,225);
view3 = new Image(300,225);
view4 = new Image(300,225);
view5 = new Image(300,225);
view6 = new Image(300,225);
```

```
    view7 = new Image(300,225);
    view8 = new Image(300,225);
    view1.src = "http://www.ebayhacks.com/pictures/view1.jpg";
    view2.src = "http://www.ebayhacks.com/pictures/view2.jpg";
    view3.src = "http://www.ebayhacks.com/pictures/view3.jpg";
    view4.src = "http://www.ebayhacks.com/pictures/view4.jpg";
    view5.src = "http://www.ebayhacks.com/pictures/view5.jpg";
    view6.src = "http://www.ebayhacks.com/pictures/view6.jpg";
    view7.src = "http://www.ebayhacks.com/pictures/view7.jpg";
❷  view8.src = "http://www.ebayhacks.com/pictures/view8.jpg";

❸  slider = new Image(20,20);
    thumb = new Image(20,20);
    slider.src = "http://www.ebayhacks.com/pictures/slider.gif";
❹  thumb.src = "http://www.ebayhacks.com/pictures/thumb.gif";

    function rotate(img) {
❺    document.images['view'].src = eval("view" + img + ".src");
❻    document.images[lastimg].src = slider.src;
❼    document.images[img].src = thumb.src;
❽    lastimg = eval(img);
    }
    // --></script>

    <table width=300 cellpadding=10 cellspacing=0 border=1>
    <tr><td>
❾    <img src="http://www.ebayhacks.com/pictures/view1.jpg" width=300
    height=225 border=0 name="view">
    </td></tr>
    <tr><td align=center>
      <nobr>
❿    <img
        src="http://www.ebayhacks.com/pictures/slider.gif" width=20
          height=20 name="1" onMouseOver="rotate('1');"><img
        src="http://www.ebayhacks.com/pictures/slider.gif" width=20
          height=20 name="2" onMouseOver="rotate('2');"><img
        src="http://www.ebayhacks.com/pictures/slider.gif" width=20
          height=20 name="3" onMouseOver="rotate('3');"><img
        src="http://www.ebayhacks.com/pictures/slider.gif" width=20
          height=20 name="4" onMouseOver="rotate('4');"><img
        src="http://www.ebayhacks.com/pictures/slider.gif" width=20
          height=20 name="5" onMouseOver="rotate('5');"><img
        src="http://www.ebayhacks.com/pictures/slider.gif" width=20
          height=20 name="6" onMouseOver="rotate('6');"><img
        src="http://www.ebayhacks.com/pictures/slider.gif" width=20
          height=20 name="7" onMouseOver="rotate('7');"><img
        src="http://www.ebayhacks.com/pictures/slider.gif" width=20
          height=20 name="8" onMouseOver="rotate('8');">
      </nobr><br>
        Move the slider to rotate the object
    </td></tr>
    </table>
```

Here's how it works. A table holds the first frame of the animation ❾ and, beneath it, a series of images that make up the slider bar ❿. As the mouse is moved across each section of the slider bar, the JavaScript code replaces the image with the corresponding view of the object, as shown in Figure 5-12.

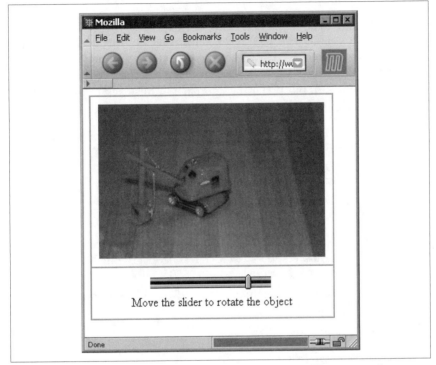

Figure 5-12. Move your mouse over the slider to flip between different views of your item

The bulk of the JavaScript code is simply used to preload the images: the eight frames in this example appear from line ❶ to ❷, followed by the two images used for the slider bar from line ❸ to ❹. You'll want to replace the URLs in these lines with the addresses of your own images, and the dimensions with the dimensions of your frames. If you have fewer or more than eight frames, you'll need to remove or add lines accordingly, as well as change the number of slider bar segments on line ❿.

The rotate( ) function is what does all the work. First, on line ❺, a new photo is placed into the "view" image (so named on line ❾). The script knows which photo to use because of the img variable, passed to the function from the onMouseOver event in each slider bar section on line ❿.

Further down, on line ❼, the current section of the slider bar is "highlighted" by replacing the "empty" slider bar section image with a "full" slider image. Finally, the current position is recorded into the lastimg variable ❽ so that the next time the function runs, it can make this section "empty" again, as it does on line ❻.

Hacking the Hack

Ultimately, the photo album produced by this code is similar to the one in "Construct an Interactive Photo Album" [Hack #61]. The only things that specifically make the image "rotate" are the collection of photos you use and the fact that the images are preloaded to make it responsive. If you want a photo album instead, but prefer the approach in this hack to the aforementioned photo album hack, you can simply replace the slider bar segments with thumbnails.

The sample code rotates the object as the mouse moves over the slider. If you prefer to have the slider move only when clicked, change the <img> tags (one for each slider bar segment) on line ❿ from this:

```
<img src="http://www.ebayhacks.com/pictures/slider.gif" width=20
     height=20 name="3" onMouseOver="rotate('3');">
```

to this:

```
<img src="http://www.ebayhacks.com/pictures/slider.gif" width=20
     height=20 name="3" onClick="rotate('3');">
```

To have the image rotate automatically, add this code immediately above line ❶:

```
setTimeout('autorotate()', 500);

function autorotate() {
    img = lastimg + 1;
    if (img > 8) { img = 1; }
    rotate(img);
    setTimeout('autorotate()', 500);
}
```

where 500 is the number of milliseconds to wait between frames (signifying a half second). Specify 200 for a fifth of a second, 1000 for a full second, and so on.

HACK #63 Create a Photo Collage

Combine multiple photos into a single image for convenience.

When you choose to "Host Your Own Photos" [Hack #59], eBay allows you to specify only a single image URL to appear beneath your auction description. If you have any additional photos, you'll have to include them directly in the description with HTML, using any of several different methods described elsewhere in this chapter. But you also have the option of combining all your photos into a single image file, thus completely eliminating the need to use thumbnails or a photo album to organize multiple pictures.

A single collage of your photos is easy to build, and ultimately requires less work to insert into your auctions. It also gives you fuller control over the presentation of your photos, allowing you to easily emphasize the most important pictures.

You don't have to host your own photos to take advantage of this hack. However, if you use eBay's Picture Services to host your photos, you'll be limited to their cramped 400×300 standard size, which is really too small for a photo collage. And while the "supersize" option would indeed remedy this, it will end up costing more than hosting multiple photos separately.

To build a collage, start with the most prominent photo of your item, properly cropped and resized, as explained at the beginning of this chapter. Then, use your image editor to increase the canvas size to accommodate additional photos. Most users are more accustomed to scrolling web pages up and down, rather than side to side, so you'll usually want to orient your photos vertically rather than horizontally. For example, if you're combining three 600×450 photos, make the canvas at least 700×1400.

Next, place your additional images on the newly enlarged canvas. In most image editors, you can do this via copy-and-paste. First, open one of the images you want to place in the new canvas, select the entire image area (Ctrl-A), and copy the image to the clipboard (Ctrl-C). Then, paste the image into your new canvas (Ctrl-V) and use the mouse to position it. (See the next section for some shortcuts for Photoshop users.)

Figure 5-13 shows a completed photo collage. Here, a black background was used to make the collage a bit more striking. You can use white if you want the photos to blend in more smoothly with the surrounding auction. You may want to avoid brightly colored backgrounds, however, as they can be hard on the eyes.

When you're done, crop out any unused background (except for perhaps a nice thin border). If needed, shrink the collage down so it isn't too large (see the beginning of this chapter for details). Finally, save it as a JPG file and you're ready to go!

Photoshop Shortcuts

Adobe Photoshop has a few nice features that can make collages much easier and quicker to create.

Figure 5-13. A photo collage combines several photos into a single image file, producing a rather striking effect

First, you can create a macro (Action) to increase the canvas size and turn the original photo into a floating layer. (You can also download this macro at *www.ebayhacks.com*.) Here's how to do it:

1. Open a sample photo in Photoshop. Any file will do, as long as it's smaller than 1000 × 1000 pixels.

2. Show the Actions palette by going to Window → Actions.

3. Record a new action by clicking the little arrow button at the top-right of the Actions palette, type a name like "Increase Canvas Size," and click Record.

4. Click the little black/white icon below the color swatches to reset the colors to black and white.

5. Press Ctrl-A to select all.

6. Press Ctrl-X to cut the selection to the clipboard.

7. Go to Image → Canvas Size, type arbitrarily large numbers for the new width and height (try 1000 and 1000), and click OK. (You can use larger numbers if you think you'll need them.)

8. Press Ctrl-V to paste the image back into the newly enlarged canvas.

9. Press the square "Stop" button at the bottom of the Actions palette.

10. Click the little arrow button at the top-right of the Actions palette and select Button Mode.

From now on, to increase the canvas size and float the image, all you need to do is click the Increase Canvas Size button on the Actions palette.

Once the canvas size has been increased, the next step is to paste other images onto the collage. But Photoshop has a shortcut for this, too. Just open the other photos and use the Move tool to drag them from their own document windows onto the newly enlarged canvas (no fussing with copy-and-paste).

You can then press Ctrl-T to begin a free transform and resize the photo in place (hold the Shift key to preserve the aspect ratio). When you're done, select any tool on the toolbox to commit the Free Transform.

Finally, go to Layer → Flatten Image to combine all the floating layers so that the file can be saved as a JPG. Or, to preserve the floating layers, go to File → Save for Web (Photoshop 7.x and later only) and save the file there instead.

HACK #64 Create a Good Gallery Photo

Prepare your gallery photos to use the postage stamp–sized area to its fullest potential.

The Gallery upgrade, described in "The Strategy of Listing Upgrades" [Hack #36], places a photo next to your item in search results and category listings. All that's required (aside from the small fee) is that you provide a Gallery photo.

When your listing goes live, eBay automatically processes the photo by performing the following tasks:

- The image file is converted to the JPG file format.
- The photo is resized so that the larger dimension is 96 pixels.
- The photo is padded with whitespace to make it a square 96×96 pixels.
- The image file is hosted on eBay's server, making it accessible at:
    ```
    http://thumbs.ebay.com/pict/3135403486.jpg
    ```
    where 3135403486 is the item number.

The closer your photo is to the final size of 96×96, the less of a hatchet job eBay's servers will have to do, and the better your gallery photo will look.

The best auction photo (described in "How to Keep Your Item from Looking Pathetic" [Hack #55]) will not necessarily be the best gallery photo, so you'll most likely want to prepare two different images.

For starters, your gallery photo must be square and without any superfluous background or borders. Figure 5-14 shows a few examples of gallery photos, both good and bad.

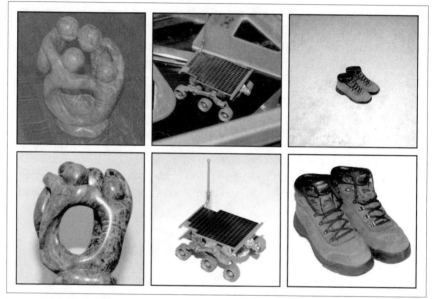

Figure 5-14. Gallery photo examples; the bad ones are shown on the first row, with their good counterparts shown immediately beneath them on the second row

The easiest way to create a good square image is to use the rectangular selection tool of your image editor software and specify a 1:1 aspect ratio. Then, simply draw a box around your image, and the software will automatically impose a square shape.

> It's likely that your photo will not fit perfectly into the square shape. In this case, it's better to slightly crop your object than to leave extra space around it. This way, the resulting object will be bigger and will look like it's trying to break out of the bounding box.

Figure 5-15 shows a well-drawn selection rectangle around an object—before cropping—in Adobe Photoshop.

Figure 5-15. Your gallery photo will look best if you slightly crop your item, rather than leave blank space around it; specify a 1:1 aspect ratio to ensure a perfectly square shape

When you're happy with the box you've drawn, just crop the image to your selection (Image → Crop in Photoshop, or Image → Crop to Selection in Paint Shop Pro) and resize the image to 96×96 pixels. When you're done, save it as a JPG file.

Finally, you'll need to host the photo on a web server, as described in "Host Your Own Photos" [Hack #59]. Unfortunately, those using eBay Picture Services will be forced to use their first auction photo as the gallery photo, in which case you probably don't want to make it the size of a postage stamp.

Completing Transactions
Hacks 65–71

When an auction ends, it's the seller's job to guide their customers through the rest of the transaction. The hacks in this chapter cover the seller's various tasks after the auction has ended.

Simple transactions typically involve one or more emails to the high bidder (as described in "Sending Payment Instructions" [Hack #66]), accepting payment (as described in "Protect Yourself While Accepting Payments" [Hack #67]), and shipping (as described in "Cheap, Fast Shipping Without Waiting in Line" [Hack #68]).

HACK
#65
Keep Track of Items You've Sold

Use a simple spreadsheet to record the details of all your closed auctions.

eBay is not your keeper. They won't pick up your room, they won't do your homework, and they won't keep permanent records of your completed auctions.

If you sell on eBay, you'll need to keep some semblance of records of all the items you've sold. You'll need to keep track of who your high bidders are, whether or not they've paid, and whether or not you've shipped. It's very easy to do, and all that's required is a spreadsheet or database (suitable applications include Microsoft Excel and Microsoft Access, respectively, both included with Microsoft Office). If you're not sure which one to use, see the "Spreadsheet or Database?" sidebar.

If you're diligent about it, you'll never forget to send payment instructions again. You'll always know who has paid (and who hasn't), and you'll know at a glance which items still need to be packed up and shipped.

Spreadsheet or Database?

Both spreadsheets and databases represent data in a table, a convenient format for keeping track of your auctions. But each type of application has strengths and weaknesses, so you should choose the one that best reflects your needs.

First, if it's too difficult to keep records, then you won't do it. So make sure to choose an application with which you're familiar and comfortable. If you use Excel every day but fear databases, then that comfort level trumps the rest of the considerations that follow (at least for the time being).

A spreadsheet requires minimal setup; just type the column headers explained here across the top, and then start entering the details of your auctions. Spreadsheets are flexible in that they impose few limits on the structure or type of data you enter. For instance, you can drag-and-drop rows to rearrange them, placing multiple auctions won by the same bidder together.

A database is more rigid, enforcing strict rules on the types of information you can place in the various fields. But that rigidity affords certain perks that just aren't available with a spreadsheet. For instance, you can run queries on a database to view sales trends, total spent on eBay fees, and so on, or run reports to make mailing labels. And databases can be much more easily linked to applications (see Chapter 8), making them more scalable. Setup is a little more involved, but if you're comfortable using a database, it's probably the better choice.

The Fields

Start by creating a spreadsheet with following columns (or a database with the following fields):

Field name	Data type	Description
End Date	Date	Closing date of the auction.
Item Number	Text	Auction number. In Excel, you can paste the full URL of the auction here, and Excel will create a hyperlink. Next, remove everything *except* the item number. You can then click the item number to view the auction page.
Title	Text	Auction title or brief description.
Closing Price	Currency	The exact amount of the winning bid, not including shipping or any other fees or charges.
Shipping Cost	Currency	The estimated cost to ship, as quoted to the bidder. If the actual cost to ship is different, include the difference in the "Fees" column; see "Cheap, Fast Shipping Without Waiting in Line" [Hack #68] for a way to make sure this never happens.

Field name	Data type	Description
High Bidder	Text	The user ID of the high bidder. If it's a Dutch auction and you have more than one bidder, include a separate entry (row) for each bidder.
Email Address	Text	The email address of the high bidder. It's important to record this separately from the bidder's user ID, especially if the customer uses a different address than the one registered with eBay.
Contacted?	Yes/No	Mark with a ✓ when you've sent payment instructions.
Wrote Back?	Yes/No	Mark with a ✓ the first time the bidder writes you.
Have Address?	Yes/No	Mark with a ✓ as soon as you have the bidder's mailing address.
Paid?	Currency	The full amount of the bidder's payment. It should equal "Closing Price" + "Shipping Cost," but you could subtract any applicable PayPal fees, for instance, so you have a record of exactly how much money you've taken in. Or use the "Fees" field, below.
Shipped?	Text	Paste the tracking number here as soon as you have shipped the package.
Fees	Currency	Optional. Any applicable fees imposed by eBay, PayPal, your credit card merchant account, etc.
Notes	Memo	Any applicable notes, such as the method of shipping, any special requests made by the customer, or related auctions. Also handy for recording the date of a Non-Paying Bidder alert, as described in "Dealing with Stragglers, Deadbeats, and Returns" [Hack #71].

If you're using a spreadsheet, you can set the data type of a field by first selecting the entire column by clicking the column header, and then going to Format → Cells → Number tab.

If you're using a database and want to print mailing labels, you'll also want to add fields for the customer's Name, Address, City, State/Province, Zip Code, and Country. Refer to your database documentation for details on reports and how they can be used to make mailing labels.

How to Use It

Every time one of your auctions ends, add a row to your spreadsheet or database and fill it with the details of the auction. Keep track of the progress of the transaction: place a ✓ in the "Contacted?" column when you send payment instructions, another in the "Wrote Back?" column when the bidder first contacts you, and yet another in the "Have Address?" column when you receive the bidder's full shipping address. Do the same for the "Paid?" and "Shipped?" fields. See Figure 6-1 for an example of how it should look.

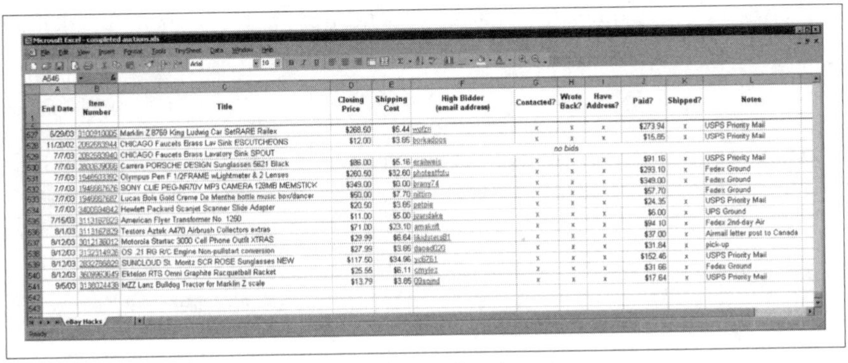

Figure 6-1. *Keep track of the status of all your closed auctions*

Automation

At first, it may seem like a royal pain in the keister to have to write all this stuff down, but it'll quickly get easier. Plus, you'll find that any time you spend on it will be compensated by the time saved in not having to repeatedly wade through your email to figure out who hasn't paid yet.

But for very busy sellers, the task of keeping the spreadsheet or database up to date will quickly get out of hand, and you'll want something less cumbersome. See "Streamlining Checkout and Payment" [Hack #75] and "Obtaining Sales Records" [Hack #76] for some extra-cost, third-party tools that will keep records for you.

But if you're a hacker—and I think that you are—you'll probably want to bypass the commercial solutions in favor of something you build yourself. In that case, see "Automatically Keep Track of Auctions You've Sold" [Hack #87] for a custom eBay API-based solution.

HACK #66 Sending Payment Instructions

How to communicate essential information to your bidders and avoid misunderstandings.

When an auction ends, it is your responsibility as the seller to guide your bidders through the rest of the transaction. Although eBay, by default, will send a notification email to bidders when they've won an auction, you should never rely solely on that email—or your auction description, for that matter—to communicate all the information your bidders need to know to send payment.

Instead, send a payment-instructions email to your customers, making sure to include all of the following:

- Thank the customer for bidding on and purchasing your item. Include the title and item number of the auction (or auctions) your customer has purchased.

- Tell the customer how much shipping will cost (even if it's already specified in the auction) and explain exactly which shipping method you'll be using. (Your customers have a right to know what they're paying for.)

 You can get the winning bidder's location (and zip code if they're in the U.S.) on the Bid History page, allowing you to determine the shipping cost before waiting for the bidder to send his or her street address.

- Calculate the total, including shipping, tax, and any handling fees, and clearly tell your customer how much he or she is supposed to pay. Don't make your customers do any math, because they'll most likely get it wrong. In most cases, you'll have all the tools you need to calculate a customer's total before you send the email.

  If your customer has purchased more than one item from you and you're willing to ship them together, add these up as well, and make it clear that you're doing so.

- Carefully explain the types of payment you accept, even if it's noted elsewhere. It's important to be clear on this point; otherwise, your bidders will most likely send you something you can't accept. See "Protect Yourself While Accepting Payments" **[Hack #67]** for considerations.

- Instruct your customer to email you if he or she has any questions. (As much as you probably don't need to be bothered with lots of stupid questions, the last thing you want is for your customers to leave negative feedback instead of writing you first.)

The Email

Here's a concise email that does it all:

Congratulations! You're the high bidder for the Antique Toy Steam Shovel (eBay #3136272129). Shipping will be $4.50 for Priority Mail shipping, bringing the total to $68.44.

The types of payment I accept are listed in the auction description and on my "About Me" page at eBay. Payment can be made in any of the following ways:

– If you have a free PayPal account, you can pay with your credit card or with an electronic bank account transfer. Just click the PayPal logo in the auction you've won.

– If you'd like to pay directly with your Visa, Mastercard, or American Express, you can use my private, secure server at:

https://www.ebayhacks.com/checkout.html

– If you'd like to pay with BidPay, or if you'd like to send a money order or cashier's check (sorry, no personal or business checks), send it to:

Acme Auctions
123 Fake Street
Springfield, 90125

Either way, please send a confirmation email mentioning how you intend to pay as soon as you get this email. Thanks for bidding!

Naturally, the details of your auction and the terms you choose will be different, but the premise will be the same. Here, the tone is friendly, and an effort has been made to make the instructions as clear as possible (separate paragraphs and hyphens as makeshift bullets are especially helpful).

Note also that the final price of the auction is nowhere to be found in this letter—only the cost to ship and the total amount to pay are specified. This is an effective way to prevent customers from mistakenly (or intentionally) omitting the shipping cost when sending payment.

Automatic Payment Instructions

A few tools are available to help automate the payment instructions email:

eBay Invoice. Click "Create an invoice" on the completed auction page to email payment instructions to your bidder. Although this accomplishes the same thing as the custom email above, in practice it is not any more convenient. It also works only with eBay's checkout system, which doesn't allow you to prioritize payment methods or set certain restrictions. See "Opting Out of Checkout" [Hack #49] for details.

PayPal Winning Buyer Notification. If you accept PayPal payments or, more specifically, if you *only* accept PayPal payments, you can instruct PayPal to automatically send payment instructions to your bidders as soon as your auctions end.

To set it up, log in to *www.paypal.com*, and go to My Account → Profile → Selling Preferences → Auctions. Your eBay user ID should appear in the list (click Add if it doesn't). Next, click "off" or "on" in the Winning Buyer Notification column, and you'll see the Winning Buyer Notification page, as shown in Figure 6-2.

The Hacker's Approach. See "Streamlining Communications" [Hack #74] for some advanced approaches to automating the payment-instructions email.

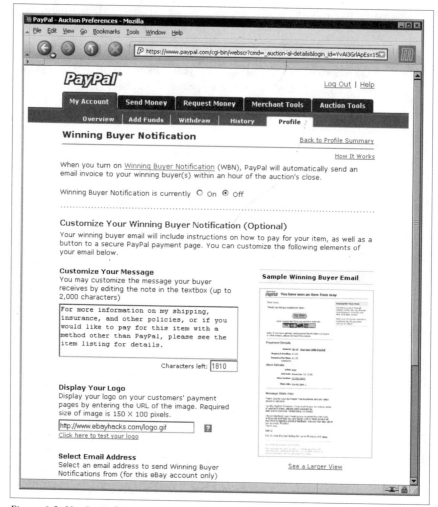

Figure 6-2. Use PayPal's Winning Buyer Notification feature to automatically send somewhat customizable payment instructions emails to your bidders

HACK
#67   Protect Yourself While Accepting Payments

Reduce your odds of getting burned by setting firm policies about the types of payments you accept.

Just as bidders must be cautious when sending money, as described in "Send Payment Quickly and Safely" [Hack #29], sellers must be careful about the payments they receive. A little common sense is all that's required to avoid fraudulent payments, payments that can be reversed, and payments that require excessive fees to process.

Fortunately, it's the seller who sets the rules, at least when it comes to payment terms. Before you start selling, and especially before you send payment instructions to your customers, you'll need to develop a strict policy regarding the types of payments you'll accept.

PayPal. PayPal goes further than just about any other payment service to protect its sellers from fraudulent payments (such as those made with a stolen credit card). But in order to qualify for PayPal's Seller Protection Policy, you'll need to do each and every one of the following:

- Have a Premier or Business account, not a Personal account, as described in "Send Payment Quickly and Safely" [Hack #29].

- Verify your account, which involves nothing more than linking an ordinary bank account with your PayPal account and "confirming" it by having PayPal make two small deposits into it (which you get to keep).

- Ship only to a customer's *confirmed* street address, as described in the "Shipping to Confirmed Addresses" sidebar. You can see whether or not a buyer used a confirmed address in the transaction details, found at *www.paypal.com* and in the payment notification email.

- Always ship with a tracking number, as described in "Cheap, Fast Shipping Without Waiting in Line" [Hack #68], and do so promptly. Make sure to keep records of all tracking numbers for a minimum of six months.

Assuming you're diligent about these rules and you respond quickly if one of your charges is disputed, you'll never be held responsible for buyer fraud. If a specific transaction doesn't qualify for PayPal's Seller Protection Policy, PayPal will pull the money out of your checking account or freeze your PayPal account until the matter is resolved.

Every time I've encountered a seller who refuses to accept PayPal, it's because he or she never bothered to read the fine print of the Seller Protection Policy and as a result was burned by at least one fraudulent transaction.

Personal and business checks. If you're smart, you'll never accept a check as payment for an auction. Checks can bounce, buyers can stop payment, and most sellers have no way of determining if a check is even valid. If you must accept checks, ship only after the check has cleared (which usually takes about two weeks). If you want to accept payments only via postal mail, you're better off restricting such payments to money orders and cashier's checks.

Shipping to Confirmed Addresses

Probably the stickiest of all the requirements of PayPal's Seller Protection Policy involves confirmed addresses. The problem is one of diplomacy more than anything else.

Many PayPal members don't have confirmed addresses, don't know how to confirm their addresses, and don't know why they need to. What makes it worse is that PayPal doesn't do an adequate job of explaining confirmed addresses to their members, so it's often left to sellers to educate their customers.

First, make sure to note in your auction description and your payment-instructions email that you accept PayPal payments only with confirmed addresses (if that's indeed what you decide to do). If you then encounter a buyer who is confused about confirmed addresses, you can explain the procedure (below) or simply instruct him to go to *paypal.com*, click Help, and search for "confirm address."

There are two ways to confirm one's street address at PayPal:

- Add a credit card to the PayPal account. The credit card billing address is then added as a confirmed address. This takes about a minute.

or:

- If the buyer can't (or won't) link a credit card to his PayPal account, he can still use PayPal's Alternative Address Confirmation as long as he has a "verified" PayPal account, has been a PayPal member for more than 90 days, and has a "Buyer Reputation Number" of more than 10. The buyer then sends a fax to PayPal, at which point PayPal sends a confirmation code to the street address the member is trying to confirm. This process takes about a week.

Probably the biggest hurdle is that only PayPal members in the United States can confirm their addresses, which means that you aren't protected by PayPal's Seller Protection Policy if you ship to a PayPal member in any other country. See "Selling and Shipping Internationally" [Hack #69] for details.

You can configure PayPal to automatically block all incoming payments that don't have confirmed addresses by going to My Account → Profile → Payment Receiving Preferences. Although this seems like a drastic step, it will eliminate the need to repeatedly refund payments from bidders who can't follow directions.

Money orders, cashier's checks, and BidPay. Money orders and cashier's checks aren't like personal checks; they don't bounce and they can't be as easily stopped, so in that regard they're more like cash. There's still the possibility of fraud, however, so if you want to be on the safe side, always have a bank teller inspect the money order or cashier's check. BidPay is an exception to this, since sellers can check the validity of payments they receive by going to *www.bidpay.com.*

Credit cards. If you accept credit cards directly through a merchant account, as described in "Streamlining Checkout and Payment" [Hack #75], you will always run the risk of chargebacks. Most credit card companies regard this as the cost of doing business, and will gladly pass that cost on to you.

If someone pays you with a stolen credit card, or if the customer simply forgets that they've bought something from you, the charge can be disputed through the cardholder's credit card company, as described in "Dealing with Disappointment: Getting Refunds" [Hack #32]. The company that issues your merchant account will then notify you of the chargeback, and will assess a nonrefundable chargeback fee to your account in addition to the amount of the original charge.

You can reduce the likelihood of chargebacks by setting the following policies:

- Ship only to the cardholder's billing address. When processing the charge, verify that the address the bidder provided matches the one on file with his or her credit card company.

- Always ship with a tracking number, as described in "Cheap, Fast Shipping Without Waiting in Line" [Hack #68], and ship promptly. Keep records of all tracking numbers for a minimum of six months.

- Require that your customers provide the CVV code, the three-digit number (four digits for American Express) that appears after the card number, typically on the back of the card. This extra bit of information will help insure that the customer actually has the card in his or her possession, especially in the event of a chargeback.

- Be extremely careful when accepting payments from buyers in other countries. Not only is the risk of fraud increased, but your ability to defend yourself against chargebacks will be compromised.

- Consider accepting credit card payments only from bidders with a certain minimum feedback rating, say 20 or 50. Make that requirement higher for international credit card payments.

International payments. See "Selling and Shipping Internationally" [Hack #69] for ways to protect yourself when receiving payments from other countries.

Cheap, Fast Shipping Without Waiting in Line

#68   Generate prepaid shipping labels online to save money and time.

"Three things in life are certain: death, taxes, and long lines at the post office."

You know the drill. Take your package down to the post office. Stand in line. Stand in line some more. Then, watch while your package is weighed, listen to your shipping options, and pick whichever one is cheapest. Go home, and do it all again next week. But the worst part is that it's completely unnecessary.

Most major couriers—and nearly all couriers in the United States—offer online shipping services. Here's how it typically works:

1. Go to your courier's web site and sign up for an account; at this time, you'll enter your mailing address and, optionally, payment information. You'll need to do this only once. See the next section for courier-specific tips.

> Before you're ready to ship, you can get a shipping cost quote from any courier web site. Do this before sending a total to the high bidder (see "Sending Payment Instructions" [Hack #66]), and you'll never underestimate shipping costs again.

2. Enter your recipient's address into a form, as well as the weight and dimensions of the package. (To avoid typos, make sure to use copy-and-paste rather than typing your customer's address by hand.) The return address is filled in automatically. Figure 6-3 shows the FedEx Ship Manager; note that the return address, which isn't shown, is filled in automatically.

3. Print out a prepaid shipping label and affix the label on your package.

4. Drop off your package at a local customer counter or, for an extra charge, schedule a pickup. You can find the closest drop-off location on the courier's web site.

5. Track the package using the tracking number generated with your label. Make sure to keep permanent records of all your tracking numbers; if your customer claims the package never arrived, you'll need to be able to track it.

The entire process takes about a minute, and requires no waiting in line and no guesswork. See "Selling and Shipping Internationally" [Hack #69] for any additional forms you might need when shipping to other countries.

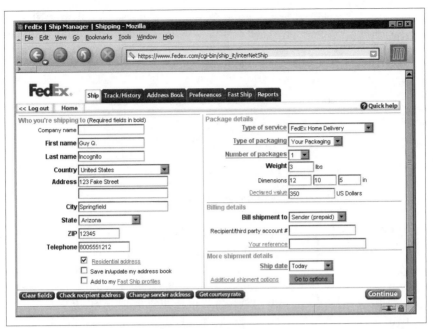

Figure 6-3. The FedEx Ship Manager lets you print out a prepaid shipping label in about a minute

This procedure can also be used if you're the customer; see "Save Money on Shipping" [Hack #31] for a way to quickly send a prepaid label to the seller.

Courier Notes

Here are some tips and considerations for the "big three" shippers:

United States Postal Service (USPS).   Not only can you print prepaid labels from the U.S. Postal Service web site (*sss-web.usps.com*), you actually get a better deal if you do so. The Delivery Confirmation option, which adds a tracking number to most types of postal mail for an extra charge, is free if you print your mailing labels online. Another perk of USPS is that you can print a label without postage and use ordinary stamps instead; this is useful for those who can't or don't want to pay with a credit card.

Due to postal regulations, any package weighing one pound or more must be handed to a postal employee inside the branch (albeit usually without having to wait in line). Only packages weighing less than one pound can be dropped in mailboxes.

You can get special labels designed especially for USPS Click-N-Ship by going to *www.labeluniverse.com/USPS.html*. But if you want to save money, you can simply use ordinary paper and a lot of tape (just make sure not to tape over the barcode).

> If you have a choice, never use USPS third class (standard) shipping. Although it may be slightly cheaper than Priority Mail, it often takes up to a month to deliver, even within the same state (despite what the USPS web site says). If you're shipping something heavy, use FedEx Ground or UPS Ground instead. The only time when third-class postal mail should be used is when you have no other choice, such as when shipping certain types of chemicals.

Probably the biggest drawback to USPS Click-N-Ship is that, at least at the time of this writing, ordinary international shipments are not supported (unless you want to pay extra for Global Express Mail). This means that if you're shipping to another country, you'll have to use FedEx or UPS if you don't want to wait in line at the post office.

Federal Express (FedEx). Shipping with a FedEx account number is one of the slickest systems around. Even when you're not using FedEx Ship Manager (*www.fedex.com*), you can simply hand-write your account number on a FedEx Express airbill or FedEx Ground form.

The FedEx Ship Manager, shown back in Figure 6-3, allows you to send any package to just about any destination around the world. When you've filled out the required fields, click Get Courtesy Rate to see the estimated shipping cost on the fly.

United Parcel Service (UPS). UPS has gone to great lengths to integrate its services with eBay and PayPal. For instance, eBay's calculated shipping feature (see "Put a Shipping Cost Calculator in Your Auction" [Hack #45]) is provided by a UPS subsidiary.

Although you can ship from the UPS web site (*www.ups.com*), it is probably more convenient (and no more expensive) to ship directly from PayPal. Start by logging in to PayPal and going to My Account → Profile → Shipping Preferences to choose the types of transactions for which the "Ship" button will appear in your transaction list. Then, click the History tab and you'll see the Ship button next to applicable transactions; click Ship to generate a UPS label for that customer. Figure 6-4 shows the PayPal shipping form, which conveniently enters the customer's address for you. (Note that this is available only for buyers in the United States.)

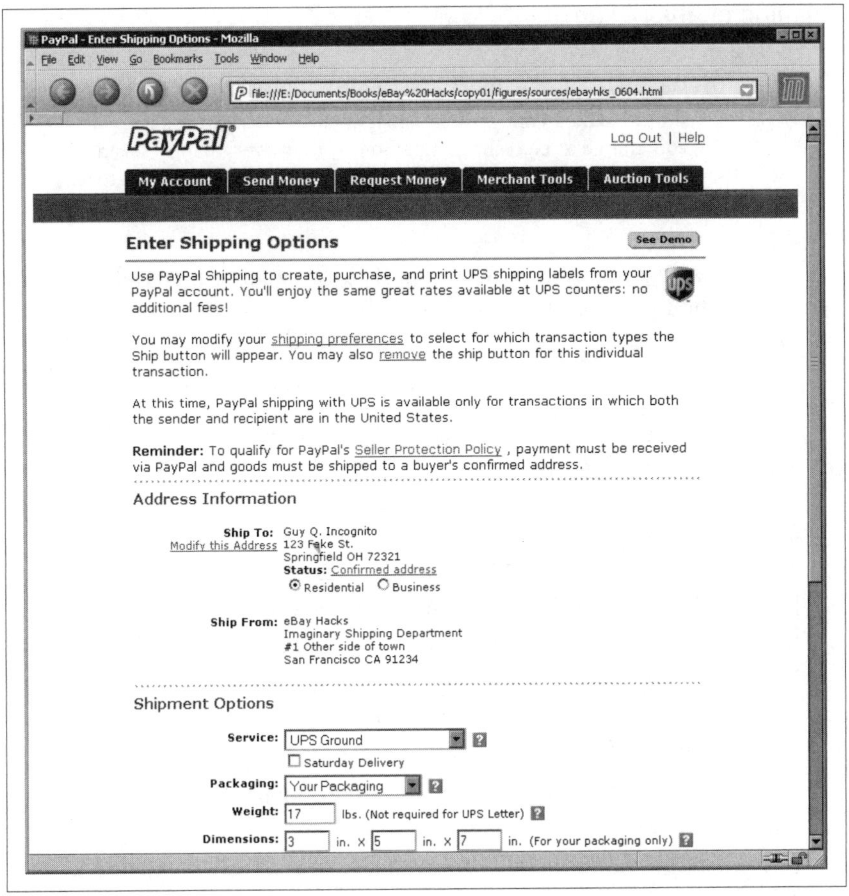

![PayPal Enter Shipping Options screenshot]

Figure 6-4. PayPal Shipping lets you create a prepaid UPS label without having to type the customer's address

You'll be covered under PayPal's Buyer Protection policy only if you ship to a customer's "confirmed" address, as described in "Protect Yourself While Accepting Payments" [Hack #67].

When you're done, PayPal will even email the tracking numbers to your customers so they can track their packages themselves.

Shipping on the Cheap

If buyers pay for shipping (and they usually do), then why should sellers care how much it costs to ship a package? If you charge a fixed shipping amount, then every penny saved is a penny earned. And if you charge the exact amount to ship, then you'll get more bids for being able to ship for less.

The other major shipping expense comes from packing materials, both in the cost of the materials themselves and the impact they have on the total shipping cost.

Here are some tips for saving money with packing materials:

- The number-one rule is to never throw out packaging materials; recycle and reuse them as much as possible. Not only will you save money, but you'll help reduce the increased strain on landfills caused by the growing popularity of eBay and mail-order shipping in general.

- Air is the best packing material on earth—it's lightweight, an excellent heat insulator, and extremely cheap. Bubble wrap and foam peanuts are terrific examples, and can be reused again and again. Tip: use clear trash bags to collect foam peanuts from packages you receive.

- Don't throw out form-fitted styrofoam. Instead, break it apart and use the fragments to fill space in your own packages.

- Most couriers will not only provide free cardboard boxes of all sizes, but they will even send them to you free of charge if you ask.

- Buy packing tape in bulk to save money. (Avoid independent packing/shipping stores, which usually grossly overcharge for packing materials.) Better yet, use a courier that provides free tape; if you're shipping with USPS Priority Mail, for example, you can use all the "Priority Mail" tape you want for free.

- Don't use newspaper or shredded paper to wrap or cushion your items. It's much heavier than foam peanuts, the ink can rub off, and it won't protect your items nearly as well as bubble wrap.

- Finally, when using prepaid shipping labels, you can place them in clear, self-adhesive "airbill" sleeves, freely available from couriers like FedEx and UPS, thus saving the time and expense otherwise spent on wads of packing tape.

Selling and Shipping Internationally

A few extra tools and tips to make shipping to customers in other countries go more smoothly.

"Nothing so liberalizes a man and expands the kindly instincts that nature put in him as travel and contact with many kinds of people." – Mark Twain, 1867

With some practice, your international shipments will be nearly as easy as domestic ones. But it takes a little experience to know how to accept payments from customers in other countries, how to ship to other countries, and how to avoid fraud from deadbeats in other countries. Fortunately, the payoff is substantial: expanding your business to include bidders all around the world, while not without its risks, will make trading on eBay more interesting, more challenging, and more profitable.

Accepting International Payments

When you send payment instructions to customers in other countries, there are a few considerations you'll need to make in addition to those outlined in "Sending Payment Instructions" **[Hack #66]**.

First, always keep the language barrier in mind. If your bidder's native language is different from yours, keep your sentences short and avoid slang. Bidders in other countries expect you to write in your own language, but they will usually not have perfect command of it. If you find that the bidder is having a hard time understanding you, you can always try including a translation of your instructions, as described in "International Transactions Made Easier" **[Hack #30]**. Just make sure it's placed alongside your original text in the email, so the bidder gets the complete picture.

Second, be patient. International transactions take longer, partly because of the delays caused by time zone differences and language barriers, and partly because sending payments internationally can be difficult and time consuming.

Finally, be extremely clear about the types of payments you can accept and the types you cannot. Here are some considerations when accepting payments from other countries:

PayPal. Buyers in nearly 50 countries around the world have access to Pay-Pal, but only those in United States can confirm their addresses. This means that if you accept a payment from a non-U.S. customer, it won't be covered by PayPal's Seller Protection policy, explained in "Protect Yourself While Accepting Payments" **[Hack #67]**.

Credit cards.   The incidence of fraud among credit card payments made by non-U.S. bidders is unfortunately much higher than payments originating from the United States. For this reason, you may wish to impose a limit, either on the amount you'll accept or on the minimum feedback rating of customers from whom you'll take a credit card. If you contact your merchant account provider, they'll probably tell you the same thing; see "Streamlining Checkout and Payment" [Hack #75] for details.

Payments by mail.   Any payment received by postal mail is subject to the terms imposed by your bank. Before you instruct an international bidder to mail you a money order, for instance, make sure your bank will accept payment, and try to determine if any additional fees will be incurred. In most cases, an international *postal* money order will be accepted without additional fees. But probably the best way is to use BidPay, introduced in "Send Payment Quickly and Safely" [Hack #29], which allows a buyer in one country to send a payment in the seller's native currency.

Although eBay does a fair job in converting currencies right on the auction page, the conversion rates they use are not necessarily the same as those used by the buyer's or seller's bank. To give your customers a more accurate estimate of how much they'll need to send you in their own native currency, contact your bank to get the latest exchange rates. Or use the Oanda Currency Converter at *www.oanda.com/converter/classic* for a quick estimate.

Shipping to Other Countries

In many ways, shipping internationally is no different from shipping domestically. It just usually costs a lot more and takes a lot longer.

Most couriers offer a different assortment of shipping options for international shipments, all of which are explained on your courier's web site. Regardless of the courier or shipping option you choose, though, you'll need to include the appropriate customs forms:

United States Postal Service (USPS).   Include customs form 2976 with all uninsured international packages, or form 2976-A (inside a 2976-E envelope) if you're insuring your package. You can get these forms at your local post office branch. Go to *ircalc.usps.gov* for exclusions and restrictions.

FedEx and UPS.   International shipments with these couriers require a commercial invoice, a generic form where you'll describe the individual contents of the package and specify their value and country of origin. Then, depending on the destination country, you'll need to include three to five copies along with the original. Place all forms in a single clear pouch, the same kind as is used for shipping labels. You can download a blank commercial invoice form in Adobe Acrobat format from *ups.com* or *fedex.com* in their respective "international documents" sections.

It's important to understand that somewhat different forms and procedures may be required for different countries. If you've never shipped to a particular country before, make sure to contact the courier and ascertain any restrictions or additional requirements that may apply your package. For example, according to UPS, no packages shipped to Mexico may contain any products made in China. And according to FedEx, packages to Canada require one original and five copies of the commercial invoice, packages to Puerto Rico require only three copies, while some other countries require only originals (no copies). In other words, there's no hard-and-fast formula that applies in all situations.

Denied Parties

If you really want to be on the safe side, you might also consider researching so-called "denied parties." For example, FedEx offers the Denied Party Screening tool, which searches for your customer's name among governmental lists of countries, individuals, companies, and other organizations that have had economic and trade sanctions imposed against them. You can try this out by going to *https://gtm.fedex.com/cgi-bin/gtm_dps.cgi*.

Expectation Management

When shipping internationally, take a moment to prepare your customers for any delays (expected or otherwise) that the package might encounter before it arrives. For example, the United States Postal Service web site (*www.usps.com*) estimates that a one-pound package sent from the U.S. to the United Kingdom via airmail parcel post will take anywhere from 4 to 10 days. In practice, however, it may take two or three times as long, given the delays imposed by customs and other unforeseen circumstances.

For this reason, a delivery that takes two weeks might be seen in two different lights, depending on what you've told the customer. If the customer expects the package in 10 days, then she'll be disappointed, and you may be thanked with negative feedback for shipping too slowly. But if you say it will take a month, the recipient will be pleasantly surprised when it gets there in half the time. See "Expectation Management" [Hack #39] for more information.

Damage Control Before and After You Ship
HACK #70 How to handle problems discovered by either you or the customer.

"A diplomat is a person who can tell you to go to hell in such a way that you actually look forward to the trip."
– Caskie Stinnett, 1960

So you're packing up an item to ship to a customer, and you suddenly discover a scratch, scrape, hole, discoloration, or missing part that you hadn't noticed and hadn't mentioned in the auction description. Sure, you can pack it up, ship it, and hope the bidder never notices. But he will, and you know it.

The best approach involves a quick preemptive email to the bidder, like one of the following:

- "I just noticed a nick on the back of the item while I was packing it. Let me know if you no longer want it, and I'll refund your money. Otherwise, I'll ship right away." **Give your customer a way out.** In most cases, if the problem is minor, the customer will still want the item. Not only will this note make you appear honest, but your customer will have a more realistic expectation about the condition of the item, and less of a reason to return it when it finally arrives.

- "While packing up your item, I discovered a flaw I hadn't noticed when writing up the auction description. I've attached a photo. If you still want it, I'd be happy to send it to you along with a partial refund. Or, if you're no longer interested, I'll refund your payment in full." **The photo gives the customer additional information** with which he can make an informed decision, and, again, helps set a more reasonable expectation. And the partial refund is an excellent compromise that will both sweeten the deal for the customer and save you the trouble and expense of having to relist the item.

- "I was called out of town for a few days, and I had to leave before I got a chance to ship your package. I shipped your package this morning and upgraded it to second-day air for no extra charge. I'm sorry for the delay; please let me know when the package arrives." **Damage control** isn't just for physical damage; it's for dealing with snags in any part of the transaction. Not only should you contact customers before they receive a late package, you should make some concession to help compensate for the delay. For instance, a free shipping upgrade will cost you very little, but will go a long way toward making your customer happy with the product when it finally does arrive.

- "I was getting ready to pack your item, but I couldn't find some of the parts that were listed in the auction description. I apologize for the inconvenience, and have refunded your payment." This is the best approach if you're reasonably certain the customer will no longer want the item, as it doesn't even suggest the possibility. Assuming you're sufficiently apologetic and your tone is sincere, the customer will be understanding, and will quickly release you of your obligation without further inquiry or negative feedback.

The goal in each case is not only to set a reasonable expectation with the customer, as described in "Expectation Management" [Hack #39], but to save you money, time, and aggravation. The last thing you want is to go to the trouble and expense of shipping an item, only to have the customer complain and ultimately return it to you. Not only would you have to refund the shipping fees (assuming that you're at fault), but you'd be stuck with negative feedback and an item you then have to resell.

If you instead refund the customer's money *before* shipping, you'll still be stuck with the item, but you won't get negative feedback, you won't lose money in shipping costs, and you won't have to go through the hassle of dealing with an unsatisfied customer.

And don't forget the partial refund, either. By refunding some of your customer's money, either by a small token amount or perhaps by shipping for free, you'll still be able to complete the sale and the buyer will be happy to get his product for a little less.

If you end up refunding some or all of the customer's payment, make sure to apply for a credit for the appropriate final-value fees, as described in "Dealing with Stragglers, Deadbeats, and Returns" [Hack #71].

After the Fact

If the customer has already received the package, any hopes of setting a reasonable expectation will be dashed. But you can still try to ensure that your customer will be happy with his or her purchase.

The typical scenario involves a customer who isn't happy with an item for whatever reason. Some customers will be more understanding and reasonable than others, but it's up to you to set the tone for the rest of the transaction and deal with the problem appropriately.

When you receive a complaint, take the following steps:

1. Check out the customer's feedback rating and look for signs that he has harassed other sellers. A customer with glowing feedback can be much

more readily trusted than one whom other sellers have found to be unreasonable or uncooperative.

2. See if the customer has left feedback for you yet. If not, you'll still have a chance at coming out of this unscathed. Otherwise, you might understandably be less willing to compromise, given that there's seemingly nothing in it for you. But don't forget that feedback can be retracted, as described in "Remove Unwanted Feedback" [Hack #6], so there's still a chance that you could make things right for both you and the bidder.

3. Double-check your auction description for a mention of the problem. If the customer's complaint is addressed in your description, then all you need to do is—kindly—inform the bidder that the problem was explained in the auction. A seller should never be held responsible for a complaint based solely on the buyer not having read the auction description.

4. Examine your photos of the item to see if you can corroborate (or refute) the seller's story. It will be up to your judgment as to how clearly the problem was illustrated by your photos, and how you wish to proceed.

5. Offer a partial refund commensurate with the severity of the problem. If the customer is happy to accept, you won't have to take the item back and refund all the customer's money.

   So how do you calculate the amount of a partial refund? One way is to take the difference between the amount the customer paid and the estimated amount the customer would've paid had he or she known about the specific problem. Barring that, a token refund of the shipping cost, for example, may be all it takes to make the bidder happy.

6. If the customer rejects the partial refund, then it's up to you whether or not to give the customer a full refund and whether or not you include the cost of shipping. It's generally accepted that the seller refunds shipping charges if the seller is at fault; otherwise, the customer is entitled to nothing more than a refund of the final bid price.

Watch out for fraud when handing out refunds. Some people will buy an item to replace a defective one they already have, only to return the defective unit to the unsuspecting seller and effectively get the item fixed for free. Make sure to inspect both the item and the customer's feedback profile for signs of fraud.

Note that you should never ask the bidder to cover eBay's fees if they return an item, mostly because you can apply for a credit for any final-value fees, as described in "Dealing with Stragglers, Deadbeats, and Returns" [Hack #71].

HACK #71 Dealing with Stragglers, Deadbeats, and Returns

Filing non-paying bidder alerts and credit requests in the event of a failed transaction.

Although sellers are responsible for paying all fees associated with an auction, eBay is not unreasonable about refunding those fees when it comes to returns, deadbeat bidders, and other extenuating circumstances.

Regardless of the terms of a failed transaction, every seller can complete the following two-step process to recover any final-value fees associated with an auction. Unfortunately, listing fees are nonrefundable, but they are never very large.

Non-Paying Bidder Alert

If a bidder never pays, if a bidder returns an item, or if you and the bidder settle a transaction for less than the final bid price, the first (and sometimes only) step is to file a Non-Paying Bidder Alert.

> This is different from the "payment reminder," available in the Selling tab of My eBay. Sending a payment reminder is optional, and is not a prerequisite to using the Non-Paying Bidder form. A Non-Paying Bidder Alert can be filed only after 7 days (and no more than 45 days) have passed since the end of the auction.

Start by going to Site Map → Request Final Value Fee Credit → Non-Paying Bidder Alert (*cgi3.ebay.com/aw-cgi/eBayISAPI.dll?NPBComplaintForm*), and enter the eBay item number as instructed.

You'll be presented with a list of reasons. The reason you choose here will have a very real effect on the way eBay handles the rest of the process. There are effectively three different scenarios:

1. *Urge the bidder to pay.* If you choose any of the following options, an email will be sent to the bidder reminding him of his obligation to pay. This will also enable you to subsequently use the Final Value Fee Credit Request Form, discussed in the next section. The options are:

    - High bidder didn't contact you.
    - High bidder refused the item.
    - High bidder didn't send payment.

- High bidder sent payment, but check bounced or payment was stopped.

- High bidder didn't comply with seller's terms and conditions stated in listing.

- One or more of your Dutch auction bidders backed out of sale.

2. *Cancel the transaction.* Choose either one of the following to end the process here and get a refund immediately:

- High bidder paid for item and returned it. You issued a refund to bidder.

- Both parties mutually agreed not to complete the transaction.

3. *Apply for a partial credit.* Use one of the following options if the transaction was successful, but the amount you ultimately received from the customer was less than the final bid price (for example, if you issued a partial refund, as described in "Damage Control Before and After You Ship" [Hack #70]). As with reason #2, your refund will be immediate, and the process will end here.

- Sale price to high bidder was actually lower than the final high bid.

- High bidder in Dutch auction did not complete the transaction. You sold the item to another bidder.

Final Value Fee Credit Request Form

If the action you took when filing the Non-Paying Bidder Alert resulted in a warning email being sent to the bidder, you are obligated to give the customer another 10 days to comply and send payment in full. If the bidder still hasn't paid after those 10 days, then you can follow up by filing a Final Value Fee Credit Request. (Note that credit requests will be denied if 60 days have passed since the end of the auction.)

 When you complete a Final Value Fee Credit Request, the bidder involved will receive a Non-Paying Bidder Warning. A bidder who receives three such warnings will be suspended from eBay. For this reason, you should be diligent about following through for deadbeat bidders. Likewise, you should be extremely careful about filing undeserved credit requests to harass bidders or save money on listing fees, lest you be suspended yourself.

Go to Site Map → Request Final Value Fee Credit → Request Your Final Value Fee Credit (*cgi3.ebay.com/aw-cgi/eBayISAPI.dll?CreditRequest*), and enter the eBay item number in the form shown in Figure 6-5.

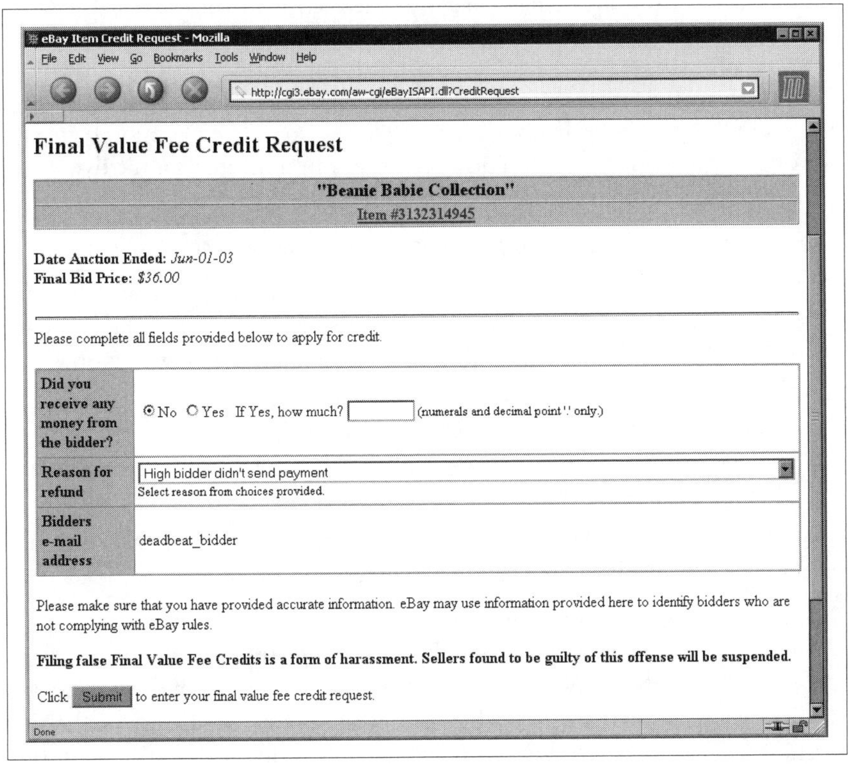

Figure 6-5. *Use the Final Value Fee Credit Request Form to get most of your fees back after a failed transaction*

Here, you'll be presented with the same assortment of reasons that appeared on the Non-Paying Bidder Alert Form, plus a field in which to specify how much money—if any—you received from the bidder. Click Submit when you're done, and eBay will credit the appropriate amount to your account.

Your credit will take effect immediately. To see how much money has been credited, go to My eBay → Accounts → View Account Status.

Relisting and Other Options

When all is said and done, you'll most likely still have the item, which means you'll want to relist it and try to sell it again.

> Before you relist, make sure to add the deadbeat bidder from the first round to your Blocked Bidder List, as described in "Keeping Out Deadbeat Bidders" **[Hack #54]**. You can also see if any of the other bidders on the auction are still interested by using the Second Chance Offer on your My eBay Selling page.

You can relist any item on eBay by going to the completed auction page and clicking "Relist your item." You can relist multiple items quickly in the Unsold Items section of your My eBay Selling tab.

Relisting in this way has three advantages over creating a new listing:

- You don't have to enter all the auction details again; eBay will do it for you. All you need to do is click Go To Review to jump to the last page of the form, and then click Submit Listing to start the new auction.

- If you turn on the Relisted Item Link option, a prominent link will be placed on the old auction, directing any customers who happen to see it to the new auction page. It's a great way to get a little extra free advertising for your item.

- If the first auction failed because it didn't receive any bids or the reserve wasn't met, eBay will waive the listing fees for the relisted auction.

Silver lining clause: More often than not, an auction that is relisted after a deadbeat bidder backs out usually closes at a higher price the second time. Why? First, two back-to-back 7-day auctions have twice the exposure (14 days) of a single 7-day auction; if you do it right, anyone who visits the first auction will see a link to the relisted auction. Second, any unsuccessful bidders on the first auction are likely to return and bid more aggressively on the second auction, especially if you're selling something rare. Third, a diligent seller is likely to improve the auction description the second time around, which can result in a higher price.

Running a Business on eBay
Hacks 72–81

No two people or companies do business in exactly the same way, but there is always common ground when it comes to saving money and time. This chapter illustrates some of the tools—available both for free and at extra cost—that sellers have at their disposal for increasing automation in their businesses, and shows how these tools can be hacked to better suit your needs.

A Word About PowerSellers

eBay recognizes sellers who meet certain sales quotas as "PowerSellers" and awards them a few extra perks, most relating to enhanced technical and customer support. Whether or not they're the "pillars of our community" as eBay claims (*pages.ebay.com/services/buyandsell/powersellers.html*) is a matter left to the pundits. But for many sellers running businesses on eBay, the PowerSellers program is a benchmark worth achieving.

> Give it some thought before placing the PowerSeller logo in your auctions as eBay suggests. Although the program as a whole can be valuable to sellers, the logo itself can send a message to bidders that you're a big, faceless organization, and they'll be lucky if they receive any personal attention from you at all. The personal touch, after all, is what attracts many bidders to eBay.

It's worth noting that the hacks in this chapter are suitable for all sellers, whether they're Titanium-level PowerSellers moving $150,000 worth of merchandise every month, or hobbyists trading a few low-cost items every couple of weeks.

HACK #72   eBay Stores

Open an eBay Store to build a more aggressive presence on eBay and on the Web.

For sellers who want their presence on eBay to be more than just a collection of running auctions, eBay allows you to open a *Storefront*, complete with the following perks:

Longer-lasting items. You'll be able to create fixed-price listings that last 30, 60, 90, or even 120 days. These listings don't show up in standard eBay search results, but are shown to buyers who enter your store through any of your eBay listings.

> Your standard eBay auctions will show up alongside your eBay Stores listings as long as they started after you opened your storefront.

Lower listing fees. eBay Stores items cost only 5 cents for each 30 days they appear in your store.

Search for your store. A search box appears at the top of your personal category listings, allowing customers to search through only your listings. See "Allow Visitors to Search Through Your Auctions" [Hack #46].

Create your own categories. Include up to 11 custom categories in your store. Although these categories aren't associated with eBay's standard auction categories, they allow you to easily organize the listings in your own store. For instance, if you're selling photographic equipment, you can have a Lenses category and a Film category, making it easy for a customer who has just purchased a camera from you to pick up a few accessories to go along with it.

Listing management tools. Use eBay's Merchandising Manager and Store Seller Reporting to generate monthly reports on your Sales and Marketplace data, helping you stay on top of your competition.

Build a stable presence on eBay. An official storefront will help make your business look more reputable to customers. See "Improve Your Trustworthiness Quickly" [Hack #7] for further information.

Aside from the expected listing and final-value fees, eBay Stores require an extra-cost monthly subscription. You can get the details and sign up at *stores.ebay.com*.

How Customers Will Find You

Once you've opened an eBay Store, a red sales-tag icon will appear next to your user ID anywhere it appears on eBay. A bidder looking at one of your eBay listings can click the icon to enter your store and shop among your items.

You'll also receive a tidy URL in this format:

```
www.ebaystores.com/storename
```

You can then easily include links to your store in your auction descriptions, your About Me page (see "Make Good Use of the About Me Page" [Hack #48]), and any emails you send to customers. Also, any customers who go to *www. ebaystores.com* will be able to browse through the various stores, as well as search for specific items through all storefronts.

But probably the biggest advantage of eBay stores over ordinary eBay listings is that since an individual listing can last for several months, it will stick around long enough to show up in search engines like Google. This means that anyone who goes to *www.google.com* and searches for antique back-scratchers may see the seven different varieties you're currently selling.

Alternatives

eBay Stores is essentially a "turnkey" solution, allowing any seller to open a prefabricated, fully functional store in just a few minutes, but it's not the only site offering such an option. Other sites offering similar services include Yahoo Stores (*stores.yahoo.com*) and Vendio Stores (*shop.vendio.com*).

HACK #73 Streamlining Listings

Use eBay Turbo Lister to upload more listings in less time.

The Sell Your Item form introduced in Chapter 4 is a simple but limited auction listing tool, adequate only for creating a few new listings at a time. It's hopelessly cumbersome for anyone needing to upload a large number of listings or otherwise automate the listing process.

eBay's own Turbo Lister application is what they call a "bulk listing tool," but in many ways it is simply a more convenient way to create eBay auctions. Turbo Lister, available at *pages.ebay.com/turbo_lister*, is completely free to download and use, and operates on any Windows machine (Mac and Unix are not supported).

Although Turbo Lister provides all the same listing options available at *eBay.com*, it sometimes takes a little while (often a few weeks) for eBay to update the software with new features and categories. To make sure Turbo Lister is always up to date, go to Tools → Options → Advanced Options, and turn on the "Automatically download updates when I start the program" option.

Setting Up Turbo Lister

One of Turbo Lister's biggest strengths is that it effectively eliminates the need to enter the same information again and again. Before you use Turbo Lister, take a moment to specify default values by going to Tools → Options, as shown in Figure 7-1.

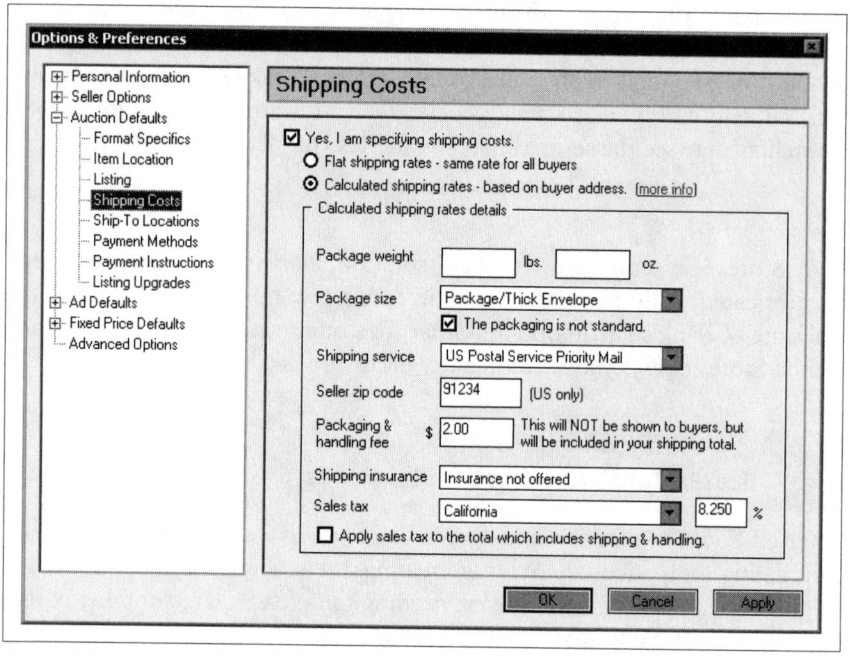

Figure 7-1. Use Turbo Lister's Options & Preferences box to set the defaults for your auctions

The more auction details you specify here, the less work you'll have to do for each listing. For instance, select Auction Defaults → Listing to create an auction description template to be used for all newly created items.

Creating Listings

Ironically, Turbo Lister's listing creation tool starts with a multipage wizard, not unlike eBay's Sell Your Item form. The good news, however, is that you have to use it only once.

Start by clicking the Create New button on the toolbar (or go to File → New → Item) and follow the prompts. If you like, you can fill in all the fields as though you were selling a single item, or just click Next repeatedly to get through the wizard and click Save when you're done. Your new listing will then appear under the Item Inventory tab, awaiting upload.

But the best part is where you can go from here. Instead of going through the wizard each time you want to create a new listing, you can simply duplicate an existing item and modify it as needed. Click the Duplicate button on the toolbar (or go to Edit → Duplicate), specify the number of duplicates to create, and click OK. This makes it remarkably easy to create dozens or even hundreds of similar listings in a fraction of the time it would take without Turbo Lister. Then, double-click any entry to show the Edit Item – Auction Details window, shown in Figure 7-2.

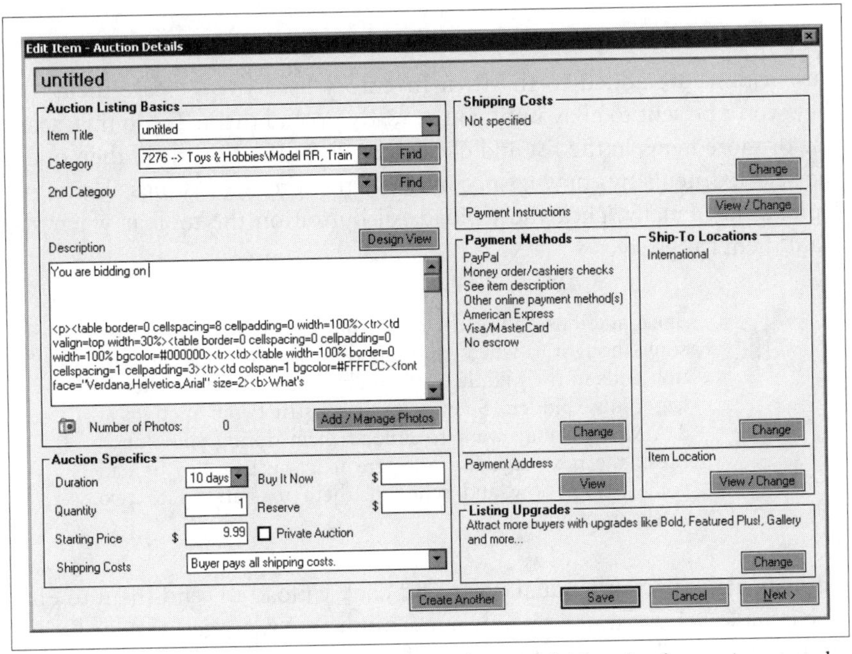

Figure 7-2. The Edit Item – Auction Details window, available only after you've created a listing, allows you to modify all aspects of a listing on one page

A few things to note about this window:

- You can specify the category (or categories) in any of three ways. Click Find to browse the entire category tree. Or, type a category number right in the Category and 2nd Category boxes, and press the Tab key to validate it. Finally, choose among your most recently used categories from the drop-down listbox.

- Click Design View in the Edit Item – Auction Details window to modify the auction description with the WYSIWYG editor. Flip to the HTML View and Preview tabs to edit the HTML directly and see what your auction will look like, respectively.

- Click Add/Manage Photos to specify one or more pictures for the item. Just like eBay's Sell Your Item form, you can either host the photos on your own server [Hack #59]) or use eBay's Picture Services. To switch between the two options, click "Change photo hosting" under Other Tasks.

- Click Create Another to duplicate the current item without having to return to the previous window.

Uploading Listings

New listings are added to the Item Inventory list as you create them, but they won't be sent to eBay until you're ready upload them. To do this, select one or more items in the list and click Upload. Turbo Lister will then queue the selected items by *copying* (not moving) them to the Listings Waiting to Upload tab. Finally, click the Upload All button on the toolbar when you want them to "go live."

Since auctions end at the same time of day they start, give some thought to when you upload them. After all, if an auction ends in the middle of the night, you will have far fewer last-minute bidders. So even if you construct your auctions at 2 A.M., you may want to upload them during your lunch break the next day. For an extra fee, you can also upload your listings now and schedule them to start up to two weeks from now.

You can also select individual items and click Upload to send them to eBay in batches, each separated by only a few minutes. By staggering your listings in this way, you'll facilitate further bidding by last-minute bidders who may want to purchase more than one item from you.

Another strength of Turbo Lister is that it maintains a non-expiring archive of every auction you've ever created with it. This allows you to upload the same item several or even hundreds of times. It can also be very helpful to have access to old listings; I sometimes reuse descriptions for similar items I've sold in the past, which can be a great time saver.

Using Folders

Use folders to organize your items. If you don't see the folder list on the left, click the Show Folders button on the toolbar.

Go to File → New → Folder, and then drag-and-drop one or more items into the new folder. Since Turbo Lister doesn't differentiate between items that have been uploaded and those that haven't, you might want to create an "Uploaded" folder and a "Pending" folder for precisely that purpose.

Seller's Assistant Pro

Once an item has been uploaded to eBay, Turbo Lister's role in that auction ends. There are plenty of tools you can use to conduct any post-auction tasks, but you may instead wish to use an integrated tool that follows the progress of an auction from conception to completion.

One such alternative is eBay Seller's Assistant Pro (*pages.ebay.com/sellers_ assistant/pro.html*), shown in Figure 7-3, which is available for a monthly fee. Although its interface is somewhat more crude than Turbo Lister, it provides much more complete auction management.

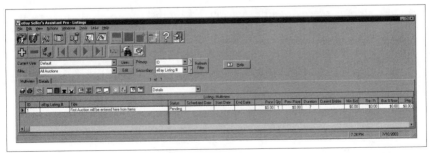

Figure 7-3. eBay Seller's Assistant Pro combines auction creation with post-auction management tools

Essentially, Seller's Assistant Pro combines Turbo Lister with the auction-tracking spreadsheet discussed in "Keep Track of Items You've Sold" [Hack #65], and adds some of the post-auction automation discussed in "Streamlining Checkout and Payment" [Hack #75] and "Streamlining Communications" [Hack #74].

See Also

Turbo Lister uses the eBay API to upload new listings. To build your own auction listing tool, see "Submit an Auction Listing" [Hack #88]. See Chapter 8 for details on the eBay API.

Also available at extra cost is Vendio Sales Manager (*www.vendio.com*), which comes with its own listing designer, inventory management, and image hosting services. One nice perk is that it will schedule eBay listings at no extra charge.

Before Turbo Lister, there was Mister Lister. Although it's now defunct, this non-API predecessor was quite popular. If you've used Mister Lister in the past, you can import your old Mister Lister collections into Turbo Lister by going to File → Import Items → From Mister Lister. However, note that any collections created with a version of Mister Lister released before May 2001 will not be readable by Turbo Lister.

HACK #74   Streamlining Communications
Use templates to send prewritten emails to your bidders.

As a seller, it is your responsibility to guide your bidders, helping them send payments and complete your transactions. You are the teacher as well as the seller, and—unfortunately—you'll get blamed when something goes wrong.

The email you send to your winning bidders after an auction has ended, as discussed in "Sending Payment Instructions" [Hack #66], must communicate several different pieces of information, including the total amount to pay, the methods of payment you accept, and how to actually send payment. As a busy seller, you'll want to do everything you can to simplify this task so that notifying dozens or even hundreds of bidders takes no more time than notifying a single one. Here are three different approaches that offer three different levels of automation.

The Simple Approach

As stated at the beginning of this chapter, sellers have different needs and different capabilities. The simplest way to streamline repetitive emails is to use the Stationery feature of your email program (instructions for Eudora and Outlook follow).

Eudora (eudora.com). To start, go to Tools → Stationery. Right-click an empty area of the Stationery window, and select New. Type the subject line and body text that you'd like to send to an average bidder, and close the Untitled window when you're done. Eudora will prompt you for a filename in which to save the stationery; thereafter, your stationery will appear in the Stationery window. Simply double-click your stationery to send it to a new customer.

 Your email should be readable by as many bidders as possible. For this reason, avoid using special fonts, colors, and especially pictures in your stationery.

Outlook or Outlook Express (microsoft.com). Go to Message → New Message. Type the subject line and body text that you'd like to send to an average bidder, and then go to File → Save as Stationery when you're done. To send a message with your stationery, go to Message → New Message Using → Select Stationery, find your newly created stationery in the folder, and then click OK.

The Hacker's Approach

This next approach involves a template, an HTML form, and a Perl script, all of which must be installed on a web server, even if it's a local server on your own machine. A seller enters a few specifics into the form, and the Perl script places them into the template and mails it to the bidder.

Start with this simple HTML form (replace the URL in the first line with the address of your script):

```
<form method="post" action="http://www.ebayhacks.com/cgi-bin/mail.pl">
Item Number: <input name="item" size=15>
<br>
Title: <input name="title" size=30>
<br>
Email address: <input name="email" size=30>
<p>
High bid: <input name="highbid" size=8>
<br>
Shipping: <input name="shipping" size=8>
<p>
<input type="submit" value="Send">
</form>
```

Next, the template should look something like this:

```
Congratulations! You're the high bidder for the
<insert title here>
 (ebay #
<insert item here>
).  Shipping will be
<insert shipping here>
, bringing the total to
```

```
<insert total here>
```
. The types of payment I accept are listed in the auction description and on my "About Me" page at eBay. Payment can be made in any of the following ways:

- If you have a free PayPal account, you can pay with your credit card or with an electronic bank account transfer. Just click the PayPal logo in the auction you've won.

- If you'd like to pay directly with your Visa, Mastercard, or American Express, you can use my private, secure server at: https://www.ebayhacks.com/checkout.html

- If you'd like to pay with BidPay, or if you'd like to send a money order or cashier's check (sorry, no personal or business checks), send them to: Acme Auctions, 123 Fake Street, Springfield, 90125

Either way, please send a confirmation email mentioning how you intend to pay as soon as you get this email. Thanks for bidding!

Customize the template to your heart's content and then save it into a plain text file. Note the special placeholders—on their own lines—into which the script places relevant information when the template is parsed. Use the following Perl script, *mail.pl*, to tie it all together.

 This script requires the *cgi-lib.pl* Perl library (*http://cgi-lib. berkeley.edu/*), used to parse the arguments passed from the HTML form.

```perl
#!/usr/bin/perl

require("cgi-lib.pl");
&ReadParse;

$myemail = "paybot\@ebayhacks.com";
$template = "/usr/local/home/template.txt";
$returnurl = "http://www.ebayhacks.com/contactform.html";

if (($in{'item'} eq "") || ($in{'title'} eq "") || ($in{'email'} eq "")
        || ($in{'highbid'} eq "") || ($in{'shipping'} eq "")) {
  print "Content-type: text/html\n\n";
  print "Please fill out all the fields.\n";
  exit;
}

open(MAIL,"|/usr/sbin/sendmail -t");
print MAIL "To: $in{'email'}\n";
print MAIL "From: $myemail\n";
print MAIL "Reply-To: $myemail\n";
print MAIL "Subject: $in{'title'}\n\n";
```

```
open (COVER, "$template");
  while ( $line = <COVER> ) {
    if ($line eq "<insert title here>") { print MAIL $in{'title'}; }
    elsif ($line eq "<insert item here>") { print MAIL $in{'item'}; }
    elsif ($line eq "<insert shipping here>") { print MAIL $in{'shipping'}; }
    elsif ($line eq "<insert total here>") {
                  print MAIL $in{'highbid'} + $in{'shipping'}; }
    elsif ($line eq "") { print MAIL "\n\n"; }
    else {
      if ($line eq "\n") { $line = "$line\n"; }
              else { chomp $line; }
      print MAIL $line;
    }
  }
close(COVER);
close(MAIL);
print "Location: $returnurl\n\n";
```

This script is fairly crude, but it does the job. Make sure to change the
$myemail, $template, and $returnurl variables to reflect your email address,
the location of your template file, and the URL of your HTML form, respectively.

To make this even more automated, tie the script in with the eBay API,
which, when given an item number, will be able to retrieve the title, the
email address of the high bidder, and the amounts of the high bid and applicable shipping charges. See Chapter 8 for details on the eBay API.

The Business Approach

Sellers who need to send payment instructions to hundreds or thousands of
bidders will not have the time to process them individually. This situation
requires auction management software, typically available for an additional
monthly fee. A few examples include:

- eBay's own Selling Manager, discussed in "Obtaining Sales Records"
  [Hack #76]
- eBay Seller's Assistant Pro, discussed in "Streamlining Listings" [Hack #73].
- Auctiva Manager (eBud), a component of Auctiva Pro (*www.auctiva.
  com*)
- Andale Checkout (*www.andale.com*) and Vendio Checkout (*www.
  vendio.com*), both discussed in "Streamlining Checkout and Payment"
  [Hack #75]

Streamlining Checkout and Payment

HACK #75

Use an off-eBay checkout system to integrate payments with shipping and accounting.

In the old days, any seller who wanted to accept credit cards had to get a credit card merchant account. Now, payment services like PayPal, BidPay, and C2IT have made merchant accounts largely unnecessary for everyone but the largest sellers.

But if there's any single truth when it comes to accepting payments on eBay, it's this: the more types of payment you accept, the more bids you'll get.

> If you decide to use an off-eBay checkout system, you may wish to disable eBay's own checkout, as described in "Opting Out of Checkout" [Hack #49]. Otherwise, your bidders may skip your preferred checkout in haste, and instead simply use the method with which they're most accustomed.

But there are still reasons to get a merchant account. For instance, sellers who do a lot of business may be able to get a better discount rate as a credit card merchant than they could through PayPal, which essentially means that they'll get to keep a larger percentage of the payments they receive. And anyone who sells merchandise outside of eBay will not want to limit their transactions only to PayPal.

Getting a Merchant Account

This is one thing that eBay won't do for you, and one thing that requires more than spending five minutes filling out a form on some web site. The best way to start is by contacting your bank and asking them to recommend a merchant account provider with which they're affiliated.

A representative will then talk to you and request lots of information about you and your business to help them establish your identity. You'll discuss payment plans and discount rates; don't be afraid to ask questions. When all is said and done, you'll be given a terminal or other means of entering credit card information, and you'll be ready to accept credit card payments.

Be warned—setting up a merchant account is not cheap, and is not for the faint of heart. Also, be extremely wary of Internet and email ads for merchant accounts.

See "Protect Yourself While Accepting Payments" [Hack #67] for some of the steps you should take to prevent chargebacks and unnecessary fees.

Accepting Credit Card Payments

Once you get your merchant account, the next step is to provide the means for your customers to transmit their credit card numbers and related information to you. This involves an HTML form and a backend script on a public web server. Let's start with a simple order form:

```
<form action="http://www.ebayhacks.com/cgi-bin/checkout.pl"
          method=post name="ccform" onSubmit="return confirmation();">
<table border><tr><td width=50% valign=top>
  <table border=0 width=100%>
  <tr><td align=right valign=top>eBay auction number(s):</td>
  <td align=left valign=top><input size=12 name="invoice"></td></tr>
  <tr><td align=right valign=top>Total amount of payment:</td>
  <td align=left valign=top><input size=12 name="total"></td></tr>
  <tr><td align=right valign=top>Method of Payment:</td>

  <td align=left valign=top>
  <select name="paytype"><option selected>(please make a selection)
    <option>Visa<option>MasterCard<option>American Express</select>
  </td></tr>
  <tr><td align=right valign=top>Credit card number:</td>
  <td align=left valign=top><input size=25 name="ccnumber"></td></tr>
  <tr><td align=right valign=top>CVV code:<br>(3-4 digits after
                   your CC number, on the back of the card)</td>
  <td align=left valign=top><input size=4 maxlength=4 name="cvv"></td></tr>
  <tr><td align=right valign=top>Expiration Date:</td>
  <td align=left valign=top>
    <select name="expiremonth"><option selected value="??">(Month)
    <option value="01">1<option value="02">2<option value="03">3
    <option value="04">4<option value="05">5<option value="06">6
    <option value="07">7<option value="08">8<option value="09">9
    <option value="10">10<option value="11">11<option value="12">12
    </select>
    <select name="expireyear"><option selected value="????">(Year)
    <option>2003<option>2004<option>2005<option>2006<option>2007
    <option>2008<option>2009<option>2010<option>2011<option>2012
    <option>2013<option>2014<option>2015<option>2016<option>2017
    </select>
  </td></tr></table>
</td><td width=50% valign=top>
  <table width=100%>
  <tr><td align=right valign=top>First Name:</td>
  <td align=left valign=top><input name="firstname" size=15></td></tr>
  <tr><td align=right valign=top>Last Name:</td>
  <td align=left valign=top><input name="lastname" size=15></td></tr>
  <tr><td align=right valign=top>E-mail Address:</td>
  <td align=left valign=top><input name="email" size=30></td></tr>
  <tr><td align=right valign=top>Mailing Address:</td>
  <td align=left valign=top><input name="address1" size=30>
    <input name="address2" maxlength=50 size=30></td></tr>
  <tr><td align=right valign=top>City:</td>
  <td align=left valign=top><input name="city" size=25></td></tr>
```

```
<tr><td align=right valign=top>State/Province:</td>
<td align=left valign=top><input name="state" size=4></td></tr>
<tr><td align=right valign=top>Zip:</td>
<td align=left valign=top><input name="zip" size=10></td></tr>
<tr><td align=right valign=top>Country:</td>
<td align=left valign=top><input name="country" size=25></td></tr>

<tr><td></td><td align=left valign=top>
  <input type="submit" value="Complete Your Order">
</td></tr></table>
</td></tr></table>
```

Place this HTML form on your public web server. You'll need to make sure your server supports SSL (Secure Sockets Layer), so the information your customers enter can be safely submitted to your server, as described in "Send Payment Quickly and Safely" [Hack #29].

Next, install the following backend Perl script, *checkout.pl*, to process the incoming data and store it in a file.

> This script requires the *cgi-lib.pl* Perl library (*http://cgi-lib. berkeley.edu/*), used to parse the arguments passed from the HTML form.

```perl
#!/usr/bin/perl

require("cgi-lib.pl");
&ReadParse;

$checkoutdir = "/usr/local/home";
$myemail = "checkout\@ebayhacks.com";
$ordernum = time;

# *** empty fields ***
if ((!keys(%in)) || ($in{'firstname'} eq "") || ($in{'lastname'} eq "")
    || ($in{'address1'} eq "") || ($in{'city'} eq "") || ($in{'zip'} eq "")
    || (($in{'state'} eq "") && ($in{'country'} eq "")) ||
    ($in{'paytype'} eq "(please make a selection)")
    || ($in{'ccnumber'} eq "") || ($in{'cvv'} eq "") ||
    ($in{'expiremonth'} eq "??") || ($in{'expireyear'} eq "????")) {
  print &PrintHeader;
  print "<b>Error:</b> Please fill out all the fields and try again.\n";
  exit;
}

# *** write data file ***
open(OUTFILE,">$checkoutdir/$ordernum.txt");

  print OUTFILE "[checkout]\r\n";
  print OUTFILE "email=$in{'email'}\r\n";
```

(circled markers: ① &ReadParse; ② $checkoutdir block; ③ empty fields if block; ④ open OUTFILE)

```
     print OUTFILE "firstname=$in{'firstname'}\r\n";
     print OUTFILE "lastname=$in{'lastname'}\r\n";
     print OUTFILE "address1=$in{'address1'}\r\n";
     print OUTFILE "address2=$in{'address2'}\r\n";
     print OUTFILE "city=$in{'city'}\r\n";
     print OUTFILE "state=$in{'state'}\r\n";
     print OUTFILE "zip=$in{'zip'}\r\n";
     print OUTFILE "country=$in{'country'}\r\n";
     print OUTFILE "invoice=$in{'invoice'}\r\n";
     print OUTFILE "total=$in{'total'}\r\n";
     print OUTFILE "paytype=$in{'paytype'}\r\n";
❺   print OUTFILE "cc=" . &formatccnumber($in{'ccnumber'}) . "\r\n";
     print OUTFILE "cvv=$in{'cvv'}\r\n";
     print OUTFILE "expiremonth=$in{'expiremonth'}\r\n";
     print OUTFILE "expireyear=$in{'expireyear'}\r\n";
   close(OUTFILE);

❻ open(MAIL,"|/usr/sbin/sendmail -t");
     print MAIL "To: $in{'email'}\n";
     print MAIL "From: $myemail\n";
     print MAIL "Reply-To: $myemail\n";
     print MAIL "Subject: Order Confirmation\n\n";
     print MAIL "Your payment information has been received.\n";
     print MAIL "Here are the details of your order:\n\n";
     print MAIL "   Name: $in{'firstname'} $in{'lastname'}\n";
     print MAIL "Address: $in{'address1'}\n";
     if ($in{'address2'} ne "") { print MAIL "         $in{'address2'}\n"; }
     print MAIL "         $in{'city'}, $in{'state'}  $in{'zip'}\n";
     print MAIL "         \U$in{'country'}\n\n";
     if (substr($in{'total'},0,1) ne "\$") { $in{'total'} = "\$$in{'total'}"; }
     print MAIL "US$in{'total'} will be charged to your $in{'paytype'}.\n\n";
     print MAIL "Your item(s) will be shipped as soon as possible.  If you\n";
     print MAIL "have any questions, please send them to $myemail\n";
   close(MAIL);

❼ open(MAIL,"|/usr/sbin/sendmail -t");
     print MAIL "To: $myemail\n";
     print MAIL "From: $in{'email'}\n";
     print MAIL "Reply-To: $in{'email'}\n";
     print MAIL "Subject: $in{'product'} Registration\n";
     print MAIL "A customer, $in{'firstname'} $in{'lastname'}, has\n";
     print MAIL "submitted a payment: order number #$ordernum.\n";
   close(MAIL);

❽ print &PrintHeader;
   print "Thank you for your order.\n";
   print "You will receive a confirmation email shortly.\n";
   exit;

❾ sub formatccnumber{

   $cc = "";
```

```
$pos = 0;
for ($i = 0; $i < length($_[0]); $i++) {
  if ("0123456789" =~ substr($_[0], $i, 1)) {
    $cc = $cc . substr($_[0], $i, 1);
    $pos++;
    if ($pos / 4 == int($pos / 4)) { $cc = $cc . " "; }
  }
}
return $cc;
}
```

This script is pretty straightforward. Using the *cgi-lib.pl* module, the script parses ❶ the incoming data into variables. Next, some custom variables are declared ❷, which you'll want to modify to reflect your system.

A single if statement ❸ checks for empty fields and spits out a generic error message if any problems are found; you'll probably want to expand this to provide more specific and appropriate error messages to your customers. The next section ❹ stores the data in a text file, but you can customize this to suit your needs.

> Note that on line ❺, the credit card number is modified by the formatccnumber function ❾, which does nothing more than insert spaces between every four digits and throw out anything else. You'll most likely want to supplement this with code that encodes the number, so you're never storing a raw credit card number on a server that can be compromised by an intruder.

After the information is stored, three more tasks are performed: a confirmation email is sent to the customer ❻, a notification email is sent to the seller ❼, and a brief confirmation page is shown in the browser window ❽.

How to Use It

With these two elements in place, all that's left is to publicize the URL of your checkout form. You'll notice that in both "Sending Payment Instructions" [Hack #66] and "Streamlining Communications" [Hack #74], the example payment-instructions email contains a link to a custom order form, complete with the https:// prefix, signifying a secure SSL connection.

When a customer places an order with your checkout form, you'll be sent an automatic email, and a new order record file will appear in the directory you specified on line ❶. You can further automate this hack by linking the script with your inventory system or setting it up to automatically print a prepaid shipping label, as described in "Cheap, Fast Shipping Without Waiting in Line" [Hack #68].

Checkout Providers

Those who don't want to create their own checkout systems may prefer an extra-cost, all-in-one "turnkey" solution, like any of the following.

Andale Checkout. The goal of a service like Andale Checkout (*www.andale.com*) is to effectively eliminate the back-and-forth emails between buyers and sellers, a necessity if you sell more than 100 items a week. Figure 7-4 shows what your customers will see when they use Andale Checkout to pay.

Figure 7-4. What your customers see when they pay via Andale Checkout

Andale Checkout also keeps records of your current and past sales, and offers additional automation such as invoice and shipping label printing and post-sale communications with customers.

Vendio Checkout.   Similar to Andale Checkout, Vendio Checkout is available with several of Vendio's subscription-based services, such as Sales Manager (*www.vendio.com*).

Selling Manager.   eBay's own Selling Manager (*pages.ebay.com/selling_ manager*), discussed in "Obtaining Sales Records" [Hack #76], and Seller's Assistant Pro (*pages.ebay.com/sellers_assistant/pro.html*), discussed in "Streamlining Listings" [Hack #73], both rely on eBay's checkout system, but provide additional post-auction tools and automation not otherwise available.

HACK #76   Obtaining Sales Records

Extract detailed accounting data from My eBay, or do it automatically with eBay's Selling Manager.

Sellers pay the bills at eBay. Fees are assessed for listings and upgrades (see "The Strategy of Listing Upgrades" [Hack #36]), and eBay gets a percentage of the final value of each successfully completed auction.

Any eBay user can check his or her account by going to My eBay → Accounts → Account Status. The fees are broken down individually and cross-referenced by item number. So to see exactly how much a particular auction cost you, just search for the item number, add up the corresponding amounts shown in the Debit column, and subtract any corresponding entries in the Credit column.

A more convenient approach is to use a spreadsheet to organize the data. First, go back and turn off Pagination and choose the appropriate date range. Click Submit and save the resulting page to an HTML file (File → Save As in your browser).

> If you want to remove the images and search box from the page, open the HTML file in a text editor and do a few search-and-replace operations before importing it into Excel. Replace every occurrence of <img with <ximg, and every occurrence of <input with <xinput. Save the file when you're done.

Open the page in a web-capable spreadsheet like Microsoft Excel. Highlight all the rows above the table (about 30 rows), and remove them (Edit → Delete). Do the same for all cells below the table. Finally, sort the listing by item number. Select the entire sheet (Ctrl-A), go to Data → Sort, choose "Item" in the first box, and then click OK.

It's not pretty, but it does the job in less than two minutes, and it's free.

Step Up to Selling Manager

For a monthly fee, you can have access to eBay's Selling Manager tool. Among other things, Selling Manager keeps an archive of past sales for up to four months, allowing you to download a sales history in a more convenient CSV (comma-separated value) format than the spreadsheet hack discussed earlier. CSV files can be easily imported into any spreadsheet, database, or accounting program.

Selling Manager simply appears as a tab in My eBay, replacing the Selling tab discussed in "Keep Track of Items You've Sold" [Hack #65]. See Figure 7-5.

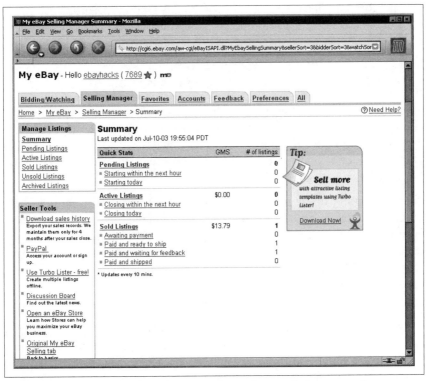

Figure 7-5. Selling Manager provides more robust sales records for an extra fee

You can subscribe to Selling Manager by going to *pages.ebay.com/selling_ manager*. eBay offers a free 30-day trial, and is even kind enough to remind you a few days before the trial period ends. Selling Manager can also be used for more general-purpose auction management, as discussed in "Streamlining Communications" [Hack #74].

One of the drawbacks of Selling Manager is that it won't migrate any of your past completed auctions to the new format; only currently running auctions and auctions that have ended *after* you upgrade will ever appear in Selling Manager. However, you can always click "Original My eBay Selling tab" to temporarily revert to the old interface to view older completed auctions.

Alternatives

If you prefer to do your accounting and reporting off-eBay, you can use Andale Reports (*www.andale.com*) or Auctiva eBud (*www.auctiva.com*), both of which offer some additional functionality at some additional cost.

 Make Money by Linking to eBay

#77   Earn affiliate kickbacks without even selling anything on eBay.

Like many e-commerce sites, eBay offers an affiliate program, wherein they pay you money for each new eBay member who signs up through the links on your site. If you're promoting your eBay auctions off-site, as described in "List Your Auctions on Another Site" [Hack #78], you can make it even more lucrative by making all the links affiliate links.

Start by signing up at *pages.ebay.com/affiliate*. You'll find a few different affiliate programs, each with different requirements and benefits (there's even one just for "eBay Stores" [Hack #72]). But the "Commission Junction" link is probably the most applicable, as it offers kickbacks for new user registrations as well as individual bids. There's no fee to apply.

Creating Links with Commission Junction

eBay is one of many affiliate sites partnered with Commission Junction, a fact that will become all too clear when you first try to create links. You'll have to dig a bit just to find eBay on the site. The quickest way is to go to Get Links → By Relationship → My Advertisers, and you'll see a list of sites with whom you've signed up. (If you join Commission Junction through eBay, you'll be automatically signed up as an eBay affiliate.)

You may see references to cryptic terms like "EPC," followed by dollar amounts that look like fees. EPC is marketing lingo for "Average Earnings Per One Hundred Clicks" and translates to the money they expect you to earn through your affiliate links.

Click View Links to show the assortment of links and banners you can use (there were 152 at the time of this writing). The listing can be sorted by clicking the column headers; click "7 Day EPC," for instance, to show the links that, statistically, are supposed to earn the most money.

Hacking the Links

But as we learned in *How to Lie with Statistics* by Darrell Huff, "There is terror in numbers." Instead of using the links that Commission Junction tells you to use, you might want to use the links that will further your specific interests and have the least impact on your site. One of the most useful is Link ID 7169491, "Customizable eBay Destination," which lets you link to any specific page at eBay. For a shortcut to the page used to create this link, just go to *pages.ebay.com/affiliate/cjflexiblelink.html*, shown in Figure 7-6.

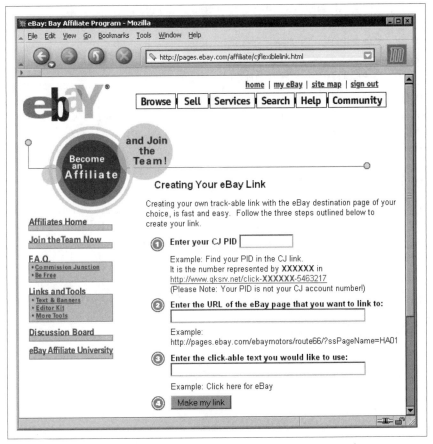

Figure 7-6. Create links to specific pages with the Creating Your eBay Link page

After entering the address of a specific category, the URL you'll get will look something like this:

```
http://www.qksrv.net/click-xxxxxxx-5463217?loc=http%3A//listings.ebay.com/
aw/plistings/list/all/category19116/index.html
```

where *xxxxxxx* is the CJ PID, a seven-digit number representing your Commission Junction account (but not the same as your account number, paradoxically). Likewise, a link to a list of all your auctions will look like this:

```
http://www.qksrv.net/click-xxxxxxx-5463217?loc=http%3A//cgi6.ebay.com/ws/
eBayISAPI.dll%3FViewSellersOtherItems%26userid%3Dusername
```

where *username* is your eBay user ID. Note that some of the special characters had to be converted to hex codes to keep them from interfering with the link. For instance, the colon (:) becomes %3A, the ampersand (&) becomes %26, the question mark (?) becomes %3F, and the equals sign (=) becomes %3D.

If you feel like doing this simple conversion manually, you can create your links without having to repeatedly return to the Creating Your eBay Link page. For instance, a link to a specific auction will look like this:

```
http://www.qksrv.net/click-xxxxxxx-5463217?loc=http%3A//cgi.ebay.com/ws/
eBayISAPI.dll%3FViewItem%26item%3Ditemnumber
```

where *itemnumber* is the item number of your auction. You can even use these links right in your eBay auctions, as described in "List Your Other Auctions in the Description" **[Hack #47]**. For a more automated approach, see "List Your Auctions on Another Site" **[Hack #78]**.

A Simplified Search Box

Among the 150+ link types are several search boxes you can put on your site. Unfortunately, each one comes in static banner used to advertise eBay. To place a simple search box with no banner on your site, just use this HTML form:

```
<form action="http://www.qksrv.net/interactive" method="get"">
<input type=hidden name="MfcISAPICommand" value="GetResult">
<input type=hidden name=ht value=1>
<input type=hidden name="SortProperty" value="MetaEndSort">
<input type="hidden" name="url"
                value="http://search.ebay.com/search/search.dll">
<input type="hidden" name="pid" value="xxxxxxx">
<input type="hidden" name="aid" value="yyyyyyy">

Search eBay for:
<input type="text" name="query" size="12" maxlength="100" value="">
<input type="submit" value="Search" name="submit">
</form>
```

The only things you have to customize are the pid and aid fields; replace *xxxxxxx* and *yyyyyyy* with the respective codes provided by Commission Junction. See "Allow Visitors to Search Through Your Auctions" **[Hack #46]** for details on making this box look like the standard eBay search box.

HACK #78 List Your Auctions on Another Site

Use the eBay Editor Kit and Merchant Kit to promote your auctions off-eBay.

Once you've signed up with one of eBay's affiliate programs, as described in "Make Money by Linking to eBay" **[Hack #77]**, you can use either of eBay's two tools for creating lists of auctions on your own site. Not only will this help promote your auctions and increase traffic to specific items, but you'll make money for each new user who signs up and for each bid that is placed as a result of your links.

The Editor Kit

The Editor Kit couldn't be slicker. Just go to *cgi3.ebay.com/ws/eBayISAPI. dll?EKCreate* and fill out the fields, as shown in Figure 7-7.

Select Commission Junction in the Provider box and enter your CJ ID in the Tracking ID field. The rest of the fields should be self-explanatory, and the only one that is required is the Search Term. If you want to limit the search to your own auctions, type your eBay user ID in the "Show items of the following sellers" box.

When you're done, click Preview to show the JavaScript code and the resulting search box, shown in Figure 7-8.

The big drawback to the Editor Kit is that it only shows results of a keyword search; you can't leave the Search Term field blank in order to show all your auctions. Instead, you can use either eBay Stores **[Hack #72]** or the Merchant Kit, next, to promote your overall business on eBay.

The Merchant Kit

Like the Editor Kit, the Merchant Kit creates simple JavaScript snippets, but centers around category listings rather than search results.

Start by going to *pages.ebay.com/api/merchantkit.html*, and simply use the Merchant Kit, shown in Figure 7-9, to create your code.

The code is little more than a URL that can be easily tweaked without having to return to the Merchant Kit. The resulting box, shown in Figure 7-10, lists all your auctions, optionally filtered by category.

Sniplet Creator - Mozilla

File Edit View Go Bookmarks Tools Window Help

http://cgi3.ebay.com/ws/eBayISAPI.dll?EKCreate

home | sign out | services | site map | help ?

Browse   Search   Sell   My eBay   Community   Powered By IBM

Create Your Editor Kit   Download User's Guide

* = Required

Tracking Services

Provider *   Commission Junction ▼   Become an eBay affiliate

Tracking ID   1337296   Help for Tracking and Payment
                    If you choose Mediaplex as your Provider, please contact your eBay account
                    manager for your Tracking ID

Commission   What is SID?
Junction SID   Enter up to 30 alpha-numeric characters as your tracking code for this Editor Kit
                    (e.g., U2 DVD 1, Harry Potter).

Search Criteria

At least one of the first three search criteria are required.*

Search term   camera   Tips
                    ☐ Search title **and** description to find more items

eBay Seller IDs   ebayhacks
                                        See items only from these sellers.
                    Enter up to 10 User IDs separated by commas (example: userid1,userid2)

Category numbers

                    Enter up to 10 category numbers separated by commas. See all Category
                    numbers

Price range   Minimum $ Maximum $
                    Enter non-decimal numbers only (example: 1, 17, 255)

Additional options ☐ Show items with Gallery images only
                    ☐ Show Buy It Now items only

Figure 7-7. Use the Editor Kit to create a custom search results listing for use on your own site

Accept PayPal Payments from Your Own Site

#79   Integrate PayPal into your web site with a simple HTML form.

PayPal is more than a standalone auction payment service—it's an engine that you can use to power transactions on or off eBay. Any site that sells products can accept PayPal payments, and can do so without forcing customers to type an email address and an amount into their browser windows.

Product	Price	Bids	Time Left
USB CABLE for OLYMPUS CAMEDIA digital camera	**$8.95**	-	2h 06m
Kodak Leather Like Digital Camera Bag	**$2.95**	-	2h 07m
~NEW~ EN-EL3 Li-Ion Camera Battery Nikon D100	**$9.99**	-	2h 07m
USB Cable for Toshiba PDR-2300 Camera	**$6.90**	-	2h 07m
Polaroid PhotoMax Digital 320 Camera	**$5.00**	1	2h 08m
NEW CASIO EXILIM EX-Z3 DIGITAL CAMERA W/ DOCK	**$300.00**	8	2h 08m
USB Cable for Canon PowerShot Pro90 IS Camera	**$12.90**	*Buy It Now*	2h 08m
Olympus IS-1 Quartzdate Auto 35mm camera ED	**$31.00**	4	2h 09m
DIGITAL CAMERA 3 CAMERAS IN ONE w/video NEW !	**$34.99**	-	2h 09m
FED-2 Russian Camera LEICA copy 35mm NR	**$10.50**	2	2h 09m
ZORKI-4 Russian Camera Leica copy /industar50	**$24.99**	-	2h 09m
View all 37698 items on eBay			*disclaimer*

Figure 7-8. The code produced by the Editor Kit will create this dynamic listing on your site

Somewhat like an API, PayPal provides an HTTP interface to their payment system that works just like the Pay Now button at the top of completed eBay auctions. This allows you, as the seller, to specify an amount, a product name, and any other bits of information you'd like to associate with the payment.

Any seller can accept PayPal payments through their HTTP interface; no special agreement or settings are necessary, other than a basic PayPal account. There are two ways to integrate PayPal into your site.

Just a Link

The simpler of the two methods involves nothing more than a link placed on your site. For instance, this URL:

```
https://www.paypal.com/xclick/business=paybot@ebayhacks.com&item_
name=wicket&amount=58.00&no_note=1
```

specifies the email address (paybot@ebayhacks.com), the product name (wicket), and the amount ($58.00). If you want to link the URL to an image (like the PayPal logo), use this code:

```
<a href="https://www.paypal.com/xclick/business=paybot@ebayhacks.com&item_
name=wicket&amount=58.00&no_note=1"><img src="https://www.paypal.com/images/
x-click-but01.gif" border=0></a>
```

Other Pay Now button images are available at PayPal. When your customers click the link, they will see a window like the one in Figure 7-11.

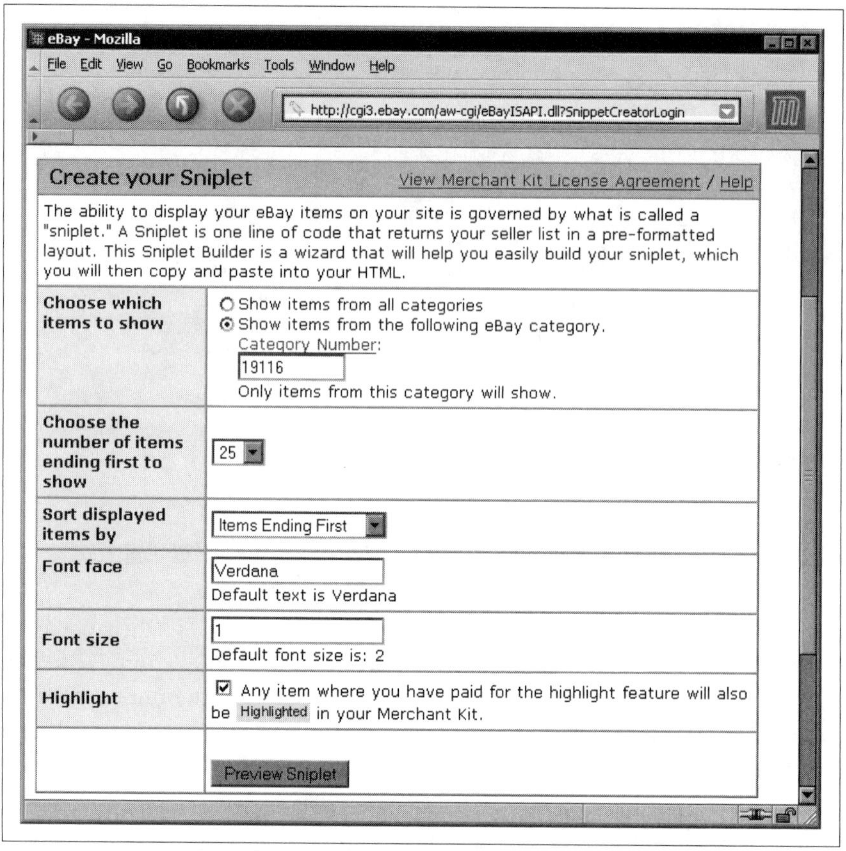

Figure 7-9. The Merchant Kit has only a few options, but the code it creates is not limited by search terms

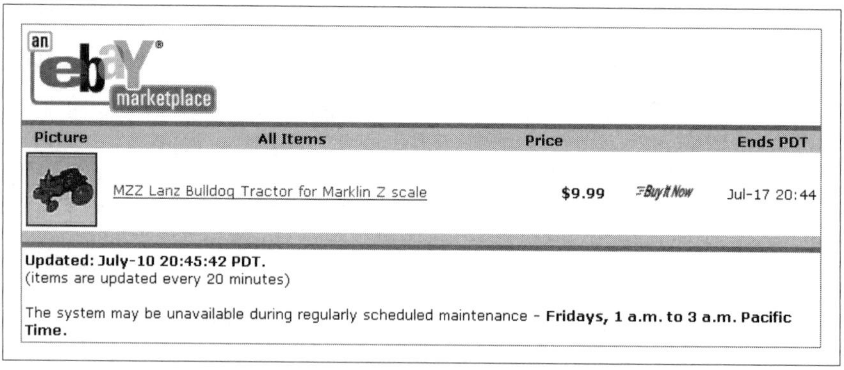

Figure 7-10. Use the Merchant Kit to produce dynamic listings of all your auctions on any site

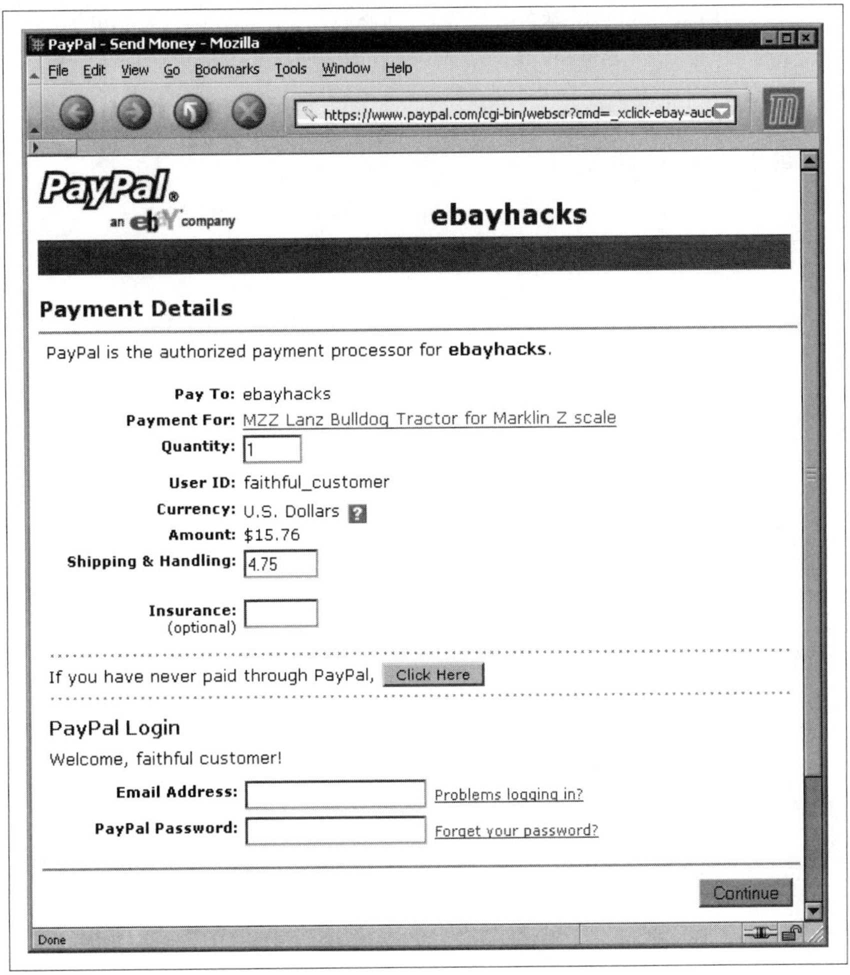

Figure 7-11. The PayPal checkout counter shows your product and the price

When your customers click Continue, the only thing they'll be able to change on the next page is the funding source and the shipping address. If you want your customers to be able to enter a note or special instructions, remove the &no_note=1 parameter from the URL.

> Look out for devious customers who might try to short-change you by altering the amount in the URL. Make sure to verify the amount before shipping your product. Use a form (described next) for a slightly more tamper-proof solution.

You can further customize your customers' experience by including additional fields in the URL, many of which are discussed in the next section.

The Form

The more robust approach requires a little more code:

```
<form action="https://www.paypal.com/cgi-bin/webscr" method="post">
<input type="hidden" name="cmd" value="_xclick">
<input type="hidden" name="business" value="paybot@ebayhacks.com">
<input type="hidden" name="return"
                 value="http://www.ebayhacks.com/thankyou.html">
<input type="hidden" name="cancel_return"
                 value="http://www.ebayhacks.com/cancelled.html">
<input type="hidden" name="no_note" value="1">
<input type="hidden" name="item_name" value="Extra-Strenth Wicket">
<input type="hidden" name="item_number" value="63123">
<input type="hidden" name="amount" value="$77.00">
<input type="hidden" name="on0" value="Name">
<input type="hidden" name="on1" value="Color">

Please type your name:
<input name="os0" value="" maxlength=60 size=22>
<p>
Please choose a color
<select name="os1">
  <option>Mustard Yellow
  <option>Metallic Puce
  <option>Chartreuse
  <option>Clear
  <option>Candy Apple Gray
</select>
<p>

<input type="submit" name="submit" value="Continue...">
</form>
```

The advantages of the form interface are clear: in addition to the standard fields (listed at the beginning in the hidden <input> tags), you can include up to two custom fields to be filled out by your customers. The names of the custom fields are specified in the hidden on0 and on1 fields, and their contents are specified in the os0 and os1 fields. In the example, the custom fields, name and color, are comprised of a standard text box and a drop-down list box, respectively.

Also new in this form are the return and cancel_return fields, which contain the URLs to which your customers will be sent when they complete (or cancel) the payment process, and the item_number field, which can be your stock number (SKU) or part number.

If you don't want to build the form yourself, PayPal will do it for you. Go to Merchant Tools → Website Payments → Buy Now Buttons to choose the options you want and review the resulting HTML code.

Shopping Cart

PayPal also supports a shopping cart interface in which customers can specify—and pay for—multiple items from your store. The code is nearly identical to the form in the previous section, except for two fields. First, change the contents of the cmd field to _cart (with the underscore), like this:

```
<input type="hidden" name="cmd" value="_cart">
```

Next, add the following new field:

```
<input type="hidden" name="add" value="1">
```

Finally, change the caption of the submit button like this:

```
<input type="submit" name="submit" value="Add to Cart...">
```

When your customers add items to their shopping carts, they'll see a page like the one in Figure 7-12.

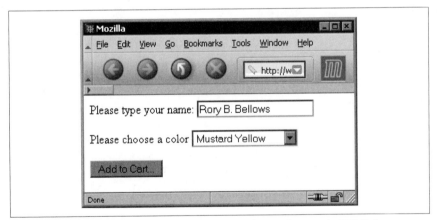

Figure 7-12. Integrate a PayPal shopping cart interface with a simple HTML form

See Also

You'll be notified of any completed sales with a payment notification email to your registered PayPal email address. To eliminate the human interaction required to process the emails and further integrate your business with Pay-Pal, you can use Instant Payment Notification, as described in "Process Pay-Pal Payments Automatically" [Hack #80].

Also, see "Opting Out of Checkout" [Hack #49] for details on controlling the integration of PayPal with your completed auctions.

HACK #80 Process PayPal Payments Automatically

Use Instant Payment Notification to fulfill orders without human intervention.

When a bidder pays for an auction with PayPal or completes an order from your online store (see "Accept PayPal Payments from Your Own Site" [Hack #79]), PayPal notifies you with a single email. Since the last thing any busy seller wants to do is deal with a bunch of emails, PayPal offers the free Instant Payment Notification (IPN) feature.

Setting Up IPN

The premise is pretty simple: as soon as a payment is received, PayPal contacts your server and submits all the details of the transaction to your script. Your script then processes and stores the data in whatever way you see fit.

To start using IPN, all you need to do is enable the feature and specify the URL of your script. Log into PayPal and go to My Account → Profile → Instant Payment Notification Preferences. Click Edit to change the current settings.

The Script

The following Perl script[*] does everything required to accept IPN notifications; all you need to do is modify the $workdir variable to reflect a valid path on your server.

> This script requires the LWP::UserAgent Perl module by Alan E. Derhaag, available at *search.cpan.org/perldoc?LWP:: UserAgent*, necessary to facilitate communication with the PayPal server. See "Create a Search Robot" [Hack #17] for installation instructions.

```
#!/usr/bin/perl
$workdir = "/usr/local/home";

read (STDIN, $query, $ENV{'CONTENT_LENGTH'});
$query .= '&cmd=_notify-validate';

use LWP::UserAgent;
```

---

[*] Portions based on sample code by PayPal and David W. Van Abel (*Perlsources.com*).

```
    $ua = new LWP::UserAgent;
    $req = new HTTP::Request 'POST','http://www.paypal.com/cgi-bin/webscr';
    $req->content_type('application/x-www-form-urlencoded');
    $req->content($query);
❸   $res = $ua->request($req);

❹   @pairs = split(/&/, $query);
    $count = 0;
    foreach $pair (@pairs) {
      ($name, $value) = split(/=/, $pair);
      $value =~ tr/+/ /;
      $value =~ s/%([a-fA-F0-9][a-fA-F0-9])/pack("C", hex($1))/eg;
      $variable{$name} = $value;
      $count++;
    }

❺   if ($variable{'payment_status'} ne "Completed") { &SendOK(); }
❻   if (-e "$workdir/$variable{'txn_id'}.txt") { &SendOK(); }

❼   open(OUTFILE,">$workdir/$variable{'txn_id'}.txt");
      print OUTFILE "[ipn_data]\r\n";
      print OUTFILE "email=$variable{'payer_email'}\r\n";
      print OUTFILE "firstname=$variable{'first_name'}\r\n";
      print OUTFILE "lastname=$variable{'last_name'}\r\n";
      print OUTFILE "address1=$variable{'address_street'}\r\n";
      print OUTFILE "address2=$variable{'address_status'}\r\n";
      print OUTFILE "city=$variable{'address_city'}\r\n";
      print OUTFILE "state=$variable{'address_state'}\r\n";
      print OUTFILE "zip=$variable{'address_zip'}\r\n";
      print OUTFILE "country=$variable{'address_country'}\r\n";
      print OUTFILE "product=$variable{'item_name'}\r\n";
      print OUTFILE "quantity=$variable{'quantity'}\r\n";
      print OUTFILE "total=$variable{'payment_gross'}\r\n";
      print OUTFILE "custom1=$variable{'option_selection1'}\r\n";
      print OUTFILE "custom2=$variable{'option_selection2'}\r\n";
    close(OUTFILE);
❽   &SendOK();


    sub SendOK() {
❾     print "content-type: text/plain\n\nOK\n";
      exit;
    }
```

Here's how it works. First, the data received from PayPal ❶ is appended
with an additional variable ❷, and then sent back to PayPal for validation ❸.
This will prevent an unscrupulous user from attempting to trick your server
into thinking an order has been received. Immediately thereafter, PayPal
returns the data, and the script parses it into separate variables ❹.

Next, the script checks to see if the transaction status is "Completed" ❺ and if the transaction ID (txn_id) has been processed already ❻. If either test fails, the script quits by way of the SendOK function.

Finally, the script writes the pertinent information to a file ❼, the name of which is simply the transaction ID. You'll undoubtedly want to change the fields that are recorded, the format of the file, and the path ($workdir) in which the files are stored.

To ensure that your server is properly notified of the transaction, PayPal sends the data repeatedly until it receives an OK signal ❾ from your script. Furthermore, a single transaction can trigger a bunch of notifications, which is why you'll need to filter out incomplete or duplicate entries (lines ❺ and ❻).

Hacking the Script

Ultimately, the only thing this script does is read the data received from IPN, validate it, and store it in a text file. The format of the file in this example is that of a Windows INI Configuration File, making it easy for a Windows application to read the data using the GetPrivateProfileString API call.

Naturally, you can store the data in whatever format you choose, including a database or even a specially formatted email. IPN is commonly used for automatic order fulfillment, wherein the server sends the customer a software registration key, subscription password, or other electronically transmitted product. But you can also use IPN to integrate incoming payments with your shipping system to produce prepaid shipping labels automatically (see "Cheap, Fast Shipping Without Waiting in Line" [Hack #68]).

PayPal email notifications can sometimes be unreliable, either taking a while to show up or not showing up at all. You can remedy this by supplementing it with your own email notification, such as the following (placed immediately before line ❽):

```
open(MAIL,"|/usr/sbin/sendmail -t");
  print MAIL "To: $variable{'receiver_email'}\n";
  print MAIL "From: $variable{'payer_email'}\n";
  print MAIL "Reply-To: $variable{'payer_email'}\n";
  print MAIL "Subject: New IPN Order Received\n\n";
  print MAIL "Order $variable{'txn_id'} has been received via IPN\n";
  print MAIL "and stored in file $workdir/$variable{'txn_id'}.txt\n";
close(MAIL);
```

See Also

Full documentation, including a list of all supported fields, is available in the PayPal Instant Payment Notification Manual, available at *www.paypal.com.*

Further examples and commercial versions of the script are available from a variety of sources, including *www.ipnhosting.com*, *www.paypalipn.com*, and *www.perlsources.com*.

IPN is sometimes used in conjunction with off-eBay web sites that accept PayPal payments, as described in "Accept PayPal Payments from Your Own Site" [Hack #79].

#81 Keep Tabs on the eBay Community

Use the Forums, Announcement boards, and New Feature Previews to keep up with the eBay community.

eBay is constantly revising their web site, policies, features, and associated fees; as a seller on eBay, you have a vested interest in how these changes shape your business. Since even the most minor changes can have an impact (positive or negative), you should stay connected to the eBay community to ensure that you're aware of potential problems and prepared for upcoming changes.

General Announcements Board. *http://www2.ebay.com/aw/marketing.shtml*

> Go to Site Map → News & Announcements for previews of new features, new category announcements, policy changes, and updates to eBay's various tools and services.

System Announcements Board. *http://www2.ebay.com/aw/announce.shtml*

> Go to Site Map → News & Announcements → System when something on eBay stops working, to see if there's an explanation here. Scheduled maintenance and unscheduled outages are also documented on this page.

Calendar. *http://pages.ebay.com/community/events/*

> Go to Site Map → Calendar for a listing of this month's workshops, tradeshows, "Share your Wares" events, Street Faires, eBay Live conferences, and eBay University seminars.

eBay Community Newsletter. *http://pages.ebay.com/community/chatter/*

> Go to Site Map → News & Announcements → Newsletter to read "The Chatter," a monthly e-zine produced by eBay staff members, complete with articles, announcements, and even a *Member Spotlight*.

Discussion Forums. *http://pages.ebay.com/community/boards/*

> Go to Site Map → Discussion, Help and Chat → Discussion Boards to discuss nearly all aspects of eBay with other members. Among the roughly 70 specialized forums are "Checkout," "Search," "International Trading," and my favorite, "Soapbox."

Use the boards to ask questions, offer help to other eBay users, and voice your opinions (and objections) regarding eBay policies, changes, and trends. For instance, when eBay's controversial Checkout feature was introduced (see "Opting Out of Checkout" [Hack #49]), eBay's then-new Checkout forum was crammed with thousands of complaints from members (including several makeshift "petitions" started by particularly outraged sellers).

Forums are comprised of *threads*, each of which starts as a single message. Any member can start a new thread or add to an existing thread. When new threads are created or old threads are updated with new additions, they're moved to the top of the list.

> Some people post to their own threads to move them to the top in the hopes of invigorating them, which is why you may occasionally see a post with nothing more than "Bump" in the message body.

When eBay staff members post to a forum (and they do), their names are shown in a pink-colored stripe, which is why you may occasionally see references to "Pinks" by some of the forum regulars.

API Forums. *http://developer.ebay.com/DevZone/community/forums.asp*

This is a special section of the forums for those working with the eBay API, discussed in Chapter 8.

The eBay API
Hacks 82–100

eBay is more than just a web site. It's a platform upon which you can build your own applications and with which you can extend your business.

The eBay API (Application Programming Interface) is a set of functions you can integrate with your applications to communicate directly with eBay. Use the API to retrieve details about an auction, perform searches, list a seller's current items, and even create new auction listings. Think of the API as a "back door" of sorts, a way for developers to interact with the eBay engine and auction database without using the standard web interface.

The possibilities of such a system are limitless. Businesses can use the eBay API to link their inventory and sales databases with auctions, cutting out most of the labor that would otherwise be involved in selling large numbers of items. Developers can use the API to construct auction management applications for themselves, their companies, or even for commercial sale. And, of course, individual buyers and sellers on eBay can use the API to do a little friendly hacking, as described throughout the rest of this chapter.

How the eBay API Works

The underlying process of placing a call to the API is conceptually quite simple. First, your program sends an XML string to eBay with the name of the API call and any additional required fields. Here's an example XML request for the GetSearchResults function:

```
<?xml version='1.0' encoding='iso-8859-1'?>
<request>
  <RequestUserId>my_user_id</RequestUserId>
  <RequestPassword>my_password</RequestPassword>
  <ErrorLevel>1</ErrorLevel>
  <DetailLevel>0</DetailLevel>
  <Verb>GetSearchResults</Verb>
  <SiteId>0</SiteId>
```

```
<Query>![CDATA[*abbey road*]]</Query>
</request>
```

eBay then responds with more XML, from which your application extracts the desired data. The components of the input and output XML will vary with the particular function and the needs of the application, but the overall methodology is the same regardless of the API call being used.

Every single XML request sent to eBay must contain three developer-specific keys, DevID, AppID, and CertID, all of which are provided to you when you join eBay's Developers Program.

Getting Started

Before you can start using the eBay API, you'll need to sign up at *developer. ebay.com*. There are four different license types (or "tiers"):

Individual. This is the free license designed for individual developers. It includes full access to all API calls, but limits usage to only 50 calls per day. The only tangible cost is Certification, as described in "Climbing Out of the Sandbox" **[Hack #82]**.

Developers using the Individual license have no access to developer technical support (though they can access developer forums), nor can they use Platform Notifications (see "Send Automatic Emails to High Bidders" **[Hack #93]**) or sell their programs commercially.

Basic. The lowest commercial tier, Basic includes 30,000 calls per month (significantly more than the 50 allotted to Individual developers), with a nominal charge for additional calls. But it also has an annual fee and a higher certification cost, all offset by the ability to create commercial applications (like auction management tools).

Professional. The Professional tier is similar to the Basic tier, but with a more expensive annual membership fee, less expensive API usage fees, and more free technical support incidents.

Enterprise. The highest commercial tier, Enterprise differs from the Basic and Professional tiers only in the fees and number of free technical support incidents.

Once you've signed up, you can log in and download the eBay API SDK (Software Development Kit).

Although the SDK comes with documentation, the online API Technical Documentation at *developer.ebay.com/ DevZone/docs/API_Doc/* is the best source for technical information about the API.

Using the Scripts in This Chapter

All of the example scripts in this chapter are written in Perl. Not only is Perl code concise and extremely easy to read, but Perl interpreters are freely available for nearly every computing platform on Earth.

Every script in this chapter relies on the following two scripts. Make sure all your scripts are stored in the same directory. As with all the scripts in this book, you can download them from *www.ebayhacks.com/*.

ebay.pl. This script contains the common code used in all scripts in this chapter, including the aptly named call_api function.

```perl
#!/usr/bin/perl
use LWP::UserAgent;
use HTTP::Request;
use HTTP::Headers;
use XML::Simple;
require 'config.pl';

sub call_api {
  my ($arg) = @_;
  return undef unless $arg->{Verb};
  $arg->{RequestUserId} = $user_id unless defined $arg->{RequestUserId};
  $arg->Ã{RequestPassword} = $password
                              unless defined $arg->{RequestPassword};
  $arg->{DetailLevel} = "0" unless defined $arg->{DetailLevel};
  $arg->{ErrorLevel} = "1" unless defined $arg->{ErrorLevel};

  my $ua   = LWP::UserAgent->new;
  my $head = HTTP::Headers->new
      ('X-EBAY-API-COMPATIBILITY-LEVEL' => $compat_level,
       'X-EBAY-API-SESSION-CERTIFICATE' => "$dev_id;$app_id;$cert_id",
                 'X-EBAY-API-DEV-NAME' => $dev_id,
                 'X-EBAY-API-APP-NAME' => $app_id,
                'X-EBAY-API-CERT-NAME' => $cert_id,
                'X-EBAY-API-CALL-NAME' => $arg->{Verb},
                   'X-EBAY-API-SITEID' => $site_id,
             'X-EBAY-API-DETAIL-LEVEL' => $arg->{DetailLevel}
  );

  my $body = XMLout($arg,
                  keeproot => 1,
                   keyattr => undef,
                    noattr => 1,
                  rootname => 'request',
                   xmldecl => 1);
  print STDERR "calling: $body" if $DEBUG;
  my $req = HTTP::Request->new("POST", $api_url, $head, $body);
  my $rsp = $ua->request($req);
  print STDERR "response: $rsp->content" if $DEBUG;
  return undef if !$rsp->is_success;
```

```
    return XMLin($rsp->content,
                   forcearray => [qw/Error Item FeedbackDetailItem/],
                   keyattr => undef);
}

sub print_error {
  my ($xml) = @_;
  foreach (@{$xml->{Errors}{Error}}) {
    print "$_->{Severity}: $_->{LongMessage}\n";
  }
}

sub formatdate {
  ($sec,$min,$hour,$mday,$mon,$year,$wday,$yday,$isdst) = gmtime($_[0]);
  $year = $year + 1900;
  $mon = $mon + 1;
  return sprintf("%0.4d-%0.2d-%0.2d %0.2d:%0.2d:%0.2d",
                                     $year,$mon,$mday,$hour,$min,$sec);
}

return true;
```

config.pl. Next, the *config.pl* script is used to store personal information such as the developer keys eBay sends you, your username and password, and other variables used throughout this chapter.

```
#!/usr/bin/perl
$api_url      = 'https://temp-sandbox.ebay.com/ws/api.dll';
$itemurl      = "http://cgi.ebay.com/ws/eBayISAPI.dll?ViewItem&item=";
$compat_level = 309;
$site_id      = 0; # US
$DEBUG        = 0;

$dev_id       = 'your_DevID';
$app_id       = 'your_AppID';
$cert_id      = 'your_CertID';
$user_id      = 'your_ebay_user_id';
$password     = 'your_ebay_password';
$selleremail  = "your_email_address";
$localdir     = "a_path_on_your_hard_disk";

return true;
```

Make sure to fill in all the "your" fields in *config.pl* with your own information. eBay will provide the DevID, AppID, and CertID keys when you join the eBay Developers Program. If you're outside the U.S., change $site_id accordingly. See "Climbing Out of the Sandbox" **[Hack #82]** for more information on the Compatibility Level ($compat_level). Finally, the two URL variables shouldn't have to be changed.

Nearly everything in Perl (and the eBay API, for that matter) is case sensitive. Always mind your upper- and lowercase when working with the scripts in this chapter.

Special thanks to Todd Larason, without whose help this chapter would not have been possible.

Climbing Out of the Sandbox

#82 Dealing with certification and going "live."

eBay is understandably protective about any access it permits through its API. To that end, they provide the Sandbox, a "dummy" eBay site with which you can test your programs to your heart's content.

The Sandbox is located at *cgi.sandbox.ebay.com/*, and looks (and acts) just like eBay.com. Although it's nearly fully functional (some features don't work at all), its auction and user databases are completely separate from the main eBay site.

The idea is that you can create user accounts, list items, bid, and even check out, all without incurring the fees and API call limits that would otherwise prevent you from freely testing your application or scripts.

Although the Sandbox is not bug-free and is often a few months behind eBay.com when it comes to new features and interface changes, it's stable where it counts. It's accepted as fact that any code that works in the Sandbox will work on the live eBay.com site.

Certification

Before your application goes "live," meaning that it can be used on what eBay calls the "production servers" (not just the Sandbox), you must complete certification.

Now, the fact that certification is a required step and costs money ($100 for Individual-tier developers) may make it seem more like a barrier than a service. However, eBay's reasoning is that it ultimately benefits developers as much as it benefits eBay.

For developers working under the Individual license, the certification fee is the only tangible cost of entry to going live.

First and foremost, certification involves testing your script or application to ensure that it operates efficiently and causes minimal impact on the performance of eBay.com. Certification also permits developers to display the eBay Certified Developer Logo in their applications; while this may not mean so much to individual developers (it is not even available under the Individual license), it is absolutely vital for those creating commercial applications to gain the confidence of their customers.

Here's how certification works:

1. Review the certification requirements (see the next section).

2. Submit the API Usage Document (available at *developer.ebay.com*), which helps provide the certification "test team" with enough information to understand how your product will be accessing the eBay API and eBay content.

3. Submit a Certification Request.

4. eBay works with you to test your application, which essentially involves hooking it up to a special debug server and analyzing the traffic it generates.

5. Provided that you've met the certification requirements, eBay estimates that your program should be certified within a week.

6. Recertification is necessary only if your application substantially changes the way it uses the API.

Certification Requirements

The following requirements must be met by your application in order for it to pass certification:

Error Handling. Make sure you look for and handle any errors received from API calls. For instance, if you're using a single API call repeatedly, make sure the loop halts if an error is encountered. All of the scripts in this chapter incorporate some degree of error checking.

Efficiency. One of the primary reasons for certification is to ensure that your application or script handles communication with eBay responsibly and efficiently. See "Cache Auction Data to Improve API Efficiency" [Hack #99] for details.

Compatibility Levels. The eBay API is constantly changing and evolving to keep up with eBay.com. It's important to keep track of these changes, especially if you're using some of the more obscure fields or API calls listed in the documentation. The Compatibility Level ($compat_level) specified in *config.pl* ensures that these changes won't affect your program, at least until eBay removes support for your compatibility level (which they do periodically).

For instance, the Seller.User.Sunglasses field was replaced with the Seller.User.NewUser and Seller.User.UserIdChanged fields as of API version 305, to correspond with changes to the main eBay site. If your program were to submit an API call with compatibility level 309, you wouldn't have access to the Seller.User.Sunglasses field.

> All the scripts in this book reflect compatibility level 309. If you encounter a script or function that doesn't work for you, refer to the API documentation for possible changes associated with later compatibility levels.

Specific call requirements. In addition to the previous rather general requirements, certification also requires certain procedures to be followed with regard to many of the individual API calls. Here are a few examples:

GetFeedback
> Every time your application retrieves comments from a feedback profile, it should cache or record the data so that it retrieves only newly added feedback records each time. See "Negative Feedback Notification" [Hack #96] for details.

GetItem
> You should use GetItem (described in "Retrieve Details About an Auction" [Hack #84]) only if the information you need cannot be retrieved through more efficient means such as GetSellerList (described in "Automatically Keep Track of Auctions You've Sold" [Hack #87]).

GetSellerList
> Use the GetSellerList call only to retrieve listing data for the first time; use GetSellerEvents to subsequently retrieve price changes, bids, item revisions, or other changes that might have occurred since the auction data was last retrieved.

License requirements. Finally, your application must fall within the limits of your license agreement. For instance, if you're working under the free Individual license, you can't redistribute your applications (nor would you want to, given the number of API calls that would be required by hundreds of users).

As the API gains popularity, it remains to be seen how strict the certification requirements will remain, and how rigorously eBay will enforce recertification for large changes to your code.

API Searches

#83   Perform reliable searches with GetSearchResults.

In "Create a Search Robot" [Hack #17], a Perl script is used to perform an automated eBay search and then email new listings as they're discovered. Although the script serves a valuable function, it has the notable handicap of relying entirely on "scraping" (via the WWW::Search::eBay module) to retrieve its search results.

Scraping involves parsing standard web pages in order to retrieve the desired data. As you might expect, any changes to eBay's search pages, even minor ones, will break the script until the WWW::Search::eBay module on which it relies is updated to work with the new version.

The API, on the other hand, provides an officially supported interface to eBay's search engine, which means that scripts based on the API will be much more robust and nearly invulnerable to changes in eBay's search pages.

A Simple Search

Here's a simple Perl script, *search.pl*, that performs a search and displays the results.

```perl
#!/usr/bin/perl
require 'ebay.pl';

use Getopt::Std;
getopts('d');
$keywords = shift @ARGV or die "Usage: $0 [-d] keywords";

PAGE:
while (1) {
  my $rsp = call_api({ Verb => 'GetSearchResults',
                       DetailLevel => 0,
                       Query => $keywords,
             SearchInDescription => $opt_d ? 1 : 0,
                       Skip => $page_number * 100,
  });
  if ($rsp->{Errors}) {
    print_error($rsp);
    last PAGE;
  }
  foreach (@{$rsp->{Search}{Items}{Item}}) {
    my %i = %$_;
    ($price, $time, $title, $id) = @i{qw/CurrentPrice EndTime Title Id/};
    print "($id) $title [\$$price, ends $time]\n";
  }
```

❶ PAGE:

❷ my $rsp = call_api({ Verb => 'GetSearchResults',

❸ foreach (@{$rsp->{Search}{Items}{Item}}) {

❹ ($price, $time, $title, $id) = @i{qw/CurrentPrice EndTime Title Id/};

```
⑤   last PAGE unless $rsp->{Search}{HasMoreItems};
      $page_number++;
    }
```

Given that searches can return hundreds or even thousands of results, the GetSearchResults API call (line ②) divides the results into pages, not unlike the search pages at eBay.com. The loop, which begins on line ①, repeatedly resubmits the call, downloading a maximum of 100 results each time, until $rsp->{Search}{HasMoreItems} is false, on line ③. That means that if there are 768 matching listings, you'll need to retrieve 8 pages, or make 8 API calls.

> Your script might not need to retrieve all matching search results, as this one does. Instead, you may be content to search until a single auction is found, or perhaps to search only the auctions that have started in the last 24 hours. See the API documentation for more ways to limit the result set.

For each page that is found, a secondary loop, line ⑤, iterates through the result set for the current page, extracts relevant data (line ④), and prints it out.

Performing a Search

Run the script to perform a title search, like this:

```
search.pl keyword
```

where *keyword* is the word you're looking for. To search for multiple keywords, enclose them in single quotes, like this:

```
search.pl 'wool mittens'
```

Or to search titles and descriptions, type:

```
search.pl -d 'wool mittens'
```

But the real beauty of API searches is how they can be used in an automated fashion.

Revising the Robot

Now, if we tie the API search into the script from "Create a Search Robot" [Hack #17], we get the following new, more robust search robot script:

```perl
#!/usr/bin/perl
require 'ebay.pl';

$searchstring = "railex";
$searchdesc = 0;
```

```perl
$localfile = "search.txt";
$a = 0;

# *** perform search ***
PAGE:
while (1) {
  my $rsp =  call_api({ Verb => 'GetSearchResults',
                  DetailLevel => 0,
                        Query => $keywords,
          SearchInDescription => $opt_d ? 1 : 0,
          Skip                => $page_number * 100,
  });
  if ($rsp->{Errors}) {
    print_error($rsp);
    last PAGE;
  }
  $current_time = $rsp->{eBayTime};

  foreach (@{$rsp->{Search}{Items}{Item}}) {
    my %i = %$_;
    ($title[$a], $itemnumber[$a]) = @i{qw/Title Id/};
    write;
  }
  last PAGE unless $rsp->{Search}{HasMoreItems};
  $page_number++;
}

# *** eliminate entries already in file ***
open (INFILE,"$localdir/$localfile");
  while ( $line = <INFILE> ) {
    for ($b = $a; $b >= 1; $b--) {
      if ($line =~ $itemnumber[$b]) {
        splice @itemnumber, $b, 1;
        splice @title, $b, 1;
      }
    }
  }
close (INFILE);
$a = @itemnumber - 1;
if ($a == 0) { exit; }

# *** save any remaining new entries to file ***
open (OUTFILE,">>$localdir/$localfile");
  for ($b = 1; $b <= $a; $b++) {
    print OUTFILE "$itemnumber[$b]\n";
  }
close (OUTFILE);

# *** send email with new entries found ***
open(MAIL,"|/usr/sbin/sendmail -t");
  print MAIL "To: $selleremail\n";
  print MAIL "From: $selleremail\n";
  print MAIL "Subject: New $searchstring items found\n\n";
```

```
print MAIL "The following new items have been listed on eBay:\n";
for ($b = 1; $b <= $a; $b++) {
  print MAIL "$title[$b]\n";
  print MAIL "http://cgi.ebay.com/ws/eBayISAPI.dll?
                          ViewItem&item=$itemnumber[$b]\n\n";

}
close(MAIL);
```

Note that the only difference in the search portion of this script is that the title and item number are stored in $title[$a] and $itemnumber[$a] arrays instead of being printed out.

If you end up scheduling this script as described in "Create a Search Robot" [Hack #17], you may not need to retrieve all matching search results each time. Probably the best way is to set the Order input value to MetaStartSort, which will retrieve newly listed items first. Then, assuming you've scheduled your search robot to run every 24 hours, you could then stop retrieving results as soon as an auction older than 24 hours is encountered. Use the $yesterday variable, introduced in "Automatically Keep Track of Auctions You've Won" [Hack #85], to do your date calculations.

HACK #84 Retrieve Details About an Auction

Use the GetItem API call to get listing details.

The GetItem API call is used to retrieve all the details of a listing, including the title, description, starting price, category, and about 180 other individual bits of information.

Here's a simple script that, when provided with the item number, returns the title, seller ID, amount of time left, number of bids, and the current price.

```
#!/usr/bin/perl
require 'ebay.pl';

$item_id = shift @ARGV or die "Usage: $0 itemnumber";

my $rsp = call_api({ Verb => 'GetItem',
                DetailLevel => 0,
                    Id => $item_id
});

if ($rsp->{Errors}) {
  print_error($rsp)
} else {
  my %i = %{$rsp->{Item}[0]};
  my ($price, $currency, $bids, $time_left, $seller, $title) =
          @i{qw/CurrentPrice CurrencyId BidCount TimeLeft Seller Title/};
```

❸ $d = $time_left->{Days};
        $h = $time_left->{Hours};
        $m = $time_left->{Minutes};
        $s = $time_left->{Seconds};
        $seller_id = $seller->{User}{UserId};
        $seller_fb = $seller->{User}{Feedback}{Score};

        print "Item #$item_id: $title\n";
        print "For sale by $seller_id ($seller_fb)\n";
        print "Currently at $currency$price, $bids bids\n";

        if ($d > 0) { print "$d days, $h hours left.\n"; }
        elsif ($h > 0) { print "$h hours, $m minutes left.\n"; }
        elsif ($s > 0) { print "$m minutes, $s seconds left.\n"; }
        else { print "auction ended.\n"; }
    }

This script is fairly straightforward. The GetItem API call is submitted on line ❶, and the desired fields are extracted on line ❷. Naturally, you can specify any of the 180+ field names specified in the API documentation (look up GetItem → Return Values in the index), as long as the variables on the left side of the equals sign on line ❷ match up with the field names on the right.

Note that some variables are hashes (which eBay calls container nodes), from which relevant data must be extracted. For instance, in the documentation you'll see entries for TimeLeft as well as TimeLeft.Days, TimeLeft.Hours, TimeLeft.Minutes, and TimeLeft.Seconds. In Perl, these elements of the hash are accessed with the -> arrow (infix dereference) operator, as shown on line ❸.

Using the Script

To use the script, simply specify the item number, like this:

    getitem.pl 3136272129

and you'll get output like this:

    Item #3136272129: Little Red Steam Shovel
    For sale by ebayhacker
    Currently at $71.00, 9 bids
    1 days, 22 hours left.

However, you'll find it much more useful when used in conjunction with other scripts, like the ones in "Automatically Keep Track of Auctions You've Won" [Hack #85] and "Automatically Keep Track of Auctions You've Sold" [Hack #87].

DetailLevel

The DetailLevel field in the API call on line ❶ determines how much information is retrieved. In most cases, a value of 0 is sufficient. However, if you want to retrieve the description, you'll need to raise this to at least 2. See "Spellcheck All Your Auctions" [Hack #90] for an example.

Provided that you're the seller or the high bidder and the auction is completed, you can retrieve the HighBidder.User.Email and Seller.User.Email fields by specifying a detail level of at least 8, as shown in "Automatically Keep Track of Auctions You've Sold" [Hack #87].

The DetailLevel tag is used for most API calls, but its usage isn't necessarily the same for all of them. In most cases, a higher detail level will result in more data received (and more time taken), but for some API calls, a high detail level (usually 32 and above) is used for special "abbreviated" result sets. Regardless, if you're not getting the results you expect from an API call, make sure you supply the appropriate DetailLevel, as instructed by the API documentation.

HACK #85 Automatically Keep Track of Auctions You've Won

Maintain a permanent record of everything you've ever purchased.

Since eBay keeps auctions on site only for about 90 days and lists them in My eBay for only 30 days, all bidders should maintain permanent, off-site records of the items they've purchased.

As long as you keep all email you've received, as described in the Preface of this book, you'll always have records of the item numbers, titles, seller IDs and email addresses, and closing prices of the items you've won. But this data is stored in a less-than-convenient format, and the descriptions aren't stored at all.

Here's a script that will automatically retrieve and store details for every auction you've won:

```
    #!/usr/bin/perl
    require 'ebay.pl';

❶   $today = &formatdate(time);
❷   $yesterday = &formatdate(time - 86400);

❸   my $rsp = call_api({ Verb => 'GetBidderList',
                  DetailLevel => 32,
                       UserId => $user_id,
                       SiteId => $site_id,
                  EndTimeFrom => $yesterday,
```

```
                    EndTimeTo => $today,
  });

  if ($rsp->{Errors}) {
    print_error($rsp);
  } else {
    foreach (@{$rsp->{BidderList}{Item}}) {
      my %i = %$_;
❹    ($highbidder, $title, $id) = @i{qw/HighBidderUserId Title Id/};

❺    if ((! -e "$localdir/$id") && ($highbidder eq $user_id)) {
❻      my $rsp = call_api({ Verb => 'GetItem',
                        DetailLevel => 2,
                                Id => $id
      });

      if ($rsp->{Errors}) {
        print_error($rsp)
      } else {
      my %i = %{$rsp->{Item}[0]};
❼      my ($price, $currency, $seller, $title, $description) =
                @i{qw/CurrentPrice CurrencyId Seller Title Description/};

❽       open (OUTFILE,">$localdir/$id");
         print OUTFILE "[$id]\n";
         print OUTFILE "title=$title\n";
         print OUTFILE "seller=".$seller->{User}{UserId}."\n";
         print OUTFILE "price=$currency$price\n";
         print OUTFILE "description=$description\n";
       close (OUTFILE);
      }
    }
   }
  }
```

The GetBidderList API verb, called on line ❸, returns a maximum of 200
items, but doesn't support paging like GetSearchResults (see "API Searches"
[Hack #83]). This means that we need to be a little creative. So instead of trying
to grab as many listings as possible, we grab only the auctions that have
ended in a certain interval, say, a day. (If you bid infrequently, you can
change this to a week or even a month, and help keep down your API calls).
So, we set the EndTimeTo and EndTimeFrom fields to today's and yesterday's
dates, respectively. The formatdate subroutine is used on lines ❶ and ❷ to
convert the Perl dates to something eBay understands.

Next, the script runs through the list of auctions you've bid on and retrieves
❹ the high bidder, title, and item number for each. (We don't actually use
the title here, but it's nice to have.)

On line ❺, a check is performed to see if the auction has been recorded previously and if you're indeed the high bidder. Note that since we're using a `DetailLevel` of 32 (specified on line ❸), we get back an "abbreviated results set" from which, as the documentation explains, the user ID of the high bidder is retrieved with the `HighBidderUserId` tag. We could also use a `DetailLevel` of 0, but we'd have to deal with the `HighBidder` hash (see "Retrieve Details About an Auction" [Hack #84] for more information on container nodes). Refer to the API documentation for the somewhat confusing circumstances surrounding the `DetailLevel` tag with regards to `GetBidderList`.

Finally, the auction details for each item are retrieved with `GetItem` (line ❻ and then line ❼). Note that the `DetailLevel` for this call is set to 2 to retrieve the descriptions as well, as described in "Retrieve Details About an Auction" [Hack #84].

> The `$description` variable contains the raw description, including any HTML code. See "Spellcheck All Your Auctions" [Hack #90] for details on extracting plain text from HTML code.

Line ❽ then saves the retrieved data into a file, named for the item number of the listing. Naturally, you can retrieve and store as many or as few fields as you like and store them in whatever format is convenient, such as a database, comma-delimited (CSV) text file, or the generic format used here.

See "Create a Search Robot" [Hack #17] for information on scheduling the script to run at regular intervals. Since the script retrieves only auctions that have ended in the last 24 hours, this script should be run once a day, every day. If you want to run it less (or more) often, just change the `EndTimeTo` and `EndTimeFrom` fields accordingly.

HACK #86 Track Items in Your Watching List
Link an off-eBay auction tracker with eBay's Items I'm Watching list.

eBay provides the Items I'm Watching list (in My eBay → Bidding/Watching) to help you keep track of auctions on which you haven't yet bid. A corresponding API call, `GetWatchList`, allows you to access the contents of that list.

But the Items I'm Watching list is rather limited and can be replaced with a custom tracking list, as described in "Keep Track of Auctions Outside of eBay" [Hack #24]. Although the hack works, there are two simple ways to use the eBay API to make the script more robust and efficient:

- Retrieve the title and end date with the GetItem API call instead of using the flakier method of extracting them from the auction page title.

- Supplement the tracking list with any auctions in the Items I'm Watching list.

The following is a revised auction tracking script with both of these improvements.

> This script requires all the Perl modules specified in "Keep Track of Auctions Outside of eBay" [Hack #24], as well as Time::Local, by Tom Christiansen, Graham Barr, and Dave Rolsky (*search.cpan.org/perldoc?Time::Local*), used to convert dates retrieved from the API from GMT to local time.

```perl
#!/usr/bin/perl
require 'ebay.pl';
use Time::ParseDate;
use Time::Local;
use POSIX qw(strftime);
require("cgi-lib.pl");

&ReadParse;
$selfurl = "http://www.ebayhacks.com/exec/track.pl";
$localfile = "ebaylist.txt";
$timeoffset = 0;
@formatting=("color=#EE0000 STYLE=font-weight:bold",
             "color=#000000 STYLE=font-weight:bold", "color=#000000");
$i = 0;
$exists = 0;
$numlevels = 2;

# *** read stored list ***
open (INFILE,"$localdir/$localfile");
  while ( $line = <INFILE> ) {
    $line =~ s/\s+$//;
    $i++;
    ($enddate[$i],$priority[$i],$item[$i],$title[$i])=split(",", $line, 4);
    if (($item[$i] ne "") && ($item[$i] eq $in{'item'})) { $exists = $i; }
  }
close (INFILE);

# *** add latest auction if specified ***
if (($in{'auction'} =~ "ebay.com") && ($in{'item'} != "") && ($exists==0)) {
  my $rsp = call_api({ Verb => 'GetItem',
                 DetailLevel => 0,
                         Id => $in{'item'}
  });
```
❶

```
        if (! $rsp->{Errors}) {
          $i++;
          $item[$i] = $in{'item'};
❷       $title[$i] = $rsp->{Item}[0]{Title};
          $priority[$i] = 2;
❸       $enddate[$i] = timegm(localtime(parsedate($rsp->{Item}[0]{EndTime})));
        }
      }
      elsif (($in{'do'} eq "promote")) {
        $priority[$exists]--;
        if ($priority[$exists] < 0) { $priority[$exists] = 0; }
      }
      elsif (($in{'do'} eq "demote")) {
        $priority[$exists]++;
        if ($priority[$exists] > 2) { $priority[$exists] = 2; }
      }
      elsif (($in{'do'} eq "delete")) {
        splice @enddate, $exists, 1;
        splice @priority, $exists, 1;
        splice @item, $exists, 1;
        splice @title, $exists, 1;
        $i--;
      }

      # *** scan watch list ***
❹     my $rsp = call_api({ Verb => 'GetWatchList',
                    DetailLevel => 0,
                        UserId => $user_id,
                        SiteId => $site_id,
      });
      if (! $rsp->{Errors}) {
❺       $ebaytime = $rsp->{EBayTime};
        foreach (@{$rsp->{WatchList}{Items}{Item}}) {
          my %ii = %$_;
          ($id, $title, $timeleft) = @ii{qw/Id Title TimeLeft/};

          $seconds_left = $timeleft->{Days}*86400 +
                          $timeleft->{Hours}*3600 +
                          $timeleft->{Minutes}*60 +
                          $timeleft->{Seconds};
❻       $alreadythere = grep /$id/, @item;

          if ($alreadythere == 0) {
            $i++;
            $item[$i] = $id;
            $title[$i] = $title;
            $priority[$i] = 2;
❼         $enddate[$i] =
                      timegm(localtime(parsedate($ebaytime) + $seconds_left));
            $in{'do'} = "silentadd";
          }
```

```
    }
  }

  # *** update list ***
  if (($in{'do'} ne "")) {
    open (OUTFILE,">$localdir/$localfile");
      for ($j = 1; $j <= $i; $j++) {
        print OUTFILE "$enddate[$j],$priority[$j],$item[$j],$title[$j]\n";
      }
    close (OUTFILE);

    if ($in{'do'} ne "silentadd") {
      print "Location: $selfurl\n\n";
      exit( 0);
    }
  }

  # *** sort list ***
  @idx = sort criteria 0 .. $i;

  # *** display list ***
  print "Content-type: text/html\n\n";
  print "<table border cellspacing=0 cellpadding=6>\n";

  for ($j = 1; $j <= $i; $j++) {
    $formatteddate = strftime("%a, %b %d - %l:%M:%S %p",
                                       localtime($enddate[$idx[$j]]));
    $formattedtitle = "<a href=\"$itemurl$item[$idx[$j]]\" target=\"_blank\">
          <font $formatting[$priority[$idx[$j]]]>$title[$idx[$j]]</font></a>";

    if (strftime("%v", localtime($enddate[$idx[$j]])) eq
                                strftime("%v", localtime(time))) {
      $formattedtitle = "<li>" . $formattedtitle;

    }
    if ($enddate[$idx[$j]] < time) {
      $formattedtitle = "<strike>" . $formattedtitle . "</strike>";

    }
    else {
      $timeleft = ($enddate[$idx[$j]] - time) / 60 + ($timeoffset * 60);
      if ($timeleft < 24 * 60) {
        $hoursleft = int($timeleft / 60);
        $minleft = int($timeleft - ($hoursleft * 60));
        if ($minleft < 10) { $minleft = "0" . $minleft; }
        $formattedtitle = $formattedtitle .
                      " <font size=-1>($hoursleft:$minleft left)</font>";

      }
    }

    print "<tr><td>$formattedtitle</td>";
    print "<td><font size=-1>$formatteddate</font></td>";
```

```
    print "<td><a href=\"$selfurl?item=$item[$idx[$j]]&do=promote\">+</a>";

    print " | <a href=\"$selfurl?item=$item[$idx[$j]]&do=demote\">-</a>";
    print " | <a href=\"$selfurl?item=$item[$idx[$j]]&do=delete\">x</a></td>";
    print "</tr>\n";
  }

  print "</table>\n";

  sub criteria {
    # *** sorting criteria subroutine ***
    return ($priority[$a] <=> $priority[$b] or $enddate[$a] <=> $enddate[$b])
  }
```

Although much of this script is documented in "Keep Track of Auctions Outside of eBay" [Hack #24], a few minor changes have been made to accommodate the new portions that deal with the API. In other words, it's the same, but different.

First, when a new listing is added through the JavaScript link (from [Hack #24]), only the item number, $in{'item'}, is used. The GetItem API call (line ❶) uses the item number to retrieve the title ❷ and end date ❸. Note that the end date has to be converted from GMT to local time, with the help of the timegm function in Time::Local. This process is much more robust and reliable (albeit ultimately a little slower) than the original method of parsing the page title.

Next, the GetWatchList API call retrieves the contents of your Items I'm Watching list ❹, and checks to see if the item number is already in the list ❻.

Unfortunately, the result set doesn't include EndTime, so unless we want to call GetItem a bunch of times, we need to be a little creative. All we have to do is retrieve eBay time from the EBayTime field (line ❺; note the capitalization) and add it to TimeLeft ❼ for each auction. (It kind of feels like cheating, but it works.) Once again, this time needs to be converted from GMT to local time.

> Every time you "watch" a new auction, just reload *track.pl* to import it into your list. Note that at the time of this writing there was no way to modify the watching list, so the script will simply retrieve the same list over and over. Presumably, you'll want to clear out the Items I'm Watching list (My eBay → Bidding/Watching) as soon as they appear in your tracking list.

See "Generate a Custom Gallery" [Hack #94] for details on setting up this script in your *cgi-bin* directory.

HACK
#87
Automatically Keep Track of Auctions You've Sold

Retrieve and store completed auction data without typing.

As explained in "Keep Track of Items You've Sold" [Hack #65], it's vital for every seller to keep permanent, off-site records of every single auction he or she has sold.

This script, when run every day at the same time (as described in "Create a Search Robot" [Hack #17]), does it all:

```perl
#!/usr/bin/perl
require 'ebay.pl';

$today = &formatdate(time);
$yesterday = &formatdate(time - 86400);

my $page_number = 1;
PAGE:
while (1) {
    my $rsp = call_api({ Verb => 'GetSellerList',
                    DetailLevel => 8,
                        UserId => $user_id,
                    EndTimeFrom => $yesterday,
                      EndTimeTo => $today,
                     PageNumber => $page_number
    });

    if ($rsp->{Errors}) {
      print_error($rsp);
      last PAGE;
    }
    foreach (@{$rsp->{SellerList}{Item}}) {
      my %i = %$_;
      ($id, $enddate, $title, $currency, $price, $highbidder) =
            @i{qw/Id EndTime Title CurrencyId CurrentPrice HighBidder/};

      if (! -e "$localdir/$id") {
        open (OUTFILE,">$localdir/$id");
          print OUTFILE "[Details]\n";
          print OUTFILE "enddate=$enddate\n";
          print OUTFILE "itemnumber=$id\n";
          print OUTFILE "title=$title\n";
          print OUTFILE "price=$currency$price\n";
          print OUTFILE "bidder=".$highbidder->{User}{UserId}."\n";
          print OUTFILE "bidderemail=".$highbidder->{User}{Email}."\n";
        close (OUTFILE);
      }
    }
    last PAGE unless $rsp->{SellerList}{HasMoreItems};
    $page_number++;
}
```

This script works similarly to the one in "Automatically Keep Track of Auctions You've Won" [Hack #85], but it retrieves a list of auctions *by seller* that have ended between the specified dates. Here are a few important things to note about this script:

- Unlike the GetBidderList API call, which is limited to only 200 results, GetSellerList supports paging, and when used properly, will continue to retrieve results until you've got them all.

- Since the DetailLevel input field (discussed in "Retrieve Details About an Auction" [Hack #84]) is set to 8, the GetSellerList retrieves all relevant information about an auction so we don't have to issue separate GetItem calls. This means we can retrieve the auction details for hundreds of listings with only one or two API calls.

- The fields saved correspond to those listed in "Keep Track of Items You've Sold" [Hack #65], with the exception of the shipping charge (see below) and any fields you'd normally enter manually (such as whether or not the bidder has yet paid).

- If you've specified a fixed shipping charge in the listing or are using the Calculated Shipping option, you can retrieve this information with the GetItemShipping API call. Also of interest is GetShippingRates, a non-item-specific function that helps determine the shipping rates for different combinations of destination zip codes, package types, weights, and shipping services.

HACK #88 Submit an Auction Listing

Use AddItem to start new listings and make scheduling easier.

eBay's Turbo Lister, introduced in "Streamlining Listings" [Hack #73], is an API-based tool used to submit new listings to eBay. It provides a complete interface with which the user can create and modify listings, as well as a database engine that stores them. (Factoid: 35% of eBay listings are reportedly submitted with the API, including those uploaded with Turbo Lister.)

All the work is done by the AddItem API call, illustrated by this extremely simple script:

```perl
#!/usr/bin/perl
require 'ebay.pl';

$category    = shift @ARGV;
$title       = shift @ARGV;
$description = shift @ARGV;
$minimum_bid = shift @ARGV;
defined($minimum_bid)
        or die "Usage: $0 category title description minimumbid";
```

```
         $country = 'us';
         $location = 'My home town';
         $duration = 7;
         $quantity = 1;
         $currency = 1;
```
❶   ```
     my $rsp = call_api({ Verb => 'AddItem',
                      DetailLevel => 0,
                           SiteId => $site_id,
                         Category => $category,
         CheckoutDetailsSpecified => 0,
                          Country => $country,
                         Currency => $currency,
                      Description => $description,
                         Duration => $duration,
                         Location => $location,
                       MinimumBid => $minimum_bid,
                     PaymentOther => 1,
                         Quantity => $quantity,
                           Region => 0,
                            Title => $title,
     });
     if ($rsp->{Errors}) {
         print_error($rsp)
     } else {
```
❷    ```
         print "New listing created: #$rsp->{Item}[0]{Id}\n";
         print "Ends $rsp->{Item}[0]{EndTime}\n";
     }
```

The simplest way to use this script is to call it from the command line, like this:

```
additem.pl 7276 'Little Red Steam Shovel' 'My description...' 5.00
```

However, it will probably make more sense to call it from another script or program, especially since you'll likely want more of a description than simply "My description…" and more options than the four required by this sample script.

Although AddItem calls do not count against your daily (or monthly) API call allotment, the listing fees normally associated with starting new auctions still apply. The same goes for the RelistItem call, discussed in "Automatically Relist Unsuccessful Auctions" **[Hack #92]**.

Hacking the Hack

Of the more than 120 individual input fields supported by the AddItem call, only 11 are required: Category, CheckoutDetailsSpecified, Country, Currency, Description, Duration, Location, MinimumBid, Quantity, Region, and

Title. But when submitting a live listing, you'll most likely want to include as many options as possible, everything from the shipping charges to the extra-cost listing upgrades. Refer to the API documentation for a complete listing, and place any additional fields alongside the others on line ❶.

As discussed in "Cache Auction Data to Improve API Efficiency" [Hack #99], it's important to save as much retrieved information as possible so that you can reduce the number of subsequent API calls needed. If you submit listings only with the AddItem API call (never through eBay.com), you should record the item numbers it returns ($rsp->{Item}[0]{Id}) for further use. This would reduce (or eliminate) your need for the GetSellerList API call— used in so many of the hacks in this chapter—at least when it comes to retrieving a listing of your own auctions.

See Also

The eBay API SDK comes with the eBay Sample Selling Application, a Microsoft Visual Studio .NET–based listing creation tool similar to Turbo Lister. Those interested in creating a similar tool will want to poke around in the included C source code.

Automate Auction Revisions

HACK #89

Simplify the task of revising several auctions at once with the ReviseItem API call.

Once an auction has started, you can normally change most aspects of the listing using the procedure outlined in "Make Changes to Running Auctions" [Hack #50]. But it's also possible to submit a revision using the API.

ReviseItem

Let's start with a simple script, *reviseitem.pl*, that will let you change any aspect of an active listing:

```perl
#!/usr/bin/perl
require 'ebay.pl';

my $item_id = shift @ARGV;
my %ARGS    = @ARGV;

my @options = qw/AdditionalShippingCosts AmEx AutoPay BoldTitle
  BuyItNowPrice CashOnPickupAccepted Category Category2 CCAccepted
  CheckoutDetailsSpecified CheckoutInstructions COD Counter Description
  Discover Duration Escrow EscrowBySeller Featured Gallery GalleryFeatured
  GalleryURL GiftExpressShipping GiftWrap Highlight InsuranceOption
  InsuranceFee LayoutId Location MinimumBid MoneyXferAccepted
  MoneyXferAcceptedinCheckout MOCashiers PackageHandlingCosts
```

```
PaymentOther PaymentOtherOnline PaymentSeeDescription PayPalAccepted
PayPalEmailAddress PersonalCheck PhotoCount PhotoDisplayType PictureURL
Private Quantity Region ReservePrice SalesTaxPercent SalesTaxState
SellerPays ShipFromZipCode ShippingHandlingCosts ShippingInTax
ShippingIrregular ShippingOption ShippingPackage ShippingService
ShippingType ShipToAfrica ShipToAsia ShipToCaribbean ShipToEurope
ShipToLatinAmerica ShipToMiddleEast ShipToNorthAmerica ShipToOceania
ShipToSouthAmerica SuperFeatured ThemeId Title VisaMaster WeightMajor
WeightMinor WeightUnit/;

my %args = ( Verb => 'ReviseItem',
      DetailLevel => 0,
         SiteId => $site_id,
         ItemId => $item_id);
   foreach (@options) {
      $args{$_} = $ARGS{$_} if defined $ARGS{$_};
}

my $rsp = call_api(\%args);
if ($rsp->{Errors}) {
   print_error($rsp)
} else {
   print "Revised item #$rsp->{Item}[0]{Id}\n";
}
```

To use the script from the command line, include only the item number and the fields you want to change. For example, to change the title, type:

```
reviseitem.pl 4500205202 Title 'This is My New Title'
```

(Notice the single quotes used around text with spaces.) To change the starting bid to $8.50, type:

```
reviseitem.pl 4500205202 MinimumBid 8.50
```

To add the Bold listing upgrade (as described in "The Strategy of Listing Upgrades" [Hack #36]), type:

```
reviseitem.pl 4500205202 BoldTitle 1
```

where 1 means on (or true) and 0 means off (or false).

> Note that the field names (Title, MinimumBid, and BoldTitle) are all case sensitive; make sure to type them exactly as they appear in the script.

Revisions made through the API follow the same rules as those made through eBay.com; for instance, you can't change your title if the item has received bids. See "Make Changes to Running Auctions" [Hack #50] for details.

AddToItemDescription

If the item has received bids, the number of changes you'll be able to make will be diminished greatly. But, just like on eBay.com, you can add to the item description with the API, using the *addtodescription.pl* script:

```perl
#!/usr/bin/perl
require 'ebay.pl';

my $item_id = shift @ARGV;
my $addition = shift @ARGV;

my $rsp = call_api({ Verb => 'AddToItemDescription',
                DetailLevel => 0,
                   ItemId => $item_id,
                   SiteId => $site_id,
                Description => $addition
});

if ($rsp->{Errors}) {
  print_error($rsp)
} else {
  print "Successfully added to the description.\n";
}
```

This much-simpler script is used somewhat like the first one. For instance:

```
addtodescription.pl 4500205202 'Just a quick note.'
```

will add the following to the end of your auction description:

```
------------------------------------------------------------------------
On Nov-28-54 at 12:11:06 PDT, seller added the following information:
Just a quick note.
```

Note that you probably want to use this only if your item has received bids.

Let's Automate

The power of the API lies in its ability to turn a laborious task into a simple one. Combining these scripts with our ability to retrieve a list of all running auctions, you can create a script, *reviseall.pl*, that will make the same revision to an arbitrary number of listings in a single step:

```perl
#!/usr/bin/perl
require 'ebay.pl';

$today = &formatdate(time);
$tendays = &formatdate(time + 864000);

my $page_number = 1;
PAGE:
while (1) {
    my $rsp = call_api({ Verb => 'GetSellerList',
```

```
                          DetailLevel => 0,
                               UserId => $user_id,
                          EndTimeFrom => $today,
                            EndTimeTo => $tendays,
                           PageNumber => $page_number
            });

            if ($rsp->{Errors}) {
              print_error($rsp);
              last PAGE;
            }
            foreach (@{$rsp->{SellerList}{Item}}) {
              my %i = %$_;
              $id = @i{qw/Id/};

              if ($ARGV[0] eq "AddToDescription") {
                system './addtodescription.pl', $id, $ARGV[1];
              } else {
                system './reviseitem.pl', $id, @ARGV;
              }
            }
            last PAGE unless $rsp->{SellerList}{HasMoreItems};
            $page_number++;
        }
```

This script requires the *reviseitem.pl* and *addtodescription.pl* scripts listed earlier in this hack. To submit a global change, type:

```
reviseall.pl BoldTitle 1
```

Note that the syntax is the same as *reviseitem.pl* except that the item number is obviously not required, since the changes apply to all running auctions.

There are many things you can do with this tool. For example, you can inform all your potential customers that you'll be out of town:

```
reviseall.pl AddToDescription 'Note to customers: I will be out of town from
    August 3rd to the 6th, and will respond to all questions when I return.'
```

Add the American Express option to all your auctions:

```
reviseall.pl AmEx 1
```

Change the shipping surcharge to $4.50 for all your auctions:

```
reviseall.pl CheckoutDetailsSpecified 1
reviseall.pl ShippingHandlingCosts 4.50
```

It's important to note that all revisions are absolute. That is, if you change the shipping surcharge to $4.50, that change will be made regardless of the original amount entered for each listing. If you want to do more complex revisions, such as lowering the starting bid or reserve price by 15% for items that have not yet received bids, you'll either have to raise the DetailLevel value for GetSellerList, as in the script in "Automatically Keep Track of Auctions You've Sold" [Hack #87], or use the GetItem API call, as described in "Spellcheck All Your Auctions" [Hack #90]. Refer to the API documentation for details.

HACK #90 Spellcheck All Your Auctions

Ensure that your titles and descriptions are spelled correctly.

The success of any auction is largely due to how readily it can be found in eBay searches. As described in Chapter 2, eBay searches show only exact matches (with very few exceptions), which means, among other things, that spelling most definitely counts.

Neither eBay's Sell Your Item form nor Turbo Lister supports spellchecking of any kind. So it's left to sellers to scrutinize their titles and auction descriptions, and to obnoxious bidders to point out any mistakes. Once again, the API comes to the rescue.

The Script

The following script requires the following modules and programs:

Module/program name	Available at
HTML::FormatText (by Sean M. Burke)	search.cpan.org/perldoc?HTML::FormatText
HTML::TreeBuilder (by Sean M. Burke)	search.cpan.org/perldoc?HTML::TreeBuilder
HTML::Entities (by Gisle Aas)	search.cpan.org/perldoc?HTML::Entities
Lingua::Ispell (by John Porter)	search.cpan.org/perldoc?Lingua::Ispell
ispell program (by Geoff Kuenning)	fmg-www.cs.ucla.edu/geoff/ispell.html

```perl
#!/usr/bin/perl
require 'ebay.pl';

require HTML::TreeBuilder;
require HTML::FormatText;
use Lingua::Ispell qw( spellcheck );
Lingua::Ispell::allow_compounds(1);

$out1 = "";
$outall = "";
$numchecked = 0;
$numfound = 0;

$today = &formatdate(time);
$yesterday = &formatdate(time - 86400);

my $page_number = 1;
PAGE:
```

```
        while (1) {
❶          my $rsp = call_api({ Verb => 'GetSellerList',
                       DetailLevel => 0,
                            UserId => $user_id,
                     StartTimeFrom => $yesterday,
                       StartTimeTo => $today,
                        PageNumber => $page_number
           });

           if ($rsp->{Errors}) {
             print_error($rsp);
             last PAGE;
           }
           foreach (@{$rsp->{SellerList}{Item}}) {
             my %i = %$_;
             $id = @i{qw/Id/};

             if (! -e "$localdir/$id") {
               my $rsp = call_api({ Verb => 'GetItem',
                         DetailLevel => 2,
                                  Id => $id
               });

               if ($rsp->{Errors}) {
                 print_error($rsp)
               } else {
                 my %i = %{$rsp->{Item}[0]};
                 my ($title, $description) = @i{qw/Title Description/};

❷                $spellthis = $title . " " . $description;
❸                $tree = HTML::TreeBuilder->new_from_content($spellthis);
                 $formatter = HTML::FormatText->new();
                 $spellthat = $formatter->format($tree);
❹                $tree = $tree->delete;

❺                for my $r ( spellcheck( $spellthat ) ) {
                   if ( $r->{'type'} eq 'miss' ) {
                     $out1 = $out1."'$r->{'term'}'";
                     $out1 = $out1." - near misses: @{$r->{'misses'}}\n";
                     $numfound++;
                   }
                   elsif ( $r->{'type'} eq 'guess' ) {
                     $out1 = $out1."'$r->{'term'}'";
                     $out1 = $out1." - guesses: @{$r->{'guesses'}}\n";
                     $numfound++;
                   }
                   elsif ( $r->{'type'} eq 'none' ) {
                     $out1 = $out1."'$r->{'term'}'";
                     $out1 = $out1." - no match.\n";
                     $numfound++;
                   }
                 }
               }
```

```
      $numchecked++;
      if ($out1 ne "") {
        $outall = $outall."Errors in #$id '$title':\n";
        $outall = $outall."$out1\n\n";
        $out1 = "";
      }


    }
  }
}
last PAGE unless $rsp->{SellerList}{HasMoreItems};
$page_number++;
}
```

❻ ```print "$numfound spelling errors found in $numchecked auctions:\n\n";
   print "$outall\n";```

This script is based on the one in "Automatically Keep Track of Auctions You've Sold" [Hack #87], but has a few important additions and changes.

First, instead of listing recently completed auctions, the GetSellerList API call (line ❶) is used to retrieve auctions that have started in the last 24 hours. This will work perfectly if the script is run every 24 hours, say, at 3:00 P.M. every day, as described in "Create a Search Robot" [Hack #17].

Second, since we want the auction descriptions, we need to use the GetItem API call for each auction we spellcheck. This means that spellchecking a dozen auctions will require 13 API calls: one call to retrieve the list, and one for each auction.

The code actually responsible for performing spellcheck starts on line ❷, where the title and description are concatenated into a single variable, $spellthis, so that only one spellcheck is necessary for each auction. Next, the HTML::FormatText module is used (lines ❸ to ❹) to convert any HTML-formatted text to plain text.

Finally, the Lingua::Ispell module ❺ uses the external *ispell* program to perform a spellcheck on $spellthat (the cleaned-up version of $spellthis). As errors are found, suggestions are recorded into the $out1 variable, which is merged with $outall and displayed when the spellcheck is complete.

Hacking the Hack

Here are a few things you might want to do with this script:

- Instead of simply printing out the results of the spellcheck, as the script does on line ❻, you can quite easily have the results emailed to you. See "Send Automatic Emails to High Bidders" [Hack #93] for an example.

- Currently, the script performs a spellcheck on every running auction started in the last 24 hours. If you run the script every 24 hours, then this won't pose a problem. But if you choose to run the script manually and therefore specify a broader range of dates, you may wish to include error checking to prevent the script from needlessly checking the same auction twice.

- If you're especially daring, you can have the spellchecker submit the revisions for you, although I would never trust a spellchecker to know how to spell all the weird names of my items.

Negative Feedback Bidder Alert

HACK
#91

Have a script automatically notify you if an eBay member with negative feedback has bid on one of your auctions.

One of the best ways to keep deadbeat bidders away is to monitor your auctions and look for potential troublemakers, namely those with negative feedback ratings. (For information on deadbeat bidders, canceling bids, and blocking bidders, see "Keeping Out Deadbeat Bidders" [Hack #54].)

This script scans through your currently running auctions and notifies you via email whenever a high bidder has a feedback rating of less than zero.

```perl
#!/usr/bin/perl
require 'ebay.pl';

$today = &formatdate(time);
$tendays = &formatdate(time + 864000);

my $page_number = 1;
PAGE:
while (1) {
    my $rsp = call_api({ Verb => 'GetSellerList',
                    DetailLevel => 8,
                         UserId => $user_id,
                    EndTimeFrom => $today,
                      EndTimeTo => $tendays,
                     PageNumber => $page_number
    });

    if ($rsp->{Errors}) {
      print_error($rsp);
      last PAGE;
    }
    foreach (@{$rsp->{SellerList}{Item}}) {
      my %i = %$_;
      ($id, $bidder) = @i{qw/Id HighBidder/};
```

```
    if ($bidder->{User}{Feedback}{Score} < 0) {
      open(MAIL,"|/usr/sbin/sendmail -t");
      print MAIL "To: $selleremail\n";
      print MAIL "From: $selleremail\n";
      print MAIL "Subject: Negative Feedback Bidder Alert\n\n";
      print MAIL "A bidder with negative feedback has placed a bid on
                                    one of your auctions:\n";
      print MAIL "$itemurl$id\n";
      close(MAIL);
    }
  }
  last PAGE unless $rsp->{SellerList}{HasMoreItems};
  $page_number++;
}
```

This script is similar to the one in "Automatically Keep Track of Auctions
You've Sold" [Hack #87], with the notable exception that listings are retrieved
for auctions ending any time in the *next* 10 days. This is an easy way to filter
out completed auctions, and illustrates how to use the input fields (such as
EndTimeFrom and EndTimeTo) to your advantage.

> See the discussion of GetSellerEvents in the API documenta-
> tion for a way to retrieve only those listings that have under-
> gone price changes in the past 48 hours, typically as the
> result of bids placed.

To use this script, make sure to modify the $selleremail variable to reflect
your own email address. Note that if we had issued a separate GetItem API
call for each auction (or even just one of the auctions), as is necessary in
some of the other scripts in this chapter (like "Spellcheck All Your Auctions" [Hack #90]), we could have retrieved the seller's email address automatically.

See "Negative Feedback Notification" [Hack #96] for a script that notifies you
when a user has left a negative or neutral feedback comment for you.

HACK #92 Automatically Relist Unsuccessful Auctions

**Save time by automatically relisting auctions that have received no bids or
have a reserve that wasn't met.**

Most of the time, when an auction ends without receiving any bids or with a
reserve that wasn't met, sellers end up relisting the item. But this can be
rather laborious, especially if you have more than a few auctions to relist.

The following script will relist for you, and when run on a regular basis, say, every day, you'll never have to manually relist an auction again.

```perl
#!/usr/bin/perl
require 'ebay.pl';

$localfile = "autorelist.txt";
$today = &formatdate(time);
$yesterday = &formatdate(time - 86400);

my $page_number = 1;
PAGE:
while (1) {
    my $rsp = call_api({ Verb => 'GetSellerList',
                  DetailLevel => 8,
                       UserId => $user_id,
                  EndTimeFrom => $yesterday,
                    EndTimeTo => $today,
                   PageNumber => $page_number
    });

    if ($rsp->{Errors}) {
      print_error($rsp);
      last PAGE;
    }
    foreach (@{$rsp->{SellerList}{Item}}) {
      my %i = %$_;
      ($id, $bidder) = @i{qw/Id HighBidder/};

      if ($bidder->{User}{Email} !~ "\@") {
        open (INFILE,"$localdir/$localfile");
          while ( $line = <INFILE> ) {
            if ($line eq "$id\n") { goto SKIP; }
          }
        close (INFILE);

        my $rsp = call_api({Verb => 'RelistItem',
                      DetailLevel => 0,
                           SiteId => $site_id,
                           ItemId => $id
        });

        if ($rsp->{Errors}) {
          print_error($rsp)
        } else {
          print "Relisted item $id as #$rsp->{Item}[0]{Id}\n";

          open (OUTFILE,">>$localdir/$localfile");
            print OUTFILE "$id\n";
          close (OUTFILE);
        }
```

```
        }
    }
    SKIP:
    last PAGE unless $rsp->{SellerList}{HasMoreItems};
    $page_number++;
}
```

This script starts by listing all your auctions that have ended in the last 24 hours, similarly to "Automatically Keep Track of Auctions You've Sold" [Hack #87]. For information on scheduling this script to run at regular intervals, see "Create a Search Robot" [Hack #17]. If you decide to have the script run less frequently, say, once a week, make sure to increase the window of dates accordingly for which auctions are retrieved.

The script determines that an auction ended unsuccessfully if the high bidder's email address is not specified, or, more specifically, that the email address field does not contain an @ sign (line ②). For auctions that have received no bids, the HighBidder.User.Email field will be empty, or, if the reserve wasn't met, it will be set to "Invalid Request."

Then, the script checks to see if the auction has been previously relisted ③; if it hasn't, the script proceeds to relist the auction ④. If the relist operation is successful, a confirmation is shown and the auction number is recorded ⑤ into the filename specified on line ①. (Note that there's no need to use the VerifyAddItem API call to confirm a successful relist, since the script already checks for errors.)

Hacking the Hack

If you don't want to automatically relist each and every unsuccessful auction, you can set restrictions. For example, you may not wish to relist any item under five dollars or any item that has already been relisted three times.

One thing you can do to improve the success of your relisted auctions is to lower the starting bid and/or reserve price. Now, if you don't explicitly specify the value of a particular option for the relisted auction, the script will simply use the value from the original auction. But, for example, if you specify a new starting bid or reserve price (perhaps 15% lower than the previous values) on line ④, those values will be used for the new auction. Most of the input arguments available for the AddItem API call (discussed in "Submit an Auction Listing" [Hack #88]) can be used in RelistItem as well; see the API documentation for details.

HACK
#93
Send Automatic Emails to High Bidders

Send payment instructions to your customers automatically.

Here's a simple script that will scan all your auctions that have ended in the last 24 hours and send a payment-instructions email to each high bidder.

> This script requires the email template from "Streamlining Communications" **[Hack #74]**; just place it in the directory specified by $localdir in your *config.pl* include file.

```perl
#!/usr/bin/perl
require 'ebay.pl';

$template = "template.txt";

$today = &formatdate(time);
$yesterday = &formatdate(time - 864000);

my $page_number = 1;
PAGE:
while (1) {
    my $rsp = call_api({ Verb => 'GetSellerList',
                     DetailLevel => 8,
                          UserId => $user_id,
                     EndTimeFrom => $yesterday,
                       EndTimeTo => $today,
                      PageNumber => $page_number
    });

    if ($rsp->{Errors}) {
      print_error($rsp);
      last PAGE;
    }
    foreach (@{$rsp->{SellerList}{Item}}) {
      my %i = %$_;
      ($id, $title, $currency, $price, $highbidder, $checkout) =
              @i{qw/Id Title CurrencyId CurrentPrice HighBidder Checkout/};

      $bidderemail = $highbidder->{User}{Email};
      if ($bidderemail =~ "\@") {
        $shipping = $checkout->{Details}{ShippingHandlingCosts};
        $total = $price + $shipping;

        open(MAIL,"|/usr/sbin/sendmail -t");
        print MAIL "To: $bidderemail\n";
        print MAIL "From: $selleremail\n";
        print MAIL "Reply-To: $selleremail\n";
        print MAIL "Subject: $title\n\n";
```

```
open (COVER, "$localdir/$template");
  while ( $line = <COVER> ) {
    if ($line eq "<insert title here>\n") { print MAIL $title; }
    elsif ($line eq "<insert item here>\n") { print MAIL $id; }
    elsif ($line eq "<insert shipping here>\n") {
            print MAIL $currency . sprintf("%0.2f", $shipping); }
    elsif ($line eq "<insert total here>\n") {
            print MAIL $currency . sprintf("%0.2f", $total); }
    else {
      if ($line eq "\n") { $line = "$line\n"; }
            else { chomp $line; }
      print MAIL $line;
    }
  }
  close(COVER);
  close(MAIL);
  }
}
last PAGE unless $rsp->{SellerList}{HasMoreItems};
$page_number++;
}
```

The amount charged for shipping is taken from the Checkout.Details. ShippingHandlingCosts field, which is suitable if you've specified fixed shipping costs. If you're using eBay's Calculated Shipping feature, as described in "Put a Shipping Cost Calculator in Your Auction" [Hack #45], then you'll need to use the GetShippingRates function. Simply pass it these fields (all children of Checkout.Details), and it will give you the same information your winning bidder sees:

```
ShipFromZipCode, ShipToZipCode, ShippingPackage,
WeightUnit, WeightMajor, and WeightMinor
```

Note also that this script will need to be modified in order to accommodate Dutch auctions. Use the GetHighBidders API call to retrieve multiple high bidders and the quantities they purchased for any single Dutch auction. Naturally, you'll need to supplement the shipping cost calculations to account for any per-item shipping expenses.

AuctionEndOfAuction Notifications

The script in this hack retrieves the list of completed auctions for the last 24 hours, just like most of the other scripts in this chapter that use GetSellerList. (Refer to "Automatically Keep Track of Auctions You've Won" [Hack #85] for details on scheduling and running the script at regular intervals.)

There is another approach, however. If you sign up to receive notifications, such as AuctionEndOfAuction, CheckoutBuyerRequestsTotal, AuctionCheckout-Complete, and FixedPriceEndOfTransaction, eBay's server will send the appropriate information to you as soon as the event is triggered, and you can then do your post-auction processing on an auction-by-auction basis.

Unfortunately, notifications are not available to developers with the free Individual license (discussed at the beginning of this chapter), but if you're operating under a Basic, Professional, or Enterprise license, you can sign up to receive notifications at *developer.ebay.com*. Look up "Getting Started with eBay Platform Notifications" in the API documentation for details.

HACK #94   Generate a Custom Gallery

Insert a list of your running auctions, with photos, into your auction descriptions.

One of the ways to advertise your other auctions in any given auction description is to use a gallery—a scrolling viewport with thumbnail photos of all your running auctions—as described in "List Your Other Auctions in the Description" [Hack #47]. Aside from the commercial versions, there's a way to create a custom gallery using the eBay API.

First, include this code in your description:

```
<iframe src="http://www.ebayhacks.com/cgi-bin/gallery.pl"
                      style="width:100%;margin:0;border:0;">
```

The URL referenced in this iframe (see "Dynamic Text in Auction Descriptions" [Hack #51]) should point to your own server and *cgi-bin* directory. See the "Using CGI Scripts" sidebar if you're not sure how to do this.

Here's the script that generates a simple gallery:

```
#!/usr/bin/perl
require 'ebay.pl';
```

❶
```
print "Content-type: text/html\n\n";
print "<html><script type=\"text/javascript\">\n";
print "function resizeIframe() {\n";
print "parent.document.getElementById('myIframe').height=";
print "document.getElementById('myContent').scrollHeight;\n";
print "}</script></head>\n";
print "<body style=\"margin:0;border:none\"\n";
print "onLoad=\"resizeIframe()\" onResize=\"resizeIframe()\">\n";
print "<div id=\"myContent\">\n";

$today = &formatdate(time);
$tendays = &formatdate(time + 864000);
```

Using CGI Scripts

Every web server has a dedicated folder (directory) in which scripts or programs are placed. Instead of displaying the *contents* of the scripts, as would happen with ordinary HTML files, the web server software runs the scripts and displays their *output* instead. This special script directory is typically called *cgi-bin*, wherein CGI stands for "common gateway interface." Refer to your web server software's documentation for details on setting up a *cgi-bin* directory, or contact your administrator (ISP) if you're renting space on someone else's web server.

Now, copying the Perl scripts discussed throughout this book into your *cgi-bin* directory is easy enough; the hard part can be making them work.

Provided that the scripts are in the correct location, all you need to do on Unix systems is to make them executable, like this:

```
chmod +x gallery.pl
```

where gallery.pl is the filename of the script.

On Windows systems, each Perl script must have a filename that ends with *.pl*. Then, you'll need to associate the *.pl* filename extension with your Perl interpreter. In most cases, this will be done for you when you install Perl.

The last step is to reference the script with the proper URL, like this:

```
http://www.ebayhacks.com/cgi-bin/gallery.pl
```

where www.ebayhacks.com is the address of your server, cgi-bin is the public name of your *cgi-bin* directory (not always the same as the private name), and gallery.pl is the filename of your script. If all goes well, you should see the output of the script in your web browser. (It's important to note that not all Perl scripts in this book are CGI scripts.)

If you get an error when you try to run the script from your browser, try running it from the command line instead to see more-detailed error messages.

```
my $page_number = 1;
PAGE:
while (1) {
    my $rsp = call_api({ Verb => 'GetSellerList',
                  DetailLevel => 32,
                       UserId => $user_id,
                  EndTimeFrom => $today,
                    EndTimeTo => $tendays,
                   PageNumber => $page_number
    });

    if ($rsp->{Errors}) { last PAGE; }
    foreach (@{$rsp->{SellerList}{Item}}) {
```

```
           my %i = %$_;
           ($id, $title, $gallery) = @i{qw/Id Title GalleryURL/};

❷         $gallery = undef if ref $gallery;
           if (defined $gallery) {
             print "<table width=96 align=left><tr><td align=center>";
             print "<a href=\"$itemurl$id\" target=\"_blank\">";
             print "<img src=\"$gallery\" width=96 height=96></a>";
             print "<br><font size=-2>$title</font></td></tr></table>\n";
           }
         }
         SKIP:
         last PAGE unless $rsp->{SellerList}{HasMoreItems};
         $page_number++;
       }
❸   print "</div></body></html>\n";
```

Note that only auctions for which you've added the Gallery listing upgrade
and specified a gallery image (as described in "The Strategy of Listing
Upgrades" [Hack #36]) will appear, as shown in Figure 8-1.

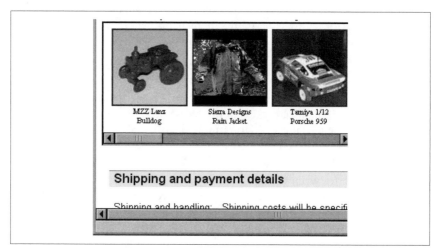

Figure 8-1. The gallery.pl script will display a scrolling list of all your current items

If you're not using the Gallery upgrade, you can specify your own images.
Simply replace line ❷ with this:

```
$gallery = "http://www.ebayhacks.com/images/$id.jpg";
```

where http://www.ebayhacks.com is the address of your server and /images is
the directory containing your personal gallery images (in JPG format). Name
the images after your auction numbers (e.g., *4500205199.jpg*), and you're
good to go!

This gallery script will be run and the GetSellerList API call will be used every time the auction page is loaded, which is probably much more often than necessary. This is an example of when it makes sense to "Cache Auction Data to Improve API Efficiency" [Hack #99].

Leaving Feedback
#95

Use the LeaveFeedback API call to more easily leave feedback.

The eBay API includes extensive support both for leaving feedback for other users and for retrieving comments from your own feedback profile.

Here's a sample script used to leave feedback for another user with whom you've had a transaction (save it as *leavefeedback.pl*):

```perl
#!/usr/bin/perl
require 'ebay.pl';

$item_id      = shift @ARGV;
$target_user  = shift @ARGV;
$comment_type = shift @ARGV;
$comment      = shift @ARGV;

defined($comment) && $comment_type =~ m:^(positive|negative|neutral)$:
        or die "Usage: $0 item user positive/negative/neutral comment";

my $rsp = call_api({ Verb => 'LeaveFeedback',
                DetailLevel => 0,
                     ItemId => $item_id,
                 TargetUser => $target_user,
                CommentType => $comment_type,
                    Comment => $comment});
if ($rsp->{Errors}) {
    print_error($rsp)
} else {
    print "Status: $rsp->{LeaveFeedback}{Status}";
}
```

You can leave feedback with this script by calling it from the command line, like this:

```
leavefeedback.pl item other_user positive 'Smooth transaction'
```

where *item* is the item number of the transaction and *other_user* is the user ID of the user for whom you're leaving feedback.

The `LeaveFeedback` API call follows the same rules as does eBay.com, namely that you can leave feedback only for a user with whom you're involved in a transaction. When testing this feature in the Sandbox (see "Climbing Out of the Sandbox" [Hack #82]), you'll need to set up two users and a handful of auctions. If the seller has a feedback rating of less than 10, however, you won't be able to use the Buy-It-Now feature. Instead, start an ordinary auction, bid on it with the other user ID, and then end the auction early.

See Also

- This script is required by "Automatic Reciprocal Feedback" [Hack #97].
- See "Negative Feedback Notification" [Hack #96] for a script that retrieves feedback comments from your profile.

HACK #96   Negative Feedback Notification

Have a script notify you whenever you've received negative feedback.

Given the importance of feedback, especially to sellers, it's a good idea to routinely check your feedback profile for complaints or comments that should be addressed, as discussed in "Replies and Followups to Feedback" [Hack #4]. But doing this every day, especially for sellers who receive dozens or even hundreds of feedback comments every week, can be a chore.

This script routinely scans your feedback profile and notifies you of any new negative or neutral feedback you've received.

```perl
#!/usr/bin/perl
require 'ebay.pl';

$localfile = "feedbackalert.txt";
%roles = ('S', 'seller', 'B', 'buyer');

my $rsp = call_api({ Verb => 'GetFeedback',
                DetailLevel => 1,
                    UserId => $user_id,
                    SiteId => $site_id,
                StartingPage => $page_number,
                ItemsPerPage => 1
});
$totalcomments = $rsp->{Feedback}{FeedbackDetailItemTotal};

$oldtotal = 0;
if (-e "$localdir/$localfile") {
  open (INFILE,"$localdir/$localfile");
    $oldtotal = <INFILE>;
```

❶ (beside `my $rsp = call_api...`)

❷ (beside `$oldtotal = <INFILE>;`)

```
      close (INFILE);
    }

❸   $newcomments = $totalcomments - $oldtotal;
    if ($newcomments == 0) { exit; }

    if ($newcomments > 200) {
      $num_pages = int($newcomments / 200) + 1;
      $page_size = 200;
    } else {
      $num_pages = 1;
      $page_size = $newcomments;
    }

    PAGE:
    for (my $page_number = 1; $page_number <= $num_pages; $page_number++) {
❹     my $rsp = call_api({ Verb => 'GetFeedback',
                    DetailLevel => 1,
                        UserId => $user_id,
                        SiteId => $site_id,
                    StartingPage => $page_number,
                    ItemsPerPage => $page_size
      });

      if ($rsp->{Errors}) {
        print_error($rsp);
        last PAGE;
      }

      FEEDBACK:
      foreach (@{$rsp->{Feedback}{FeedbackDetail}{FeedbackDetailItem}}) {
        my %i = %$_;
        ($text, $type, $from, $item, $id, $role) = @i{qw/CommentText CommentType
                      CommentingUser ItemNumber TransactionId FeedbackRole/};

❺       if (($type eq "Complaint") || ($type eq "Neutral")) {
          open (INFILE,"$localdir/$localfile");
            while ( $line = <INFILE> ) {
              if ($line eq "$id\n") { next FEEDBACK; }
            }
          close (INFILE);

          open(MAIL,"|/usr/sbin/sendmail -t");
          print MAIL "To: $selleremail\n";
          print MAIL "From: $selleremail\n";
          print MAIL "Subject: Negative Feedback Alert\n\n";
          print MAIL "A ".$roles{"$role"}.", $from, has left this feedback:\n";
          print MAIL "$type: '$text'\n";
          print MAIL "regarding this transaction:\n";
          print MAIL "$itemurl$item\n";
❻         close(MAIL);
        }
```

```
    }
  }

  open (OUTFILE,">$localdir/$localfile");
❼ print OUTFILE $totalcomments;

  close (OUTFILE);
```

What may seem like an unnecessary extra call at the beginning of the script (line ❶) is actually quite necessary to achieve compliance with eBay's Production Access Rules. This call retrieves a single comment entirely for the purpose of determining the total number of feedback comments in the profile, $totalcomments.

The number of new comments ($newcomments, line ❸) is calculated by subtracting the previous total ($oldtotal, line ❷) from the current total. Then, all new comments are retrieved with the second GetFeedback API call on line ❹.

All this needs to be done because GetFeedback doesn't support the EndTimeFrom or EndTimeTo arguments (possibly signifying the dates that feedback comments were left) that are supported by most of the other API calls discussed in this chapter. Paradoxically, adding an extra call (line ❶) prevents the script from issuing too many calls later on. Since the script doesn't need to download the entire feedback profile every time, you also don't need to cache feedback, as eBay suggests.

The script then iterates through the profile and sends an email every time a new negative or neutral feedback comment is encountered. Finally, the script records the new total (line ❼).

> To automate this script, schedule it to run regularly (every day, every week, etc.), as described in "Create a Search Robot" **[Hack #17]**.

See "Negative Feedback Bidder Alert" **[Hack #91]** for a script to notify you when a user with a negative feedback rating bids on one of your auctions.

Automatic Reciprocal Feedback
HACK #97

Leave automatic feedback for any customer who has left positive feedback for you.

As much as you should respond quickly to any complaints lodged against you in your feedback profile, you'll also want to leave positive reciprocal feedback for each and every positive comment you receive from buyers, as suggested by "Withholding Feedback" **[Hack #5]**. As you might expect, this is also something that can be done with the eBay API.

But let's add a little spice to the mix. Instead of leaving the same feedback comment every time, let's have the script choose a random comment. Start by creating a plain-text file with a handful of positive comments, one on each line:

```
Lightning-fast payment. Reliable buyer. Thanks for your business!
Quick to pay, friendly emails. This eBayer makes selling a pleasure!
Very fast payment, good communication. All-around excellent customer!
```

Save the file as *prefabpraise.txt* and place it in the directory specified in your *config.pl* file (discussed at the beginning of this chapter).

Next, take the script from "Negative Feedback Notification" [Hack #96] and replace the code between line ❺ and line ❻ with this code:

```
if ($type eq "Praise") {
  open (INFILE,"$localdir/prefabpraise.txt");
    @line = <INFILE>;
  close (INFILE);
  chomp @line;
  $lines = @line;
  $choice = int rand ($lines);

  system './leavefeedback.pl', $item, $from, 'positive', $choice;
}
```

Or, if you want a single script to leave positive reciprocal feedback *and* notify you of negative feedback, just place this code *before* line ❺.

Note that this script requires the *leavefeedback.pl* script from "Leaving Feedback" [Hack #95].

HACK #98 Queue API Calls

How to work around eBay's API call limit.

Developers working under the Individual license, explained at the beginning of this chapter, have a strict limit as to the number of eBay calls they are allowed to make each day.

Provided that your application uses the API efficiently, as described in "Cache Auction Data to Improve API Efficiency" [Hack #99], this shouldn't pose a problem. And as the theory goes, anyone needing more than 50 API calls per day is probably running a business on eBay and can justify one of the higher developer tiers.

Consider the following scenario. As a seller, you might have 55 separate auctions ending on a single day. If you use the script in "Automatically Keep Track of Auctions You've Sold" [Hack #87], you can retrieve sufficient data for all your recently closed auctions with only a single GetSellerList call. But if you use the script in "Spellcheck All Your Auctions" [Hack #90], you'll need a minimum of 56 calls: one to retrieve the list of auctions, and 55 more to retrieve the individual auction descriptions. All you need is to run this single script just once to exceed your API quota for the day.

If you feel that exceeding your quota is a possibility, you can take some extra steps to ensure both that your software understands this limit, and that if your software reaches the limit, it can queue additional API calls and complete its work the next day.

The first step is to begin recording your API call usage. Probably the best way to do this is by adding a counter to the call_api subroutine in the *ebay.pl* script listed at the beginning of this chapter. The counter code might look something like this:

```
   open (INFILE,"$localdir/apiquota.txt");
❶     my %count = map { split(/,/, $_) } <INFILE>;
   close (INFILE);
   chomp %count;

   my ($today, $dummy) = split(/ /, &formatdate(time));
❷  $count{$today}++;
   open (OUTFILE,">$localdir/apiquota.txt");
     while (($date,$count) = each %count) {
❸       print OUTFILE "$date,$count\n";
     }
   close (OUTFILE);

❹  if ( $count{$today} > 50 ) {
      ...
      # queue this API call for later processing
      ...
      return undef;
      exit;
   }
```

Here's how it works. The script retrieves the counts (line ❶) for all recorded days from the *apiquota.txt* file (located in the directory specified by $localdir in your *config.pl* script). It then adds 1 to today's count (line ❷) and writes the updated data back to the file (line ❸).

Finally, if today's count is above 50 (line ❹), it runs some code you provide (sorry, I'm not going to do *all* the work for you!) to queue the next API call. You could, for example, set up a temporary cron job, as described in "Create a Search Robot" [Hack #17], to run another script that resubmits queued API calls.

If nothing else, this nifty snippet of code records accounting data for your API usage. After a few days of using the API, your *apiquota.txt* file will look something like this:

```
2005-07-11,3
2005-07-12,11
2005-07-13,0
2005-07-14,60
2005-07-15,4
```

This shows that on July 14, 2005, 60 calls were made, while only 4 calls were made the next day. (Note that since the data is manipulated as a hash by this script, the records won't necessarily be recorded in order in the file.)

HACK #99 Cache Auction Data to Improve API Efficiency

Reduce the number of API calls your program makes and work within your daily API allotment.

One of the requirements of certification, as described in "Climbing Out of the Sandbox" [Hack #82], is that your application or script does not make more calls or retrieve more data than is absolutely necessary. This is typically accomplished in any of three ways:

- Restricting the result set to a specific date range, as described in "Automatically Keep Track of Auctions You've Won" [Hack #85].

- Download only new entries by comparing the current total of entries with the total you recorded the last time the call was used, as described in "Negative Feedback Notification" [Hack #96].

- Caching retrieved data so that it doesn't have to be retrieved again, as described in this hack.

Which data you cache and how you do it depends on the type of data you're working with.

Caching Input

Probably the most useful place to start is by recording the item numbers of all auctions you're currently selling. Assuming you're using GetItem to upload your listings to eBay (see "Submit an Auction Listing" [Hack #88]), you can simply save the resulting item number in a file, like this:

```
open (OUTFILE,">>$localdir/auctionlist.txt");
  print OUTFILE "$rsp->{Item}[0]{Id},$rsp->{Item}[0]{EndTime}\n";
close (OUTFILE);
```

Eventually, the file will look like this:

```
4500207651,2005-07-15 20:43:32
4500207783,2005-07-16 08:14:18
4500208002,2005-07-18 19:00:31
```

with each line containing one item number and one end date, separated by a comma. Then, instead of using the GetSellerList API call found in many hacks in this chapter, you can simply load the list, like this:

```
open (INFILE,"$localdir/auctionlist.txt");
  my %items = map { split(/,/, $_) } <INFILE>;
close (INFILE);
chomp %items;
```

which will create a hash of item numbers and end times. To fill an array with all the item numbers, use the keys function:

```
@itemnumbers = keys %items;
```

To retrieve the end date for a single auction, reference the hash like this:

```
$endtime = $items{'4500207783'}
```

Naturally, if you want to store more than just item numbers and end times, you'll need a more complex storage system, but the methodology will be the same.

Not only will this approach significantly reduce your API usage, it will end up being a lot faster than repeatedly downloading large amounts of data from eBay.

Caching Output

Another case where caching can reduce API usage and improve performance is when it comes to the output your program generates. For example, the script in "Generate a Custom Gallery" [Hack #94] generates a web page with a listing of your currently running auctions (with pictures). But instead of generating the same page every time, you can redirect the output to a static HTML file and then run the script every so often to generate the file.

 You can schedule the script to run at regular intervals or, better yet, run the script every time an auction starts or ends (using, among other things, the notifications discussed in "Send Automatic Emails to High Bidders" [Hack #93]).

A simple conversion to the *gallery.pl* script will make it cache its own output. First, add this line immediately before line ❶:

```
open (OUTFILE,">/some_directory/gallery.html");
```

where /some_directory is the full path to the gallery.html file. Next, remove line ❶ entirely:

```
print "Content-type: text/html\n\n";
```

Then, you'll need to convert all print statements in the script so that their output is redirected to the open file. For example, change:

```
print "<html><script type=\"text/javascript\">\n";
```

to:

```
print OUTFILE "<html><script type=\"text/javascript\">\n";
```

Finally, at the end of the script, after line ❸, close the file like this:

```
close (OUTFILE);
```

That should do it. All that's left to do at this point is to change the URL in the <iframe> tag to reflect the address of the static page, like this:

```
<iframe src="http://www.ebayhacks.com/gallery.html"
                 style="width:100%;margin:0;border:0;">
```

With this approach, your customers see a cached list of auctions every time your custom gallery is loaded. Not only will this eliminate the unnecessary API calls, but the page will load much faster as well.

HACK 100   Working Without the eBay API

Programming eBay outside the confines of the eBay API.

Consider the API to be a gift from the gods at eBay. At least in theory, the existence of the API puts an end to the need for scrapers, parsers, and other kludges.

For example, the script in "Keep Track of Auctions Outside of eBay" [Hack #24] retrieves auction information by parsing the title of the auction page. While this works most of the time, it is susceptible to failure from even the smallest changes. Now, consider the alternative script in "Track Items in Your Watching List" [Hack #86], which accomplishes the same task with more robust API calls. The API version will continue to work even if eBay dramatically changes the formatting of their auction pages (which, in fact, they did on July 7, 2003).

But the API comes at a cost. Quite a bit of setup is required (not to mention certification) before you can use the API, and it often ends up being somewhat slower than some simple parsers.

So here are some extra, non-API tools you can use to supplement (or take the place of) your API-based code.

Note that all of these come with the standard "don't do this" clause. Not only are these types of tools unreliable by their very nature, but they also violate eBay policies.

WWW::Search::eBay.   This Perl module, written by Glenn Wood and available at *search.cpan.org/perldoc?WWW::Search::eBay*, scrapes eBay search pages and returns the results. See "Create a Search Robot" [Hack #17] for a working example. Note that updated versions can also be found at *alumni.caltech.edu/~glenwood/SOFTWARE/*.

php eBay List.   This PHP script, available at *www.aeoninteractive.net*, parses your About Me page to obtain a list of your currently running auctions, which you can then list on your own site. See "List Your Auctions on Another Site" [Hack #78] for the official way to do this (and make money to boot).

grep.   This little Perl function (also a program found on any Unix system) allows you to search text or a file for a particular string of characters. If you download any page from eBay.com using lwp-download, you can build your own scraper with grep in just a few lines of code.

Index

localization, 37
lockout function (JavaScript), 193
logging in using a link, 57
lots (see bundle, selling items as)
LWP::UserAgent Perl module, 270

M

market, investigating, 102
merchandise, problems with, 97
    (see also returning merchandise)
merchant accounts, 252
Merchant Kit, 263
Microsoft Office HTML Filter, 130
minimum bid, 73
Mister Lister, 248
money, 85
    saving on packing materials, 230
    (see also payments)
money orders, 224
    international postal, 92
MS Paint, 180
multiple auctions
    leaving feedback for, 7
    listings (see listings, streamlining)
Multiple Sellers search, 35
My eBay Bidding/Watching tab, 66
My Favorite Categories page, 40
My Favorite Searches list, 40
    creating, 42
My Favorite Sellers page, 40

N

negative feedback, 2
    alert, eBay API, 304–305
    avoiding, 9–11
    new users and, 18
    notifying when negative feedback is
        received, 314–316
    retaliation (see retaliation for negative
        feedback)
nested tables, 129
Netscape/Mozilla Composer, 130
neutral feedback, 3
new users, 17
    negative feedback, 18
newsletter, 273
non-API tools, 321
Non-Paying Bidder Alert, 237, 238

norightclick function (JavaScript), 193
notification of being high bidder, 220
NSLookup program, 84

O

online shipping-cost calculators, 93
opening bids, small, 56
OR searches, 24
outbidding highest bidder, 75

P

packing materials, money saving
        tips, 230
pages
    backgrounds, 131
    frames, 132–136
    viewing hard-to-read, 138
Paint, 180
Paint Shop Pro, 180
passwords, 57
paying too much, 63
Payment Instructions box, 162
payments
    BidPay, 88
    C2IT, 88
    credit cards, 89
    electronic, 85
    options, 223
    sending, 85–90
    sending instructions, 219–221
    setting firm policies, 222–225
    (see also PayPal)
PayPal, 86–88
    accepting payments on your own
        site, 264–270
        more robust approach, 268
    checkout counter, 267
    disabling, 160–162
    Instant Payment Notification
        Manual, 272
    international bidders, 231
    processing payments
        automatically, 270–273
    refunds, 99
    Seller Protection Policy, 223
    shopping cart, 269
    signing up, 86
    total payment calculations, 90
    Winning Buyer Notification, 221

Colophon

Our look is the result of reader comments, our own experimentation, and feedback from distribution channels. Distinctive covers complement our distinctive approach to technical topics, breathing personality and life into potentially dry subjects.

The tool on the cover of *eBay Hacks* is a corkscrew ...

Emily Quill was the production editor and copyeditor for *eBay Hacks*. Sarah Sherman, Matt Hutchinson, and Claire Cloutier provided quality control. Jamie Peppard, Mary Agner, Phil Dangler, and James Quill provided production assistance. Julie Hawks wrote the index.

Emma Colby designed the cover of this book, based on a series design by Edie Freedman. The cover image is a photograph taken from the Stockbyte Work Tools CD. Emma Colby produced the cover layout with Quark-XPress 4.1 using Adobe's Helvetica Neue and ITC Garamond fonts.

David Futato designed the interior layout. This book was converted by Joe Wizda, Andrew Savikas, and Julie Hawks to FrameMaker 5.5.6 with a format conversion tool created by Erik Ray, Jason McIntosh, Neil Walls, and Mike Sierra that uses Perl and XML technologies. The text font is Linotype Birka; the heading font is Adobe Helvetica Neue Condensed; and the code font is LucasFont's TheSans Mono Condensed. The illustrations that appear in the book were produced by Robert Romano and Jessamyn Read using Macromedia FreeHand 9 and Adobe Photoshop 6. This colophon was written by David Futato.